# The Invisible University

Postdoctoral Education in the United States

Report of a Study Conducted
under the Auspices of the
NATIONAL RESEARCH COUNCIL

NATIONAL ACADEMY OF SCIENCES
Washington, D.C. 1969

Standard Book Number 309-01730-0

*Available from*
Printing and Publishing Office
National Academy of Sciences
2101 Constitution Avenue
Washington, D. C. 20418

Library of Congress Catalog Card Number 70-601489

# Foreword

Postdoctoral studies fulfill the desire of the advanced scholar to pursue research for a time often in close association with a distinguished mentor or colleague. They provide education-capping experiences for the younger scholar and reinvigoration and new directions for the established investigator.

One of the earliest formal recognitions of the importance of postdoctoral studies in the United States was the establishment in 1919 of the National Research Fellowship Program by the National Research Council with the support of the Rockefeller Foundation. Over 1,300 young scientists in the physical, mathematical, biological, and medical sciences received fellowship awards for postdoctoral research in the three decades during which the program was in operation. The fellows were selected for unusual ability and for promise of future leadership in scientific research. They went on to distinguished careers in educational institutions and industrial and governmental laboratories, taking with them their enthusiasm for research and their high competence. The program played a major role in establishing for the United States the eminence in science that it now enjoys.

Postdoctoral studies have undergone major growth since World War II. At an increasing rate, new PhD's have sought temporary postdoctoral research appointments as a preliminary to careers in universities and, to a lesser extent, in industry and government. Increasingly, universities have expected those appointed to their faculties to have had postdoctoral research experience and,

## FOREWORD

in turn, they have been willing to serve as hosts to postdoctoral scholars. More established investigators also have sought the renewal provided by postdoctoral studies and have continued to seek such opportunities. Interest in postdoctoral studies is strongest in the fields of the natural sciences, but it is increasing in the social and behavioral sciences, in the humanities, and in some of the professional fields. With the impetus given by the availability of federal research funds during the last two decades, postdoctoral studies have reached institutional status and may justifiably be referred to as the newest stratum of higher education in this country.

The present report is the result of a concern within the National Research Council and elsewhere about the scope of postdoctoral education in the United States. Although postdoctoral appointees were present on many campuses, their numbers and functions were not known nationally and, in many instances, were not even known to the host universities. Postdoctoral education, as the title of this report suggests, had grown to institutional status without study or planning. In the absence of information, the costs and benefits of this development to the universities, to the postdoctoral appointees, and to the nation could not be adequately assessed. The financial uncertainties associated with reductions in the federal research budget during the last several years added to the urgency of the need for information.

A national study of postdoctoral education in the United States was first suggested by Sanborn C. Brown of the Massachusetts Institute of Technology. Sponsored by the National Research Council and housed administratively within the Office of Scientific Personnel, the study got under way in 1966. It is indicative of the widespread interest in the problem that financial support was provided by five agencies of the federal government and by the Alfred P. Sloan Foundation.

An advisory committee, representative of the academic community and of other sectors affected by postdoctoral education, determined policies for the study and established directions for it. The members included Sanborn C. Brown, Chairman, Massachusetts Institute of Technology; G. M. Almy, University of Illinois; Kenneth E. Clark, University of Rochester; Bryce Crawford, Jr., University of Minnesota; H. Bentley Glass, State University of New York; Thomas F. Jones, University of South Carolina; Arthur R. Kantrowitz, AVCO-Everett Research Laboratory; Eugene M. Landis, Harvard Medical School; H. W. Magoun, University of California; John Perry Miller, Yale University; Hans Neurath, University of Washington; Colin S. Pittendrigh, Princeton University; Moody E. Prior, Northwestern University; and Gordon T. Whyburn, University of Virginia. Members of the committee were generous with their time, and we are greatly indebted to them. They were assisted by consultants drawn from the academic world, from industry, and from government. A series of conferences, interviews, and interim reports provided further

## FOREWORD

means of registering a wide spectrum of opinions and evaluations during the course of the study.

Staff leadership during the first half-year was provided by Robert A. Alberty, then at the University of Wisconsin and now at Massachusetts Institute of Technology, who served as the first director and gave the project its initial impetus. He was succeeded as director in March 1967 by Richard B. Curtis of Indiana University, who was given leave of absence by his university to serve as full-time director of the study. Dr. Curtis carried out the analysis of results, the interviewing, and the consultations reported here and was the principal author of this report, with the close collaboration of the advisory committee. We are exceedingly grateful to him for his hard work and insightful leadership.

Other staff responsibilities were met by Robert K. Weatherall of Massachusetts Institute of Technology, who served as associate director for institutional studies, and by Lindsey R. Harmon of the Office of Scientific Personnel, who was associate director for manpower studies. M. H. Trytten and William C. Kelly of the Office of Scientific Personnel provided general administrative supervision of the study.

The information, evaluations, conclusions, and recommendations contained here are offered to all who are concerned with postdoctoral education. It is hoped that the report will lead to greater understanding of a rapidly developing sector of higher education.

FREDERICK SEITZ, *President*
National Academy of Sciences

April 15, 1969

# Acknowledgments

This study was made possible by the financial support of the Alfred P. Sloan Foundation, the National Institute of General Medical Sciences, the National Endowment for the Humanities, the National Science Foundation, the National Aeronautics and Space Administration, and the United States Office of Education. Their assistance is gratefully acknowledged. The program officers of each have been most helpful throughout the course of the study.

The Committee on Science and Public Policy of the National Academy of Sciences has provided encouragement and advice. In particular, Harry Eagle and Mark G. Inghram of that committee sat with the Advisory Committee and served as wise counselors.

In an undertaking of this magnitude it is impossible to thank individually everyone who has made a contribution. Thanks are owed to the many postdoctoral appointees, departmental chairmen, faculty members, university administrators, directors of research in industrial and government laboratories, and foundation or agency officers, who provided helpful information. Special acknowledgment must be made of the assistance of approximately 400 coordinators for the study, appointed at each of the responding universities and organizations by their presidents. The Director and Associate Director were graciously received on twenty university campuses and at a number of industrial laboratories and scholarly organizations. Several dozen program officers

## ACKNOWLEDGMENTS

in federal agencies provided information as to their policies on postdoctoral appointments.

Several groups of individuals assisted the study by providing advice on various aspects of the postdoctoral phenomenon. From the social sciences were O. Meredith Wilson (Center for Advanced Study on the Behavioral Sciences), Robert E. Lane (Yale), Donald W. Taylor (Yale), Elbridge Sibley (Social Science Research Council), Gardner Lindzey (University of Texas), Raymond J. Balester (National Institute of Mental Health), and Charles R. Wright (National Science Foundation). In the humanities were Virgil Whitaker (Stanford University), C. Hugh Holman (University of North Carolina), Frank Ryder (Indiana University), John Fisher (Modern Language Association), Frederick Burkhardt (American Council of Learned Societies), Gordon Ray (Guggenheim Foundation), Barnaby Keeney (National Endowment for the Humanities), and James H. Blessing (National Endowment for the Humanities). In the study of the costs of postdoctoral education advice was provided by Adrian Harris (University of California at Los Angeles), George Pake (Washington University at St. Louis), Marshall Sittig (Princeton University), Rashi Fein (then of the Brookings Institution and now at Harvard University), Carl Kaysen (Institute for Advanced Study), and William Bowen (Princeton University).

Raymond Bowers (then at the Office of Science and Technology and now at Cornell University) provided invaluable advice in the organization of the project. Francis Colligan (Department of State), Charles V. Kidd (then at the Office of Science and Technology; now at the Association of American Universities) and André Rheault (Education and World Affairs) helped with the problem of foreign postdoctorals. Assistance in the area of the postdoctoral fellows in medicine was provided by Robert Berson (Association of American Medical Colleges), by Leland Powers (Association of American Medical Colleges), by Walter Wiggins (American Medical Association), by Herbert Rosenberg (National Institutes of Health), and especially by Howard H. Hiatt (Harvard Medical School) and Jonathan Rhoads (University of Pennsylvania).

John Caffrey (American Council on Education), Harriet Zuckerman (Columbia University), Lewis Slack (American Institute of Physics), and Alice Shurcliff (Education and World Affairs) provided useful data and information.

# Preface

For many graduate students in science today there is little question about the nature of their first positions after they receive their PhD's. They will seek to work full time in research for a year or two with a senior investigator. If the graduate student is pointing toward a career as a faculty member at one of the established universities, such a postdoctoral appointment will be almost required to acquire new skills and experience in research and to join the pool from which new appointments in the major universities are almost always made. The period spent in such an apprentice role is for the most part an enjoyable one for the young scholar. He is relieved from the predoctoral pressures of graduate requirements and almost poverty-level stipends.

The mentor of such young men finds them almost indispensable. Knowing that his laboratory is in the charge of one or more of these recent PhD's, the faculty member is able to attend to his other responsibilities of teaching and committee work. The research goes on, with higher quality (and quantity) and the professor's contribution can be more in the realm of ideas than in day-by-day mechanics. Furthermore, these bright young scientists often bring ideas and techniques from other laboratories that the faculty member himself might find it necessary to take a leave of absence to learn.

In view of this almost idyllic relationship it is perhaps not surprising that at the beginning of the study, I was asked by a senior professor in physics why a study was necessary. He expressed the opinion that postdoctoral education was perhaps the best part of higher education; it had grown naturally out of the needs of the participants without any interference by deans. The system was working satisfactorily. Why rock the boat?

A similar objection came from the education officer of a major foundation. He wondered why one should study postdoctorals when graduate and undergraduate education were both much larger and were probably in much worse shape.

In a sense the postdoctoral phenomenon needs study just because it has been so successful. Increasing numbers of postdoctoral students have caused them to become visible beyond the laboratory and the library. But it would be more accurate to say that the larger community has become aware of them without really seeing them. It is this awareness without insight that is responsible for the study.

In brief, the purpose of the study was to provide the basic facts about postdoctoral study as it exists in the United States today so that those entrusted with academic, administrative, and legislative responsibilities could better cope with perceived problems. Beyond this, however, the study was conceived to inform the participants, both the postdoctoral appointee and the faculty mentor, of the actual situation in which they are involved and of the forces that have brought it into existence and that are likely to lead to change. In answer to the professor mentioned above, the boat had already been rocked. It was hoped that the study would enable all those concerned to find a new position of stability.

In a more personal vein, I would like to express my appreciation to the National Research Council-National Academy of Sciences for all the support they gave me during the course of the study. In particular I am grateful to Dr. M. H. Trytten and Dr. William C. Kelly for their guidance and untiring efforts to provide me with the staff, facilities, and assistance necessary to complete the task. The Advisory Committee was an extraordinary group of dedicated leaders in higher education and research. Without their encouragement and timely suggestions this report and the study on which it is based would not have been nearly so significant. I am especially grateful for the opportunity to have worked with Robert K. Weatherall, the Associate Director of the study. Not only was he responsible for the historical research and for his share of the design of the study, but throughout the study his wit and sensibility and organizing skills were indispensable.

Finally, I want to express particular thanks for the distaff contribution to the completion of this report—to Mrs. Mary Alice McDonough for organizing the flow of questionnaires and materials, Miss Jane Howard for recording lengthy meetings, Mrs. Doris Rogowski and her staff for coding the questionnaires, Dr. Joan Creager for translating prose questions into programming instructions, Mrs. Aida Perez for the programming, Mrs. Judith Cleary for correcting my grammatical mistakes and awkward phrases, Miss Clarebeth Maguire for organizing the manuscript and preparing the graphics, and my wife who, without complaint, put up with my frequent trips between Bloomington and Washington.

RICHARD B. CURTIS
*Study Director*
April 1969

# Contents

**CHAPTER 1**

INTRODUCTION ... 1

**CHAPTER 2**

AN HISTORICAL VIEW ... 7

Beginnings of Doctoral and Postdoctoral Research in the
   United States ... 7
Research in the Medical Schools ... 10
National Research Fellowships ... 16
International Fellowships ... 21
Fellowships in the Humanities and Social Sciences ... 22
The Association of American Universities ... 26
The Federal Government ... 27
   National Cancer Institute, 27
   National Institutes of Health, 29
   National Science Foundation, 33
Career Awards in the Medical Sciences ... 34
Epilogue ... 37

**CHAPTER 3**

THE STUDY ... 39

The Available Facts ... 40
Definition of Postdoctoral Appointment ... 41
Strategy of the Study ... 45

CONTENTS

CHAPTER 4

THE DEMOGRAPHY OF POSTDOCTORAL EDUCATION 49

The Composition of the Postdoctoral Population 51
The Postdoctoral in U.S. Academic Institutions 54
   Immediate PhD Postdoctorals, 58
   Intermediate PhD Postdoctorals, 94
   Senior PhD Postdoctorals, 98
   Long-Term PhD Postdoctorals, 101
   Post-Professional-Doctorates (MD's), 105
The Postdoctoral in Nonacademic Institutions 115
   Nonprofit Institutions, 118
   Industrial Laboratories, 119
   Federal Government Laboratories, 122
   Postdoctorals Abroad, 124


CHAPTER 5

IMPLICATIONS FOR THE POSTDOCTORAL 126

Comments of Former Postdoctorals 128
Quantitative Aspects of the Postdoctoral Experience 133


CHAPTER 6

IMPLICATIONS FOR ACADEMIC INSTITUTIONS 143

Effect on the Department 149
Teaching by Postdoctorals 161
Contribution to Research 170
   Implications for the Research Group, 177
Recruitment of Postdoctorals as Faculty 179
Implications for the Disciplines 183
Summary 193


CHAPTER 7

IMPLICATIONS FOR NONACADEMIC INSTITUTIONS 194

Employment of New Doctorate Recipients 195
Research Funds and Recruitment of Postdoctorals 197

## CHAPTER 8

### THE FOREIGN POSTDOCTORAL — 205

Impact on United States Universities — 207
Countries of Origin — 212
Return to Countries of Origin — 217

## CHAPTER 9

### THE FINANCES OF POSTDOCTORAL EDUCATION — 224

Stipends — 225
University Costs — 230
Sources of Support — 233

## CHAPTER 10

### CONCLUSIONS AND RECOMMENDATIONS — 241

Summary — 254

## APPENDIX A

### THE QUESTIONNAIRES — 259

1. Postdoctoral Census Questionnaire — 259
2. Departmental Questionnaire — 263
3. Faculty Questionnaire — 267
4. Postdoctoral Experience Questionnaire — 272
5. Institutional Questionnaire — 278

## APPENDIX B

### COMPILATIONS OF DATA — 283

1. Fine Field Distribution of Postdoctorals — 283
2. Distribution of Postdoctorals among Universities — 296
3. Distribution of Foreign Postdoctorals by Country — 304

## APPENDIX C

### BIBLIOGRAPHY — 309

# Tables and Figures

CHAPTER **2**

TABLES

1 Number of National Research (NRC) Fellows holding teaching positions in 1950, by field — 19
2 Number of NIH postdoctoral and special fellowships, fiscal years 1946-1967 — 30
3 Appropriations for NIH training grant programs, fiscal years 1946-1967 — 31
4 Number of NSF regular and senior postdoctoral fellowships and science faculty fellowships, 1953-1969 — 35

FIGURES

1 Percentage of PhD recipients receiving National Research (NRC) Fellowships, by field, 1920-1939, and percentage of 1967 PhD's receiving postdoctoral appointments — 18

CHAPTER **4**

TABLES

5 Number of postdoctorals by level of appointment and percent foreign — 52

## TABLES AND FIGURES

| | | |
|---|---|---|
| 6 | Number of postdoctorals by field and percent foreign | 54 |
| 7 | Concentration of postdoctorals among academic institutions in selected fields | 57 |
| 8 | Percentage of academic institutions having postdoctorals by type of institution and department | 58 |
| 9 | Distribution of postdoctorals at U.S. academic institutions by level of appointment and field | 59 |
| 10 | Number of PhD's and percentage taking immediate postdoctoral appointment, by field of doctorate, 1962–1967 | 60 |
| 11 | Next anticipated employer of immediate U.S. postdoctorals, by type of host institution | 62 |
| 12 | Next anticipated employer of immediate U.S. postdoctorals at universities, by field | 63 |
| 13 | Work activity of assistant professors in selected departments, by type of academic institution | 66 |
| 14 | Immediate previous experience of newly appointed junior faculty in selected departments, by type of academic institution | 68 |
| 15 | Geographic location of immediate postdoctorals (with U.S. baccalaureates) at three training levels, all host institutions | 73 |
| 16 | Migration of immediate postdoctorals at U.S. academic institutions from PhD to postdoctoral institution for selected fields | 74 |
| 17 | Percentage of PhD's taking postdoctoral appointments in selected fields, by type of PhD institution | 76 |
| 18 | Migration of postdoctorals by reputation of PhD and postdoctoral institutions, by field | 77 |
| 19 | Mean years elapsed (total time) from baccalaureate to doctorate for PhD postdoctorals in selected broad fields, by type of academic institution | 78 |
| 20 | Average quality index of postdoctorals at academic institutions, by type of postdoctoral institution, by field | 80 |
| 21 | Average quality index of postdoctorals at academic institutions, by type of doctoral institution, by field | 82 |
| 22 | Field and subfield changes of immediate U.S. postdoctorals, all host institutions | 84 |
| 23 | Types of appointment of all postdoctorals at U.S. academic institutions: A comparison between departmental and postdoctoral responses | 91 |
| 24 | Distribution of intermediate postdoctorals among host institutions, by field and citizenship | 96 |

TABLES AND FIGURES

| | | |
|---|---|---|
| 25 | Percentage of intermediate postdoctorals at academic and nonacademic host institutions on employment leave, by field and citizenship | 97 |
| 26 | Distribution of senior postdoctorals among host institutions, by field and citizenship | 100 |
| 27 | Number and percentage of long-term postdoctorals at U.S. academic institutions, by sex and citizenship | 105 |
| 28 | Comparison between Office of Scientific Personnel (OSP) census and AMA data on postdoctorals in the clinical specialties at U.S. medical schools | 106 |
| 29 | Enrollment of postdoctorals at U.S. academic institutions in regular courses and in degree programs, by field and citizenship | 107 |
| 30 | Distribution of post-MD's among fields, by type of host institution and citizenship | 113 |
| 31 | Anticipated employment of post-MD's, by citizenship and level of degree | 114 |

FIGURES

| | | |
|---|---|---|
| 2 | Profile of U.S. postdoctorals | 50 |
| 3 | Distribution of 1967 postdoctorals among U.S. academic institutions and comparison to 1960-66 PhD production and 1966 federal academic science obligations | 56 |
| 4 | Geographic location of PhD institutions and academic host institutions of immediate postdoctorals | 72 |
| 5 | Percentage of immediate postdoctorals, by field of PhD, who changed from the field or subfield of their PhD's | 85 |
| 6 | Types of appointment of postdoctorals at U.S. academic institutions | 92 |
| 7 | Percentage of enrollees, by level, in dentistry, medicine, and basic medical sciences, 1966–67 | 110 |
| 8 | Distribution of U.S. and foreign post-MD's, by degree level, postdoctoral field, and host institution | 112 |
| 9 | Nonacademic host institutions: Percentage of postdoctorals by field of postdoctoral, sex and citizenship, and level of appointment | 116 |

CHAPTER 5

TABLES

| | | |
|---|---|---|
| 32 | Type of employer in 1967 of natural scientists, by postdoctoral background, PhD's of 1950, 1955, and 1960 | 134 |

TABLES AND FIGURES

| 33 | Rank or position in 1967 of academic scientists (U.S. males only), by year of PhD and postdoctoral background | 136 |
|---|---|---|
| 34 | Type of work activity in 1967 of academic scientists (U.S. males only), by PhD year and postdoctoral background | 136 |
| 35 | Research activity of academic scientists (U.S. males only), by year of PhD and postdoctoral background | 137 |

FIGURES

| 10 | Evaluation of immediate postdoctoral experience by academic scientists (U.S. males only) | 140 |
|---|---|---|
| 11 | Evaluation of delayed postdoctoral experience by academic scientists (U.S. males only) | 141 |

CHAPTER 6

TABLES

| 36 | Participation in postdoctoral education in three fields, by type of academic institution | 144 |
|---|---|---|
| 37 | Faculty and students in selected graduate departments with and without postdoctorals, by type of academic institution | 154 |
| 38 | Graduate degrees granted per year per faculty member in departments with and without postdoctorals, by type of academic institution | 156 |
| 39 | First employment of 1967 doctorates from departments with and without postdoctorals | 157 |
| 40 | Percentage of faculty with postdoctoral background and percentage who are postdoctoral mentors in departments with and without postdoctorals | 158 |
| 41 | Previous position of newly appointed junior faculty in departments with and without postdoctorals | 160 |
| 42 | Degree of faculty involvement in research in departments with and without postdoctorals | 162 |
| 43 | Involvement of postdoctorals in teaching, by citizenship and field | 167 |
| 44 | Percentage of postdoctorals who teach, by level and types of teaching and by citizenship | 168 |
| 45 | Evaluation by the chairmen of doctoral departments without postdoctorals of the desirability of having postdoctorals | 175 |
| 46 | Composition and size of research groups with and without postdoctorals, by field | 176 |

xxii
TABLES AND FIGURES

| | | |
|---|---|---|
| 47 | PhD production by research groups with and without postdoctorals, by field | 178 |
| 48 | Average amount of research support per research group with and without postdoctorals, by field and type of academic institution | 180 |

FIGURES

| | | |
|---|---|---|
| 12 | Percentage of departments by highest level of educational activity, by type of academic institution | 150 |
| 13 | Faculty time and departmental space requirements for postdoctorals as compared with requirements for graduate students | 159 |
| 14 | Percentage of postdoctorals who teach, by level and type of teaching and by citizenship | 169 |
| 15 | Contribution of research group—graduate students, postdoctorals, professional research staff—to natural science professors' teaching responsibilities | 171 |
| 16 | Contribution of research group—graduate students, postdoctorals, professional research staff—to faculty research in the natural sciences | 174 |

CHAPTER 7

FIGURES

| | | |
|---|---|---|
| 17 | Percentage of 1965–66 PhD's in selected fields from the 30 leading universities entering various employment categories | 196 |
| 18 | Percentage of 1965–66 PhD's from the 30 leading universities by type of employer, including postdoctorals distributed according to their subsequent employers | 198 |

CHAPTER 8

TABLES

| | | |
|---|---|---|
| 49 | PhD postdoctorals at U.S. academic institutions, by type of institution and citizenship | 209 |
| 50 | Distribution of foreign postdoctorals among U.S. academic institutions, by GNP rating of foreign country of origin | 210 |
| 51 | Percentage of foreign postdoctorals by field, from six leading countries | 214 |
| 52 | Future location as projected by 1967 foreign postdoctorals and present location of 1961–62 foreign postdoctorals | 221 |

TABLES AND FIGURES

## FIGURES

| | | |
|---|---|---|
| 19 | Number of postdoctorals from the 13 countries that were the source of three-quarters of all foreign postdoctorals | 213 |
| 20 | Previous training of foreign postdoctorals compared with American postdoctorals, by per capita GNP of foreign country, all fields combined | 218 |
| 21 | Relevance of the foreign postdoctorals' experiences to their countries' needs, by per capita GNP of country of origin | 220 |

CHAPTER 9

## TABLES

| | | |
|---|---|---|
| 53 | Number and percentage of postdoctorals, by reported source of support | 234 |
| 54 | Number of postdoctorals, by source of support and postdoctoral field | 235 |
| 55 | Number of postdoctorals, by source of support and type of host institution | 236 |
| 56 | Number of postdoctorals, by source of support and level of appointment | 238 |
| 57 | Number of postdoctorals, by source of support and citizenship | 239 |

## FIGURES

| | | |
|---|---|---|
| 22 | Median annual (12-month) stipends of postdoctorals compared with salaries of assistant professors, by field, 1967 | 227 |
| 23 | Annual (12-month) stipend of postdoctorals by citizenship, type of host institution, and level of postdoctoral appointment | 229 |

CHAPTER 10

## TABLE

| | | |
|---|---|---|
| 58 | A comparison of the physics and chemistry postdoctoral population in 1967 and 1968 | 249 |

CHAPTER 1
# Introduction

To an increasing extent, the doctorate is no longer the terminal point for advanced education in the United States. Each year significant numbers of doctoral recipients, especially in the sciences, seek temporary positions where they may augment their education and experience in research before accepting more permanent employment. Others, more senior, take leaves of absence from their employment to obtain a similar experience. Although most of these postdoctoral scholars are at universities, they may be found in government laboratories, at nonprofit research institutions, in hospitals, at archeological digs, and at industrial laboratories.

At some universities postdoctorals have been familiar figures for many years, but they have never before existed in such large numbers or at so many institutions. In several university departments they outnumber the faculty; occasionally they outnumber the students. In the division of biology at the California Institute of Technology, which has long been a center of postdoctoral education, postdoctorals outnumbered professors four to one in 1967-68.[1] At the Harvard Medical School in 1967-68 there were more postdoctoral research fellows than medical students.[2]

The postdoctoral scholar is not easy to describe. He can be a doctor of philosophy (PhD) or, quite a different matter, a doctor of medicine (MD).

---

[1] *A Report for the Year 1967-68 on the Research and Other Activities of the Division of Biology at the California Institute of Technology,* Pasadena, California, pp. 6-9.
[2] Harvard Medical School, *Dean's Report for 1967-68,* pp. 13, 28.

## 2
INTRODUCTION

Sometimes he has both degrees. Occasionally, his doctorate is in veterinary medicine, law, or education, or he may be a scholar with the intellectual qualifications of a doctorate but without the degree. In each case he has come to the status of postdoctoral scholar by a different academic route. He has pursued a different training, with different objectives.

The postdoctoral scholar with a PhD is most often a young natural scientist who has recently completed his doctoral dissertation. He has completed his formal education, but believes that he can benefit from continuing his research for awhile under an experienced mentor—often a colleague of his dissertation adviser at another institution. But he may also be a social scientist or, more rarely, a humanist. Often he is an older scholar. A good percentage of the postdoctoral population consists of faculty members who have taken leave from their institutions to study in a colleague's laboratory or in a library that offers resources they need.

The postdoctoral scholar with an MD is usually well advanced in a specialty. He has often completed the internship and residency training required for practice in his field but he wants further training in an area that concerns him. His ultimate aim may be practice in his specialty or an academic career—a career for which his training, primarily oriented toward practice, has not prepared him. But there are also postdoctoral scholars with the MD who have not completed residency training and perhaps never will. They have decided early that they want a career in teaching and research rather than in practice. Typically their interest is not in clinical medicine but in the sciences basic to medicine, such as biochemistry, microbiology, or physiology. If they had made their decisions still earlier, they might have studied for a PhD instead of an MD.

A postdoctoral scholar's status is not always clear from his title. His appointment is characteristically transitional and temporary but it merges with that of the research staff member whose appointment is considered more or less permanent. On many campuses the title of research associate is given both to short-term postdoctoral scholars receiving support from research project funds and to long-term research staff. The title of postdoctoral fellow is equally imprecise. Many postdoctoral scholars are the holders of fellowships for which they have competed successfully on a regional or national basis. The title of fellow has meaning in this case and, because it is a distinction to win a competitive fellowship, it adds a certain luster. But the same title is often given to a postdoctoral scholar supported by other means. To avoid complication, there is advantage in turning the adjective into a noun and calling him simply "a postdoctoral." This is how we refer to him in this report.

One important characteristic of the postdoctoral population is its close association with distinguished institutions. Although postdoctorals can be found at almost 200 universities, over half of them are at only 17 institutions. In in-

# INTRODUCTION

dividual fields the concentration is even greater. One fourth of the postdoctorals in the engineering, mathematics, and physical sciences are at only six universities, all of which rank among the top seven in quality, as measured by Cartter.[3] Similarly, only five schools account for a third of the postdoctorals in the clinical specialties. Characteristic also is an association between postdoctorals and distinguished mentors. It is not difficult to find internationally known investigators serving as mentors to as many as a dozen postdoctorals.

Postdoctorals are found, in varying numbers, in virtually all fields of study—preponderantly in the natural and medical sciences, but also in the social sciences and the humanities. As will be seen from the chapters that follow, a very large proportion of the total population is foreign.

Many postdoctorals have gone on to distinguished careers. A notable example is the French Nobel prizewinner, Jacques Monod, who as a young investigator held a postdoctoral fellowship at the California Institute of Technology. It was as a postdoctoral that an American Nobel Laureate, James D. Watson, did the work that made his reputation.

In 1967 the total number of individuals holding temporary appointments for the purpose of continued education and experience in research (our definition of a postdoctoral) was approximately 16,000. That this large a number of holders of the doctorate should be welcome at several hundred different host institutions implies that something is very right about postdoctoral study. The eagerness with which former postdoctorals are sought by university departments for faculty positions suggests that the experience and/or the selectivity of the postdoctoral appointment makes this group particularly attractive. Both the participants and the subsequent employers seem to consider postdoctoral education a success.

This does not mean that no problems exist. As we shall see in the first chapter, the problem in the past was to establish the idea of postdoctoral education in the minds of the participants and potential participants. The problems of today are more diffuse and result as much from the successes of the past as the failures of the present. For all concerned, whether host institution, sponsoring agency, or the general public, the numbers involved raise important questions.

For almost a decade, university presidents have been concerned about the ever increasing number of postdoctoral appointments on campus. Neither student nor faculty, the postdoctoral appointees have been virtually invisible to anyone outside their departments. Their major impact on the campus at large is the space they require. Departments have asked the administration for additional space when a head count of faculty and graduate students

---

[3] H. W. Magoun, The Cartter Report on Quality in Graduate Education, *Journal of Higher Education*, Vol. XXXVII, No. 9, December 1966.

would indicate that the present laboratories were not yet filled. The problem is aggravated at state universities by the lack of recognition by state budget offices of the legal existence of postdoctorals. Few universities are able to acquire building funds based on the number of postdoctorals in a department.

The situation is made more awkward in that few universities have initiated postdoctoral activity by design. When asked why his university encourages postdoctoral education, one graduate dean replied: "I am not sure we could be said to have a rationale; we permit rather than promote postdoctoral study." For the most part, postdoctorals come to a university provided with their own support, seeking the use of certain facilities, or they come as employees under a faculty research grant. The administration is aware that the faculty member wants the postdoctoral in his laboratory to assist with his research, but it seldom asks why the postdoctoral seeks such a position. Unlike undergraduate and graduate education, postdoctoral education is, with few exceptions, not consciously or intentionally undertaken by the university.

Most universities suspect, but are not sure, that having postdoctorals on campus is costing them money. This is especially true of the postdoctoral who comes with little more than his stipend from some federal agency or private foundation. Few postdoctorals pay tuition, but they all consume faculty time and academic space. There is no general agreement on whether they are the most senior students or the most junior faculty members. Not knowing the role of the postdoctoral, the universities cannot agree how the activity should be classified in their budgets.

There are also questions raised by those outside the academic community. Since the Congress appropriates the funds that support most of the activity, its opinion is especially important. The Reuss Report[4] suggested that the shortage of teachers, especially in the sciences, is a consequence of young PhD's being deflected from teaching into research by the availability of postdoctoral appointments. The problem is made more intense by the circumstance, as the Subcommittee sees it, that "the abler graduate students and young postdoctorals go into research—the less able teach."

The federal agencies react somewhat differently from the Congress. Charged primarily with promoting research, the various groups—ranging from the Department of Defense (DOD) and the National Institutes of Health (NIH) through the independent agencies, such as the National Science Foundation (NSF) and the National Aeronautics and Space Administration (NASA)—have evolved a number of programs affecting the postdoctoral population. Some, through fellowship programs like those of NSF and NIH, support postdoctorals

---

[4]*Conflicts Between the Federal Research Programs and the Nation's Goals for Higher Education,* Report of the Research and Technical Programs Subcommittee of the Committee on Government Operations, House Report No. 1158, 1965.

directly in order to produce a core of highly creative researchers. Others, by means of research contracts and grants awarded to universities to support faculty research, contribute funds to pay for postdoctorals who are hired to assist the faculty members. There is no coordination of postdoctoral support between these two disparate mechanisms, even when both instruments issue from the same agency. Consequently, in these days of curtailed growth (or even reduction) of federal research funds to universities, the agencies are hard pressed to establish priorities and to strike a balance between research and training.

Most people involved with postdoctorals are aware of the fairly large numbers of foreign citizens within the group. Those who are concerned about research output tend to be indifferent to the nationality of the researcher; those who are concerned with training are troubled by the use of federal funds to support scientists who will not remain in this country. From a different point of view, both the Congress and the Department of State have been discussing the so-called "brain drain." To the extent that it exists, the foreign postdoctoral is clearly an important component. Implicit in all of these attitudes and concerns are questions concerning the numbers of foreign postdoctorals.

After academic institutions, the major employer of physical science doctorates is industry. A deficit of college and university faculty, resulting from the growth of undergraduate education and the insufficient output of the graduate schools, is reflected in a shortage of top scientific talent in the industrial research laboratories. There is some suspicion among industrialists that the expansion of postdoctoral education in the universities is responsible for aggravating the manpower squeeze. The recruiting officer of a major industrial firm has expressed concern over the large number of science graduates who are hired by universities to do research with funds supplied by the federal agencies. Others have suggested that the availability of postdoctorals has enabled universities, with their lower overheads, to compete successfully for federal research contracts that might otherwise have gone to industry. Still others have expressed concern that postdoctoral education in the university setting only further insulates the young doctorate from applied problems, making him more unlikely to choose industrial research as a vocation. The question is, of course, how valid are these criticisms?

Finally there are the questions raised by society at large. In the face of rising costs, both state legislatures and boards of trustees are beginning to question university administrators more closely on various aspects of their programs. Although undergraduate education is recognized as essential and desirable, some state university presidents find that they must constantly defend the concept of graduate education by illustrating the contribution it makes to the state and nation. In this setting postdoctoral education appears

## INTRODUCTION

esoteric and even gratuitous. Is the postdoctoral indulging a luxury or is he receiving a critically important experience and thereby fulfilling a national need?

Although the dimensions of postdoctoral education have increased steadily, particularly since World War II, this is the first time that it has been the subject of a comprehensive study. Bernard Berelson, in his well-known *Graduate Education in the United States*, published in 1960, devoted ten pages to postdoctoral education. "There is so much postdoctoral training," he noted, "that many people are becoming perplexed or even alarmed at where it is all going to end."[5] At the request of the Association of American Universities he went on to take a closer look at postdoctoral education, examining it particularly on the campuses of the 41-member institutions of the Association. A summary of his report was published in the spring of 1962.[6] In the medical sciences, at the same time, there was concern over the impact of large numbers of research fellows on the structure of medical education and the medical profession. The Division of Medical Sciences of the National Academy of Sciences obtained funds in 1957 for a study of the role of postdoctoral fellowships in academic medicine. This study, conducted until his death by Arthur S. Cain, Jr., and completed by Lois G. Bowen, bore fruit in a long report published in 1961 in the *Journal of Medical Education*.[7] A number of studies have been made of the postdoctoral population at particular institutions and postdoctoral education increasingly finds a place in surveys of individual research fields. But there has not hitherto been a study of the whole scope of postdoctoral education, embracing all institutions and all fields.

In this report we have attempted to answer the questions raised above. We begin with a review of the history of postdoctoral education since it first began in this country more than fifty years ago. The succeeding chapters consider in detail the composition of this population; the significance of postdoctoral education for the individual, for the department, and for the institution of which he is temporarily a member; the character of postdoctoral education in different fields of study; the manner in which it is supported and provided for; and its cost. We conclude the report with recommendations based on our findings.

---

[5] Bernard Berelson, *Graduate Education in the United States*, McGraw-Hill, New York, 1960, p. 190.
[6] Bernard Berelson, Postdoctoral Work in American Universities: A Recent Survey, *Journal of Higher Education*, Vol. XXXIII, No. 3, March 1962, pp. 119-130.
[7] Arthur S. Cain, Jr. and Lois G. Bowen, The Role of Postdoctoral Fellowships in Academic Medicine, *The Journal of Medical Education*, Vol. 36, No. 10, Part 2, October 1961, pp. 1351-1556.

CHAPTER **2**
# An Historical View

The instinct of the scholar to carry his education as far as he can at the centers of learning in his field is as old as the university itself. Thomas Aquinas in the 13th century left the University of Naples for Paris and Cologne to study under Albertus Magnus. To get the best training in medicine available in the 16th century Andreas Vesalius went from Louvain to Paris and thence to Padua, "that most famous university of the whole world,"[1] as he called it. In more recent times, Ernest Rutherford, recipient of the best education his native New Zealand could give, seized the opportunity of a grant for further study to pursue research in physics in England under J. J. Thomson. At its best, postdoctoral education represents an ancient prescription for excellence.

## Beginnings of Doctoral and Postdoctoral Research in the United States

The men who developed the American university as a teaching and research institution a century ago intended it to be a place where learning would continue through a man's lifetime. Teachers and students alike were to learn by

---

[1] Andreas Vesalius, *De Humani Corporis Fabrica*, 1543, the preface.

doing research. Attainment of the PhD was not to be any sort of stopping point. "What are we aiming at?" asked Daniel Coit Gilman in his inaugural address as first president of Johns Hopkins in 1876. He answered, in part: "The encouragement of research; the promotion of young men; and the advancement of individual scholars, who by their excellence will advance the sciences they pursue, and the society where they dwell."[2]

President Gilman offered twenty fellowships annually to attract and support young men starting research careers. The first fellows chosen in 1876 included four who already had their PhD's.[3] The others were candidates for the doctorate but all had the same long-range objective. As a fellow of the following year recalled, "The Johns Hopkins fellowship in those days did not seem a routine matter, an every-day step in the regular process toward a doctorate or a professorship, but a rare and peculiar opportunity for study and research, eagerly seized by men who had been hungering and thirsting for such a possibility."[4]

The faculty also were encouraged to develop as creative scholars. The psychologist G. Stanley Hall, a professor at Johns Hopkins before he became the first president of Clark University, thought that Gilman "nowhere showed more sagacity than in applying individual stimuli and checks, so that in this sense and to this extent he was a spiritual father of many of his faculty, the author of their careers, and for years made the institution the paradise and seminarium of young specialists. This made stagnation impossible, and the growth of professors there in their work was, I believe, without precedent."[5] When Hall opened Clark University in 1889 he said boldly: "We are a school for professors, where leisure, method, and incentive train select men to higher and more productive efficiency than before."[6]

At the University of Chicago, founded in 1890, President William Rainey Harper ventured to limit the claims of classroom teaching on a faculty member's time. "It is proposed in this institution," Harper wrote, "to make the work of investigation primary, the work of giving instruction secondary."[7] For the sake of research, heavy teaching loads were avoided and arrangements were made to excuse faculty members from their teaching duties entirely from time to time. The commitment to research also found expression in the titles of appointments. The faculty was formally divided into scholars, fellows, and docents as well as instructors, lecturers, and professors.

---

[2] Quoted by W. Carson Ryan, *Studies in Early Graduate Education*, No. 31, Carnegie Foundation for the Advancement of Teaching, New York, 1939, p. 28.
[3] John C. French, *A History of the University Founded by Johns Hopkins*, The Johns Hopkins Press, Baltimore, 1946, p. 41.
[4] Fabian Franklin, *The Life of Daniel Coit Gilman*, Dodd, New York, 1910, p. 228.
[5] Quoted by Ryan, *op cit.*, p. 39.
[6] *Ibid.*, p. 48.
[7] *Ibid.*, p. 126.

## BEGINNINGS OF DOCTORAL AND POSTDOCTORAL RESEARCH

The eighties and nineties was a period of rapidly rising student enrollments across the nation and of run-away growth in PhD programs. Graduate enrollments grew tenfold. In 1877-78 only a handful of institutions granted the PhD. Their graduate population totaled little more than four hundred. By 1896-97 there were 146 PhD-granting institutions with a collective graduate enrollment of 4,392. The pressures of expansion subjected the universities to financial strains that made it difficult to give strong support to postdoctoral and faculty research. At the 1901 meeting of the recently constituted Association of American Universities, Dean Harry P. Judson of Chicago commented on the support that fellowships had given to doctoral study and lamented that "the number of research fellowships offered to those who have made the doctorate is as yet inconsiderable." He urged the endowment of "a considerable number of research fellowships . . . to be granted only to those who have already on foot an investigation which promises results."[8] Four years later he fought a proposal that Chicago balance its budget by increasing teaching loads; if it took this course, he argued, it would ". . . sink to the level of the many institutions which, while really large colleges, are adding a small portion of advanced work in the hands of overburdened teachers."[9]

There were those who felt that reasonable teaching loads were the key to the matter, rather than fellowships. At the seventh annual meeting of the Association of American Universities in 1906, a morning was devoted to the topic, "To what extent should the university investigator be relieved from teaching?" President David Starr Jordan of Stanford offered the view that there was too much conceit of research—"not all who talk of research, even in Germany, shall enter the kingdom"—but he concluded:

The university should recognize the necessity of research to university men, and in a much greater degree than is now the case in any American university. It should provide for this by furnishing all needed appliances, material, books, clerical help, artists, assistants, leisure, and freedom. . . . Men should not be encouraged to undertake research in order to gain professorships. Rather they should gain professorships in order to make research fruitful. A university need not provide for research fellowships or research professorships.[10]

In his annual report for 1910, the President of the Carnegie Foundation for the Advancement of Teaching, Henry S. Pritchett, looked critically at the contribution of the growing graduate student population to research.

The graduate school had its rise ostensibly in a desire to promote research. As a matter of fact, it is engaged in the main in training teachers who desire degrees. The develop-

---

[8] Association of American Universities, *Journal of Proceedings and Addresses, First and Second Annual Conferences, 1900 and 1901*, pp. 40, 41.
[9] Quoted by Richard J. Storr, *Harper's University: The Beginnings*, University of Chicago Press, Chicago, 1966, p. 353.
[10] Association of American Universities, *Journal of Proceedings and Addresses, Seventh Annual Conference*, 1906, pp. 25, 28, 29.

ment of true research has had no relation to the enormous growth of the graduate school. Indeed, in many institutions the creation of a graduate school has practically put an end to research. . . . In some graduate schools men who, in a perfectly natural way, would have developed into research men have been forced to give up the work of research in order to hold seminars and to find new themes for constantly growing armies of aspirants for the degree of doctor of philosophy. It is true that both the appreciation of research and the disposition toward research have grown in American colleges, but in no such proportion as the graduate school has grown, and the growth of one has had too little to do with the growth of the other.[11]

In 1913 the American Association for the Advancement of Science appointed a Committee of One Hundred to consider the state of scientific research in America. It was a blue-ribbon group including representatives from the leading research institutions of the day. At a meeting the following year the chairman, Edward C. Pickering, pointed to the small sums appropriated by universities for research. "If a tenth of the money used for teaching was employed in research," he said, "Americans would soon take their proper places among the great men of science of the world." A subcommittee that included the surgeon, Harvey Cushing, and the geneticist, Thomas Hunt Morgan, suggested that

. . . in order to encourage the original minds in America, there should be more research professorships and research assistantships of high grade, which would raise their holders above the worry and inefficiency caused by financial need. . . . The finding of the really promising man (who must possess not only originality, but also sound judgment and intellectual honesty) is not easy, because it often involves the gift of prophecy on the part of the searcher. Nevertheless, it seems to us that all those in each of our larger institutions for learning who are really interested in research of the highest kind, either individually or grouped together as a voluntary committee, should keep their eyes open for persons possessing in high degree the happy combination of qualities desired and should urge upon presidents and governing boards the importance of supporting these persons so as to make it possible for them to yield their best fruit in discovery.[12]

## Research in the Medical Schools

Medical research was handicapped by the poor training received by many MD's. Abraham Flexner's famous report of 1910 on medical education in the United States and Canada is an eloquent account of the deplorable condition of undergraduate medical education at this time.[13] At many schools students

---

[11] *Sixth Annual Report of the President and of the Treasurer*, The Carnegie Foundation for the Advancement of Teaching, 1911, pp. 104, 105.
[12] *Science*, February 26, 1915, Vol. XLI, No. 1052, pp. 316, 319.
[13] Abraham Flexner, *Medical Education in the United States and Canada*, Bulletin No. 4, The Carnegie Foundation for the Advancement of Teaching, 1910, p. 56.

got little grounding in the sciences basic to medicine and little exposure to clinical cases. The lecture theater played too large a part in medical education, the laboratory and ward much too small a part.

Taking a year's appointment as a hospital intern was not yet the rule for young medical graduates. "House surgeons" and "house physicians," on the pattern of today's interns, were appointed at the New York Hospital soon after its inception in 1791 and at Bellevue in 1806, but during most of the nineteenth century the concept of the internship as an educational opportunity made little headway.[14] In 1904 the American Medical Association estimated that less than 50 percent of medical graduates took an internship before starting private practice.[15] Those who sought the opportunity were, one observer said, the more studious element, "men of high and noble aspirations, intent on making records for themselves in their professional career; men with pronounced taste for the academic side of medicine."[16] It seemed increasingly scandalous that a student could go directly from the lecture theater to the treatment of his first patient, and in 1905 the American Medical Association voted that an internship year should be a regular part of medical training. This did not make it so, however. It was five years before a medical school, the College of Medicine and Surgery of the University of Minnesota, made a year's internship a requirement for graduation. The first state to make it a requirement for practice, Pennsylvania, took the step in 1914. Even in 1920 only six states required it.[17] But by this time the importance of an internship year was gaining acceptance, and a decade later virtually every medical graduate served an internship, whether required of him or not.[18]

A year's internship, however, could not meet the needs of men who wished to achieve the highest level of medical competence. "Training for the higher clinical careers," wrote the distinguished Johns Hopkins pathologist, William H. Welch, in 1907, "requires a long apprenticeship after graduation from medical school and after the ordinary hospital internship, and is best secured by prolonged service in a hospital as resident physician or surgeon under conditions which secure more thorough practical experience and better opportunities for scientific study and investigation than those which now exist under the customary arrangement of the medical staff of our hospitals."[19] Residencies of this description were available at the Johns Hopkins Hospital and at some other university hospitals but they were few in total number. Many

---

[14]*Internships and Residencies in New York City, 1934-37, Their Place in Medical Education*, The Commonwealth Fund, 1938, p. 27.
[15]*Journal of the American Medical Association*, Vol. 43, August 13, 1904, p. 469.
[16]*Ibid.*, Vol. 50, May 2, 1908, p. 1395.
[17]*Ibid.*, Vol. 63, Sept. 19, 1914, p. 1049; Vol. 74, April 17, 1920, p. 1099.
[18]*Ibid.*, Vol. 99, August 27, 1932, p. 743.
[19]*Ibid.*, Vol. 49, August 17, 1907, p. 534.

## AN HISTORICAL VIEW

MD's interested in advanced medical training sought it in Europe. Residencies at European teaching hospitals were advertised in the American medical journals.

Some who wished to see more provision for advanced medical training in the United States looked to the graduate schools to provide it. The graduate schools, it was felt, had the necessary respect for research and, as institutions dedicated to scholarship, were in the best position to maintain scholarly standards. In 1914 the University of Minnesota under President George E. Vincent (later president of the Rockefeller Foundation) initiated graduate degrees in medicine on the pattern of the university's graduate degrees in the arts and sciences. Six three-year teaching fellowships were established for the support of candidates. The following year the university signed an agreement with the Mayo Foundation in Rochester permitting students to work for the degrees in the clinics and laboratories of either institution. Thirty clinical fellows or residents at the Foundation officially became fellows in the university. The graduate work at Rochester was placed under the direction of a committee chaired by the dean of the graduate school.[20]

What was intended by graduate work in medicine was made clear in a report presented to the university regents:

> In graduate work of any kind research plays a large part. Originality and ability to conduct investigation must be demonstrated. The studies of a medical graduate in any given specialty should consist of: (1) Further work in the fundamental sciences of anatomy, physiology, etc.; (2) adequate practice in the technical procedures of diagnosis and treatment; (3) a thorough acquaintance with the literature of the specialty and related branches; (4) original investigation relating to his specialty.... Investigators are trained by doing original work under critical and inspired leadership. This is the prime function of the graduate school.[21]

Development of the program was delayed by World War I but after the war it attracted large numbers of applicants. As many as one thousand applied annually to study at Rochester. About 60 a year were awarded fellowships. The great majority came for advanced training in surgery. Roughly one in six was interested in internal medicine. Only a scattering were interested in work in the basic medical sciences.[22] By 1934 a total of 1,098 students had spent an average of four years on fellowship appointments at Rochester. Most had held fellowships that were service appointments in the clinic, at least in part; only 123 had held strictly research appointments. The program was not intended as preparation for academic work as against clinical practice. Neverthe-

---

[20] Helen Clapesattle, *The Doctors Mayo*, University of Minnesota Press, 1941, p. 643.
[21] *Journal of the American Medical Association*, Vol. 64, March 6 and June 12, 1915, pp. 790-794, 2009-2011.
[22] *Journal of the American Medical Association*, Vol. 74, March 27, 1920, p. 912.

less, 700 or so of the fellows later became teachers in medical schools and in other institutions.[23] It appears that about half of them completed the requirements for a degree in the graduate school, normally a master's degree but in some cases a PhD. Other advanced students received graduate degrees for their work at the university.[24]

Few graduate schools, however, followed Minnesota's initiative, and the medical schools were slow to devise any program beyond the MD. Lacking help from the universities, medical practitioners devised means of their own to promote higher levels of competence. As early as 1908 members of the American Ophthalmological Society urged the desirability of a special examination for the certification of practitioners in their field. It was suggested that the Society could require an advanced degree for membership, but this idea was not taken up. One objection, it is interesting to note, was that if the medical schools responded by starting advanced degree programs there would be as many standards for the degree as there were schools. The Society appointed a joint committee with the American Academy of Ophthalmology and Otolaryngology and the section on ophthalmology of the American Medical Association to look for a solution. In 1915 the committee recommended that the three groups establish together an examining board to certify to competence in the specialty. It was hoped that the board's certificates, while they would have no legal standing, would become the recognized mark of proficiency in the field. The committee's recommendations were accepted, and in 1916 the first specialty board examinations in ophthalmology were held in Memphis, Tennessee. In due time other specialty groups followed the ophthalmologists' example. A specialty board for otolaryngology was set up in 1924, for obstetrics and gynecology in 1930, for dermatology and syphilology in 1932, and for pediatrics in 1933.[25]

Hospital service provided the means to prepare for the board examinations. The increasing complexity of medical techniques put hospitals more and more at the center of medical practice. Diseases which had once been treated by a visiting physician in the home were now best treated in the hospital. The hospital was no longer feared, as it had been in the nineteenth century, as an institution of last resort, where a patient went when treatment at home failed. The number of hospital beds rapidly increased, creating a rising demand for resident house staff. A residency at a well-equipped hospital with a varied case load

---

[23] Association of American Universities, *Journal of Proceedings and Address of the Thirty-sixth Annual Conference*, 1934, p. 64.
[24] *Bulletin of the University of Minnesota*, The President's Report for the Years 1932-1934, pp. 178, 272, 278.
[25] Graduate Medical Education, *Report of the Commission on Graduate Medical Education*, Chicago, 1940, pp. 204-207; *Journal of the American Medical Association*, Vol. 65, Oct. 16, 1915, p. 1328; Vol. 68, March 10, 1917, p. 790.

## AN HISTORICAL VIEW

could offer an excellent training to a young MD who wished to develop his competence, and hospitals looking for house staff organized their residencies to serve this second function.

In 1925 the Council on Medical Education and Hospitals of the American Medical Association started listing residencies that they believed offered satisfactory educational opportunities. Its first list included only 35 hospitals, one of them a hospital in Paris. Many of the hospitals on the list were closely associated with medical schools, but others were not. Discussing the features it looked for in a satisfactory residency, the Council expressed the view that a hospital offering residencies in a specialty

> ... should provide (a) review courses in anatomy, pathology and the other basic preclinical sciences ... (b) clinics in which students can have the opportunity personally to examine patients ... (c) courses of operative and laboratory technique; and (d)–to be assigned only when the student's previous training will warrant–assistantships in which, under the supervision of a physician who is recognized as an expert in the particular specialty, he can gradually assume responsibility in the diagnosis and therapeutic or operative treatment of the sick. Opportunity should be provided also for research work in the chosen specialty bearing on both the fundamental sciences and clinical fields. [26]

In 1928, after a careful canvass, the Council published a list of 1,136 residencies at 292 hospitals.[27] Additions to the list during the next ten years doubled the number of approved hospitals and tripled the number of approved residencies.

In 1939 the Council set forth in detail what it considered to be the essentials of an approved hospital residency or fellowship. A residency was defined as a service appointment "of one or more years following an approved internship ... designed primarily to meet the requirements for certification of special practice."[28] It characterized a fellowship in this context as "a form of apprenticeship which in some cases is indistinguishable from a residency, although it usually offers greater opportunity for the study of basic sciences and research. Ordinarily a fellowship is a university rather than a hospital appointment."[29] The Council made no distinction in the essentials of a residency or fellowship training program. Both residents and fellows, it thought, "should be given an opportunity to contribute to the hospital service by some investigative work. This may take the form of research in the hospital laboratories or wards, summaries of medical literature, or the preparation of statistical analyses derived from the hospital record department. The members of the resident staff should likewise be encouraged to engage in teaching activi-

---

[26] *Journal of the American Medical Association*, Vol. 85, August 22, 1915, pp. 595–598.
[27] *Ibid.*, Vol. 90, March 24, 1928, pp. 911, 920, 922–979.
[28] *Ibid.*, Vol. 112, March 11, 1939, p. 926.
[29] *Ibid.*, April 8, 1939, pp. 1386–1392.

ties, particularly in relation to the training of medical students, interns, and nurses."

Residencies served well as a means of providing advanced clinical training but offered little opportunity to the man whose area of interest lay in the preclinical sciences. In 1920 the professor of physiology at Yale complained bitterly of the small encouragement given to men in these fields. Believing that the preclinical and clinical men on the staff of a medical school should work as a team, regarding each other as equals, he thought that "no man of the PhD variety should be allowed in the preclinical chairs." However, "no man of ability with the MD degree will in fact strive for them or stay in them, against the immensely greater opportunities and advantages offered now, and to be offered in even richer measure in the future, by the clinical departments. Unless something pretty radical is done and done soon, either these chairs will be filled by men with the PhD or they will be vacant. To get young men into the medical sciences through the avenue of the PhD," he continued, "is, under present conditions, a cruel proposition. They get in; they cannot get out, as an MD could; and there is then nothing for them to do but to accept the starvation wages, perhaps a half of the pay of men no older nor more loyal and industrious in the clinical chairs . . . it is more like a cemetery than a career."[30] He spoke with feeling, as a PhD man himself.

Widespread agreement that the preclinical sciences were in trouble led to the appointment of a committee by the National Research Council, then recently established, to study the situation. Information it received from preclinical department heads at 68 medical schools convinced the committee that there was indeed "a great paucity of satisfactory assistants in the preclinical departments," that "insufficient immediate and prospective financial support" was largely responsible, and that the shortage of assistants was "seriously hampering the development of the preclinical sciences, and, through them, of medicine as a whole." The committee offered a suggestion that had been made to it in a number of places, that preclinical departments should have at their disposal "a number of attractive assistantships and research fellowships so that a man who wished to obtain additional training in one of the fundamental medical sciences, either for the purpose of better preparing himself for practice or for a post in a clinical department, would find no financial obstacle in his way." The committee speculated that "some of the men availing themselves of such appointments might become sufficiently interested to give up their first intentions and become full-time members of a department of a preclinical science."[31]

---

[30]*Ibid.*, Vol. 74, May 15, 1920, pp. 1415, 1416.
[31]*Ibid.*, Vol. 74, April 17, 1920, pp. 1117-1122.

## National Research Fellowships

The National Research Council was established by the National Academy of Sciences in 1916 to help organize the country's scientific resources to meet the threat of war. Its work during World War I demonstrated its usefulness as an agency for coordinating scientific research, and in 1918 President Woodrow Wilson asked the Academy to perpetuate the Council as a peacetime institution.[32] One of the first peacetime tasks to which it turned was the task outlined earlier by the Committee of One Hundred of identifying and encouraging young researchers in science. Discussions between the executive officer of the Council, Robert A. Millikan, and the president of the Rockefeller Foundation, George E. Vincent, on the merits of a national program of postdoctoral research fellowships led to a grant by the Foundation of $500,000 to be used by the Council over five years in support of research fellowships in physics and chemistry. The grant was announced in March 1919; the first 13 fellows were selected before the end of the year.

The stated purpose of the fellowship was threefold: to open a scientific career to a larger number of investigators and to give investigators a more thorough training in research, to increase knowledge relating to the fundamental principles of physics and chemistry "upon which the progress of all the sciences and the development of industry depend," and to create more favorable conditions for research in the educational institutions of the country. On the last point the Council was most specific.

National Research Fellows will be permitted to conduct their investigations at institutions that will cooperate in meeting their needs. These needs differ widely from those of students seeking only instruction. Able investigators, actively engaged in productive research, are needed to inspire and guide the work of the Fellows. Research laboratories, adequately manned with assistants and mechanicians, and amply supplied with instruments, machine tools, and other facilities, are indispensable, and funds to provide supplies and to satisfy the constantly recurrent demands of research must be available. Above all, there must exist the stimulating atmosphere found only in institutions that have brought together a group of men devoted to the advancement of science through pursuit of research.

The fellowships were to be awarded preferably, but not exclusively, to United States citizens who had had the equivalent of doctoral training. Individuals were to be appointed initially for one year but were to be eligible for reappointment. They were to devote themselves entirely to research, except that during the academic year they could devote up to one fifth of their time to teaching (including preparation time), if teaching would benefit them educationally, or to attendance of advanced courses of study. It was hoped, by

---

[32]*National Research Council Bulletin*, Vol. 1, Part 1, No. 1, 1918, pp. 22, 23.

the award of the fellowships, "to confirm a number of the most promising workers in research by enabling them to continue their research work immediately after taking their doctorates, at which time it is believed they are best qualified to continue any fundamental research."[33]

In 1922 the Rockefeller Foundation and the Rockefeller-endowed General Education Board, acting in concert, pledged $500,000 for similar fellowships in the medical sciences, with emphasis on the preclinical sciences. In 1923 the Foundation pledged $325,000 for fellowships in the biological sciences. All three programs were continued when the initial grants were spent, and they received repeated extensions thereafter.

Until the advent of large-scale federal programs for postdoctoral education in the 1950's, the Rockefeller Foundation, through the National Research Council, provided the single most effective means for the development of young American scientists as creative investigators. The record of the National Research Fellowships is remarkable. A study made in 1950 of the 1,359 individuals who had been fellows between 1919 and 1949 found that 65 had been elected to the National Academy of Sciences and 3 had won Nobel prizes.[34] Several others have been Nobel prizewinners since. Of 500 scientists newly starred as leaders in research in the 1937 and 1943 editions of the directory, *American Men of Science*, more than half had been postdoctorals, most of them National Research Fellows. Eighty-five percent said that their postdoctoral experience had contributed much to their later scientific achievement, 15 percent that it had contributed moderately. In saying so they attached as much significance to their postdoctoral as to their graduate work.[35] There can be no question but that the National Research Fellowships played a major part in strengthening American science. Robert A. Millikan made the judgment in 1950 that the fellowships had been "the most effective agency in the scientific development of American life and civilization" in his lifetime.[36] The Rockefeller Foundation's investment in the fellowships totaled about $5 million.

Although the number of fellows appointed each year during the twenties and thirties now seems small, it constituted a significant percentage of all PhD recipients in those years. Figure 1 shows the percentage of PhD recipi-

---

[33] *Proceedings of the National Academy of Sciences*, Vol. 5, 1919, pp. 313–315; *Bulletin of the National Research Council*, Vol. I, 1919-1921, p. 24; Myron J. Rand, *The Scientific Monthly*, Vol. 73, No. 2, August 1951, pp. 71–73.
[34] Myron J. Rand, *The Scientific Monthly*, Vol. 73, No. 2, August 1951, p. 79.
[35] Stephen Sargent Visher, *Scientists Starred, 1903-1943, in American Men of Science*, The Johns Hopkins Press, 1947, pp. 361, 530.
[36] R. A. Millikan, *The Autobiography of Robert A. Millikan*, Prentice-Hall, New York, 1950, p. 213.

## 18
AN HISTORICAL VIEW

### FIGURE 1
Percentage of PhD Recipients Receiving National Research (NRC) Fellowships, by Field, 1920-1939, and Percentage of 1967 PhD's Receiving Postdoctoral Appointments.

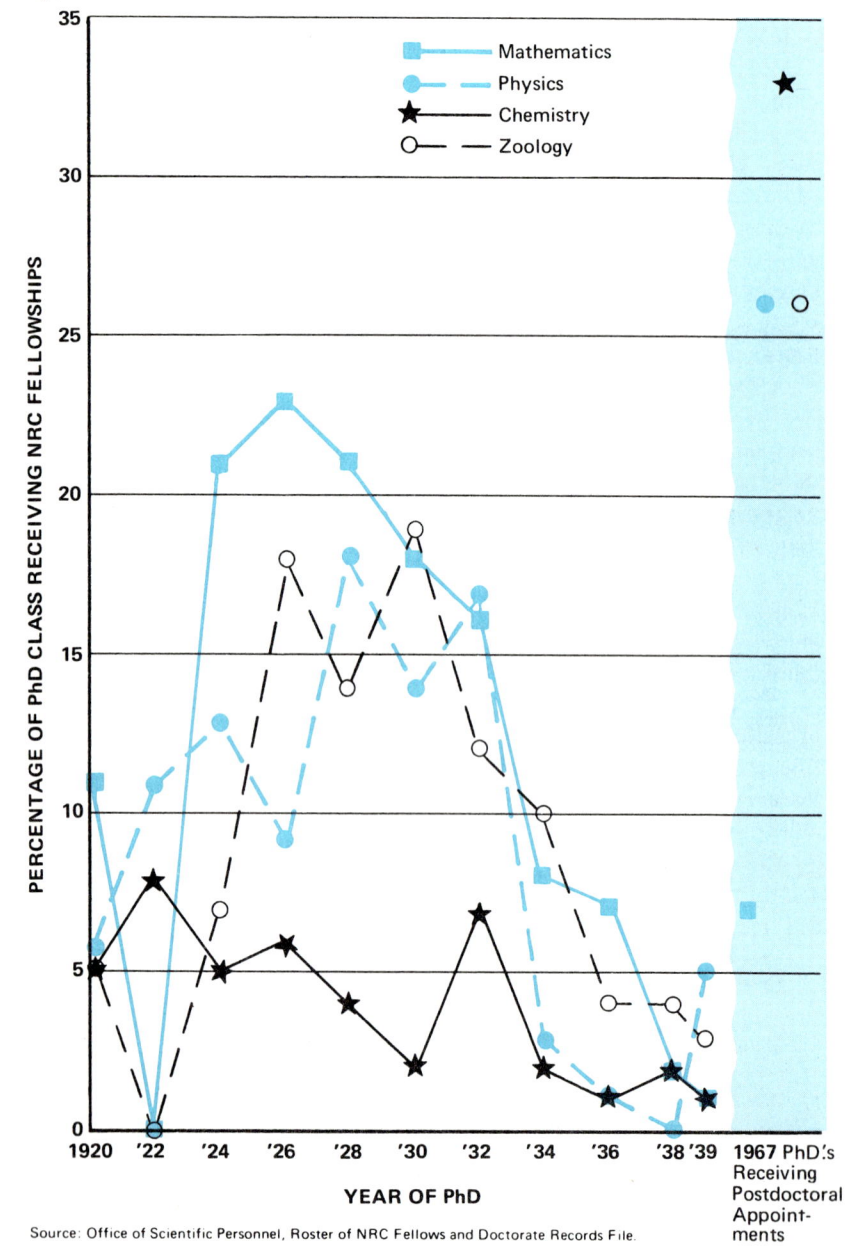

Source: Office of Scientific Personnel, Roster of NRC Fellows and Doctorate Records File.

ents in chemistry, physics, mathematics, and zoology in the twenties and thirties who received National Research Fellowships, compared with the percentage of PhD recipients in these fields in the sixties taking postdoctoral appointments after graduation. The percentages are of the same order of magnitude.[37]

Most of the fellows in the medical sciences were MD's, but a significant number were PhD's. Although most of the MD's used their fellowships to pursue research in the preclinical sciences, a few did clinical research. The selectors for the medical fellowships set their sights on men who planned to make their careers in academic medicine and excluded candidates who had no interest in teaching. They pressed host universities to provide the medical fellows with suitable opportunities for part-time teaching as well as for research.[38]

As it turned out, however, a majority of the fellows in all three programs became professors. Table 1 shows the number of former National Research fellows who were teaching in 1950.

Of the 1,146 fellows chosen between 1919 and 1938, 263 (23 percent) took their fellowships overseas. Another 70 pursued their work at nonacademic research centers like the Carnegie Institution, the National Bureau of

TABLE 1 Number of National Research (NRC) Fellows Holding Teaching Positions in 1950, by Field

| Field | Number of Fellows | Number in Teaching | % in Teaching |
|---|---|---|---|
| Mathematics | 126 | 109 | 86.5 |
| Astronomy | 16 | 10 | 62.5 |
| Physics | 196 | 103 | 52.6 |
| Chemistry | 229 | 104 | 45.5 |
| Geology and Geography | 15 | 8 | 53.3 |
| Zoology | 164 | 111 | 67.7 |
| Botany | 112 | 70 | 62.5 |
| Agriculture | 41 | 25 | 61.0 |
| Forestry | 8 | 4 | 50.0 |
| Anthropology | 27 | 16 | 59.2 |
| Psychology | 93 | 67 | 72.0 |
| *Natural Sciences Total* | 1,027 | 627 | 61.1 |
| *Medical Sciences Total* | 332 | 239 | 72.0 |
| *All* | 1,359 | 866 | 63.8 |

Source: Myron J. Rand, *The Scientific Monthly,* Vol. 73, No. 2, August 1951, p. 79.

---

[37] In contrast to the comment by Myron Rand, *op. cit.*, p. 72.
[38] National Research Council, *Fellowships in Medicine. List of Fellows in Medicine Past and Active, June 1922 to December 1931*, Washington, D.C., *passim.*

AN HISTORICAL VIEW

Standards, and the Rockefeller Institute. Most, however, held their fellowships in university laboratories in this country. The 14 leading host universities with the number of fellows attending each for a part or all of their tenure,[39] were the following:

| | |
|---|---|
| Harvard | 218 |
| Princeton | 117 |
| Chicago | 105 |
| California Institute of Technology | 93 |
| Johns Hopkins | 72 |
| California (all campuses) | 65 |
| Yale | 62 |
| Columbia | 53 |
| Cornell | 40 |
| Pennsylvania | 29 |
| MIT | 27 |
| Michigan | 25 |
| Stanford | 23 |
| Minnesota | 17 |

For the most part, these were also the universities making the largest investment in research at the time. It was estimated in 1938 that $51 million had been spent on research in American universities and colleges in 1935-36, with 14 institutions probably accounting for half the total. The 14 spending the most were the following[40]:

| Spending in excess of $2 million | $1.5 to $2 million | $0.5 to $1 million |
|---|---|---|
| California | Cornell | MIT |
| Chicago | Minnesota | New York University |
| Columbia | Wisconsin | Ohio State University |
| Harvard | Yale | University of Pennsylvania |
| Illinois | | |
| Michigan | | |

At the California Institute of Technology a relatively small sum ($250,000 to $300,000) was spent to good effect in a few selected fields in 1935-36. Millikan became the Institute's administrative head in 1924; under his leadership it exemplified in high degree the National Research Council's ideal of a

---

[39] National Research Council, *National Research Fellowships, 1919-1938*, Washington, D.C., 1938, pp. 1, 2, 81-84.
[40] *Research—A National Resource; Part I, Relation of the Federal Government to Research;* Report of the Science Committee to the National Resources Committee, November 1938, pp. 177, 190.

scientific institution. It organized itself as a center of postdoctoral research, establishing fellowships of its own to support young investigators. The *Caltech Bulletin* for 1936 includes a section on Research Fellowships, listing the fellowships available to postdoctoral researchers at the Institute. The list includes the Institute's own fellowships, the National Research Fellowships, and fellowships supported by industrial sponsors. The Bulletin offers a welcome to members of the staff of other institutions "who have already received their Doctor's degree and desire to carry on special investigations." Listed after the faculty are the names of 26 postdoctorals on fellowships at the Institute.

Another institution that gave concentrated attention to postdoctoral education was the Institute for Advanced Study at Princeton. Founded in 1933, it reflected the commitment to research of its director, Abraham Flexner. "In some fields," he wrote in the Institute's bulletin, "universities provide admirable opportunities for work beyond the PhD degree but, with the exception of medicine and certain other branches, the country has not hitherto possessed an institution in which young men and women could continue their independent training beyond this stage and in which research could be carried on with adequate support without pressure of numbers or routine and unhurried by the need of obtaining practical results."[41] The Institute grew from a nucleus of scholars in mathematics, adding in due course "schools" of economics and politics and of humanistic studies. In 1936 the scholarly community at the Institute consisted of a regular staff of 20 professors, associates, and assistants, and 45 "members" present for a year or so. Albert Einstein and John von Neumann were along the regular professors; Wolfgang Pauli was a visiting professor. Many of the members were young scholars who had recently obtained the doctorate, but others were more senior. Flexner was in favor of the older man: "It is difficult to overestimate the importance of a year spent in free research and study to those who for a number of years previously have been carrying the burden of routine college and university teaching and have had to carry on their original work in such bits of time as could be snatched from their daily studies. Naturally, mature persons of this kind receive preference in the matter of admission."[42]

## International Fellowships

Besides providing support through the National Research Council for young American investigators, the Rockefeller Foundation and other Rockefeller-endowed agencies provided fellowships for foreign scientists. The Rockefeller

---

[41] *The Institute for Advanced Study, Bulletin No. 2*, Princeton, New Jersey, 1933, p. 1.
[42] *Ibid., Bulletin No. 5*, 1936, p. 6.

## AN HISTORICAL VIEW

agencies were spurred to action by the sad state of European science in the aftermath of World War I. Research centers that had attracted scientists from all over the world before the war were starved for funds. Research teams had lost valuable members. Old contacts were broken. To try to knit together again the strands of international science, Wickliffe Rose, president of the Rockefeller-endowed International Education Board, sketched out this program:

Begin with physics, chemistry, and biology; locate the inspiring productive men in each of these fields; ascertain of each of these whether he would be willing to train students from other countries; if so, ascertain how many he could take at one time; provide the equipment needed, if any, for operation on the scale desired. Provide by means of fellowships for the international migration of select students to each of these centers of inspiration and training: students to be carefully selected, and to be trained with reference to definite service in their own countries after completion of their studies.[43]

The International Education Board awarded its first fellowships in 1924. From the beginning a large proportion of the recipients chose to use their fellowships in the United States and during the first six years alone 218 foreign fellows studied at United States institutions.

### Fellowships in the Humanities and Social Sciences

Postdoctoral fellowships, so far available only to scientists, became available to scholars in all fields in 1925 with the establishment of the John Simon Guggenheim Memorial Fellowships. In choosing to endow a fellowship program as a memorial to their son, the donors, Senator and Mrs. Simon Guggenheim, were influenced by much the same motives as had prompted the establishment of the National Research Fellowships. In an outline of the purposes of the endowment, Senator Guggenheim said:

It has been my observation that just about the time a young man has finished college and is prepared to do valuable research, he is compelled to spend his whole time in teaching. Salaries are small; so he is compelled to do this in order to live, and often he loses the impulse for creative work in his subject, which should be preserved in order to make his teaching of the utmost value, and also for the sake of the value of the researches in the carrying on of civilization. I have been informed that the sabbatical year is often not taken advantage of because professors cannot go abroad on half salary and for this reason we have provided that members of teaching staffs on sabbatical leave shall be eligible for these appointments.[44]

---

[43] Quoted by Raymond B. Fosdick, *The Story of the Rockefeller Foundation*, Harper, New York, 1952, p. 148.
[44] *Outline of Purposes of the John Simon Guggenheim Memorial Foundation*, 1925.

## FELLOWSHIPS IN HUMANITIES AND SOCIAL SCIENCES

The fellowships were intended for scholars in the humanities as well as in the sciences who had already proved their capacity for independent research. They were also to be awarded to artists with demonstrated creativity. It was expected that the fellowships would ordinarily be used for study in Europe.

Seventy-eight applications were submitted to the Guggenheim Foundation in 1925 and 15 fellows were appointed. The next year about 900 candidates applied and 38 were appointed. The selection committee had set no age limits but quickly decided to restrict the field to persons between 25 and 35.

As to mature scholars who are full professors in first-rate institutions, it has seemed to the Committee that the duty of providing for such scholars is upon the institutions themselves. . . . In certain cases of younger scholars holding such full professorships, the Foundation has made grants on condition that the universities provide an equal amount. As a rule, grants to scholars more than forty years of age have been made when first-rate scholarship has appeared in an environment unfavorable to research, or where there were circumstances, such as lack of access to other funds, which made it desirable that the opportunity needed be afforded by this Foundation.[45]

By 1936 Guggenheim fellowships had been awarded to 525 United States citizens; at the time of award 334 were teachers in educational institutions and 191 were scholars and artists working on their own. Sixty-nine of the fellows in scholarly disciplines were in the physical sciences and engineering, 12 were in mathematics, 53 were in the life sciences (including medicine), 38 were in the social sciences, and 186 were in history, literature, philosophy, and languages.[46]

The example of the National Research Council suggested the formation of similar coordinating organizations for the social sciences and the humanities. Representatives of the American Economic Association, the American Sociological Society, and the American Political Science Association formed the Social Science Research Council in May 1923. The American Statistical Association, the American Psychological Association, and the American Anthropological Association joined later the same year. The American Historical Association joined in 1925.

Beardsley Ruml, director of the Laura Spelman Rockefeller Foundation, encouraged the formation of the Council and provided the support for a program of Social Science Research Council fellowships to match the National Research Fellowship program. The purpose of the fellowships was similar:

Generous as American Universities have been in helping graduate students to obtain Doctor's degrees, they have not been generous or wise in treating their young instructors.

---

[45]*Reports of the Secretary and Treasurer*, John Simon Guggenheim Memorial Foundation, New York, 1925–26 and 1927. Today, in different circumstances, older candidates are favored. Less than a third of current awards are to men under 40.
[46]*Ibid.*, 1935 and 1936, pp. 14–19.

A newly fledged doctor, appointed to a junior position in one of our departments, is usually assigned a heavy teaching schedule, when he neither knows thoroughly the subjects he has to cover, nor knows how to teach. . . . That is a most effective system for discouraging research. Only the most vigorous or the most fortunate men keep their creative faculties intact for the years when promotion enables them to command a scanty leisure. . . . Some universities have established fellowships especially for their young instructors. Others have obtained funds for supporting research programs in which young faculty members can join. Still others are seeking to cut down the teaching schedules of individuals with marked capacity for research. . . . But the need is far from met. If our few research fellowships can give the ablest among the hundreds of men who aspire to do scientific work in the social field opportunity to develop their powers while they are still in their flexible years, we may hope for large results, ultimately if not immediately.[47]

Fifteen fellowships were offered in 1925 and awards had been made to 246 persons by 1939. The recipients came from the following fields:

| | |
|---|---|
| Anthropology | 16 |
| Economics | 67 |
| Geography | 5 |
| History | 53 |
| Political Science | 35 |
| Psychology | 22 |
| Sociology | 27 |
| Miscellaneous | 21 |
| Total | 246 |

The Council made an average of 16 new awards each year, compared with 57 a year in the National Research Fellowship program.

The fellowships were intended initially to support the research of young investigators who had completed their training, but the emphasis shifted in time from supporting research to supporting further research training. A fellowship would be awarded to provide a needed opportunity for fieldwork, or to allow an investigator to strengthen his knowledge of important supporting disciplines. Some of the anthropologists, for example, used their fellowships for work in sociology; many of the sociologists sought training in statistics.[48]

The American Council of Learned Societies, formed in 1919, promoted research in the humanities. When it awarded its first postdoctoral fellowships in 1930 (with Rockefeller Foundation support), 17 scholarly associations belonged to it. They included such organizations as the Modern Language Association of America, the American Philosophical Society, and the Medieval

---

[47] Wesley C. Mitchell, quoted in the Annual Report of the Chairman, 1926, Social Science Research Council, *Political Science Quarterly*, Vol. XLI, No. 4, December 1926, pp. 16-18.
[48] *Fellows of the Social Science Research Council, 1925-1939*, Social Science Research Council, New York, 1939, pp. vii-xiii.

# FELLOWSHIPS IN HUMANITIES AND SOCIAL SCIENCES

Academy of America. Some member organizations, like the American Economic Association, were also members of the Social Science Research Council.

The American Council of Learned Societies described its fellowships as "post-doctoral fellowships in the humanities of the type already made available in other fields by the National Research Council and the Social Science Research Council." They were "to encourage research on the part of scholars who have the degree of PhD or its equivalent in training and experience, who are not over thirty-five . . . and who have already demonstrated marked aptitude for constructive scholarship." The fellowships were offered "in all fields of the humanities except the Social Sciences."[49]

The humanities fellowships were surprisingly unsuccessful. Only 48 candidates applied in the first year, when 14 awards were made. In 1931 the number of applications dropped to 26. In 1936, after 82 fellows had been selected, the program was suspended. About 330 applications were submitted during the life of the program.

Why these fellowships did not achieve the success of the fellowship programs in other fields is a matter for speculation. Dr. Waldo G. Leland, secretary of the American Council of Learned Societies, told the Association of American Universities in 1935 that the Depression was probably a factor; a fellowship was not so appealing to a potential candidate as a regular university appointment. But this can be only part of the answer, for candidates in the other programs were subject to the same economic conditions.

The Council had hoped that the fellowships might be used to encourage young scholars in undeveloped fields—Far Eastern studies, for example—but most candidates were interested in the well-trodden fields of Western history, literature, and language. The Rockefeller Foundation seems to have been disappointed by the fellows' scholarly bias. David H. Stevens, director of the Foundation's Division of the Humanities during this period, wrote later: "How was this program a credit to us? In having a sense of magnitude. In what way a discredit? By buttressing scholasticism and antiquarianism in our universities."[50] In 1934 a committee of the Rockefeller Foundation trustees wrote: "It frankly appears to your committee that a program in the humanities, based on a cloistered kind of research, is wide of the goal which the Foundation should have in mind. It is getting us facts but not necessarily followers. We have more detailed information about a great number of rather abstruse subjects, but that does not logically mean that the level of artistic and aesthetic appreciation in America has been measurably raised."[51]

---

[49] American Council of Learned Societies, *Bulletin No. 12*, December 1929, pp. 24, 65.
[50] Quoted by Raymond B. Fosdick, *op. cit.*, p. 239.
[51] *Ibid.*, p. 251.

## AN HISTORICAL VIEW

### The Association of American Universities

In 1934 a representative of the National Research Council, the chemist Charles A. Kraus, spoke to the Association of American Universities on the development of postdoctoral education since the war, a development he believed would have far-reaching influence on higher education. He pointed to the active role played by the various fellowship programs and compared this with the role of the universities: "Contrary to what might have been expected, the universities have not been instrumental either in initiating the fellowship experiment or in shaping its course. Their part has been the passive one of placing libraries and laboratories at the disposal of Fellows." He urged the universities to assume more responsibility for postdoctoral education: ". . . the fellowships represent an experiment on the part of the supporting foundations, and it is not to be expected that such support will continue indefinitely." [52]

Postdoctoral education was placed on the agenda for the Association's meeting in 1935, and again the following year. In 1936 a committee was appointed to consider ways and means of carrying out "a comprehensive study of postdoctoral education in America." [53] The committee reported in 1937 that it had considered the various types of postdoctoral education, some of their advantages and disadvantages, and certain questions of administration. It divided postdoctorals into three groups: Group I, those who had just received the PhD or its equivalent; Group II, those who had some experience (e.g., from three to five years) after receiving the doctorate; and Group III, older, established scholars. The committee suggested that there were three reasons for promoting postdoctoral education: the furthering of research, the improvement of teaching, and the development of occupational or professional proficiencies. However, these three purposes could not be completely separated; most of the national fellowship programs had as their primary purpose the furthering of research, but they were also concerned with the improvement of teaching and the acquiring of professional proficiencies.

The committee was convinced that postdoctoral education was "a potent means of furthering research in any field of knowledge" and listed six ways of providing for it: (a) full-time fellowships, (b) part-time fellowships or assistantships requiring some service in return for the stipend or facilities furnished, (c) sabbatical leaves, (d) exchange professorships, (e) symposia and conferences, and (f) short courses of intensive and advanced character. "For the training of new personnel (recent PhD's)" the committee continued, "the full-time or part-time fellowship extending for one or two years is obviously more

---

[52] Association of American Universities, *Journal of Proceedings and Addresses, 36th Annual Conference,* 1934, pp. 129-136.
[53] Association of American Universities, *Journal of Proceedings and Addresses, 38th Annual Conference,* 1936, p. 60.

desirable than the other means listed. The main purpose of such fellowships should be to give the fellow new ideas, new points of view, a stimulus and a training which will influence his later work rather than merely to provide an opportunity to complete some particular piece of work. In other words, it is the opinion of your Committee that post-doctoral fellowships for the younger men should be regarded primarily as training fellowships...."

Turning to administrative matters, the committee made this recommendation:

It is the opinion of your Committee that the objectives of training fellowships can better be accomplished by fellowships administered nationally than locally. The post-doctoral fellowships of one character or another now awarded by some universities are commendable, and your Committee is of the opinion that a larger proportion of the funds now devoted to subsidizing candidates for advanced degrees could be advantageously allocated to the support of post-doctoral fellows. However, university administered post-doctoral fellowships are likely to be limited to a smaller group of applicants, and often are limited to the institution which awards them. Your Committee believes that a need exists for a system of country-wide post-doctoral training fellowships more numerous and broader in range than are now available. [54]

## The Federal Government

### National Cancer Institute

The Association of American Universities took no further action, but the wind was changing. In April 1937, a bill was submitted in Congress for the establishment of a National Cancer Institute in the Public Health Service to conduct research on cancer and to coordinate the work of other organizations fighting the disease. Representatives of the American Society for the Control of Cancer (later to become the American Cancer Society) testified in favor of the bill and it was passed in July without a dissenting voice.

Among other provisions of the Act, the Surgeon General was authorized to provide facilities where qualified persons might receive training in the diagnosis and treatment of cancer, and to pay such trainees up to ten dollars a day. He was also authorized to establish "research fellowships in the Institute" and to pay the fellows such stipends as he thought necessary "to procure the assistance of the most brilliant and promising research fellows from the United

---

[54] Association of American Universities, *Journal of Proceedings and Addresses, 39th Annual Conference*, 1937, pp. 38-40.

## AN HISTORICAL VIEW

States or abroad."[55] The Institute appointed its first trainee in January 1938 and its first fellows later the same year.

It was the beginning of a program of federal support for the medical sciences that has had a far-reaching impact on medical education in the United States. But it was a beginning without ceremony. No one seems to have thought that the National Cancer Institute might be the precursor of other national institutes, that it might be a precedent with important consequences. The annual budget authorized for it was small—$700,000. The Rockefeller Foundation was spending much more at this time for work in medicine. Congress was spending annually more than three times as much on the eradication of tuberculosis in cattle. For a war on cancer, $700,000 must have seemed a small budget; certainly not enough to launch a revolution in education.

The Surgeon General, Dr. Thomas Parran, contracted with hospitals and universities to carry out the training provisions of the Act. The first National Cancer Institute trainee went for his training to the Western Reserve University. Physicians were appointed for two years to receive eight months' special training in each of the fields of pathology, radiology, and surgery. As is the case in many postdoctoral training programs since, research training was not a component. Candidates for the program were required to have had not less than three years of hospital experience.[56]

By 1948, 111 trainees had held appointments of one to three years at 35 universities, hospitals, and research institutes. None trained at the National Cancer Institute itself. The character of the training, however, was set by the Institute. While many trainees subsequently satisfied the requirements of specialty boards, and some received credit for degrees, this was not the purpose of the program. In 1949 the Institute issued its own certificate for completion of the training.[57]

Fewer fellowships were awarded than traineeships. Forty-three National Cancer Institute research fellows were appointed between 1938 and 1946. The fellowships were not restricted to physicians and several recipients were PhD's. The Act's authorization of fellowships "in the Institute" was not construed to mean that they had to be held at the Institute; although many of the early fellows held their awards at the Institute, many attended other institutions.[58]

---

[55] *National Cancer Institute Act*, 1937, Chapter 565 of the 75th Congress, 1st Session.
[56] *Journal of the American Medical Association*, Vol. III, Dec. 17, 1938, p. 2314.
[57] R. R. Spencer, M.D., National Cancer Institute Program of Postgraduate Training for Physicians, *Public Health Reports*, June 17, 1949, Vol. 64, No. 24, pp. 750–756.
[58] *Annual Report of the Surgeon General of the Public Health Service of the United States for the Fiscal Year 1939*, Washington, D.C., p. 83. *Research Fellows of the National Cancer Institute, January 1, 1938–April 1, 1958, P.H.S. Publication No. 658*, U.S. Dept. of Health, Education, and Welfare, 1959, pp. 1–6.

The National Cancer Institute Act provided for the appointment by the Surgeon General of a six-member National Advisory Cancer Council. However, it did not give the Council any responsibility for overseeing the fellowship and training programs. Responsibility for selecting training centers, trainees, and fellows rested effectively with the professional staff of the Institute.

### National Institutes of Health

In 1944 Congress passed an act to consolidate the many existing statutes governing the Public Health Service and to revise its organization to meet the needs of a nation again at war. Many of the changes were administrative. The National Cancer Institute, for example, was made a branch of a division of the service called the National Institute of Health. Other changes were more far-reaching. An important provision gave the Surgeon General the power from then on to award fellowships in any field "relating to the causes, diagnosis, treatment, control, and prevention of physical and mental diseases and impairments of man." [59] His authority to award training grants was still confined to the field of cancer. The establishment by Congress of other institutes on the pattern of the National Cancer Institute, however, soon extended his authority to other fields. A National Institute of Mental Health was established in 1946,[60] and a National Heart Institute and a National Institute of Dental Research followed in 1948.[61] Then in 1950 an omnibus medical research act authorized the Surgeon General to set up an Institute of Neurological Diseases and Blindness and an Institute of Arthritis and Metabolic Diseases, to set up still other institutes whenever he determined such action "necessary," and to award training grants in any institute so established.[62] In 1948 the National Institute of Health, the administrative division to which the separate research and training institutes reported, was officially renamed the National Institutes of Health.

Funding of the institutes by Congress kept pace with their growing number. Appropriations for fellowships of all kinds, predoctoral and postdoctoral, jumped from $45,000 in the fiscal year 1946 to $1.4 million in fiscal 1950. Appropriations for training programs during the same period increased from $25,000 to $6.4 million.

*NIH Postdoctoral Fellowships* In 1945 NIH was encouraged to view its mission broadly when it was asked to take over a number of medical research

---

[59] *Public Health Service Act*, 1944, Chapter 373 of the 78th Congress, 2nd Session.
[60] Public Law 587, 79th Congress, 2nd Session.
[61] Public Laws 655 and 755, 80th Congress, 2nd Session.
[62] Public Law 692, 81st Congress, 2nd Session.

## AN HISTORICAL VIEW

projects sponsored during the war by the Office of Scientific Research and Development. The following year it established a Research Grants Office to administer a continuing program of research grants. The new office was also made responsible for implementing the fellowship provisions of the Public Health Service Act of 1944.[63] In 1947 a Central Qualifications Board was set up to coordinate the review of fellowship applications submitted in different fields.

The Research Grants Office (renamed the Division of Research Grants) established three types of NIH fellowships: predoctoral, postdoctoral, and

TABLE 2  Number of NIH Postdoctoral and Special Fellowships, Fiscal Years 1946-1967

| Fiscal Year | NIH Postdoctoral Fellows | NIH Special Fellows | Total |
|---|---|---|---|
| 1946 | 2 | 2 | 4 |
| 1947 | 27 | 7 | 34 |
| 1948 | 119 | 20 | 139 |
| 1949 | 255 | 57 | 312 |
| 1950 | 268 | 38 | 306 |
| 1951 | 291 | 27 | 318 |
| 1952 | 222 | 17 | 239 |
| 1953 | 335 | 22 | 357 |
| 1954 | 426 | 36 | 462 |
| 1955 | 389 | 38 | 427 |
| 1956 | 342 | 39 | 381 |
| 1957 | 471 | 99 | 570 |
| 1958 | 482 | 94 | 576 |
| 1959 | 627 | 104 | 731 |
| 1960 | 822 | 159 | 981 |
| 1961 | 1,050 | 228 | 1,278 |
| 1962 | 1,211 | 276 | 1,487 |
| 1963 | 1,223 | 389 | 1,612 |
| 1964 | 1,190 | 425 | 1,615 |
| 1965 | 1,188 | 505 | 1,693 |
| 1966 | 1,237 | 537 | 1,774 |
| 1967[a] | 1,088 | 522 | 1,610 |

[a]Data for 1967 are partially estimated and exclude fellowships awarded by the National Institute of Mental Health. Beginning in FY 1967 NIMH was separated administratively from the other National Institutes of Health. Data for earlier years include NIMH fellowships.

Source:  Data provided by the Career Development Review Branch, Division of Research Grants, NIH.

[63]*Annual Report of the Federal Security Agency*, Section Four, United States Public Health Service, for fiscal year 1964, p. 299.

THE FEDERAL GOVERNMENT

special. The "special" category was intended for investigators who for some reason did not qualify naturally for a regular predoctoral or postdoctoral award. They might be men in highly specialized fields, distinguished foreign scientists who wished to spend a year doing research in the United States, or men with unusual qualifications. Table 2 shows the number of postdoctoral and special fellowships awarded by NIH.

*NIH Traineeships* Unfortunately figures are not available on the number of postdoctorals supported on NIH training grants during the same period. The growth in dollar appropriations for training, predoctoral and postdoctoral, is given in Table 3.

The following, however, is the number of postdoctoral trainees supported since 1963:[64]

| Fiscal Year | NIH Postdoctoral Trainees |
|---|---|
| 1963 | 5,366 |
| 1964 | 6,042 |
| 1965 | 6,534 |
| 1966 | 6,861 |

The number of trainees and of fellows cannot be compared directly because many trainees hold other awards for short periods, for example, for a summer.

TABLE 3   Appropriations for NIH Training Grant Programs, Fiscal Years 1946–1967

| Fiscal Year | Training Appropriation | Fiscal Year | Training Appropriation |
|---|---|---|---|
| 1946 | $25,000 | 1957 | $28,075,000 |
| 1947 | $250,000 | 1958 | $32,932,000 |
| 1948 | $2,810,000 | 1959 | $49,902,000 |
| 1949 | $3,930,000 | 1960 | $74,673,000 |
| 1950 | $5,415,000 | 1961 | $110,000,000 |
| 1951 | $6,652,000 | 1962 | $118,506,000 |
| 1952 | $7,392,000 | 1963 | $154,139,000 |
| 1953 | $8,184,000 | 1964 | $172,602,000 |
| 1954 | $10,813,000 | 1965 | $181,311,000 |
| 1955 | $11,051,000 | 1966 | $209,896,000 |
| 1956 | $14,502,000 | 1967 | $224,486,000 |

Source: *NIH Almanac, 1967*, p. 74.

[64] Statistics prepared by the Resources Analysis Branch, Office of Program Planning, NIH.

## AN HISTORICAL VIEW

It has been estimated that the 6,861 trainees supported in fiscal year 1966 held the equivalent of 5,300 year-long awards. The figure would probably be lower still if it included only awards held during the academic year or part of it and excluded awards held only during the summer. Even with this correction, however, the number of postdoctorals on training grants far exceeds the number on fellowships.

The large majority of postdoctoral trainees are MD's. In 1966 over 85 percent held the MD degree. Some also held a PhD, but less than 15 percent held the PhD alone. The NIH postdoctoral fellows are much more evenly divided between MD's and PhD's. In 1966 almost 45 percent of the fellows held the PhD degree or equivalent.[65]

The several institutes within NIH have pursued a variety of objectives in their training programs, and individual programs differ widely. Some programs, such as the original training program of the National Cancer Institute, are intended to provide training in needed clinical skills; others, to provide training in research. All the institutes, however, support research training to a greater or less extent. The National Institute of General Medical Sciences, established in 1962, is particularly concerned with basic research, but it has no monopoly in this area. Each of the other institutes supports basic research relevant to its mission. Unfortunately, it is not possible to determine from the available statistics how many of the trainees supported by the several institutes are in research training programs and how many are in other sorts of training.

Whatever the purpose of a training program, all the institutes follow the same criteria in selecting a hospital or university for a training grant. These criteria are "the significance and relevance of the proposed training program; [the] adequacy of the leadership, faculty, and facilities; and [the] training record of the institution and department concerned."[66] An institution must apply for a training grant to receive one and is free to set its own educational policy in providing training but, in the absence of a clear institutional policy, NIH policies set the pattern. It has seemed to some in the universities that the universities have assumed too little responsibility. Robert E. Ebert, Dean of the Harvard Medical School in 1966, made the following statement:

Although the University has become heavily involved in graduate [medical] education, it has no primary responsibility for this phase of education. The internship is the responsibility of the Council of Medical Education of the AMA. The Specialty Boards, as well as extra-university residency review committees, are responsible for the quality, content and length of residency training. The National Institutes of Health, through the mecha-

---

[65] Joseph S. Murtaugh, Director, Office of Program Planning, NIH, in *Proceedings of the Conference on Postdoctoral Fellowships and Research Associateships–in the Sciences and Engineering,* National Research Council, 1967.

[66] Administrative Policies Governing Training Grants of the National Institutes of Health, mimeographed manual, May 1, 1962, p. 5.

nism of its study sections, is responsible for the definition of [postdoctoral] fellowship training. It is true that members of medical faculties play important roles on all of these various councils and boards, but only in an extra-university capacity. Neither the profession nor the universities yet regard any of these programs as the responsibility of medical faculties. We are impelled to ask if the University can continue to assume that half of the education of a physician is not its business. Should not the faculty review the various programs of postdoctoral instruction going on within or near its walls as it does its doctoral program either for the PhD or the MD degree? Especially in the area of fellowship training, which presumably is training young men for academic medicine, the University must take a more direct responsibility.[67]

National Science Foundation

In the development of the National Institutes of Health, events outran the articulation of policy. In 1944 President Roosevelt asked Vannevar Bush, director of the war-time Office of Scientific Research and Development, to prepare a report on the federal support of science after the war. In *Science, The Endless Frontier*, published in 1945, Dr. Bush recommended the establishment of a National Research Foundation, funded by the Congress "for promoting the flow of new scientific knowledge and the development of scientific talent in our youth." He submitted a report by a medical advisory committee under the chairmanship of Walter W. Palmer of Columbia University urging the desirability of a new agency to channel funds into medical research. In the opinion of the Palmer committee none of the existing agencies of the government was "sufficiently free of specialization of interest" to warrant assigning to it the broad mission of supporting medical research across the country. "The Federal agency concerned with medical research should be created *de novo* and be independent of all existing agencies." Dr. Bush, opposed to a separate agency for medicine, recommended the establishment of a single agency serving all of science, with separate divisions for the medical and natural sciences.[68] "Science is fundamentally a unitary thing. The number of independent agencies should be kept to a minimum."

He urged that there should be another division for scientific personnel and education. It would support undergraduate scholarships and graduate fellowships, and also "fellowships for advanced training and fundamental research." He submitted a report by a committee under the chairmanship of Isaiah Bowman of Johns Hopkins that recommended a program of postdoctoral fellowships "as a direct aid to research." The Bowman committee felt that the program

---

[67] Robert E. Ebert, *Report to the President of Harvard University for 1965-66*, p. 7.
[68] Vannevar Bush, *Science, The Endless Frontier, A Report to the President*, Washington, D.C., 1945, pp. 28-34, 43-54.

## AN HISTORICAL VIEW

> ... should include awards for older men to enable really experienced investigators to develop and utilize their talents most effectively.... Research workers who have reached the status of assistant professor or above tend to remain in their own universities and their time available for research tends to become increasingly broken up. In theory, the sabbatical year gives an opportunity for intensive research or travel, but in recent years universities have been less and less able to grant such freedom from academic routine. The resulting immobility of the senior staff serves to isolate the intellectual life of a university... and the individuals concerned, lacking outside stimulation, may incline more and more to perfunctory performance of routine duties.... Fellowships large enough to meet the salaries of advanced academic personnel for periods of intensive research work at their own institutions or at other universities would be an effective means of attacking these problems.[69]

The Palmer committee also urged the need for fellowships and recommended that postdoctoral fellowships in the medical sciences be tenable for periods up to six years. The committee cautioned, however, against "the establishment of lifetime research professorships, or of protracted research fellowships, at the expense of Federal funds."[70]

Five years later Dr. Bush's recommendations were realized in the National Science Foundation. The Foundation received meager appropriations in its early days and it was two years more before it was able to mount a fellowship program. By this time the National Institutes of Health were well established as a fellowship agency. The National Science Foundation incorporated a Division of Medical Research but no funds were appropriated to the Foundation for the support of research in the medical sciences until 1959. The National Institutes of Health (NIH) quickly became the main channel of federal support in this area.

The National Science Foundation's total budget has never matched the total budget of NIH, and it has never been as large a sponsor of research training. Table 4 gives the number of fellowships the Foundation has awarded over the years for the support of postdoctoral scholars in various categories.

### Career Awards in the Medical Sciences

Conditions in the universities after World War II made an academic career in the basic medical sciences appear to be as unattractive as it had been after World War I. In 1948 the average maximum salary of instructors in the basic medical sciences who had spent three to five years in PhD training was about the same as the average wage of carpenters and bricklayers. The best they could hope for by way of promotion was a professorship paying $8,000 to

---

[69]*Ibid.*, pp. 91, 92.
[70]*Ibid.*, pp. 54, 58.

CAREER AWARDS IN THE MEDICAL SCIENCES

TABLE 4 Number of NSF Regular and Senior Postdoctoral Fellowships and Science Faculty Fellowships, 1953-1969

| Year | NSF Postdoctoral Fellowships (Regular) | NSF Senior Postdoctoral Fellowships | NSF Science Faculty Fellowships (for College Science Teachers) |
|---|---|---|---|
| 1952-53 | 38 | — | — |
| 1953-54 | 42 | — | — |
| 1954-55 | 79 | — | — |
| 1955-56 | 70 | — | — |
| 1956-57 | 98 | 52 | — |
| 1957-58 | 109 | 55 | 100 |
| 1958-59 | 151 | 76 | 216 |
| 1959-60 | 194 | 83 | 302 |
| 1960-61 | 180 | 75 | 285 |
| 1961-62 | 235 | 91 | 285 |
| 1962-63 | 245 | 92 | 325 |
| 1963-64 | 245 | 95 | 325 |
| 1964-65 | 240 | 96 | 325 |
| 1965-66 | 229 | 98 | 325 |
| 1966-67 | 230 | 95 | 326 |
| 1967-68 | 150 | 65 | 250 |
| 1968-69 | 120 | 55 | 223 |

Source: National Science Foundation, Annual Reports.

$11,000. "It is little wonder," commented a Survey Committee of the American Medical Association and the Association of American Medical Colleges, "that young physicians enter the clinical fields or the fields of research and industry instead of the medical basic sciences.... The clinical departments offer to young men a much greater range of opportunity than do the medical basic sciences. In the clinical areas a man may teach, carry on research, and keep in touch with clinical medicine. If he is not successful in obtaining a full-time position on the faculty, he may work on a part-time basis, or he can enter the practice of medicine and work for the medical school on a volunteer basis. All this constitutes stiff competition for the medical basic science fields."[71]

To improve the situation for promising young teacher–investigators in these fields, the John and Mary R. Markle Foundation launched in 1948 a program of Grants for Scholars in Academic Medicine. The grants, paying $5,000 a year for five years were to enable universities to give nominated individuals the best possible chance of developing their full powers. An applicant univer-

---

[71] John E. Deitrick and Robert C. Berson, *Medical Schools in the United States at Mid-Century*, Report of the Survey of Medical Education, 1953, p. 198.

## AN HISTORICAL VIEW

sity and its nominees were to be considered together. The university's role was described as follows:

> It involves selecting outstanding men just as their training ends but before they make a scientific reputation; steeling them against tempting positions outside their chosen field of academic medicine; protecting them from being overloaded with teaching and administrative responsibilities and contributing funds toward their support, or their research, or both. It is hoped that the security thus provided for five years will be sufficient for the Scholars to prove their ability and to become established as research workers and teachers. . . . The real interest of a medical school in encouraging scientific talent should be evident in the plan for the Scholar offered by the school when it makes a nomination. In the selection process, the plan of each school will be carefully analyzed so that nominations received from schools unable or unwilling to carry out the purposes of the scheme will be eliminated. This does not mean that the financially less fortunate medical schools will be neglected. On the contrary some of the better candidates and most thoughtful plans, we hope, will come from such sources. Quality is not dependent on income or size.[72]

Sixteen Markle Scholars were appointed in 1948. Eighteen years later, 431 scholars had been appointed in 88 schools.[73] The program still continues. A similar program of Grants for Scholars in Radiological Research was established by the James Picker Foundation in 1953, and in 1954 the American Cyanamid Company through its Lederle Laboratories Division established a program of Lederle Medical Faculty Awards.[74]

In 1956 NIH was prompted to establish its own program of five-year fellowships for investigators in the medical sciences. The need was described as follows:

> 1. There are well-recognized deficiencies in the training of physicians for careers in research. Rarely does a physician receive the rigorous training in research methodology that is typical of the PhD-type of training. Experiments devised by medical schools and designed to remedy this weakness for students who intend to enter research rather than the practice of medicine will be financed by NIH.
>
> 2. The state of the sciences basic to clinical medicine—the preclinical sciences—has for some time been a matter of concern among those who have thought extensively about medical research, medical education, and their interrelations. These fields are becoming progressively more important as the essential unity of biological and medical sciences with the physical sciences is expressed operationally in the design and execution of experiments. Despite unparalleled need for a vigorous effort in this field, research is not flourishing. The number of younger men of top caliber who aspire to research and teaching careers in medical schools is inadequate.[75]

---

[72] The John and Mary R. Markle Foundation, *1947 Annual Report*, pp. 6–10.
[73] *Ibid.*, 1965–66 Annual Report, p. 51.
[74] *Lederle Medical Faculty Awards, Eleventh Year, 1954-1965*, April 1964; *A Statement of General Principles in the Granting of the Fifteenth Annual Series of Lederle Medical Faculty Awards, 1968-1969*.
[75] *Science*, Vol. 124, No. 3233, December 14, 1956, pp. 1189, 1190.

The NIH career fellowships, called Senior Research Fellowships, were restricted to men in the preclinical sciences who, having had two years of postdoctoral training or experience, gave promise of a career in independent research and teaching and demonstrated "potential for development as an academic leader."[76] In 1961 the fellowships, redesignated Research Career Development Awards, were thrown open to investigators in any of the sciences related to health—clinical as well as preclinical. In fiscal year 1964 a total of 747 individuals held these appointments. They included 191 in clinical medicine and dentistry, 466 in the basic medical and biological sciences, and 81 in the behavioral sciences.[77]

## Epilogue

These are some of the highlights in the development to date of postdoctoral education in the United States. This account is necessarily sketchy, and many programs that have made a significant contribution have been passed over. This is particularly true of the period since World War II. No account has been given of the postdoctoral fellowship programs of the Atomic Energy Commission and of the Air Force Office of Scientific Research, of the Fulbright-Hays program, of the development of in-house postdoctoral research associateships at the National Institutes of Health and in other government research institutions, and of the programs of the many private foundations that, undaunted by the flow of federal money, have committed funds to support postdoctoral study. The postwar history of the Social Science Research Council fellowships, the re-establishment of a postdoctoral fellowship program for the humanities by the American Council of Learned Societies, and the recent entry into the field of the National Endowment for the Humanities are also an important part of the story. Equally important is the growing population of postdoctorals supported by universities on research project funds. As shown in later chapters, such postdoctorals are now the largest segment of the total postdoctoral population. How their numbers have grown cannot be told since no one has counted them previously.

The pattern postdoctoral education has followed since the war was largely set in the prewar years. As we have seen, many of the problems that concern us now were problems then: the need to support young PhD's in creative re-

---

[76] *Grant and Award Programs of the Public Health Service*, Vol. II, Policy and Information Statement on Training Programs, 1959, p. 21.
[77] *Reference Tables on Persons Receiving Support from N.I.H. Extramural Training Programs during Fiscal Year 1964*, Public Health Service, 1966, Table 8, pp. 141-243.

search, the need to provide MD's with opportunities for research training, the balance of teaching and research, the influence of the sponsoring agencies, the responsibility of the universities.

We are concerned in the following pages with a form of education that has developed over a long period, shaping itself in response to long-felt needs. It has had its setbacks, but it has survived the test of time.

CHAPTER 3

# The Study

Although postdoctoral education in the United States has been in existence almost as long as graduate education, very little quantitative information exists that describes the scope and intensity of the enterprise. In view of the large amount of educational data that has been compiled in the past, it is surprising that so little attention has been paid to postdoctoral study. Most of the data we have pertain either to particular fields or to particular programs of support; if all of these sources were assembled the record would remain incomplete.

A basic difficulty in securing information on postdoctoral education results from the fact that no formal conferring of a degree or certificate marks the completion of the postdoctoral experience. This is not to argue the desirability of such a recognition of accomplishment, but rather to suggest that in a profession where milestones are easily counted, postdoctoral activity takes place so unobtrusively and ends so indeterminably that little note is taken of the event except by the participants.

The lack of documentation also springs from a lack of consensus as to the purpose of postdoctoral education. Postdoctoral education has grown almost spontaneously (and independently) in many segments of the universities and in nonacademic environments. At most institutions there is no coordination and no contact between the postdoctoral activity in one field and that in another. As Robert Alberty, Dean of Science at MIT, remarked in a speech to the National Research Council in the spring of 1968: "The graduate students have their deans and graduate deans have their national organizations. Many universities have Vice Presidents for Research, but very few people in universities have any formal responsibilities for postdoctorals."

The lack of consensus is reflected in (and partially caused by) the numerous and uncoordinated agencies, foundations, health organizations, and professional societies supporting postdoctoral education. Each has its own well defined purpose (if the agency is complex there may be several different well defined purposes), but there is not necessarily agreement among these groups with regard to motivation. Sometimes the differences are sufficiently great that some program officers are unaware that they are supporting postdoctorals as such.

The practice of hiring postdoctorals to work on research projects at universities, supported by extramural (usually federal) funds has contributed greatly to the absence of statistics on the magnitude of the postdoctoral population. Not only do the employing institutions often fail to make a distinction between the postdoctoral research associate and the other professional and semi-professional staff being paid from these restricted funds, but some granting agencies are indifferent to the backgrounds of those the professor selects to work with. One program officer asserted that his responsibility was to purchase research as efficiently as possible; who was hired to do the work was not his concern. The result is that, with the exception of one or two federal agencies, no count has been made of the number of people at each education level who have been paid from agency funds. The new annual inventory of personnel being carried out by NSF for the interagency Committee on Academic Science and Engineering will supply these data in the future.[1] For the past and present, however, such information is unavailable.

## The Available Facts

The most comprehensive previous examination of the postdoctoral situation was made by Bernard Berelson[2] in 1960 in preparation for a report to the Association of American Universities. Berelson visited some 16 campuses, sent questionnaires to the forty-odd member institutions of the AAU, and held discussions with representatives of a number of federal agencies. In lieu of hard data, except for a few national fellowship programs, Berelson applied the

---

[1] Unfortunately the information requested of universities in this CASE Phase II study will not include those postdoctorals whose stipend is paid by a nongovernmental source, but whose research expenses are supplied from the mentor's federal contract or grant.
[2] Bernard Berelson, Postdoctoral Work in American Universities, *Journal of Higher Education*, Vol. XXXIII, No. 3, March 1962, pp. 119-130.

formula of one postdoctoral research associate for each $100,000 of federal research funds at universities. With this and other rough approximations he estimated that in 1960 there were 8,000 postdoctoral appointees in all fields at universities.

Another study was made in 1958 by Dr. Arthur S. Cain and completed, after his death, by Lois G. Bowen.[3] They reported on a comprehensive questionnaire study made of the system of medical fellowships and their impact on both the recipients and the medical institutions. Valuable in its limited areas of concern, the study is now out-of-date. The decade that has passed has seen tremendous growth, and the climate in medical schools has changed radically.

An unpublished pilot study examining many aspects of postdoctoral education at eight universities was undertaken by the National Science Foundation in 1965.

Studies at individual universities have been made by H. W. Magoun at UCLA, Robert Alberty at Wisconsin, G. M. Almy at Illinois, and John Perry Miller at Yale. In addition Myron Rand has written a short history of the National Research Council Fellowships describing the development of that important program that "contributed to the spectacular rise from mediocrity to world leadership in scientific research which the United States has accomplished during the one generation in which the fellowship experiment has been in progress."

In none of these studies is there an overview of the extent and nature of postdoctoral activity in the United States. The present study was undertaken by the National Research Council to provide that overview. The first task was to establish the boundaries of the universe to be investigated. This was no easy task, since the definition of postdoctoral education was really to be the conclusion of the study.

## Definition of Postdoctoral Appointment

Strictly speaking, *postdoctoral* is an adjective that pertains to an individual who has attained the doctor's degree. Thus, a postdoctoral appointment in precise terms refers to any formal position to which a person is appointed following his completion of the requirements for a doctor's degree. The word would most naturally be contrasted with *predoctoral*.

---

[3] Arthur S. Cain, Jr. and Lois G. Bowen, The Role of Postdoctoral Fellowships in Academic Medicine, *The Journal of Medical Education*, Vol. 36, No. 10, Part 2, October 1961, pp. 1357-1556.

However, just as *predoctoral* is generally limited to describing that period before the doctorate but after the baccalaureate, the common usage of *postdoctoral* is restricted to those holders of the doctorate who are pursuing some special experience or training beyond their formal predoctoral work. Exactly which experiences should be included or excluded is a question on which there is little agreement, although most observers would admit that holders of fellowships who are carrying on research in association with a senior investigator represent the paradigm. The problem of definition is complicated by the age and field of the individual, the variety of titles used, the institution at which the appointment is held, and, most critically, by the ambiguity in the purpose of many appointments. We shall discuss these difficulties after presenting the following definition used in this study:

This study is concerned with appointments of a temporary nature at the postdoctoral level that are intended to offer an opportunity for continued education and experience in research, usually, though not necessarily, under the supervision of a senior mentor. The appointee may have a research doctorate (e.g., PhD, ScD) or professional doctorate (e.g., MD, DVM) or other qualifications which are considered equivalent in the circumstances. A person may have more than one postdoctoral appointment during his career.

In its inquiries, the Committee on Academic Science and Engineering of the Federal Council for Science and Technology inserts the restriction that the man be within five years of his doctorate. We have avoided such a restriction for several reasons. If we set a limit that might be appropriate in the case of PhD's, many MD's who take postdoctoral work following their internships and residencies would not be included. Furthermore, in fields such as the humanities and social sciences, the pattern is to delay postdoctoral work until a period of time has passed. Some of these people would also be missed. Finally, in terms of the impact on institutions, it makes little difference if the occupants of laboratory benches or library carrels are just out of graduate school or have been employed elsewhere for some time. Our data permit us to distinguish among the age groups when it is important.

The first key word in the definition is *temporary*. There are a number of temporary postdoctoral appointments that we want to exclude or at least to amplify the conditions under which they may be included. The first is the appointment to instructor or assistant professor. These appointments are generally temporary, but ordinarily should not be considered within our definition, since they are understood to be part of a regular series of academic appointments and lead, if all goes well, to permanent positions. On the other hand, at some institutions a person may be given a fractional professorial appointment with the remainder of his support coming from a fellowship. Such people will be included in our study.

## DEFINITION OF POSTDOCTORAL APPOINTMENT

Another variation on this theme is the practice, especially in mathematics, of creating named instructorships, such as the Moore Instructorships at MIT, the Pierce Instructorships at Harvard, or the J. Willard Gibbs Instructorships at Yale, where young PhD's are given a reduced teaching load so that they may concentrate their efforts on research. It is likely that these people should be included in the study, although it is not known whether all such individuals or departments responded to our inquiries.

Another temporary appointment is that of the Visiting Professor. In this case, although the individual has often accepted the appointment to make use of the research facilities and professional contacts at the host institution, we have excluded him from our definition if he is filling a regular faculty position in the host institution. Our reasoning here is that his impact upon the budget and facilities of the institution is small; the faculty member he temporarily replaced would have used essentially the same resources. The effect of this decision on our part is to reduce the apparent number of postdoctoral positions in those fields where, for lack of extramural funds, other postdoctoral opportunities are rare. It may be one reason for the low representation of postdoctorals in the humanities and in the social sciences.

Some temporary appointments are so short as to be little more than visits. These clearly are not relevant to the study. However, it is less clear how long the visit must be before we become interested. The critical question is whether the duration is sufficient for research to be accomplished. We decided that the criterion ought to be whether a formal appointment has been made by the host institution.

Another ambiguous group is what Clark Kerr[4] has called the "unfaculty." These are the professional research personnel who are more or less permanently appointed to the research staffs of institutes and departments of universities without having regular faculty appointments. At some institutions a parallel structure of research faculty appointments is established through which these people may progress without ever attaining tenure or other faculty privileges. This group overlaps in an irregular and indefinite way with the postdoctoral population to the degree that it is difficult to draw the dividing line. From the point of view of the supporting federal agency and the director of the research group, both the professional research staff and the postdoctorals are appointed to perform research under the rubric of the contract. There is no explicit intention in either case that the appointment provide an opportunity for continued education and experience in research, although this opportunity exists. The distinction between the unfaculty and the post-

---
[4] Clark Kerr, *The Uses of the University*, Harvard University Press, Cambridge, Mass., 1964, p. 67.

doctoral is in their respective perceptions of their goals and purposes. The postdoctoral is one who intends to leave the position after an interval, having received the continued education and experience in research that *he* sought.

The second key word in the definition is *research*. There are a number of types of temporary positions that have the character of apprenticeships. These include internships and residencies for physicians, clerkships for lawyers, teaching internships in liberal arts colleges, and administrative internships in in the major universities. None of these is a postdoctoral appointment in our sense unless research training under the supervision of a senior mentor is the prime purpose of the appointment.

Related to the restriction to research is the problem of the second doctorate. What is to be done in the case of the physician who seeks a PhD or the PhD who heads for a professional doctorate? It was decided to admit the man to postdoctoral status if research was his main activity. This has the effect of denying this status to the man seeking the professional doctorate (e.g., medicine or law) and of granting it to the physician pursuing the PhD degree.

The situation for the young medical doctor is further complicated by the fact that some sources of support do not make the research distinction that we do. Thus, a man may hold a postdoctoral traineeship from the National Institutes of Health to obtain training in research or to obtain training in clinical practice. The former we include; the latter we do not.

Up to this point, much of the discussion has dealt with the university scene. In industrial, governmental, and nonprofit laboratories and libraries around the country there are positions similar to those described above in the university environment. When such positions in nonacademic organizations have the character and objectives of postdoctoral appointments in the universities, we have included them in the study.

Regardless of the host institution, a major problem in identifying postdoctorals is the bewildering array of titles that are attached to them. Although there are only four basic types of postdoctoral appointments (see page 86 for fuller discussion), the titles are often unrelated. A man supported by a fellowship generally has the word "fellow" in his title: however, a man supported on faculty research funds may be called a "fellow," a "research fellow," a "research associate," a "research assistant professor," etc. At many institutions a research associate is a young postdoctoral supported by faculty research money, while at the California Institute of Technology a research associate is a distinguished visiting scholar who does not teach, regardless of his source of support.

Differences in semantic usage have made for difficulties in collecting data. When asked how many postdoctoral students were in his department, one chairman answered, "None," when, in fact, his department leads the country in the ratio of postdoctorals to faculty (3:1). At his institution postdoctorals are counted among the faculty and consequently are not students.

In an attempt to anticipate some of the ambiguities mentioned above, a list of explicit exclusions and inclusions was attached to the definition distributed along with all questionnaires and inquiries. This list is reproduced as follows:

### EXCLUSIONS

1. Although appointments to Instructor and Assistant Professor are temporary, they are excluded because they are understood to be part of the regular series of academic appointments and lead, if all goes well, to a permanent position.
2. Visiting professor appointments are excluded if they fill regular places in the host institution's academic staff.
3. Service Research appointments which are not intended to provide an opportunity for continued education in research are excluded.
4. Internships and Residencies are excluded unless research training under supervision of a senior mentor is the prime purpose of the appointment.
5. Holders of a doctor's degree who are studying for another doctorate that does not involve research as a primary activity are excluded.

### INCLUSIONS

1. Postdoctoral appointments, supported by whatever funds, that provide an opportunity for continued education and experience in research are included.
2. Scholars on leave from other institutions are included if they come primarily to further their research experience.
3. Appointments of holders of professional doctoral degrees who are pursuing research experience are included even though they may be candidates for a second doctoral degree.
4. Appointments in government and industrial laboratories that resemble in their character and objectives postdoctoral appointments in the universities are included.
5. Persons holding fractional postdoctoral appointments are included. For example, a postdoctoral fellow with a part-time Assistant Professorship is included.
6. Appointments for a short duration are included if they are of sufficient duration to provide an opportunity for research and a formal appointment can be made.

## Strategy of the Study

In order to provide information and opinions from the whole spectrum of persons connected in some way with postdoctoral education, we found it necessary to use a wide variety of instruments and techniques to sample the pertinent components of the population. Depending on the nature of his involvement, an individual may have been asked to respond to a formal questionnaire, to an invitation to record free replies to broad inquiries, or he may have been approached through an interview. The interviews included single individuals and groups. A number of conferences were held following speeches by the Director and by members of the Advisory Committee and many reactions were obtained. It is felt that opinions of most major groups have been sampled.

Two kinds of information have been gathered: factual counts of numbers of individuals, institutions, and responses; and statements of opinion. The former were required simply to provide scope to the study; the latter to place the scope in context. Let us first consider the instruments used to collect the facts.

The fundamental question is: How many postdoctorals consistent with our definition exist? Immediately associated with that question are many others. Where are they located? In what fields do they work? Where did they get their formal education? What is their citizenship? By whom are they supported? What is the nature of their support? How much remuneration do they receive? What is the nature of their activities? Why did they seek such an appointment? What are their future plans? etc. Although some of this information can be partially gleaned from federal agencies and private funding sources, most of the data did not exist. For example, most agencies have only fragmentary information on the number of postdoctorals supported on research grants, since the receptor institutions are allowed some freedom in the selection of the kinds of personnel hired with these funds. We decided that only a census of postdoctorals would permit us to answer the questions posed. Adequate responses were received from 10,740 postdoctorals and we estimate that the total postdoctoral population in the spring of 1967 numbered 16,000.[5]

Another major question concerns the nature of the environment within which the postdoctoral is working and where he is likely to be employed following his present appointment. In both cases the location is probably an institution of higher education (as is evident from the postdoctoral census data). Accordingly, a questionnaire was designed to be answered by departmental chairmen to discover the answers to such questions as: How many faculty of what rank are in the department? What kind of background do the faculty have? How many graduate students are enrolled? How many graduate degrees are awarded? What positions do their doctoral recipients fill following their degrees? How many postdoctorals are in the department? What are the departmental policies regarding the postdoctoral? etc. Returns were received from 4,040 departments in 357 schools.[6]

---

[5] The technique used in carrying out the census and the way in which the rate of return was estimated are discussed in Appendix A-1. In view of the uncertainties in the estimation procedure the estimate of 16,000 postdoctorals could be wrong by as much as 2,000 in either direction.

[6] See Appendix A-2 for details on sampling procedures and for analysis of the returns.

## STRATEGY OF THE STUDY

Faculty members play central roles in postdoctoral education. By directing inquiries to the faculty, views were sought from mentors of postdoctorals and from those who, although involved in research, had no postdoctorals in their research group. Both views are important since the present evolution of postdoctoral study does not meet with the approval of all faculty. Answers were sought to such questions as: What is the composition of research groups in terms of graduate students, postdoctorals, professional staff, faculty coworkers, etc.? How many recent graduate degrees have been produced from the group? For what reasons are graduate students urged to take postdoctoral study? In what way do the various kinds of members of the research group contribute to the research and teaching? Does the nationality of the postdoctoral make a difference? What are the time and space requirements of a postdoctoral compared to a graduate student? etc. Completed questionnaires were received from 2,195 postdoctoral mentors and from 564 doctoral mentors without postdoctorals in their research groups.[7]

The administrative point of view was elicited through an open-ended questionnaire (see Appendix A-5) that was sent to each of the universities having postdoctorals. Questionnaires were sent to 165 schools and replies were received from 125.

The many agencies and private organizations that support nationally competitive fellowship programs were asked three questions: How many fellowships in what fields have been awarded since the inception of their program? What was their budget for postdoctoral fellowships in fiscal year 1967 (July 1, 1966 to June 30, 1967)? What purpose were they seeking to fulfill with their program?

In addition we have had commentary from directors of nonprofit, government, and industrial laboratories on the effect of the growth of postdoctoral education on their activities. Interviews have been held with program officers in the several federal agencies supporting the bulk of the research in universities to determine the part that consideration of the postdoctoral plays in their awarding research grants and contracts to universities. Twenty universities were visited and conversations were held with deans, departmental chairmen, faculty members, postdoctorals, and terminal doctoral candidates. Numerous discussions have been held with knowledgeable people in and out of the federal government and close coordination has been maintained with a number of other related studies being carried out in the National Academy of Sciences and elsewhere.

One other investigation has been made to determine the value of postdoctoral education. Many observers are of the opinion that, for the most part, those who seek and receive postdoctoral appointments are among the better

---

[7]See Appendix A-3 for sampling details and for analysis of the returns.

## THE STUDY

doctoral recipients. This study confirms that opinion on the average. Separate studies such as the report of the Commission on Human Resources and Advanced Education[8] demonstrate that, as measured by the rate at which published work is cited by others, former postdoctorals do more important research than those researchers who have not had postdoctoral appointments. The combination of these two concepts leads to the rather obvious conclusion that better PhD's do better research. Whether the postdoctoral experience is relevant to the subsequent success is left in doubt.

We have attempted to improve on existing data by selecting two samples of doctorate holders of apparent equal quality. A group of former postdoctorals was matched with an equal group of non-former-postdoctorals that was similar with regard to field distribution, to the "quality" of the PhD institution,[9] to the time lapse between the baccalaureate and the doctor's degree, and to the age of the individual. These two groups were sent questionnaires[10] and citation information was gathered from the Science Citation Index.

These then, in addition to published documents, are the inputs to the study. The exposition of our results and conclusions are found in the chapters that follow.

---

[8] *Human Resources and Higher Education*, Russell Sage Foundation, New York, in press, 1969.
[9] Allan Cartter, *An Assessment of Quality in Graduate Education*, American Council of Education, 1966.
[10] See Appendix A-4 for sampling details and response rates.

CHAPTER 4
# The Demography of Postdoctoral Education

We received usable responses to our census of postdoctorals from 10,740 persons who determined that they were included within our definition. Assuming that we had a 65 percent rate of return,[1] in the spring of 1967 there were approximately 16,000 postdoctorals including U.S. citizens either in this country or abroad and foreign nationals in this country. Compared with Berelson's estimate[2] (although he was concerned only with postdoctorals at academic institutions), the number of postdoctorals has doubled between 1960 and 1967.

The rate of doubling has not been uniform across all fields. In chemistry the numbers have doubled in five or six years,[3] while in physics the doubling required only four or five years.[4] We will examine the situation in each discipline later. For the present it is sufficient to note that until recently the number of postdoctorals has been increasing steadily since World War II.

There is evidence that the growth has now begun to level off, if not to decrease. In spite of an increase in the number of applicants, the number of fellowships awarded by the National Science Foundation has almost halved in the last three years. The Committee on Physics and Society (COMPAS) of the American Institute of Physics has reported that although the number of post-

[1] See Appendix A-1.
[2] Bernard Berelson, *Postdoctoral Work in American Universities*, pp. 119–130.
[3] NAS–NRC, *Chemistry Opportunities and Needs*, Publ. 1292, Washington, D.C., 1963.
[4] NAS–NRC, *Physics: Survey and Outlook,* Publ. 1295, Washington, D.C., 1966.

50
THE DEMOGRAPHY OF POSTDOCTORAL EDUCATION

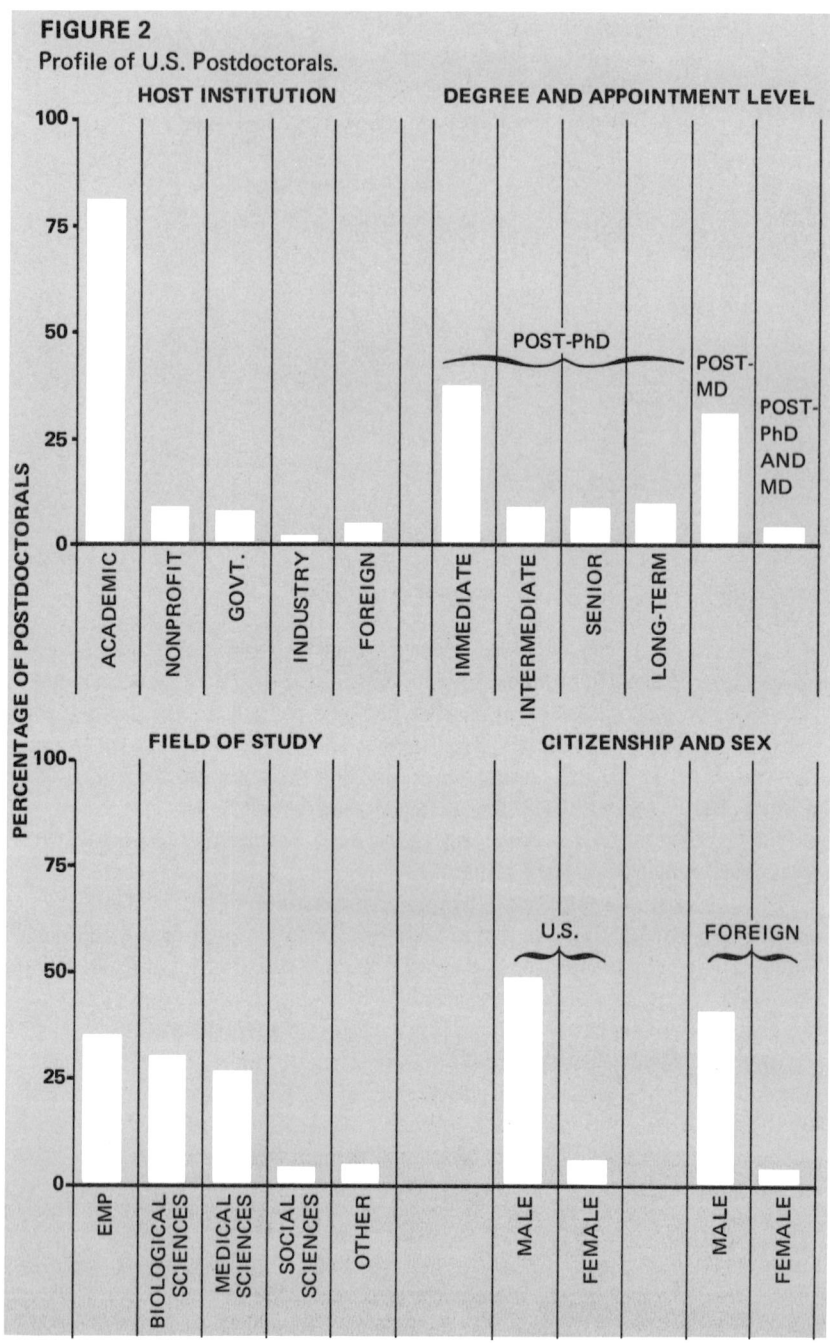

**FIGURE 2**
Profile of U.S. Postdoctorals.

Source: NRC, Office of Scientific Personnel, Postdoctoral Census Questionnaire.

doctorals in physics has increased slightly between 1965-66 and 1966-67, the figure was expected to decrease in 1968-69 as the hiring of new postdoctorals was deferred because of the uncertainty in federal support.[5] (It did decrease, by about 3 percent.) The COMPAS survey of 130 department chairmen revealed that the number of physics postdoctorals per faculty member was expected to fall from 0.34 (where it has stabilized for three years) to 0.29. (The implications of a reduction of the number of postdoctoral appointments will be pursued in Chapter 6.)

## The Composition of the Postdoctoral Population

As is shown in Figure 2, 81 percent of the postdoctorals are at academic institutions in the United States, 8 percent are at U.S. nonprofit organizations, 7 percent are at federal research establishments, 4 percent are in other countries, and only 0.4 percent are in industrial installations. Although the universities predominate as host institutions, it is important to keep in mind that significant numbers of postdoctorals have chosen other places to do research. It will become clear that the nature of the experience and the aspirations of the postdoctorals are relatively independent of the host institution.

A more significant difference among the segments of the postdoctoral population is the type of degree that the postdoctoral has earned. According to the responses to our census,[6] 62 percent hold a research doctorate only (PhD or equivalent), 31 percent hold a professional doctorate only (MD, DDS, DVM, etc.), 3 percent hold both the PhD and the MD, and 4 percent reported no doctorate.[7] Because of the different nature of the predoctoral experience, the postdoctoral activity is different for the PhD and the MD. PhD's, having had more research experience, play the role of apprentices, whereas most MD's, receiving perhaps their first research training, tend to have the status of students of research.

Another critical difference among the postdoctorals is the level of their professional seniority. An established researcher will generally neither seek

---

[5] *Survey of the Committee on Physics and Society—Report No. 1*, American Institute of Physics, February 27, 1968.

[6] Unless otherwise indicated all data will be presented in terms of what we collected from the various questionnaires. If we have not received uniform return rates from the various segments of the population, the actual distribution will differ from what is reported. Unfortunately, there is no way to correct such errors.

[7] A number of scholars receive appointments and fellowships of the postdoctoral character without having earned a doctoral degree. Some of these are from foreign countries where the doctorate has a different significance from that in the United States.

nor expect the same kind of appointment that a fresh PhD will accept, nor will their activities necessarily be the same. From this perspective, several categories are usually established. The "regular" postdoctoral with the PhD is one within five years of his PhD. The senior postdoctoral with the PhD is more than five years beyond his PhD. A similar distinction can be made among those with the MD except that we have used seven years as the dividing point. This allows the man to serve one year of internship and several years of residency before taking a postdoctoral appointment.

In this study the post-PhD categories are defined somewhat differently from those in most fellowship programs in order to group the postdoctorals in more homogeneous sets. With a complication to be described below there are three basic subcategories: immediate postdoctoral, intermediate postdoctoral, and senior postdoctoral. The immediate postdoctoral is within two years of his doctorate, the intermediate postdoctoral is between two years and five years from his doctorate, and the senior postdoctoral is more than five years from his doctorate.

A fourth category is important and overlaps those already given. This group comprises the long-term postdoctorals, defined as those who, however far from their doctorate, have spent more than two years on a postdoctoral appointment and who are not on leave from another position. It is clear that the long-term postdoctoral as we have defined him is not necessarily to be identified with the postdoctoral on indefinite appointment. Some of the long-term postdoctorals are simply completing work that has taken more than two years. The professional research appointee, since he did not perceive of himself as on a "temporary" appointment, may not have responded to our ques-

TABLE 5  Number of Postdoctorals by Level of Appointment and Percent Foreign

| Level of Appointment | Postdoctorals Number | Percent | Percent Foreign at Level |
|---|---|---|---|
| Immediate post-PhD | 3,997 | 37.2 | 44 |
| Intermediate post-PhD | 905 | 8.4 | 64 |
| Long-term post-PhD | 979 | 9.1 | 54 |
| Senior post-PhD | 815 | 7.6 | 44 |
| Recent post-MD | 2,391 | 22.3 | 26 |
| Senior post-MD | 937 | 8.7 | 52 |
| Both PhD and MD | 334 | 3.1 | 84 |
| No reported doctorate | 382 | 3.6 | 64 |
| *Total* | 10,740 | 100.0 | 45 |

Source: NRC, Office of Scientific Personnel, Postdoctoral Census Questionnaire.

tionnaire (in fact, he should not have responded). Thus the reader is cautioned that the long-term category is at best an ill-defined group.

The distribution of postdoctorals by seniority and degree type is given in Table 5. It should be noted that the immediate postdoctoral represents 60 percent of all post-PhD's (3,997 out of 6,686). This is the group that most people refer to when discussing postdoctorals. They have taken postdoctoral appointments as their first employment after completing their degree requirements. The same may be true of some of the long-term postdoctorals, but they constitute less than 14 percent of the post-PhD's. The intermediate postdoctorals have been employed elsewhere and they are either on leave of absences or are in transition to new employment.

To understand the composition of the postdoctoral population it is necessary to explore another dimension. In each discipline there exists the spectrum of levels just described and, to a lesser extent, a mixture of both post-PhD's and post-MD's.[8] Similarities across fields are not absent, but similarities within a discipline and across host institutions are often striking. Table 6 shows the distribution of the postdoctorals in the various fields.

It is clear that the social sciences and humanities do not participate in postdoctoral education to the extent that the natural sciences do. Whether these fields ought to be more involved or not is discussed in Chapter 6. It should be noted, however, that these data were collected before the National Endowment for the Humanities made its first awards.

An important categorization of the entire population can be made in terms of the citizenship of the postdoctoral. Tables 5 and 6 give the fraction of all individuals at each level and in each field who are foreign. The details of the foreign component of the population and its relation to federal and educational policy will be discussed in Chapter 8. At this point we should be reminded that international travel of scientists and scholars generally is a well established pattern. Between the end of the last century and the first third of this century many American scientists went abroad, mostly to Germany, for postdoctoral training. It is not at all unlikely that as many as half of the postdoctorals in Germany at that time were not Germans. What has changed is that the locus of scientific excellence has shifted to the United States and the availability of support in this country is now much larger. We must also remember that 8 percent of all U.S. postdoctorals (35 percent of senior postdoctorals) are abroad.

An important feature of the foreign postdoctoral population is the concentration of citizenship in only a few countries. Over half of all foreign postdoc-

---

[8] The term *post-MD* is used here and elsewhere as a generic term that includes all post-professional doctorates. The MD degree is by far the most predominant of these (approximately 95 percent).

THE DEMOGRAPHY OF POSTDOCTORAL EDUCATION

TABLE 6  Number of Postdoctorals by Field and Percent Foreign

| Postdoctoral Field | Postdoctorals Number | Percent | Percent Foreign in Field |
|---|---|---|---|
| Astronomy | 108 | 1.0 | 56 |
| Mathematics | 240 | 2.2 | 40 |
| Physics | 1,267 | 11.8 | 50 |
| Chemistry | 1,660 | 15.5 | 63 |
| Earth sciences | 189 | 1.8 | 54 |
| Engineering | 274 | 2.6 | 64 |
| EMP[a] Total | 3,738 | 34.9 | |
| Biochemistry | 1,322 | 12.3 | 51 |
| Other basic life sciences | 1,030 | 9.6 | 40 |
| Other biosciences | 907 | 8.4 | 44 |
| Agricultural sciences | 55 | 0.5 | 62 |
| Internal medicine | 1,059 | 9.9 | 36 |
| Other medical sciences | 1,166 | 10.8 | 35 |
| Allied medical sciences | 425 | 4.0 | 37 |
| Life Sciences Total | 5,964 | 55.5 | |
| Psychology | 246 | 2.3 | 11 |
| Social sciences | 196 | 1.8 | 36 |
| Social Sciences Total | 442 | 4.1 | |
| Arts and humanities | 228 | 2.1 | 23 |
| Other fields | 368 | 3.4 | 36 |
| Total | 10,740 | 100.0 | 45 |

[a] Engineering, mathematics, and physical sciences.

Source: NRC, Office of Scientific Personnel, Postdoctoral Census Questionnaire.

torals are from only five countries (United Kingdom, India, Japan, West Germany, and Canada) and 75 percent are from 13 countries. Thus, the remaining 68 countries represented account for only 1,211 postdoctorals, or slightly less than 18 postdoctorals per country. Appendix B-3 presents data for foreign postdoctorals by their country of origin.

## The Postdoctoral in U.S. Academic Institutions

In 1967 there were approximately 13,000 postdoctorals of all varieties at U.S. institutions of higher education. Of these, 8,654 responded to the census questionnaire. Of the 212 universities that had granted a PhD by 1966, only 147 or 70 percent had postdoctorals. In addition, 27 other colleges or newly formed graduate institutions had postdoctorals. Appendix B-2 contains a listing of the institutions with postdoctorals. The distribution of postdoctorals among these 174 institutions is, however, highly skewed, as is shown in Figure 3. From the curve it can be seen that 50 percent of the postdoctorals are in only 9 percent of the schools that have any postdoctorals and 80 percent of the postdoctorals are in only 25 percent of the schools. Harvard alone can claim 7 percent of the postdoctorals. In spite of the different total number of institutions in the base, the distribution of PhD production is strikingly similar. The relationship to federal funding[9] is also shown in Figure 3.

Another way of looking at the concentration is to examine the number of institutions in each field that have postdoctorals compared with the number of institutions that have granted the PhD. Table 7 gives the number of schools having half of the postdoctorals in a given field as well as the fraction of available schools these numbers represent. Although postdoctorals are most widely dispersed among the potential universities in chemistry and internal medicine, the concentration of postdoctorals among a few of the universities is almost independent of field, as can be seen in the last column. The small attention generally paid to postdoctoral activity might be explained by the fact that only at a handful of schools is the number of postdoctorals large enough to be noticeable outside of the departments.

In terms of departments, the distribution of postdoctoral activity is given in Table 8. It is not surprising that postdoctorals tend to go to the more prestigious schools.[10] What might be unexpected is that postdoctorals are present in liberal arts colleges that do not award the PhD. The percentages given for colleges at which less than half the faculty have the PhD may be inflated since the return rate may have been higher from departments with postdoctorals.

The current pattern does not differ significantly from what Berelson found in 1960. He found that the institutions in the Association of American Universities (AAU) did about two thirds of the postdoctoral work in American universities.[11] At that time the AAU had about 40 members, which would imply that approximately one fifth of all schools had 67 percent of the postdoctorals in 1960.

---

[9] A total of 298 schools received funds in excess of $12,000 in 1966 to support research from the AEC, NASA, or the Department of Defense. Since NSF and HEW contribute funds for nonresearch purposes, it is difficult to determine whether the funds from them represent research support. The fit in Figure 3 would not be nearly so close if all of the schools receiving federal support were included.
[10] The grouping of institutions by reputation is explained in Appendix B-2, which also includes summary data for postdoctorals at U.S. academic institutions.
[11] Berelson, *loc. cit.*

## THE DEMOGRAPHY OF POSTDOCTORAL EDUCATION

**FIGURE 3**

Distribution of 1967 Postdoctorals among U.S. Institutions and Comparison to 1960–66 PhD Production and 1966 Federal Academic Science Obligations.

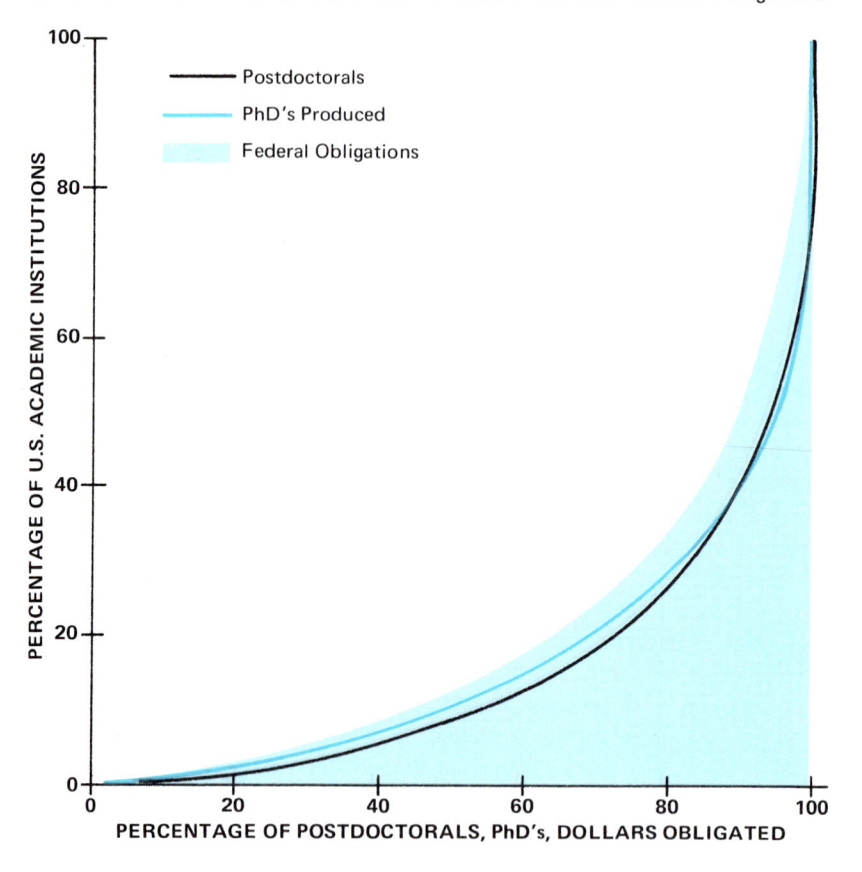

Source: NRC, Office of Scientific Personnel, Postdoctoral Census Questionnaire and Doctorate Records File. NSF, data compiled for the Committee on Academic Science and Engineering (CASE).

An adequate picture of postdoctoral activity in the universities can be obtained only if we examine the various kinds of postdoctorals there. Table 9 gives the distribution among levels in the various fields. The significance of the activity, both for the university and for the individual postdoctoral, depends on the level of appointment. Usually the young man who proceeds to a postdoctoral appointment immediately after his doctorate is motivationally and professionally different from a seasoned researcher. Moreover, he is at a much more critical point in his career than the older man. Since 84 percent of these

TABLE 7  Concentration of Postdoctorals among Academic Institutions in Selected Fields

| Postdoctoral Field | Number of Institutions Granting Doctorates | Number of Institutions Postdoctoral Hosts | Doctoral Institutions with Postdoctorals (percent) | Institutions with One-Half of Postdoctorals Number | Percent of All Granting Doctorates | Percent of All Postdoctoral Hosts |
|---|---|---|---|---|---|---|
| Mathematics | 103 | 36 | 35.0 | 6 | 5.8 | 16.7 |
| Physics and astronomy | 124 | 89 | 71.8 | 13 | 10.5 | 14.6 |
| Chemistry | 153 | 129 | 84.3 | 20 | 13.1 | 15.5 |
| Biochemistry | 141 | 93 | 66.0 | 15 | 10.6 | 16.1 |
| Biosciences | 152 | 103 | 67.8 | 14 | 9.2 | 13.6 |
| Internal medicine | 84 | 79 | 94.0 | 10 | 11.9 | 12.7 |
| Total (unduplicated) | 212 | 176 | 83.0 | 17 | 7.9 | 9.8 |

Source: NRC, Office of Scientific Personnel, Doctorate Records File and Postdoctoral Census Questionnaire.

TABLE 8 Percentage of Academic Institutions Having Postdoctorals by Type of Institution and Department

| Type of Academic Institution | Physical Sciences | Engineering | Biosciences | Basic Medical Sciences | Social Sciences | Humanities |
|---|---|---|---|---|---|---|
| Ten leading | 95 | 72 | 86 | 100 | 61 | 30 |
| Twenty other major | 78 | 57 | 79 | 97 | 36 | 18 |
| Established | 58 | 21 | 71 | 71 | 15 | 8 |
| Developing | 25 | 5 | 20 | 59 | 5 | 1 |
| Others | | | | | | |
| More than half PhD faculty | 4 | 6 | 7 | 25 | 1 | 0 |
| Less than half PhD faculty | 1 | 0 | 0 | 0 | 0 | 1 |

Source: NRC, Office of Scientific Personnel, Postdoctoral Census Questionnaire.

immediate postdoctorals have chosen to do their work at universities, we should discuss their situation next.

Immediate PhD Postdoctorals

An increasing number of PhD recipients have been selecting postdoctoral appointments as their first appointment after the doctorate. In 1962, 8.5 percent of all PhD's produced in this country went immediately into postdoctoral positions.[12] By 1967, the fraction had increased to 11.6 percent. Since the number of graduating doctorates had grown from 11,507 to 20,295 in the same time interval, this relatively small percentage change indicates almost a tripling in the number of postdoctorals.

The behavior of doctoral recipients in the various fields shows even more striking changes with time (Table 10). The percentage in physics and astronomy taking a postdoctoral appointment has moved from 16 percent of the 1962 class to 26 percent of the 1967 class. Biochemistry sent 36 percent of its doctoral recipients on to postdoctoral work in 1962; by 1967 that fraction had

[12] These data are derived from the Doctoral Records File, maintained by the Office of Scientific Personnel of the National Research Council from the annually conducted Survey of Earned Doctorates. A questionnaire is filled out by doctoral candidates when they have completed the requirements for their degrees. The respondents are asked to indicate their anticipated employment. Follow-up studies show that their responses are accurate.

TABLE 9  Distribution of Postdoctorals at U.S. Academic Institutions by Level of Appointment and Field

| Postdoctoral Field | Percentage of Postdoctorals by Level of Appointment ||||||| Total Number (100%) |
| | Post-PhD Immediate | Post-PhD Intermediate | Post-PhD Senior | Post-PhD Long-Term | Post-MD | No Doctorate Degree | |
|---|---|---|---|---|---|---|---|
| Mathematics | 54.3 | 9.7 | 22.3 | 5.7 | 1.1 | 6.9 | 175 |
| Astronomy | 64.4 | 17.8 | 5.5 | 8.2 | 0.0 | 4.1 | 73 |
| Physics | 61.4 | 12.1 | 5.4 | 14.7 | 0.1 | 6.3 | 1,034 |
| Chemistry | 63.3 | 13.0 | 6.5 | 13.6 | 0.8 | 2.7 | 1,502 |
| Earth sciences | 60.4 | 12.2 | 15.8 | 7.2 | 0.0 | 4.3 | 139 |
| Engineering | 67.1 | 11.1 | 6.2 | 8.6 | 2.5 | 4.5 | 243 |
| EMP[a] | 62.4 | 12.4 | 7.4 | 12.8 | 0.7 | 4.4 | 3,166 |
| Agricultural sciences | 52.9 | 11.8 | 11.8 | 13.7 | 5.9 | 3.9 | 51 |
| Biochemistry | 47.0 | 10.6 | 3.6 | 15.8 | 18.8 | 4.2 | 1,072 |
| Other basic medical sciences | 28.1 | 5.4 | 3.9 | 6.7 | 53.5 | 2.4 | 761 |
| Biosciences | 44.6 | 10.6 | 8.5 | 15.1 | 18.0 | 3.1 | 715 |
| *Agric. and biol. sci. Total* | 40.9 | 9.1 | 5.2 | 12.9 | 28.5 | 3.3 | 2,599 |
| Internal medicine | 5.3 | 1.2 | 0.7 | 1.6 | 89.6 | 1.5 | 810 |
| Other clinical medicine | 2.4 | 0.4 | 0.1 | 1.2 | 93.9 | 2.0 | 930 |
| Allied medical sciences | 3.9 | 0.8 | 0.8 | 0.8 | 91.2 | 2.6 | 388 |
| *Medical sciences Total* | 3.8 | 0.8 | 0.5 | 1.3 | 91.8 | 1.9 | 2,128 |
| Psychology | 58.3 | 8.9 | 14.3 | 9.5 | 6.5 | 2.4 | 168 |
| Social sciences | 32.9 | 19.7 | 22.4 | 15.1 | 2.0 | 7.9 | 152 |
| Arts and humanities | 14.0 | 20.4 | 45.9 | 8.9 | 0.6 | 10.2 | 157 |
| Education and professions | 26.1 | 7.4 | 15.4 | 8.1 | 34.2 | 9.9 | 284 |
| Total All Fields | 38.9 | 8.6 | 6.4 | 9.7 | 32.7 | 3.8 | 8,654 |

[a] Engineering, mathematics, and physical sciences.

Source: NRC, Office of Scientific Personnel, Postdoctoral Census Questionnaire.

TABLE 10  Number of PhD's and Percentage Taking Immediate Postdoctoral Appointment, by Field of Doctorate, 1962-1967

| Field of Doctorate | 1962 PhD's N | 1962 Taking Postdoct. % | 1963 PhD's N | 1963 Taking Postdoct. % | 1964 PhD's N | 1964 Taking Postdoct. % | 1965 PhD's N | 1965 Taking Postdoct. % | 1966 PhD's N | 1966 Taking Postdoct. % | 1967 PhD's N | 1967 Taking Postdoct. % |
|---|---|---|---|---|---|---|---|---|---|---|---|---|
| Mathematics | 388 | 9.2 | 484 | 8.4 | 590 | 7.0 | 684 | 7.0 | 766 | 6.6 | 828 | 6.9 |
| Physics and astronomy | 710 | 15.8 | 818 | 19.0 | 865 | 19.9 | 1,046 | 21.6 | 1,049 | 25.1 | 1,295 | 26.1 |
| Earth sciences | 249 | 7.4 | 322 | 9.6 | 312 | 7.1 | 374 | 10.2 | 399 | 14.1 | 419 | 12.3 |
| Chemistry | 1,137 | 21.9 | 1,288 | 30.4 | 1,351 | 31.8 | 1,439 | 33.2 | 1,580 | 33.0 | 1,764 | 32.6 |
| Engineering | 1,215 | 3.8 | 1,357 | 6.4 | 1,662 | 6.1 | 2,068 | 6.8 | 2,283 | 5.7 | 2,581 | 4.8 |
| Agricultural sciences | 387 | 5.8 | 373 | 9.7 | 445 | 7.3 | 480 | 10.6 | 485 | 7.0 | 517 | 8.1 |
| Biochemistry | 286 | 36.2 | 300 | 49.6 | 371 | 52.4 | 391 | 53.9 | 446 | 58.0 | 495 | 58.1 |
| Other basic medical sciences | 422 | 25.1 | 488 | 29.1 | 552 | 30.7 | 688 | 34.8 | 675 | 36.0 | 814 | 35.7 |
| Biology | 772 | 15.2 | 808 | 20.5 | 853 | 23.4 | 975 | 23.6 | 1,088 | 23.8 | 1,114 | 25.7 |
| Psychology | 857 | 8.9 | 892 | 11.1 | 1,013 | 10.4 | 955 | 14.0 | 1,133 | 13.2 | 1,293 | 12.5 |
| Social sciences | 1,437 | 2.7 | 1,575 | 2.8 | 1,820 | 2.3 | 2,028 | 2.7 | 2,178 | 2.4 | 2,597 | 2.4 |
| Arts and humanities | 1,196 | 1.4 | 1,274 | 2.2 | 1,455 | 1.7 | 1,718 | 1.5 | 1,853 | 1.1 | 2,126 | 1.3 |
| Education | 1,898 | 0.5 | 2,130 | 0.6 | 2,348 | 0.9 | 2,727 | 0.9 | 3,026 | 0.5 | 3,442 | 1.0 |
| Other fields | 553 | 2.2 | 611 | 3.1 | 687 | 2.1 | 729 | 2.2 | 904 | 2.2 | 1,010 | 2.6 |
| Total | 11,507 | 8.5 | 12,720 | 10.9 | 14,324 | 10.8 | 16,302 | 11.6 | 17,865 | 11.4 | 20,295 | 11.6 |

Source: NRC, Office of Scientific Personnel, Doctorate Records File.

increased to 58 percent. On the other hand, the fraction of new doctorates taking postdoctoral appointments in the humanities and in the social sciences has remained stable at 1 and 2 percent, respectively, and in mathematics it has dropped from 9 to 7 percent.

The drop in the number of positions funded in the 1969 fiscal year occurs in the face of a rising demand. It is to be expected that the uncertain impact of the draft on graduate enrollments will not affect the PhD production for the next three or four years.[13] Consequently, the reduction in positions will result in the failure of potential postdoctorals to realize their training goals.

An obvious question is, Why are so many seeking postdoctoral appointments? The answer is not simple. Not only is there no single answer, even for an individual, but the emphasis changes as we move from field to field. Nevertheless, it is possible to enumerate several categories of motivations that are present in varying degrees among most of the postdoctorals in the natural sciences. The humanities and the social sciences require separate treatment.

It is important to realize that only one out of nine PhD recipients seek postdoctoral appointments, and among these there is a great spread of talent, accomplishment, and background. A man who received his degree from a small university and who did his research with a relatively unknown faculty member might have a different motivation from the graduate of a major institution whose mentor was a Nobel Laureate. Moreover, a man whose field is theoretical physics is likely to perceive the requirements for his future career differently from the man in biochemistry.

The unifying theme of postdoctoral work is, by definition, research. More relevant here, however, is the commitment of virtually all the postdoctorals to research and scholarship as a career. Another almost universal feature of postdoctoral activity in the academic world is that most of the participants are anticipating an academic career. With one exception, all the postdoctorals we visited on 18 different campuses preferred to be employed subsequently in a university where they could work with graduate students and carry out research. The one exception was a man who had taken the postdoctoral appointment to determine whether he wanted a research career. He did not and is now headed for a position in a state college system. The others not only were looking to the university setting, but also were hoping to be employed in the more prestigious institutions (at least as prestigious, that is, as the university at which they were taking their postdoctoral appointment). Several at a top institution turned down faculty appointments at lesser places in order to take the postdoctoral positions. Their attitudes toward industrial careers were uniformly negative, usually because they saw such positions as lacking both the

---

[13] Except for the reduction arising from those candidates who will purposely delay completion of degree requirements until they have passed the critical 26th birthday.

# THE DEMOGRAPHY OF POSTDOCTORAL EDUCATION

TABLE 11  Next Anticipated Employer of Immediate U.S. Postdoctorals, by Type of Host Institution

| Type of Host Institution | University | College | Federal Government | Industry | Other and Unknown | Total Number (100%) |
|---|---|---|---|---|---|---|
| University | 73 | 7 | 3 | 8 | 9 | 1,749 |
| Foreign | 77 | 7 | 2 | 8 | 6 | 156 |
| Federal government | 55 | 3 | 23 | 7 | 12 | 209 |
| Industry | 53 | 6 | 0 | 35 | 6 | 17 |
| Nonprofit | 70 | 6 | 3 | 3 | 18 | 101 |
| Total    % | 71 | 6 | 5 | 8 | 10 | |
|          No. | 1,597 | 139 | 108 | 170 | 218 | 2,232 |

Source: NRC, Office of Scientific Personnel, Postdoctoral Census Questionnaire.

freedom and the student contact of the academic world. "If I had wanted an industrial job, I wouldn't have taken the postdoctoral," said one chemist. "I took a $4,000 cut in salary to come here." Another objection to nonacademic positions is the belief by many that the move is unidirectional: once one leaves the academic world, they feel, it is difficult to return. Some reluctantly admitted that, if no suitable academic position was available at the end of their appointment, they would take one in government or industry. Others, however, indicated that in such a circumstance they would try to prolong their postdoctoral appointments or that they would move down the academic hierarchy.

How much their formal responses to this question on the census questionnaire reflected the postdoctorals' desires and how much their more realistic expectations is unknown. It is possible that those interviewed were a biased sample, since their unanimity does not correspond to the replies to the questionnaire given in Tables 11 and 12. Nevertheless, 80 percent of the immediate postdoctorals at universities anticipate an academic career and even 58 percent of those who are taking their appointments in industrial or federal laboratories expect to return to a college or university. By field, physics, chemistry, and engineering have the most postdoctorals heading toward an industrial career. In physics, most of those anticipating an industrial position come from the subfields of atomic and molecular physics, solid state physics, and classical physics. Solid state physics, with 107 university-based postdoctorals, has only 15 going to industry. In nuclear and elementary particle physics, with 221 postdoctorals at academic institutions, only 9 are going to industry.

TABLE 12  Next Anticipated Employer of Immediate U.S. Postdoctorals at Universities, by Field

| Postdoctoral Field | Percentage of Immediate Postdoctorals by Type of Next Anticipated Employer |  |  |  |  | Total Number (100%) |
|---|---|---|---|---|---|---|
|  | University | College | Federal Government | Industry | Other and Unknown |  |
| Mathematics | 89.3 | 1.8 | — | 3.6 | 5.4 | 56 |
| Astronomy | 92.0 | 4.0 | — | — | 4.0 | 25 |
| Physics | 74.9 | 1.7 | 5.1 | 9.7 | 8.6 | 350 |
| Chemistry | 60.3 | 13.6 | 2.1 | 17.5 | 6.5 | 383 |
| Earth sciences | 62.2 | 2.2 | 11.1 | 2.2 | 22.2 | 45 |
| Engineering | 53.7 | 5.6 | — | 22.2 | 18.5 | 54 |
| EMP[a] Total | 68.2 | 7.0 | 3.4 | 12.7 | 8.8 | 913 |
| Agricultural sciences | 63.6 | — | 27.3 | 9.1 | — | 11 |
| Biochemistry | 76.7 | 7.4 | 3.3 | 3.3 | 9.3 | 270 |
| Other basic med. sciences | 82.4 | 3.5 | 2.1 | 2.8 | 9.2 | 142 |
| Biosciences | 81.0 | 6.7 | 2.8 | 1.7 | 7.8 | 179 |
| Medical specialities | 86.7 | 1.7 | 5.0 | — | 6.7 | 60 |
| Life Sciences Total | 79.1 | 6.1 | 3.3 | 2.8 | 8.6 | 662 |
| Psychology | 85.6 | 2.2 | — | — | 12.2 | 90 |
| Social sciences | 69.0 | 13.8 | — | — | 17.2 | 29 |
| Arts and humanities | 76.9 | 15.4 | — | — | 7.7 | 13 |
| Education and professional | 57.1 | 11.9 | — | 2.4 | 28.5 | 42 |
| Other Total | 75.3 | 7.5 | — | 0.6 | 16.7 | 174 |
| Total All Fields | 73.3 | 6.6 | 3.1 | 7.7 | 9.4 | 1,749 |

[a]Engineering, mathematics, and physical sciences.

Source: NRC, Office of Scientific Personnel, Postdoctoral Census Questionnaire.

The situation is similar in chemistry. The subfields of analytic, organic, and pharmaceutical chemistry contribute most of the postdoctorals to industrial positions, while inorganic, nuclear, and theoretical chemistry tend to retain their postdoctorals at the university. In engineering, the fields of mechanical and metallurgical engineering contribute 9 out of the 14 engineers of all kinds going into industry. Subfields such as electrical, aeronautical, and chemical engineering contribute only 3 postdoctorals to industry out of the 23 in these fields.

Although it has been suggested by some directors of industrial laboratories that the postdoctoral experience weans the young doctorate away from industrial careers, it is more likely that the career decision between the academic and the industrial environment is made earlier. Reflecting the attitude of many industrial employers that the postdoctoral experience is unnecessary, faculty members tend not to urge their better students to take postdoctoral appointments if they are headed toward industrial careers. The response of faculty (with and without postdoctorals in their groups) to the question, "How strongly do you encourage your better graduate degree candidates to take an extra year or two of postdoctoral study?" is given below:

| Anticipated Career of Doctorate Recipient | Encouragement of Postdoctoral Work by Faculty (Percent) |||||||
|---|---|---|---|---|---|---|
| | With Postdoctorals ||| Without Postdoctorals |||
| | Strong | Fairly Strong | Not Strong | Strong | Fairly Strong | Not Strong |
| Academic | 75 | 18 | 7 | 49 | 23 | 28 |
| Nonacademic | 15 | 28 | 57 | 9 | 22 | 69 |

*Reasons for Postdoctoral Work*  With this background we can examine the motivations that led the new PhD to his postdoctoral position. The typical postdoctoral in the natural sciences aspires to a lifetime of research in an academic setting where he will have students to train and where he can be a faculty member in the complete sense of the word. However, when he examines the prospect, there are several reasons why he is willing to postpone entering the community as a full-fledged member.

The first reason can be stated generally as "I am not yet prepared academically to become a professor." In part, this attitude is realistic in that the young PhD has not undertaken a complete research problem. We asked a group of 16 terminal-year graduate students from a variety of departments in a Big Ten university how many were anticipating a postdoctoral appointment. Slightly over half responded affirmatively. We then asked how many of the group had invented their own thesis topics. The correlation was perfect in this imperfect sample: All who had been assigned a thesis problem by their advisers planned to take a postdoctoral appointment; all who had come up with an acceptable research topic on their own did not feel the necessity of the additional apprenticeship. Again, dealing with this same group, we discovered that there was a strong subfield dependence for this phenomenon. The geologists and classical biologists tended to have been more independent during their thesis research, whereas those in the more mathematically complex sciences were dependent on their advisers, at least to the extent of knowing what problems were both significant and capable of being accomplished in a reasonable amount of time.

A physics professor has suggested along this line that the transition from being a student to being a professor is too abrupt. In the present system the professor, in addition to his pedagogical responsibilities, is expected to carry out independent research. Postdoctorals maintain that struggling through only one research problem is not sufficient to create the independent researcher who can be a teacher as well. Before facing students, many postdoctorals would like to shift fields slightly or to change institutions to pick up more breadth and style in their approach to research. They argue that without this experience they will tend to work the rest of their lives on their thesis problems.

In part, however, the postdoctoral who senses that he is unprepared for full faculty responsibility is less concerned about his research qualifications than about his readiness to undertake the other responsibilities of a graduate faculty member. One young man questioned whether he was ready to guide graduate students in research. He expected to learn how this was done by observing his postdoctoral mentor and by serving as a surrogate faculty member in the research group. For him the postdoctoral appointment was more like a medical internship where he would have limited responsibility in the whole scope of professorial activities.

In this vein, another response by a postdoctoral expressed the desirability of allowing time to get his first research paper published in order that he might have stature in the eyes of the graduate students. Among the other benefits of a postdoctoral appointment is the time lapse during which one's reputation can become established on the basis of one's thesis research. It is likely that this motivation depends less on the academic realities than on the insecurity of a man who has finished only one project.

A second reason for undertaking postdoctoral work that is shared by many postdoctorals is enlightening for the insight it provides into what graduate students perceive to be the life of a professor, especially before attaining tenure. It can be oversimplified by the statement: "I am not yet eager to become bogged down like the assistant professor." The assistant professor is understood to be "the low man on the totem pole," burdened with a heavy teaching assignment, faced with creating lecture notes *de novo*, forced to seek

TABLE 13  Work Activity of Assistant Professors in Selected Departments, by Type of Academic Institution

| | | Percentage of Assistant Professors by Type of Academic Institution | | | | | |
|---|---|---|---|---|---|---|---|
| | | | | | | Other Colleges and Universities | |
| Department | Work Activity | Ten Leading | Twenty Other Major | Established | Developing | More than Half PhD Faculty | Less than Half PhD Faculty |
| Physics | Research | 57 | 55 | 50 | 35 | 17 | 12 |
| | Instruction | 42 | 42 | 49 | 64 | 79 | 83 |
| | Administration | 1 | 2 | 1 | 1 | 3 | 4 |
| | Other | 0 | 1 | 0 | 0 | 1 | 1 |
| Chemistry | Research | 58 | 49 | 50 | 36 | 20 | 11 |
| | Instruction | 37 | 46 | 47 | 61 | 77 | 83 |
| | Administration | 5 | 4 | 3 | 2 | 2 | 5 |
| | Other | 0 | 1 | 0 | 1 | 1 | 1 |
| Biology | Research | 49 | 53 | 44 | 31 | 19 | 10 |
| | Instruction | 45 | 44 | 54 | 66 | 79 | 87 |
| | Administration | 4 | 2 | 2 | 2 | 1 | 2 |
| | Other | 1 | 1 | 0 | 1 | 1 | 1 |
| Humanities | Research | 19 | 25 | 21 | 11 | 8 | 5 |
| | Instruction | 76 | 73 | 74 | 86 | 88 | 91 |
| | Administration | 4 | 2 | 4 | 2 | 3 | 2 |
| | Other | 1 | 0 | 1 | 1 | 1 | 2 |

Source:  NRC, Office of Scientific Personnel, Postdoctoral Departmental Questionnaire.

extramural funds to support his research, and expected to be compiling a research record that will result in a permanent appointment. Since the teaching must come first and since the ancillary responsibilities of committee work will compete with his research, the postdoctoral seeks to get a running start at his research in the hope that the momentum will carry him through those first critical years. Lacking the confidence to expose himself to these overwhelming pressures and counterpressures, the fresh PhD seeks the intermediate stage of the postdoctoral appointment.

From his point of view, the postdoctoral years provide several useful stepping stones. In the first place, he recognizes that it is easier to do research "piggy-backing" on a faculty member's research grant than to obtain independent support. He does not have either the research record or the reputation to be able to compete successfully for his own grant. Although some sources, such as the Petroleum Research Fund, have special "starter" grants especially designed for the young new investigator, the size of the grants is seldom sufficient to enable the man to purchase major equipment items. Unless the man's field is "small" science, the various grants and fellowship programs alone are unlikely to provide him with the research environment he seeks.

Not only will the postdoctoral period enable the young researcher to establish a research record and a respectable publication list to present eventually for promotion, but that record will also make it easier to obtain a grant of his own when he joins the faculty. Finally, some anticipate accumulating a number of research problems on which they can work while serving as assistant professors. They do not expect ever again to have enough unoccupied time to be able to plot the future.

It should be pointed out that the picture drawn above is that perceived by many postdoctorals. If it is incorrect or distorted, it is nonetheless affecting the behavior of these young men. The only information that we collected that bears on the matter is given in Table 13. The chairmen of departments in all kinds of institutions of higher education were asked to describe how the average assistant professor in their departments distributed his time. Understanding that these are estimates by the chairmen, there is still an interesting shift as one moves from field to field and among the reputations and types of schools. At the top institutions in the sciences, approximately one half of an assistant professor's time is spent in research. At other schools the fraction of research time is much less and correspondingly more time is spent on instruction.

The third motivating reason for postdoctoral activity is somewhat more cynical than the others. It is a response to the academic marketplace and takes the form of the assertion that "the establishment requires that I have this experience." By only a very few is this reason given as the primary cause for

TABLE 14  Immediate Previous Experience of Newly Appointed Junior Faculty in Selected Departments, by Type of Academic Institution

| Department | Previous Experience | Percentage of New Junior Faculty by Type of Academic Institution ||||| Other Colleges and Universities ||
| | | Ten Leading | Twenty Other Major | Established | Developing | More Than Half PhD Faculty | Less Than Half PhD Faculty |
|---|---|---|---|---|---|---|---|
| Physics | Faculty member | 4 | 17 | 14 | 16 | 18 | 18 |
| | Postdoctoral | 76 | 57 | 50 | 21 | 10 | 7 |
| | New PhD | 18 | 13 | 25 | 32 | 31 | 19 |
| | Graduate student | 0 | 1 | 2 | 15 | 24 | 45 |
| | Nonacademic | 2 | 12 | 9 | 16 | 17 | 11 |
| Chemistry | Faculty member | 2 | 11 | 13 | 16 | 24 | 23 |
| | Postdoctoral | 67 | 54 | 58 | 38 | 23 | 8 |
| | New PhD | 23 | 26 | 20 | 23 | 30 | 25 |
| | Graduate student | 4 | 1 | 2 | 7 | 12 | 22 |
| | Nonacademic | 4 | 8 | 7 | 16 | 11 | 22 |
| Biology | Faculty member | 21 | 26 | 18 | 25 | 19 | 33 |
| | Postdoctoral | 44 | 41 | 44 | 18 | 13 | 1 |
| | New PhD | 16 | 24 | 26 | 34 | 34 | 16 |
| | Graduate student | 3 | 3 | 10 | 17 | 26 | 47 |
| | Nonacademic | 6 | 6 | 2 | 6 | 8 | 3 |
| Humanities | Faculty member | 21 | 28 | 32 | 31 | 36 | 33 |
| | Postdoctoral | 4 | 2 | 4 | 2 | 3 | 1 |
| | New PhD | 39 | 33 | 35 | 18 | 14 | 8 |
| | Graduate student | 35 | 37 | 27 | 46 | 43 | 52 |
| | Nonacademic | 1 | 0 | 2 | 3 | 4 | 6 |

Source:  NRC, Office of Scientific Personnel, Postdoctoral Departmental Questionnaire.

their taking a postdoctoral appointment, but most will agree that the "system" insists upon it. One man, an organic chemist at a California university, stated that he would not have taken the postdoctoral if it had been possible to get a faculty position in a "good" school without it. A biologist from a New England university of note was an instructor for the first semester of the 1967-68 academic year but became a postdoctoral the second semester not only to allow himself more time for research but also because "it is the done thing." A postdoctoral from Italy admitted that the research he is doing here is similar to what he would have been doing at home but having been a postdoctoral in the United States would increase his chance for a better job back in Italy.

The idea that it is not possible to get a faculty appointment in a major institution without a postdoctoral record is only a slight exaggeration in some fields. The rationale of department heads for preferring postdoctorals for faculty appointments will be examined in Chapter 6 but it is instructive to examine the practice of recruitment in selected fields across the spectrum of institutions. Table 14 gives the distribution of the immediate previous experience for recent appointments to the junior faculty (instructor or assistant professor) in several fields. What is striking in the sciences is the decrease in the fraction of new appointments who are postdoctorals and the corresponding increase in the percentage who are still graduate students as the reputation of the institution descends. Also of interest is the general tendency for the percentage of new faculty who are appointed directly after earning the PhD to rise as the institution goes down in reputation and then to fall for the weaker colleges. More to the point, however, is the far-from-negligible fraction of new appointments even at the top schools who are fresh PhD's. Although it is clearly advantageous to have had postdoctoral work, it is possible for the most talented young PhD's to be hired without that experience. It is curious that whereas the chemists, both postdoctorals and faculty members, spoke most often to us of the "requirement of postdoctoral work by the establishment," it is the physics departments at the better schools that tend to require it more often.

The fourth reason is obviously more appropriate to some postdoctorals than to others but, with some extension, might be made a valid rationale for postdoctoral study generally. This reason can be stated, "I want to see how research is done elsewhere." One postdoctoral who had obtained his PhD from a small technical school wanted to see what the academic world was like in a large institution. He was aware that the style of research and graduate education at a developing university was different from that at a major university, and he felt that without the postdoctoral experience he would have had a distorted idea of research generally. Somewhat the same idea was expressed by a postdoctoral in chemistry who took his PhD with a relatively young professor at a small university but who was taking his postdoctoral with an eminent scientist at a prestige school. He not only wanted to see how a top scientist did his research but he realized that he was much more likely to acquire a good faculty position with the recommendation of the better-known man. Several postdoctorals have pointed out the possibility of upward mobility in the academic world through the postdoctoral mechanism.

The final general reason given for seeking a postdoctoral appointment can be phrased, "I finished my PhD at the wrong time (or in the wrong field)." The ideal time for finishing one's doctoral work is in the late summer. Then, with no break in income, the graduate can take employment in the fall. If a man finishes in December, say, the choice positions are filled and the recruiting season is not yet open. It often happens that a man will be appointed as a research associate on his mentor's grant for the remainder of the year. From the faculty point of view the situation is ideal; his new associate is entirely familiar with the apparatus. From the postdoctoral's point of view an awkward financial situation is resolved. If a suitable appointment does not appear during the year, he might be kept on for another year. Several men have pointed out the utility of the postdoctoral appointment in providing a useful and productive way of waiting until the appropriate position opens up.

Another alternative is to make use of the postdoctoral period to change fields. One man did his doctoral work in chemistry and then decided he needed more physics than he had been able to acquire as a student. The postdoctoral appointment made this possible. Another chemist did his work at the predoctoral level in nuclear chemistry and was taking his postdoctoral in radiochemistry. He asserted that there was no other way to make the shift unless he repeated some graduate work. A professor in the field of x-ray crystallography as applied to biological structures pointed out that interdisciplinary fields, such as his, train their students at the postdoctoral level. He prefers to have his advisees complete their doctorates in chemistry or biology before joining his group.

In addition to these general reasons, there are more isolated ones. One botanist wanted to follow up some peripheral areas of his thesis research that did not appear within the dissertation. He remained at his doctoral institution since that was where his plants were. For married women the postdoctoral position is an ideal one for working in their fields either while waiting for their husbands to finish their graduate work or because their husbands are on the faculty and the nepotism rules do not permit them both to have a regular appointment.

The situation in the humanities and in the social sciences is different. As is evident from Tables 12 and 14 (p. 63 and p. 68), the postdoctorals in these areas who seek academic positions—and most of them do—would have had no difficulty in taking a faculty appointment even before finishing their doctorates. It is also the case that only a minority of the postdoctorals in these fields can be classified as immediate postdoctorals (10 percent in the humanities and 26 percent in the social sciences as compared with 53 percent in biochemistry, 71 percent in physics, and 75 percent in chemistry). Unlike the case in the natural sciences it is not the pattern for doctorates in these fields to seek postdoctoral work or to get it. Consequently, we are dealing here with individual cases rather than with general patterns. The immediate postdoctorals in these areas are people with particular research interests and with exceptional opportunities to exploit them. Almost inevitably they will be back in the classroom within the year.

When asked to check the three most important reasons for seeking a postdoctoral appointment, over 70 percent of the respondents in the natural sciences selected the following:[14]

To gain further research experience (1)
To acquire additional research techniques (4)
To work with a particular scholar (2)
To broaden my understanding of the field (3)
To carry out a piece of research on my own
To put myself at the growing edge of current research (8)
To develop further the research I did during my predoctoral training
To see work being done at other centers (7).

The other options that were checked by less than one in seven respondents were as follows (in no particular order):

To sharpen the focus of my research
To give me a free period for research before I get saddled with other responsibilities (5)
To support myself in the academic world until a suitable faculty appointment becomes available
To give me some teaching experience
To give myself a breathing spell after my formal training
To give me further time to mature (6)
To give me a chance to publish something.

That these lists should give a different impression from the discussion above is perhaps explainable by the fact that the unstructured interview permits more candor than the printed form. The choices by the faculty more closely correspond to the interviews with postdoctorals.

---

[14] The list is arranged in order of decreasing frequency of response. The parenthetical numbers following certain statements represent the order in which at least one out of seven faculty members gave as reasons for promoting postdoctoral study among their better graduate students.

72
THE DEMOGRAPHY OF POSTDOCTORAL EDUCATION

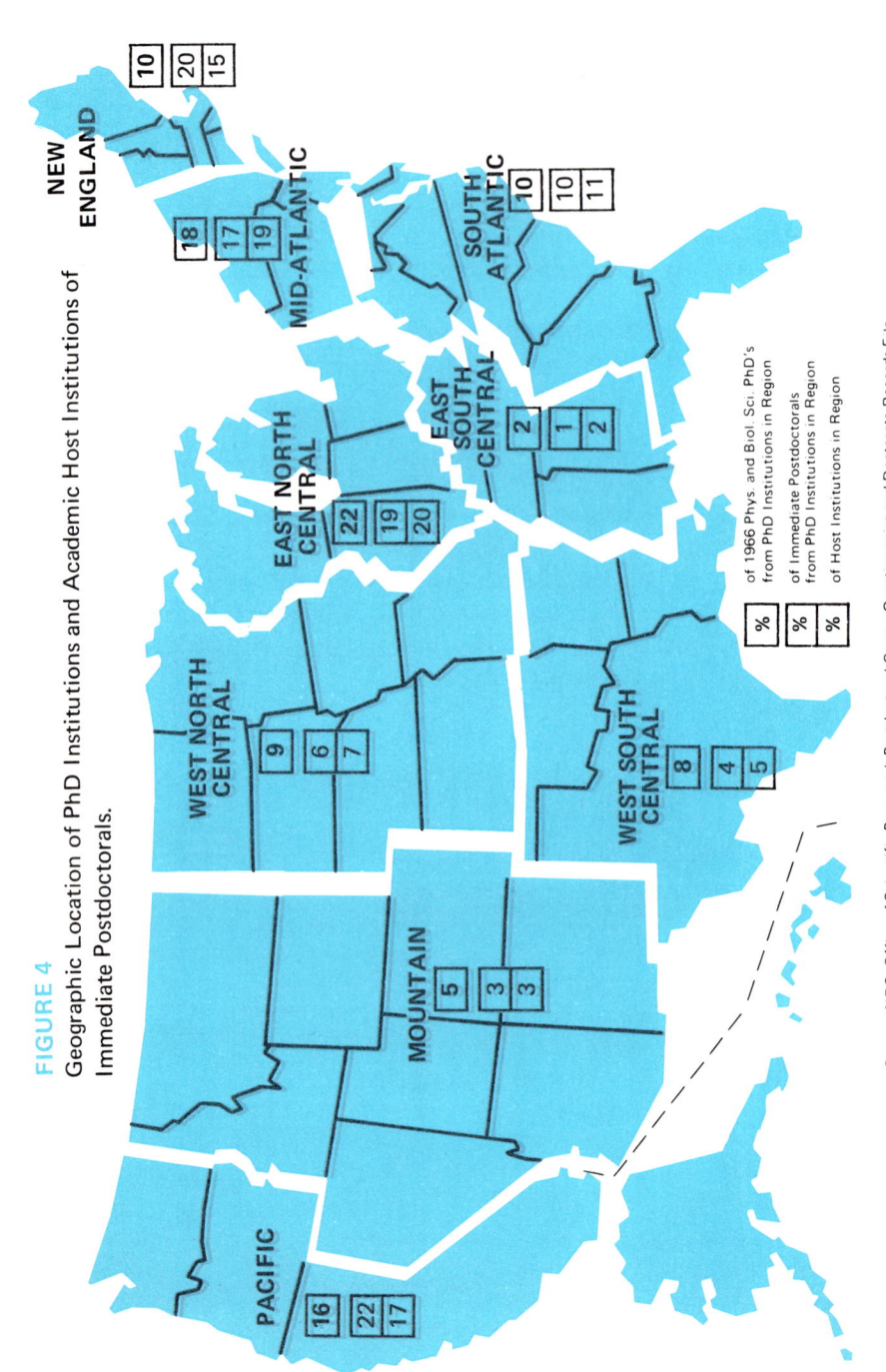

**FIGURE 4**
Geographic Location of PhD Institutions and Academic Host Institutions of Immediate Postdoctorals.

Source: NRC, Office of Scientific Personnel, Postdoctoral Census Questionnaire and Doctorate Records File.

*Geographic Mobility* Having some idea how many immediate postdoctorals there are and why they seek such positions, we now look at where they are and where they come from. We will concentrate on those with U.S. PhD's; the foreign component will be discussed later. Figure 4 gives a comparison of the geographic location of the doctoral institution of all 1966 U.S. PhD's, of the PhD institutions of immediate U.S. postdoctorals, and of the postdoctoral institutions of these same postdoctorals. It is evident that the northeast and Pacific regions consistently attract more postdoctorals than they produce, whereas the rest of the country has the reverse experience. Moreover, the eastern and western seaboards produce a larger proportion of postdoctorals than they produce PhD's. The center of the country from north to south, on the other hand, sends a smaller fraction of its doctorates on to postdoctoral work.

When we examine the geographic distribution of the immediate postdoctorals at their various educational levels (Table 15), a general pattern unfolds. As the population progresses from the baccalaureate to the PhD and from the PhD to the postdoctoral, it becomes more uniformly distributed geographically. This is true, almost without exception, in each field. The East and Midwest tend to send their baccalaureates to postdoctoral appointments in the South and West with the West being the major beneficiary. The East particularly is the baccalaureate origin of eventual postdoctorals, to a greater extent than its being a baccalaureate origin of PhD's generally. The situation in the Midwest is just the opposite.

TABLE 15 Geographic Location of Immediate Postdoctorals (with U.S. Baccalaureates) at Three Training Levels, All Host Institutions

| Geographic Area | Percentage of Immediate Postdoctorals by Location at Training Level |     |              | 1960–1966 PhD's |     |
|                 | Baccalaureate | PhD | Postdoctoral | Baccalaureate | PhD |
|---|---|---|---|---|---|
| East | 40 | 34 | 33 | 32 | 30 |
| Midwest | 26 | 27 | 20 | 32 | 34 |
| South | 17 | 18 | 19 | 20 | 18 |
| West | 16 | 20 | 21 | 16 | 18 |
| Foreign |  | 1 | 7 |  |  |
| *Total Number (100%)* | 2,261 | 2,261 | 2,261 | 80,042 | 80,042 |

Note: The Eastern area includes New England and Middle Atlantic regions; Midwest: East and West North Central regions; South: South Atlantic, East and West South Central regions; and West: Mountain and Pacific regions. See Figure 4 for states included in regions.

Source: NRC, Office of Scientific Personnel, Postdoctoral Census Questionnaire and Doctorate Records File.

## THE DEMOGRAPHY OF POSTDOCTORAL EDUCATION

It must be remarked that the data presented in Table 15 are for all immediate postdoctorals both in and out of academic institutions. If we restrict our attention to those who hold their appointments at U.S. academic institutions, the picture changes somewhat (Table 16). Except for physics, the overall flow pattern is that the South has a net loss to all other areas, the Midwest to all areas except the South, the East only to the West, and the West gains from everywhere. The major reason for the difference between this pattern and the one for all immediate postdoctorals is that the nonacademic host institutions (mainly federal government installations) are heavily concentrated in the South, whereas the South is relatively weak in academic institutions. It remains to be seen whether the conscious federal policy of placing federal labo-

TABLE 16  Migration of Immediate Postdoctorals at U.S. Academic Institutions from PhD to Postdoctoral Institution for Selected Fields

| Postdoctoral Field | Geographic Area | In Area | With PhD from Area | Net Flow into Area | Net Upward Mobility into Area |
|---|---|---|---|---|---|
| Physics | East | 148 | 171 | -23 | +9 |
|  | Midwest | 119 | 114 | +5 | +4 |
|  | South | 65 | 66 | -1 | -24 |
|  | West | 106 | 87 | +19 | +11 |
| Chemistry | East | 161 | 142 | +19 | +11 |
|  | Midwest | 123 | 135 | -12 | +46 |
|  | South | 81 | 97 | -16 | -42 |
|  | West | 92 | 83 | +9 | -15 |
| Biochemistry | East | 100 | 80 | +20 | +5 |
|  | Midwest | 92 | 110 | -18 | +34 |
|  | South | 43 | 69 | -26 | -37 |
|  | West | 83 | 59 | +24 | -2 |
| Biosciences | East | 72 | 63 | +9 | -21 |
|  | Midwest | 53 | 66 | -13 | +25 |
|  | South | 23 | 29 | -6 | -9 |
|  | West | 67 | 57 | +10 | +5 |
| *Total, all fields* | East | 729 | 674 | +55 | -4 |
|  | Midwest | 489 | 551 | -62 | +140 |
|  | South | 291 | 353 | -62 | -151 |
|  | West | 467 | 398 | +69 | +15 |

Source: NRC, Office of Scientific Personnel, Postdoctoral Census Questionnaire.

ratories in economically depressed locations will raise the level of the academic institutions there. It is evident from our data that the effect of the policy is to draw substantially more postdoctoral talent into the South than the academic institutions alone are able to attract.

Another component of this geographical flow of postdoctorals is the migration among institutions of different reputation. We assign to each postdoctoral who changes area after his doctorate a positive or negative weight, depending on his moving up or down in the reputation of the schools with which he is associated.[15] Thus, a man who received his PhD in the East from one of the ten leading institutions and who takes his postdoctoral in the South at an established institution will be given a negative weight. In a similar fashion, a man who received his PhD in the Midwest from one of the 20 other major institutions and who takes his postdoctoral in the West at one of the ten leading institutions will be assigned a positive weight. Finally, a man whose postdoctoral institution has comparable reputation with his PhD institution will carry zero weight.

The last column in Table 16 gives the net upward mobility measured in this way. Institutions in the Midwest tend to bring in postdoctorals from institutions of lesser reputation, whereas the South does the opposite; East and West show little net change. The following table gives the number of institutions in the top 30 schools in three broad fields in each area (the number in parentheses is the number of schools in the ten-leading group):

| Area | Number of Top Thirty Institutions | | |
|---|---|---|---|
| | Physical Sciences | Basic Medical Sciences | Biosciences |
| East | 13(5) | 13(4) | 9(1) |
| Midwest | 9(2) | 10(3) | 11(4) |
| South | 3(0) | 1(0) | 3(1) |
| West | 5(3) | 6(3) | 7(4) |

The direction of flow tends to equalize the geographic distribution of people with experience at more prestigious institutions. The Midwest is undoubtedly doing more than its share of upgrading, and the East is not helping as much. On the other hand, the East is relatively weaker in the biosciences and the flow in that field is also in the direction to restore the balance.

Inhibiting this tendency toward balance in quality is the uneven interest in postdoctoral education among doctoral recipients at institutions of greater and lesser repute. The significance of this variation can be seen in Table 17 in which the percentage of PhD's taking a postdoctoral is given. Chemistry and the basic medical sciences are affected least, but existing problems caused by quality differences among institutions are likely to persist in fields like mathematics, engi-

---

[15] See Appendix B-2 for the ranking of institutions.

THE DEMOGRAPHY OF POSTDOCTORAL EDUCATION

TABLE 17  Percentage of PhD's Taking Postdoctoral Appointments in Selected Fields, by Type of PhD Institution

| Postdoctoral Field | Ten Leading | Twenty Other Major | Established | Developing | Total |
|---|---|---|---|---|---|
| Physics | 35 | 31 | 23 | 10 | 26 |
| Chemistry | 34 | 37 | 36 | 24 | 33 |
| Other physical sciences | 17 | 8 | 4 | 5 | 9 |
| Engineering | 7 | 4 | 5 | 1 | 5 |
| Biochemistry | 68 | 72 | 48 | 47 | 58 |
| Other basic medical sciences | 41 | 32 | 43 | 29 | 36 |
| Biosciences | 38 | 30 | 27 | 14 | 26 |
| Social sciences | 3 | 2 | 2 | 3 | 2 |
| *Total* | 17 | 15 | 15 | 11 | 15 |

Source: NRC, Office of Scientific Personnel, Postdoctoral Census Questionnaire.

neering, and biosciences. These differences among the schools may be a result of corresponding differences in the quality of graduate students attracted to them.

The migration by field between institutions of different reputation is illustrated in Table 18. Overall, there is net upward migration. However, in some fields there is little net change. These are the physical sciences (with the exception of chemistry), engineering, and biosciences. These fields are also the fields in which fewer than half of the postdoctorals make a move involving a change in institutional reputation and they are also the fields showing the least equalization through geographic mobility. Of interest in this regard are the tables presented by Berelson[16] showing the tendency of faculty members to be hired at institutions of equal or of less reputation than their PhD institutions. Although we have no hard data, there is testimony to the ability of a man to upgrade his PhD by taking a postdoctoral appointment at a more prestigious institution. The good PhD from Harvard can expect to have little difficulty in being hired at a top institution; it is probably true that the good postdoctoral at Harvard can do the same regardless of his doctoral institution.

Not everyone changes schools after the PhD. However, the differences by field are indicative of significant differences in attitude toward postdoctoral appointments. From Table 18, we can see that chemistry and the basic medical sciences retain only one in six or seven while the other fields keep a third

---

[16] Berelson, *Graduate Education in the United States*, pp. 113-115.

TABLE 18 Migration of Postdoctorals by Reputation of PhD and Postdoctoral Institutions, by Field

| Postdoctoral Field | Moved up in Reputation of Inst. | Moved to Inst. with Same Reputation | Remained at Same Inst. | Moved down in Reputation of Inst. | Total Number (100%) |
|---|---|---|---|---|---|
| Physics | 22 | 22 | 33 | 23 | 438 |
| Chemistry | 40 | 25 | 14 | 21 | 457 |
| Other physical sciences | 23 | 24 | 29 | 24 | 147 |
| Engineering | 11 | 15 | 66 | 8 | 96 |
| Biochemistry | 42 | 24 | 18 | 16 | 318 |
| Other basic medical sciences | 37 | 25 | 16 | 22 | 146 |
| Biology | 28 | 20 | 28 | 24 | 234 |
| Social sciences | 39 | 22 | 26 | 13 | 115 |
| Total | 32 | 22 | 26 | 20 | 1,986 |

Source: NRC, Office of Scientific Personnel, Postdoctoral Census Questionnaire.

TABLE 19  Mean Years Elapsed (Total Time) from Baccalaureate to Doctorate for PhD Postdoctorals in Selected Broad Fields, by Type of Academic Institution

| Postdoctoral Field and Type of Academic Institution | Percentage of Postdoctorals Remaining at PhD Inst. | Total Years Elapsed from Baccalaureate to Doctorate | | |
|---|---|---|---|---|
| | | Postdoctorals Remaining at Same Inst. | Postdoctorals from Other Inst. | All PhD's of 1965 |
| Physical sciences | | | | |
| Ten leading | 17 | 6.1 | 5.4 | 7.1 |
| Twenty other major | 15 | 7.2 | 5.4 | 7.5 |
| Established | 14 | 6.2 | 5.6 | 7.8 |
| Developing | 10 | 8.5 | 6.1 | 8.4 |
| *Total* | 15 | 6.6 | 5.5 | 7.6 |
| Basic medical sciences | | | | |
| Ten leading | 14 | 6.8 | 5.7 | 7.4 |
| Twenty other major | 10 | 7.4 | 6.2 | 8.5 |
| Established | 17 | 7.2 | 6.8 | 8.7 |
| Developing | 20 | 8.1 | 7.3 | 8.9 |
| *Total* | 14 | 7.3 | 6.3 | 8.4 |
| Biosciences | | | | |
| Ten leading | 21 | 7.7 | 5.8 | 8.2 |
| Twenty other major | 17 | 7.3 | 6.1 | 8.5 |
| Established | 24 | 7.2 | 7.0 | 8.6 |
| Developing | 17 | 8.2 | 6.0 | 8.9 |
| *Total* | 20 | 7.5 | 6.2 | 8.5 |

Source: NRC, Office of Scientific Personnel, Postdoctoral Census Questionnaire and Doctorate Records File.

or a fourth of their postdoctorals at the PhD institution. Although the numbers are small, in engineering two thirds of the postdoctorals remain at home for their appointments. With some danger of oversimplification, these results correlate with the impression gained from talking to faculty and chairmen around the country. In those fields where relatively few remain at their PhD institutions, there tends to be more concern about the experience that the postdoctoral receives. In the other fields, the postdoctoral is seen more as a research aid than as a person to be trained. In fact, there is not much enthusiasm for postdoctoral work for any reason among the engineering faculty. Industrial experience is often seen as a much more important component of a faculty member's background.

Another aspect of what we might call the "stay-at-home" is his quality compared with the quality of those postdoctorals who are brought in from the outside. We cannot use the reputation of the PhD institution here, since the stay-at-home at the ten leading institutions will, of course, share that reputation with all those classmates who changed institutions. An alternative measure of quality is the years elapsed from baccalaureate to PhD. Although not significant in individual cases and certainly not comparable across disciplines because of differences in curricula and in predoctoral support patterns, it is probably true on the average within a field that the shorter the baccalaureate-to-PhD time lapse, the better the graduate.

Table 19 gives some data on this variable for several groups. Although even postdoctorals who remain at their doctoral institutions average a year less in achieving the PhD than graduates generally, the postdoctorals attracted from the outside have spent one year less than the stay-at-home in completing degree requirements. The migrating postdoctoral is likely, therefore, to be of higher quality than the stay-at-home, and postdoctorals generally are significantly better than the average PhD.

Even those who migrate differ, and the complaint is heard that weaker schools cannot attract postdoctorals of as high quality as those the more prestigious schools bring in. To measure this effect we have assigned a weight of 1 to graduates of the ten leading institutions, 2 to graduates of the 20 other major institutions, 3 to graduates of established institutions, and 4 to the graduates of developing institutions. Measured in this way, we see in Table 20 the average quality of postdoctorals attracted to various institutions. In every field except biosciences the ten leading institutions attract better students than the other schools. For all fields combined, the quality of the postdoctoral decreases with the reputation of the school, but the individual fields show no such neat regularity. The numbers are sufficiently small that many of the percentage differences are not statistically significant.

The other side of the question is how much the reputation of the school at which one takes a postdoctoral appointment is determined by the reputation

TABLE 20  Average Quality Index[a] of Postdoctorals at Academic Institutions, by Type of Postdoctoral Institution, by Field

Average Quality Index[a] and Number of Postdoctorals by Type of Postdoctoral Institution

| Postdoctoral Field | Ten Leading Index | Ten Leading Number | Twenty Other Major Index | Twenty Other Major Number | Established Index | Established Number | Developing Index | Developing Number |
|---|---|---|---|---|---|---|---|---|
| Physics | 1.8 | 110 | 2.2 | 77 | 2.1 | 87 | 2.1 | 24 |
| Chemistry | 2.2 | 140 | 2.6 | 115 | 2.7 | 79 | 2.8 | 58 |
| Other physical sciences | 1.8 | 50 | 1.9 | 22 | 2.0 | 22 | 1.9 | 10 |
| Engineering | 1.6 | 18 | 2.3 | 4 | 1.9 | 7 | 2.8 | 4 |
| Biochemistry | 2.3 | 95 | 2.4 | 113 | 2.8 | 35 | 2.7 | 17 |
| Other basic medical sciences | 2.5 | 32 | 2.7 | 36 | 2.5 | 32 | 2.7 | 22 |
| Biosciences | 2.4 | 48 | 2.3 | 69 | 2.0 | 28 | 2.4 | 23 |
| Social sciences | 2.4 | 40 | 2.5 | 24 | 3.0 | 13 | 2.6 | 8 |
| Total | 2.1 | 540 | 2.4 | 465 | 2.4 | 301 | 2.6 | 166 |

[a]The average quality index of postdoctorals is based on the reputation of the institutions at which the postdoctorals earned the PhD. Those who remain at their doctoral institution are not included. The highest possible index is 1.0; the lowest 4.0.

Source: NRC, Office of Scientific Personnel, Postdoctoral Census Questionnaire.

of one's PhD institution. Because of the nature of the process by which appointments are made, one should expect the correlation to be high. Usually, informal contacts between one's PhD thesis supervisor and prospective postdoctoral mentor precede any formal application. This is true even if the postdoctoral is the winner of a national fellowship. Since the weight of a professor's recommendation depends on his own reputation, and since the school's reputation is related to the professor's, it would be expected that equals tend to speak to equals. Table 21 bears out this analysis. The better the reputation of the institution of one's doctorate, the better the reputation, on the average, of one's postdoctoral institution. Again, biosciences provides the exception.[17] These results partially confirm Berelson's[18] conclusion that "there is a tendency for postdoctoral people to attend institutions like those from which they received their doctorate." It is, as we have seen, only a tendency. Approximately half of the postdoctorals migrate to schools of a reputation different from their PhD institution.

*Field Migration* Another aspect of the transition from predoctoral to postdoctoral status is the migration between fields. One of the major motivations for postdoctoral work is to enable a PhD to shift directions from his dissertation. Although this need not involve a change of fields, it often does. As one postdoctoral suggested, a change of institutions without a field change permits a person to get a new perspective, to become broadened, and to gain further experience. Of the immediate postdoctorals, 35 percent change fields and 46 percent change institutions without a change in fields[19]; 19 percent do neither.

---

[17] Since the grouping of schools by reputation is dependent on Cartter's study, which ranked schools by the quality (really reputation) of the graduate faculty, one wonders if our results for biology do not cast doubt on Cartter's results in this field.

[18] *Postdoctoral Work in American Universities, op. cit.*, p. 56.

[19] These percentages are subject to some question. The difficulty lies in determining the point at which a change of research topic becomes a field change. There may be some doubt that a physics PhD whose postdoctoral field is cytology has changed fields, if the nuclear magnetic resonance techniques that he is using on tissue *in vitro* are those that he used in his thesis research on impurities in semiconductors. On the other hand, his classmate whose thesis also dealt with the same techniques and the same class of materials and whose postdoctoral research is low temperature physics would probably be considered by most to have changed fields, particularly if he were learning cryogenic techniques anew and were concerned now with the properties of $^3$He. Unfortunately, the information available to us forces us to make the opposite decision in both cases.

Each respondent was asked to identify both his PhD and his postdoctoral field by means of a three-digit code from a specialties list attached to the questionnaire (see Appendix B-1). We determined a subfield change by observing any change in the three-digit code. Both men in the above example would have indicated solid state physics (code no. 160) for their PhD field. The former would have given cytology (code no. 522)

TABLE 21  Average Quality Index of Postdoctorals at Academic Institutions, by Type of Doctoral Institution, by Field

Average Quality Index[a] and Number of Postdoctorals by Type of Doctoral Institution

| Postdoctoral Field | Ten Leading Index | Ten Leading Number | Twenty Other Major Index | Twenty Other Major Number | Established Index | Established Number | Developing Index | Developing Number |
|---|---|---|---|---|---|---|---|---|
| Physics | 1.9 | 109 | 2.0 | 94 | 2.2 | 65 | 2.4 | 25 |
| Chemistry | 1.7 | 74 | 2.0 | 128 | 2.6 | 105 | 2.4 | 85 |
| Other physical sciences | 1.8 | 48 | 2.0 | 35 | 1.9 | 10 | 2.1 | 11 |
| Engineering | 1.6 | 11 | 1.8 | 16 | 2.6 | 5 | 4.0 | 1 |
| Biochemistry | 1.8 | 62 | 1.8 | 84 | 2.0 | 55 | 2.1 | 59 |
| Other basic medical sciences | 2.2 | 21 | 2.3 | 30 | 2.5 | 39 | 2.5 | 32 |
| Biosciences | 2.2 | 41 | 2.3 | 65 | 1.8 | 29 | 2.2 | 37 |
| Social sciences | 1.6 | 20 | 1.9 | 24 | 1.7 | 16 | 2.1 | 25 |
| Total | 1.9 | 395 | 2.0 | 479 | 2.2 | 326 | 2.3 | 272 |

[a]The average quality index of postdoctorals is based on the reputation of the institutions at which the postdoctorals hold their appointment. Those who remain at their doctoral institution are not included. The highest possible index is 1.0; the lowest 4.0.

Source: NRC, Office of Scientific Personnel, Postdoctoral Census Questionnaire.

Field changes are especially common in the rapidly developing research areas. A notable example of an investigator who undertook his postdoctoral in a field different from that of his PhD is James Watson. In his vivid memoir, *The Double Helix*,[20] he describes his experiences in attempting to learn biochemistry after his doctoral work in genetics. The breakthrough which brought him his Nobel prize occurred in an interdisciplinary field. One of his co-workers with whom he shared the prize, Francis Crick, was a physicist.

In Table 22 some data are presented on field changes by immediate postdoctorals. The fourth column contains the numbers of postdoctorals with PhD's in one of the major fields listed on the left who took their postdoctoral appointments in another of those major fields. The third column gives the number of the postdoctorals who received their PhD's in one of the major fields and who changed subfields within the major field in moving to the postdoctoral. The reason that biochemistry shows no change in this column is that biochemistry is a subfield with no finer structure in our specialties list. (See also Figure 5.)

Chemistry, engineering, and the biological sciences (with the pronounced exception of biochemistry) all suffer a net loss in PhD's to other fields. Biochemistry is the major gainer from chemistry and the other biological sciences, while physics picks up most of the engineers who change fields.

The following table displays the migration of the immediate postdoctorals among gross field groupings; the number in parentheses is the number who have remained in the same subfield:

| Postdoctoral Field | PhD Field EMP | Life Sciences | Other Fields |
|---|---|---|---|
| EMP | 1,107 (867) | 13 | 10 |
| Life sciences | 66 | 721 (451) | 25 |
| Other fields | 13 | 66 | 211 (122) |

The gross field move is an extremely limited occurrence. Of the 66 making the transition from engineering, mathematics, and physical sciences (EMP) to the biological sciences, 49 are chemistry PhD's and 38 of these changed to biochemistry. Similarly, of the 13 going in the opposite direction, 11 are moving to chemistry. Finally, of the 25 who received their PhD's in other fields and who are taking their postdoctorals in the biological sciences, 16 are psychology PhD's.

---

for his postdoctoral field while the latter would again have written solid state physics (code no. 160). Since there is a limit to the amount of fine structure one can permit in a list of specialties, we will have to be content with the possible distortions that are introduced in this way.

[20] James Watson, *The Double Helix*, Atheneum, 1968.

TABLE 22 Field and Subfield Changes of Immediate U.S. Postdoctorals, All Host Institutions

| Field | Total in Field (100%) | Immediate U.S. Postdoctorals With PhD in Same Subfield as Postdoct. N | % | With PhD in Same Field as Postdoct. N | % | With PhD in Field Other Than Postdoct. N | % | Number of PhD's in Field Changing to Different Field as Postdoctoral |
|---|---|---|---|---|---|---|---|---|
| Physics | 450 | 349 | 77 | 55 | 12 | +46 | 10 | -23 |
| Chemistry | 453 | 345 | 76 | 87 | 19 | +21 | 5 | -75 |
| Other physical sciences | 160 | 121 | 76 | 16 | 10 | +23 | 14 | -12 |
| Engineering | 67 | 52 | 77 | 12 | 18 | +3 | 5 | -39 |
| Biochemistry | 343 | 211 | 62 | | | +132 | 38 | -38 |
| Other basic medical sciences | 193 | 122 | 63 | 9 | 5 | +62 | 32 | -120 |
| Other biosciences | 276 | 118 | 43 | 77 | 28 | +81 | 29 | -105 |
| Other fields | 290 | 122 | 42 | 89 | 31 | +79 | 27 | -35 |
| *Total* | 2,232 | 1,440 | 65 | 345 | 15 | +447 | 20 | -447 |

Source: NRC, Office of Scientific Personnel, Postdoctoral Census Questionnaire.

### FIGURE 5

Percentage of Immediate Postdoctorals, by Field of PhD, Who Changed from the Field or Subfield of Their PhD's.

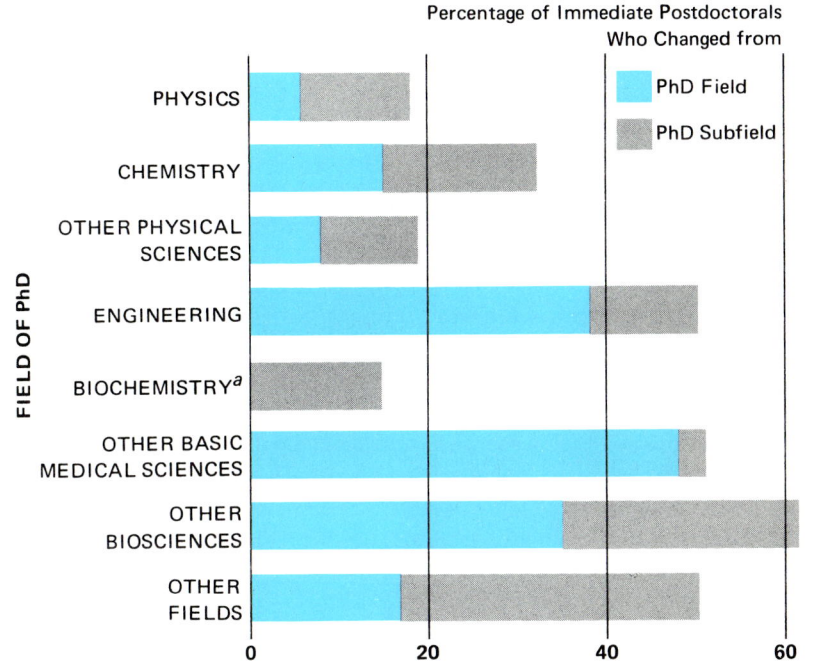

[Bar chart: horizontal bars showing Percentage of Immediate Postdoctorals Who Changed from PhD Field (blue) and PhD Subfield (gray), by Field of PhD: Physics, Chemistry, Other Physical Sciences, Engineering, Biochemistry[a], Other Basic Medical Sciences, Other Biosciences, Other Fields. X-axis: 0 to 60.]

[a] Biochemistry is a subfield in the specialties list; therefore all changes are at the subfield level.

Source: NRC, Office of Scientific Personnel, Postdoctoral Census Questionnaire.

The predominance of field-changing in the biological sciences is probably related to the specificity of those fields in comparison with the physical sciences. In the latter the mathematical nature of their principles allows students and investigators an economy of categorization. Many diverse systems and phenomena can be subsumed under a few laws or mathematical statements. As yet the phenomena with which the biological sciences are concerned have not been resolved to the point that they can be discussed in precise quantitative terms. Consequently, discoveries and understanding on one biological system may not be transferable to another system. One young English geneticist explained that her postdoctoral in biochemistry was not so much a change of fields as a change of proteins. Such considerations are important in making crossdisciplinary comparisons.

*Kinds of Support* Although there are four major support mechanisms for postdoctorals, only three play any role for immediate postdoctorals. These are the fellowship, the traineeship, and what we might designate generically as the project associateship. The fourth, the sabbatical, relates to the older postdoctoral on leave from an established position and is usually available only after an extended stay at that position. The immediate postdoctoral, almost by definition, is excluded from this latter opportunity. We shall discuss in Chapter 9 the stipends associated with these mechanisms and their policy implications. Here we shall merely describe the differences and the similarities among them and their distribution by field.

Historically, the dominant mode of support and encouragement has been the fellowship. Generally speaking, the fellow has been chosen in a national competition by a select panel. From the beginning, however, there have been locally sponsored fellowships at host institutions. Both approaches are similar in attempting to provide a period of relative financial security for the young postdoctoral during which he might gain increased sophistication in research. Except for the local programs, of course, the fellow may take his appointment at any host institution that is willing to provide him with space and where a suitable mentor is willing to supervise his activities. This provision has almost always (sometimes by the conditions of the program) led the fellow to an academic institution or to a nonprofit, quasi-academic research institute, although not necessarily in the United States.

The applicant must propose a plan of research, and this plan, along with letters of recommendation and copies of publications, constitutes the materials on which the selection is based. Much leeway is allowed in the alteration of the research plan once the tenure has begun in order to permit local conditions and unforeseen changes of direction in research findings to determine the most fruitful course of the investigation.

It is the hope of these fellowship programs that they are providing assistance and encouragement to the most promising young scholars and that their programs, like the earlier National Research Council program, which has been acclaimed for its success, will promote excellence in research in this country.

Another support mode—limited almost entirely to the life and medical sciences—is the traineeship. The competition here is among groups of faculty or even whole departments to obtain a training grant, usually from NIH, for the purpose of creating a cadre of manpower trained in a particular field. The proposal to the federal agency from the department describes the national need for people with a particular background; enumerates the facilities, research personnel, and research activities of the prospective training institution; and requests funds both for stipends and for training expenses, including research equipment and supplies. Often the proposed program extends from the predoctoral level through the postdoctoral level, although a man is relatively unlikely to stay at the same institution for work at both levels. The postdoctoral trainee is selected by the training institution rather than by an extramural panel; in particular he is selected by the faculty participants in the training grant on the basis of credentials and letters of recommendation similar to those required in the fellowship programs.

The third major support mechanism is the project associateship (often called the "research associateship"). In this case the competition is among faculty investigators for support of their research. The postdoctoral enters into the picture when the successful investigator is awarded sufficient funds to permit him to hire people at this level. Gaining an appointment as a project associate tends to be a less formal process than applying for a fellowship. An application for appointment generally follows an informal decision by the faculty member to make the appointment. This decision is based on correspondence with the PhD adviser of the prospective project associate in which the strengths and weaknesses of the candidate are explored. Papers by the candidate and a résumé of his thesis are also examined, but his area of research is established by the faculty investigator who is bound by the specifications of his grant or contract. Any formal application is filled out for the purpose of obtaining approval by the university administration to ensure that the project associate will be paid.[21] From the point of view of the granting agency, of the university administration, and often of the faculty mentor, the project associate is an employee.

In principle, then, the three mechanisms can be said to support the independent researcher, the research student, and the research employee, respectively. From these descriptions one can understand the fellow and the trainee as two different kinds of postdoctorals in our sense of the word, but the case is less clear for the project associate. He is included because in practice the distinctions of principle only partially survive. Whatever the motivation of the funding agencies, and however clearly they perceive the particular need that their funds are intended to satisfy, the postdoctorals and the faculty are relatively indifferent to the mode of support. The critical concern of the postdoctoral is to work with the particular faculty member. The major interest of the faculty is to have junior colleagues. The various mechanisms are used to maximize success for both participants.

As seen from the vantage of the terminal-year graduate student who desires to become a faculty member at a major university, there are two principal routes. The first (and less likely) is to be hired immediately after his doctorate as an assistant professor at a prestige institution. This does occur, as can be seen from Table 14 (p. 68), although it occurs infrequently. In physics, chem-

---

[21] The process described here is typical but not universal. In Chapter 6 we will examine the situation in more detail.

istry, or biology, only one in five faculty members appointed as assistant professors at the ten leading institutions came directly from graduate school. Assuming that each school appoints four men each year at that level in each field, then eight people in each field qualify annually with the PhD alone. For those to whom this opportunity presents itself, the postdoctoral fellowship is probably less attractive. The data in Table 13 (p. 66) indicate that their teaching loads are small and their research opportunities are large. Since these fortunate few are probably the most able researchers in their PhD class, their defection from the fellowship applicants means that the fellowship programs are not supporting all of the very best. This loss is only to the fellowship program; both research and higher education are served by their employment.

The other route to faculty status at a major institution is to be awarded a postdoctoral appointment. Winning a postdoctoral fellowship gives a man a number of advantages, including prestige in applying later for an academic position or for a research grant. But postdoctoral fellowships are not easy to get. Only one in nine applicants was successful for the 1969 fiscal year in the NSF program. If the faculty member with whom he wants to work has project associate funds, it may be possible to proceed informally through his PhD adviser to a guaranteed position.[22] Nothing much is lost if being a project associate entails much the same experience as being a fellow.

Although exceptions exist, the project associate is usually given more freedom than the employee status would imply, and the fellow has less freedom than the grantors intended. The faculty member is seldom comfortable in the employer-employee relationship and prefers the master-apprentice interaction instead. His research support is seldom so narrow in description that a spectrum of activities may not be allowed under the terms of the grant or contract. His own interests probably lie in several areas simultaneously. If his project associate has ideas of his own, he is permitted to follow them if they fall within the scope of the faculty member's interest.

On the other hand, the fellow will often discover that unless his research interests coincide fairly closely with those of his mentor, he will get little help. Few institutions have free space not assigned to faculty members, and consequently, the fellow's research must conform somewhat to the facilities available to his mentor. Since the fellow is not likely to have sufficient funds to pay for his research expenses,[23] he is dependent on his mentor for support from the mentor's project grant or contract. Such funds, however, are legally used only when the research is appropriate to the project.

---

[22] Indeed, once the position is guaranteed, he may be urged by his prospective postdoctoral mentor to apply for the fellowship anyway. If he wins it, the mentor will be able to hire a second postdoctoral with funds released.

[23] Some programs provide up to $1,000 for expenses. Not all of these funds are necessarily available to the fellow, and even if they were, research costs often exceed this amount.

THE POSTDOCTORAL IN U.S. ACADEMIC INSTITUTIONS

The net result of these conditions is that the distinction between the project associate and the fellow is lessened. When a research group contains both types, a faculty member is especially loath to insist on differences. This does not mean that there are none, however. The project associate, as an employee of the university, usually shares in the fringe benefits of health insurance, parking privileges, and even retirement plans. On the other hand, the fellow is granted exemption of tax liability for up to $3,600 of his stipend.

The faculty often see the training grant as a means of increasing the number of postdoctorals in the department. Since the award is at their disposal, the traineeships are used to attract able postdoctorals in the department. Once there, the postdoctoral may be urged to apply for a fellowship. If he is successful, a traineeship is released to bring another postdoctoral to the group. Although this shuffling from traineeship to fellowship or even to project associateship makes the impact of the training program difficult to measure, the individual continues to receive the experience that he sought, the faculty receive the assistance that they desire, and the manpower pool generally receives another independent researcher.

None of the above destroys all differences between the three modes of support. It merely tends to make them less severe. Fellows, after all, have been selected in a national competition and tend, on the average, to be much better researchers. Some faculty want only fellows in their group for just this reason. They argue that the national committees can do a better job of selection than the individual faculty member. As one put it, "I insist that the people who come to work with me be good enough to win in a national competition." Of course, not all faculty members have the reputation to attract fellows. Those who do tend to be at the prestige institutions.

The project associate may be a graduate of the host institution who has been kept on since he was offered no suitable outside position. As we have seen from Table 19 (p. 78), he may not be as able as the man from the outside. It is probably true that, on the average, the project associate is not as promising as the fellow. Even if this were true, the overlap in ability of the two groups is extensive.

Not only is there little difference in treatment among the fellow, the trainee, and the project associate once they are at the host institution, but the situation is confused further by the lack of consistency in the use of titles at the host institutions. Respondents to our census of postdoctorals were asked to give their title and, separately, to check the type of appointment they held. The latter options were fellowship, traineeship, sabbatical, position supported by project funds, and other. The following table gives the relationship among their responses[24]:

---

[24] 9,971 out of the 10,740 respondents provided both title and type of appointment.

## THE DEMOGRAPHY OF POSTDOCTORAL EDUCATION

| Type of | Title | | |
| --- | --- | --- | --- |
| Appointment | Fellow | Research or Project Associate | Other |
| Fellowship | 3,572 | 726 | 796 |
| Traineeship | 316 | 105 | 604 |
| Sabbatical | 23 | 43 | 93 |
| Project associateship | 326 | 2,030 | 625 |
| Other | 188 | 184 | 340 |
| Total | 4,425 | 3,088 | 2,458 |

It would appear that many postdoctorals neither know nor care what type of appointment they have as long as their checks arrive on time and they are able to do the research they want.[25] It is with little confidence, therefore, that we present the data on the types of appointment held by the postdoctorals.

Table 23 gives the distribution of all postdoctorals among the types of appointment at U.S. academic institutions as reported by the postdoctorals and as reported by the departments.[26] The departmental response is probably accurate and the lack of agreement between the two sets of data reinforces the comments made above concerning the postdoctoral attitudes toward the various modes of support at academic institutions. It is apparent that regardless of nationality, postdoctorals prefer to consider themselves as fellows, no matter what their real status may be. The reasons for this preference are many. They include the prestige of being a fellow, ignorance of the distinction between the various types, and the confusion of titles.

Concentrating now on the departmental response, and realizing that approximately 62 percent of the science postdoctorals are immediates, it is apparent (Figure 6) that postdoctorals in the engineering, mathematical, and physical sciences have fewer opportunities for fellowships than those in the biological sciences and almost no opportunity for traineeships. The burden of postdoctoral support in the EMP fields is on the research grant mechanism. This explains why current cut-backs in research funding affect the postdoctoral situation in the physical sciences so much more severely than in the other areas. It will also have a serious impact on the foreign postdoctoral in all science fields. Only in the humanities and social sciences ("other fields") are the foreigners less often project associates than the Americans.

The lesser dependence on the training-grant mechanism in the EMP fields correlates with a lesser interest among the faculty in these fields in the merits

---

[25] One young biologist told us that he had avoided a project associateship because he thought it would commit him to his mentor. Earlier in the discussion he had complained that his mentor had ignored the project outlined in his fellowship application and had required the fellow to work in an area that interested the mentor.

[26] Not all departments were asked for data so that the numbers of postdoctorals as given by the departments need not agree with the numbers from the census. On the other hand, it is difficult to reconcile the change in the ratio of foreign to U. S. between the two sources, unless our response rate from foreigners was better than from U. S. citizens.

TABLE 23 Types of Appointment of All Postdoctorals at U.S. Academic Institutions: A Comparison between Departmental and Postdoctoral Responses

| Postdoctoral Field | Source of Data | Citizenship | Fellowship | Traineeship | Project Associateship | Other | Total Number (100%) |
|---|---|---|---|---|---|---|---|
| EMP[a] sciences | Postdoctoral | U.S. | 29 | 2 | 58 | 11 | 1,257 |
|  |  | Foreign | 37 | 1 | 51 | 11 | 1,893 |
|  | Departmental | U.S. | 19 | 1 | 73 | 7 | 1,430 |
|  |  | Foreign | 11 | 0 | 81 | 8 | 1,790 |
| Biological sciences | Postdoctoral | U.S. | 51 | 20 | 21 | 7 | 1,254 |
|  |  | Foreign | 43 | 8 | 42 | 8 | 1,338 |
|  | Departmental | U.S. | 35 | 24 | 35 | 6 | 1,091 |
|  |  | Foreign | 20 | 5 | 68 | 7 | 832 |
| Medical sciences | Postdoctoral | U.S. | 67 | 26 | 2 | 5 | 1,337 |
|  |  | Foreign | 70 | 13 | 10 | 7 | 780 |
|  | Departmental | U.S. | 23 | 41 | 8 | 28 | 2,011 |
|  |  | Foreign | 35 | 18 | 19 | 28 | 638 |
| Other fields | Postdoctoral | U.S. | 53 | 10 | 14 | 22 | 517 |
|  |  | Foreign | 54 | 5 | 19 | 21 | 242 |
|  | Departmental | U.S. | 49 | 7 | 25 | 20 | 213 |
|  |  | Foreign | 62 | 0 | 12 | 26 | 94 |

[a]Engineering, mathematics, and physical sciences.

Source: NRC, Office of Scientific Personnel, Postdoctoral Census and Departmental Questionnaire.

# 92
THE DEMOGRAPHY OF POSTDOCTORAL EDUCATION

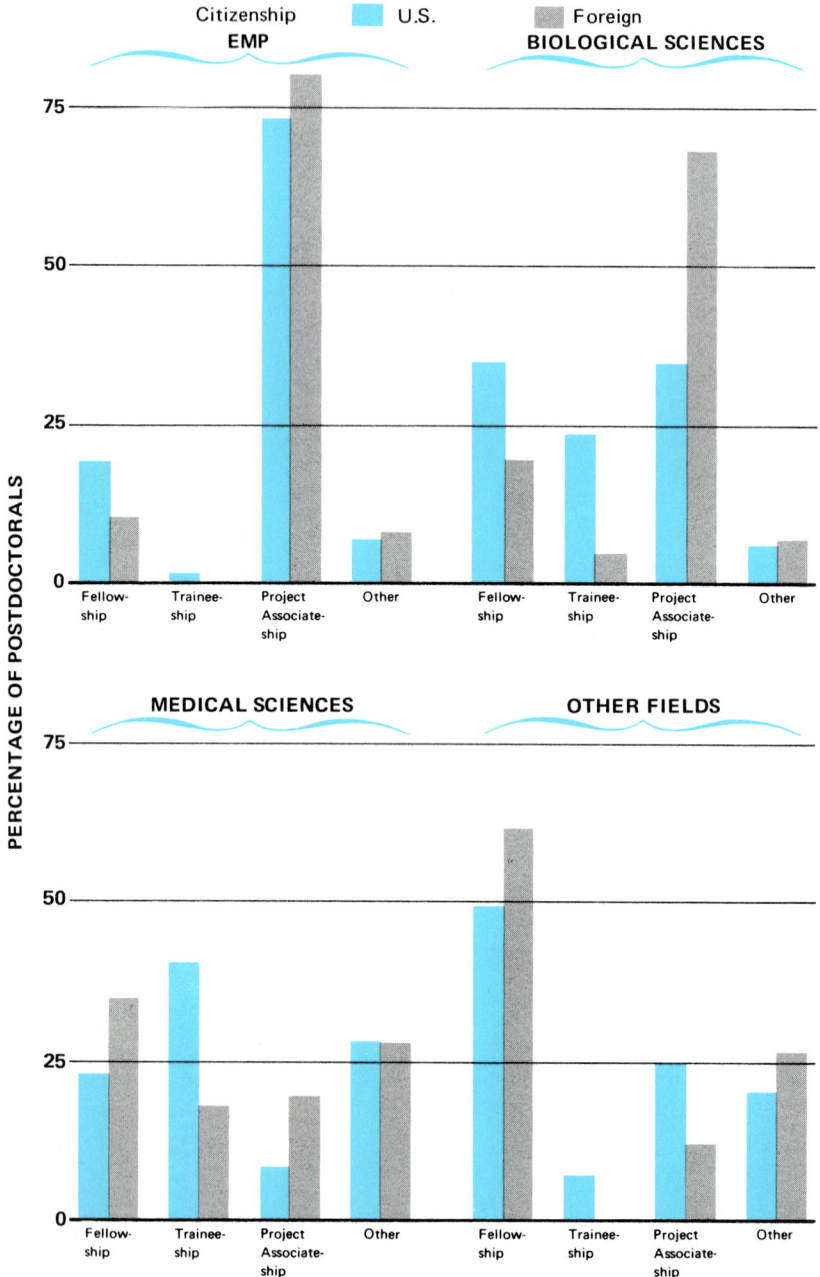

## FIGURE 6
Types of Appointment of Postdoctorals at U.S. Academic Institutions.

Source: NRC, Office of Scientific Personnel, Postdoctoral Departmental Questionnaire.

of the postdoctoral experience in preparing PhD's for research in the university setting. In preparing a training grant proposal the faculty member is forced to consider the manpower needs of the country and to design a program to help fulfill those needs. The research grant proposal, on the other hand, puts the emphasis upon accomplishing a desired research goal. Any support for postdoctorals included in the proposal must be justified by the level of effort that the research requires. Although both mechanisms are research based, the latter recognizes the postdoctoral as a "means," while the former considers him an "end." In actual practice, the situation is mixed; the trainee is also a research assistant and the project associate is receiving valuable experience. Both of these by-products, however, are less intentional than fortuitous. A mechanism is called for that ties these two together.

*Duration of Appointment* Postdoctorals spend varying amounts of time on their appointments. A few remain for an indefinite period, becoming, in our terminology, "long-term" postdoctorals. Most immediate postdoctorals, however, tend to stay three years or less, with the overall average being 1.6 years and with over 80 percent staying less than 2.3 years. Contrary to the general opinion, the foreign immediate postdoctoral does not spend any longer time on appointment than his American counterpart.

By field, the humanist spends from 0.6 years to 1.4 years, the chemist from 0.8 to 2.0 years, and the biochemist from 1.3 to 2.5 years. All other fields lie somewhere between the extremes. These figures, not surprisingly, do not differ significantly from those suggested by the faculty as optimum either for the postdoctoral's sake or for the department's. In both cases the duration recommended is from 1.4 years to 2.8 years, with biochemistry at the upper end and chemistry at the lower. At one major institution the chemistry chairman asserted that one year of postdoctoral study was enough. "The second year does not double the benefit of one year of postdoctoral study." Another chemistry chairman echoed this impression and added that "the first year rewards the postdoctoral; the second year rewards the mentor." A third chairman, also from chemistry, introduced the important proviso that the crucial determinant is that the postdoctoral stay long enough "to do something."

There is, however, much variation in the departmental attitudes toward establishing limits on the length of time that a postdoctoral may spend in the department. The top institutions tend to have a policy on duration more often than the lesser institutions and the EMP fields more often than the basis medical sciences. Only 77 departments out of 915 that reported having postdoctorals limit the tenure of postdoctorals and in no field did more than 18 percent of the departments report such a policy.

Of course there are other constraints on the duration of appointment. Fellowships are generally tenable for one year, although some programs permit a renewal for an additional year and sometimes longer. The postdoctoral's own career interest is a major cause for limiting the appointment. Most are eager to get onto the tenure ladder as assistant professors. They are quite conscious of their artificial status at most universities where they no longer think of themselves as students but are not faculty members either. The actual duration is likely to be a compromise among a number of forces including the postdoctoral's desire for faculty status, the mentor's desire for expert research assistance, the progress of the particular research problem involving both of them, and the availability of a suitable next appointment for the postdoctoral.

### Intermediate PhD Postdoctorals

The intermediate postdoctoral did not take his appointment immediately after his doctorate. Presumably he was employed elsewhere in the intervening time and then made a decision to pursue postdoctoral study. Postdoctorals in this category are of two different kinds: those who are on leave from their previous positions, and those who have resigned from their previous positions and are making a transition to new employment. The former are in a sense taking an early sabbatical, perhaps to escape the distractions from research of their regular employment and possibly to achieve new competencies in their research fields. In the humanities and social sciences, especially, this is the time when the thesis may be transformed into a book for publication. For the scientist who went immediately to an academic position following his PhD, the temporary leave allows him to pick up his research, which previously had to compete with the preparation of lecture notes and with the other demands on the time of a new assistant professor.

For others the postdoctoral appointment is a mechanism for upward mobility in the academic world. Having taken a position in a lesser institution (from which it is difficult to appear attractive to the better schools), the young PhD takes a postdoctoral appointment and essentially starts over again in the employment market. Thus, the postdoctoral position provides for the system a means of individual renewal—a second chance. This is particularly important for the PhD in science who, having tired of being a student, opted for immediate faculty status. Without the postdoctoral experience he is unlikely to receive an appointment at an institution of high prestige (see Table 14 on p. 68). Were it not for the opportunities for an intermediate postdoctoral appointment, such a man would be unable to move to a more desirable university.

These remarks apply mainly to the U.S. citizen. For the foreign citizen the intermediate postdoctoral appointment, in addition, may be simply a delayed immediate postdoctoral position. The difficulties of arranging appointments from abroad, as well as the problem of acquiring travel funds, may cause a

## THE POSTDOCTORAL IN U.S. ACADEMIC INSTITUTIONS

year or two to pass before the foreign PhD can finally get to the United States. In the meantime, of course, he has been temporarily employed. In every sense, except for the formal definition, he is an immediate postdoctoral.

The number of intermediate postdoctorals is not very large. Table 24 summarizes some of their characteristics. In the sciences over 70 percent of the intermediates are foreigners, while in the humanities and social sciences less than 30 percent are from abroad. Altogether, 72 percent of the U.S. intermediates are at universities; 14 percent are pursuing postdoctoral work abroad. In all fields combined there are only 326 U.S. intermediate postdoctorals; a small number when one realizes the important function postdoctoral study may play at this career stage.

Table 25 gives the leave status for intermediate postdoctorals. Since migration to a university is relatively difficult from a nonacademic institution, it is not surprising that a fair number of postdoctorals are on leave when taking their appointments outside the university. Again, those in the humanities and the social sciences demonstrate behavior much different from the scientists. They are much less likely to use the postdoctoral appointment as a means of changing institutions. Their main interest in an appointment is that it temporarily releases them from other time-consuming duties connected with an academic position and that it enables them to devote themselves to research. The importance of postdoctoral study at this time for these disciplines is indicated by the relatively large proportion of intermediate postdoctorals in the social sciences (other than psychology) and in the humanities. Although only 2 percent of postdoctorals at the immediate level are in these fields, they are the fields of interest of 18 percent of the postdoctorals at the intermediate level. Eighty-eight percent of the intermediate postdoctorals in those fields are on leave.

People who delay their postdoctoral appointment until the intermediate stage have had maturing experiences beyond their PhD training. Consequently, it is difficult to measure their quality compared to the immediate postdoctorals. One would expect that, having tasted regular employment, they have a clearer idea of what they want to achieve during their postdoctoral study. The maturity that some years out of graduate school have given them may compensate for whatever initial differences separated them from their colleagues who went immediately into postdoctoral study. When we compare the two groups with regard to their total baccalaureate-to-PhD time lapse, the differences are small but interesting. The mean time lapse for intermediates in the physical sciences is 6.1 years, for the basic medical sciences 7.1 years, and for the other biological sciences 6.8 years. In each case the intermediate falls midway between the immediate who migrates and the immediate who stays at home (see Table 19, p. 78). In all cases the intermediate shares with the immediate about a 1½-year advantage over the PhD population generally.

TABLE 24  Distribution of Intermediate Postdoctorals among Host Institutions, by Field and Citizenship

|  |  | Percentage of Immediate Postdoctorals by Type of Host Institution |  |  |  |  | Total Number |
|---|---|---|---|---|---|---|---|
| Postdoctoral Field | Citizenship | University | Nonprofit | Industrial | Government | Abroad | (100%) |
| EMP[a] | U.S. | 79 | 6 | 0 | 8 | 7 | 114 |
|  | Foreign | 88 | 4 | 1 | 6 | 0 | 345 |
| Biological sciences | U.S. | 69 | 6 | 0 | 7 | 18 | 100 |
|  | Foreign | 89 | 5 | 1 | 5 | 0 | 189 |
| Medical sciences | U.S. | 56 | 22 | 0 | 11 | 11 | 9 |
|  | Foreign | 86 | 14 | 0 | 0 | 0 | 14 |
| Other fields[b] | U.S. | 68 | 10 | 1 | 3 | 18 | 103 |
|  | Foreign | 90 | 10 | 0 | 0 | 0 | 31 |
| Total | U.S. | 72 | 8 | 0 | 6 | 14 | 326 |
|  | Foreign | 88 | 5 | 1 | 5 | 0 | 579 |

[a] Engineering, mathematics, and physical sciences.
[b] Includes social sciences and humanities.

Source: NRC, Office of Scientific Personnel, Postdoctoral Census Questionnaire.

TABLE 25  Percentage of Intermediate Postdoctorals at Academic and Nonacademic Host Institutions on Employment Leave, by Field and Citizenship

| | Percentage of Intermediate Postdoctorals on Employment Leave | | | |
|---|---|---|---|---|
| | U.S. Citizens at | | Citizens of Foreign Countries at | |
| Postdoctoral Field | Academic Host Inst. | Nonacademic Host Inst. | Academic Host Inst. | Nonacademic Host Inst. |
| EMP[a] | 19 | 58 | 55 | 68 |
| Biological sciences | 18 | 30 | 50 | 67 |
| Medical sciences | 20 | 0 | 50 | 0 |
| Other fields[b] | 71 | 55 | 57 | 67 |
| *Total* | 34 | 45 | 54 | 66 |

[a]Engineering, mathematics, and physical sciences.
[b]Includes social sciences and humanities.
Source: NRC, Office of Scientific Personnel, Postdoctoral Census Questionnaire.

As with the immediate postdoctorals, the usual period of time spent as a postdoctoral is from one academic year to two full years. It is shorter in the humanities and social sciences, where it seldom lasts longer than a year. Biochemistry is the longest, with two thirds of the intermediates spending from 1.2 years to 2.8 years on their appointments. For both the immediate and the intermediate the appointment is limited both by the availability of funds (especially outside the natural sciences)[27] and by the availability of a suitable position.

The intermediates look forward to academic positions even more strongly than the immediates do. Many, of course, are returning to the ones they left; others to better ones. The striking difference is in the proportion heading toward a college rather than a university. Whereas 7 percent of university-based immediates were anticipating colleges as their next employers, 15 percent of the intermediates are planning on teaching at a college. It is possible that most of these are on leave from colleges and are simply returning. Government and industry are selected less often by intermediates than by immediates, which probably reflects the preselection of the entire group of interme-

[27]Even in the physical sciences, which are dependent almost entirely on the National Science Foundation for fellowship support, there is little money for the intermediate postdoctoral. Of the 120 fellowships awarded in the 1968 NSF regular postdoctoral program, 86 went to persons who had not finished their doctorates at the time of their applications. At most, the remaining 34 fellowships went to intermediates in all the fields covered by that program.

diates. Most were previously in academic positions and are not changing their minds.

### Senior PhD Postdoctorals

Whatever doubts may exist with regard to the necessity of postdoctoral study immediately following the PhD, study or research leaves for mature scholars are universally recognized as important and desirable. After several years of teaching, research, and administration, the senior investigator is often in need of both a change of pace and the stimulation of new surroundings. For some, a leave of absence permits them the leisure to complete a book on which they have been working. For others, it is an opportunity to work with a colleague at another institution. For still others, the absence of regular duties allows them to visit libraries and other sources of original documents to pursue their research. All look forward to the experience to renew their ability to cope with their normal responsibilities.

Institutions recognize these needs and support them generally. Often the support is limited to granting leaves without pay to their staff. Many universities and some nonacademic institutions have formal sabbatical leave programs. The usual pattern is to provide a half-year's salary every seven years and to require no services for a period up to a year. The employee has the option of receiving full pay for one semester or half-pay for the entire academic year. The sabbatical leave is seldom automatic and is granted only on the submission of a proposed plan of study and research. It is understood that the professor on sabbatical may supplement his income through research grants and fellowships, but he may not be paid for services during his leave.

Although some senior investigators make use of their leave to acquire new skills, more often their motivation is to have free time to exploit their already considerable talents. They do not think of themselves as postdoctorals and it is likely that our estimates of their numbers are low. The formal fellowship programs, such as the NSF Senior Postdoctoral Fellowships, make the identification with postdoctoral study and research. Others, such as the Guggenheim Fellowships, are designed to support scholars with or without the doctorate. Humanists supported by a grant from the American Council of Learned Societies (ACLS) or social scientists who have been awarded a grant by the Social Science Research Council probably do not perceive of their activities as being "postdoctoral" in any special sense. Part of the difficulty in estimating the numbers of this group arises from our definition. If a scholar receives an ACLS grant that supports his research part-time during the academic year while he maintains his pedagogical duties, his situation is akin to that of the physicist with support from a research contract. If, on the other hand, he is released from teaching responsibilities to pursue his research, he becomes, in our definition, a postdoctoral.

Assuming, nevertheless, that our data are representative if not complete, they show that the humanists and the social scientists make much more use of the senior postdoctoral appointment than do the natural scientists. Almost half of the American senior postdoctorals are from fields outside the natural sciences. By contrast, only one in seven of the foreign senior postdoctorals are not natural scientists. Table 26 gives the distribution of senior postdoctorals among the host institutions. In striking contrast to the rest of the postdoctoral population, the American senior postdoctoral is almost as likely to travel abroad as he is to spend his time at a U. S. educational institution. In the physical and biological sciences particularly, he will be a visitor in a foreign country as often as he will be at a different U. S. university. While the American senior postdoctoral is at an academic institution abroad, the foreign senior postdoctoral is at a university here.

The distribution of senior postdoctorals among the fields may only partially reflect the availability of funds. It is also a consequence of the different nature of research in the different disciplines. Most experimental scientists at universities have their own laboratories at their universities. They are likely to slow down their research if they go on leave for a year or less.[28] Unless a humanist is extremely fortunate, his "laboratory" is distributed around the country and abroad. Once he has exploited the resources of the local library and whatever materials may be obtained through interlibrary loan, he has need for extended periods of uninterrupted time to write. It may also be necessary to see original-source documents. In either case, his research requires the leave of absence to become efficient. As we have seen earlier, the scientist often finds it necessary to take a postdoctoral appointment early in his career in order to become a productive investigator. For him a later postdoctoral is an enrichment, but seldom a necessity. The humanist is already competent in the techniques of scholarship when he receives his doctorate. His immediate need is rather for growth and contemplation, often enhanced by classroom confrontations. The delayed postdoctoral for him is necessary if he is to bring his research to fruition.

Although the senior postdoctoral may be relatively more important for the humanist than for the scientist, it is still important for the scientist. Especially if he desires to work with or near colleagues abroad, the availability of fellowships is crucial. The evidence is that there is not nearly enough money to support postdoctoral activity in the sciences for the mature investigator. All of

---

[28] This is not true for the theoretical physicist or mathematician. The association with colleagues at a different institution can be extremely fruitful, even if the duration is relatively short.

TABLE 26  Distribution of Senior Postdoctorals among Host Institutions, by Field and Citizenship

| Postdoctoral Field | Citizenship | Percentage of Senior Postdoctorals by Type of Host Institution ||||| Total Number (100%) |
| | | University | Nonprofit | Industry | Government | Foreign | |
|---|---|---|---|---|---|---|---|
| EMP[a] | U.S. | 48 | 5 | 0 | 3 | 45 | 146 |
| | Foreign | 82 | 6 | 2 | 10 | 1 | 199 |
| Biological science | U.S. | 48 | 1 | 0 | 1 | 50 | 80 |
| | Foreign | 96 | 2 | 0 | 2 | 0 | 102 |
| Medical science | U.S. | 50 | 25 | 0 | 0 | 25 | 4 |
| | Foreign | 89 | 0 | 0 | 11 | 0 | 9 |
| Other fields[b] | U.S. | 56 | 17 | 0 | 2 | 25 | 225 |
| | Foreign | 82 | 14 | 0 | 2 | 2 | 50 |
| Total | U.S. | 53 | 10 | 0 | 2 | 35 | 455 |
| | Foreign | 86 | 6 | 1 | 6 | 1 | 360 |

[a] Engineering, mathematics, and physical sciences.
[b] Includes social sciences and humanities.

Source: NRC, Office of Scientific Personnel, Postdoctoral Census Questionnaire.

the national programs have more applicants than awards. In the 1968 competition the NSF Senior Postdoctoral Program had 384 applicants for 55 awards.[29] The NATO program had 462 applicants for 39 awards. The humanists and social scientists face similar shortages in awards from their respective sources of support.

Long-Term PhD Postdoctorals

Of major concern to those entrusted with public policy questions as they relate to science education and research is the matter of the long-term postdoctoral. Whatever the values of postdoctoral activity, they seem to some observers to be abused by those individuals who make a career of being a postdoctoral. At a time when both higher education and industry are bemoaning the insufficient supply of trained manpower, the whole of postdoctoral education is open to discredit by the failure of the "eternal postdoctoral" to take a "real" position.

A number of considerations must be borne in mind. As we have seen, the average postdoctoral spends less than two years on his appointment before taking a more permanent position. Although the postdoctoral phenomenon introduces a delay in the flow of manpower, in a steady-state situation the flow is undiminished for the bulk of the postdoctorals.

In fact, it is difficult to isolate the truly perpetual postdoctoral. As indicated earlier, he may not have responded to our questionnaire, since he perceives himself to be a permanent employee rather than a temporary postdoctoral. Furthermore, there may be other factors in perpetuating a postdoctoral career other than the reluctance to leave the academic research laboratory.

If we examine the research groups at universities, we find that there are a number of different kinds of people involved, ranging from graduate students (and occasionally undergraduates) through senior faculty. In addition there are immediate and intermediate postdoctorals who are transient members of the group. Occasionally a senior scholar will be a temporary visitor. There are also the more permanent professional research staff. Some of these are technicians with varying degrees of formal training and others are holders of the doctorate who have chosen the academic research environment as their career location. This latter group is the "unfaculty" mentioned earlier. They occur primarily at the major institutions where the level of federal support of research is sufficiently massive, permitting the expectation of uninterrupted employment over an extended period. The long-term postdoctoral may be identified in part with this professional research staff, although he may also exist in less prestigious institutions.

---

[29] In 1969, due to the budgetary stringency, the NSF found it necessary to drop this program altogether.

In a study made in the spring of 1967, Kruytbosch and Messinger[30] examined the situation, as "observant participants," of the professional researcher at the University of California. The document is not free from bias and was conceived to influence policy, but it yields an interesting and informative picture of both the problems and the activities of the "unfaculty." The report raises important questions about the place of research at a university and, although the authors plead for more formal recognition and acceptance by the administration of these "temporary" and somewhat unofficial members of the community, they suggest why some of the long-term postdoctorals choose that status over being a faculty member at another (and lesser) institution.

These people are strongly committed to research and aspire to faculty positions at major institutions. The opportunities to do the kind of research that they desire are limited to a few centers. To leave those centers would require either a change of research emphasis or a diminution of research activity. Given these alternatives, they prefer being unrecognized persons at a research center to having full faculty status elsewhere. Even better, they would like their present status formalized with all the privileges of the faculty at their institution.

That they are valuable members of the research groups to which they belong is undeniable. The evidence is strong that they participate not only in the research activity but also in the administration of the grants and contracts that support the research. The longer they stay the more they are able to assist the professors. The fact that the project directors continue to find funds to support them indicates the desirability of their presence. If the object is to produce research, the professional researcher is clearly a most important component.

The question may be raised, of course, as to whether there is a more effective use that could be made of these people. Should the funding of research at universities be such as to encourage the practice of retaining professional researchers for indefinite periods? The formulation of an answer to this question requires the consideration of several complicating issues. In the first place, it must be decided whether the research being performed is itself sufficiently valuable to be supported at current levels. If so, then the question must be faced as to whether the same research could or would be performed outside of the university setting. Furthermore, except for the important question of the relevance of this kind of research to the university's mission, does it make any difference to the purchasers of the research (ultimately society at large) where it is done? If the same people are doing the same research, the alteration of titles is not a real resolution of the long-term postdoctoral problem.

---

[30]Carlos E. Kruytbosch and Sheldon L. Messinger, *Unequal Peers: Professional Researchers at Berkeley,* unpublished report, University of California, Berkeley, April 1967.

## THE POSTDOCTORAL IN U.S. ACADEMIC INSTITUTIONS

If one should decide that, for whatever reasons, the support of these people should be stopped, the question of whether they would be as usefully employed elsewhere is the next consideration. The mere possession of a PhD does not necessarily qualify a person for an academic or industrial position. Hopefully, a faculty member wants to teach and has the personal characteristics beyond formal learning and research productivity that enable him to relate pedagogically to students. Industrial laboratories require researchers who are stimulated by applied problems and who are sufficiently self-denying to be productive even when proprietary interests forbid publication and public or professional recognition. Furthermore, there are few industrial applications for elementary particle physics or fruit fly genetics. The long-term postdoctoral has been aware that there are other opportunities and for a variety of reasons, both personal and professional, he has rejected them. It may be that his greatest contribution to society is being made where he is, given his peculiar academic training and personality traits.

In lieu of a better criterion, given the data available to us, we have designated as "long-term" those postdoctorals who are in their third or later year of postdoctoral work and who are not on leave from another position. Granting the appropriateness of this definition in this area of postdoctoral activity and accepting the probable bias in the responses to our census questionnaire, it is instructive to examine the details of the group of long-term postdoctorals as we measured them. From Table 9 (p. 59) we see that there is much variation in the proportion of the postdoctorals in a given field who are long term. The physical and biological sciences have a larger share than the medical sciences, and in the fields of physics, chemistry, and biochemistry approximately one in seven of all postdoctorals are long term. These three fields also have the largest number of postdoctorals, with the result that they collectively account for sixty-two percent of all long-term postdoctorals. The situation is somewhat more complex, however, since the post-MD component by definition does not contribute to the long-term group. If we compute the percentages on the basis of the number of post-PhD's in the field there are some dramatic changes. The medical sciences have a total of only 175 post-PhD's but 27 (or 15 percent) of them are long term. The fraction of long-term postdoctorals in the biological sciences rises to 18 percent while there is little change in the physical sciences.

In addition to variation by field there is a strong dependence on sex and nationality. The following table gives the fraction of each group who are long term:

| Postdoctoral Field | U.S. Male % | U.S. Female % | Foreign (Both Sexes) % |
|---|---|---|---|
| EMP | 10 | 33 | 14 |
| Biological sciences | 9 | 27 | 14 |

## 104
THE DEMOGRAPHY OF POSTDOCTORAL EDUCATION

Thus foreigners are approximately one and one-half times as likely to be long term as U. S. males, while U. S. females are long-term postdoctorals three times as often as their male counterparts. Stated in a different way, whereas 39 percent of all postdoctorals in the biological sciences are U. S. males, only 29 percent of the long-term postdoctorals are. U. S. women constitute 9 percent of all postdoctorals in these fields, but 21 percent of the long-term postdoctorals.

The fact that U. S. males have a greater chance of obtaining faculty appointments in this country may partially explain the distribution of long-term postdoctorals. Many of the women are either faculty or student wives who are not able to receive faculty positions because of institutional rules on nepotism. There are, of course, some women who find the postdoctoral status to their liking, allowing them to do research part-time while remaining a wife and mother. Nevertheless, it is clear that the majority are simply taking the best position that is open to women who want to do research and to live with their husbands and children. This is especially true at institutions not near other research opportunities.

The foreign component shares some of the same constraints. Language difficulties as well as lack of faculty opportunities at research oriented universities for all but the very best foreign postdoctorals probably account for the attractiveness of postdoctoral appointments for those who want to prolong their stay in the United States. If we examine the fraction of postdoctorals coming from countries in the various GNP categories[31] (Table 27), we can see that it is a vast oversimplification to speak of the foreign postdoctoral as though he were member of a homogeneous group. Because they constitute more than nine-tenths of the postdoctorals from very low income countries, the Indians have been considered as a separate GNP category. Indians are twice as likely to be long-term postdoctorals as other foreign groups and they account for 27 percent of all foreign long-term postdoctorals, while constituting only 13 percent of all foreign postdoctorals. On the other hand, the postdoctorals from countries with fair per capita GNP become long-term postdoctorals even less often than U. S. males. We will examine the foreign postdoctoral in more detail in Chapter 8.

One final comment about the long-term postdoctoral is in order. As one examines Table 27, it is clear that the number of people involved is not large considering that all fields are combined. In the fields with the highest concentration of postdoctorals—physics, chemistry, and biochemistry—there are only

---

[31] For the purpose of comparison among countries, per capita gross national product (GNP) is a better (although not perfect) measure of the degree of development of a country than geographic location. Japan, for example, is better grouped with Great Britain than with the rest of Asia, if one wants to measure the sophistication and relative adequacy of higher education in the countries of the world. The countries in each group are listed in Appendix B-3.

TABLE 27  Number and Percentage of Long-Term Postdoctorals at U.S. Academic Institutions by Sex and Citizenship

| Citizenship | Male Total | Male Long-Term N | Male Long-Term % | Female Total | Female Long-Term N | Female Long-Term % | Total Total | Total Long-Term N | Total Long-Term % |
|---|---|---|---|---|---|---|---|---|---|
| Foreign (grouped by per capita GNP of country of origin) | | | | | | | | | |
| High | 2,587 | 256 | 9.9 | 203 | 28 | 13.8 | 2,790 | 284 | 10.2 |
| Fair | 275 | 13 | 4.7 | 42 | 2 | 4.8 | 317 | 15 | 4.7 |
| Low | 450 | 35 | 7.8 | 91 | 7 | 7.7 | 541 | 42 | 7.8 |
| Very low | 37 | 4 | 10.8 | 1 | 0 | 0.0 | 38 | 4 | 10.5 |
| India | 520 | 118 | 22.7 | 47 | 12 | 25.5 | 567 | 130 | 22.9 |
| Foreign Total | 3,869 | 426 | 11.1 | 384 | 49 | 12.2 | 4,253 | 475 | 11.2 |
| U.S. Total | 3,916 | 254 | 6.5 | 485 | 113 | 23.3 | 4,401 | 367 | 8.3 |
| Total | 7,785 | 680 | 8.7 | 869 | 162 | 18.6 | 8,654 | 842 | 9.7 |

Source: NRC, Office of Scientific Personnel, Postdoctoral Census Questionnaire.

61, 35, and 42 U. S. male long-term postdoctorals respectively. The national manpower picture would not change significantly if they were otherwise employed.

Post-Professional-Doctorates

The postdoctoral in the medical, dental, and other professional fields is at once different in his motivations and background from the post-PhD and also much less well defined. Since professional doctoral training is generally limited in research participation, the post-professional-doctorate is not as useful to the faculty as a research associate. It is, in fact, the purpose of postdoctoral activity in these fields more to instill the methodologies and techniques of research than to expand or to sharpen tools already possessed. Unfortunately for the purposes of our study, the definition of postdoctorals in these fields (generally the ones supported by the National Institutes of Health) is not the same as that found appropriate by NIH. Whereas we have restricted our study to those post-professional-doctorates involved primarily in research, the NIH programs are appropriately designed for physicians, surgeons, dentists, and others who desire additional training for a much wider range of activities. Thus, their "postdoctoral" fellowship and traineeship programs include individuals interested in acquiring additional clinical experience in their specialties, working toward specialty-board examinations, and receiving special residency

THE DEMOGRAPHY OF POSTDOCTORAL EDUCATION

experience, as well as those seeking research training. Since some of the activities may also include an exposure to research during a portion of the appointment, the question of inclusion or exclusion from our study becomes problematic. As mentioned in the introduction, our return rate in medical sciences is probably not only low, but more indefinite.

*Post-MD* Notwithstanding this caution with regard to the accuracy of the absolute numbers, we believe that the relative data may be sufficiently precise to describe adequately the post-MD. This confidence arises not only from the consistency of our data with the comments and opinions given in a number of interviews but also with the agreement of percentages between our census and data developed annually by the American Medical Association (AMA). Table 28 gives these data for nine leading medical schools[32] and for all others.

Because of the internship and residency requirements there is no "immediate" postdoctoral in a real sense among the post-MD's. It is difficult, therefore,

TABLE 28  Comparison between Office of Scientific Personnel (OSP) Census and AMA Data on Postdoctorals in the Clinical Specialties at U.S. Medical Schools

| Clinical Specialty and Type of School | MD-Postdoctorals in U.S. Medical Schools |  |  |  |
|---|---|---|---|---|
|  | OSP Census Data |  | AMA Data |  |
|  | Number | Percent | Number | Percent |
| Internal medicine |  |  |  |  |
| Nine leading schools | 372 | 30 | 500 | 33 |
| All others | 628 | 70 | 1,003 | 67 |
| *Total* | 900 | 100 | 1,503 | 100 |
| Other clinical medicine |  |  |  |  |
| Nine leading schools | 345 | 26 | 749 | 28 |
| All others | 962 | 74 | 1,934 | 72 |
| *Total* | 1,307 | 100 | 2,683 | 100 |
| Total |  |  |  |  |
| Nine leading schools | 617 | 28 | 1,249 | 30 |
| All others | 1,590 | 72 | 2,937 | 70 |
| *Total* | 2,207 | 100 | 4,186 | 100 |

Source: NRC, Office of Scientific Personnel, Postdoctoral Census Questionnaire; AMA.

[32]The division into nine leading medical schools and all others is admittedly arbitrary, but it is interesting to note that the same mobility picture that was produced by the reputation grouping of the graduate schools is reproduced here. Although the nine leading medical schools produce only 13 percent of the MD's, they attract 28 percent of the postdoctorals.

THE POSTDOCTORAL IN U.S. ACADEMIC INSTITUTIONS

to determine precisely what fraction of the MD's produced take a postdoctoral appointment. In 1965-66 there were 7,574 MD's produced by medical schools in the United States.[33] We collected questionnaires from 833 medical science postdoctorals who are U.S. citizens and who had received their MD's within the last seven years. Assuming an average of three years for their postdoctoral experience and estimating that our returns represent half of the total, 555 MD's per year seek postdoctoral appointments. This is only 7 percent of the MD's produced, as compared with 20 percent of the PhD's in the natural sciences.

The rationale for postdoctoral education in the clinical sciences is simple and agreed upon by all participants, both postdoctoral and mentor, as well as by the medical school administration and supporting agencies: to create faculty for medical schools. It is the general consensus that a faculty member must be involved in research if he is to be in a position to pass on to medical students the latest developments. Consequently, it is imperative that, following a long period of didactic training and supervised practice of medicine, the potential faculty member be not only introduced to research but raised to a level of proficiency and self-sufficiency. Some achieve this goal by seeking a PhD. Table 29 demonstrates that, compared to the post-PhD, the post-MD is much

TABLE 29 Enrollment of Postdoctorals at U.S. Academic Institutions in Regular Courses and in Degree Programs by Field and Citizenship

| Postdoctoral Field | Citizenship | Percentage of Postdoctorals Taking or Auditing Courses | Candidates for Second Doctorate |
|---|---|---|---|
| Physical sciences and engineering | U.S. | 41 | 0 |
|  | Foreign | 31 | 1 |
| Biological sciences Post-PhD | U.S. | 46 | 0 |
|  | Foreign | 35 | 2 |
| Post-MD | U.S. | 78 | 45 |
|  | Foreign | 47 | 19 |
| Medical specialties | U.S. | 46 | 10 |
|  | Foreign | 36 | 15 |
| Humanities and social sciences | U.S. | 46 | 1 |
|  | Foreign | 56 | 6 |

Source: NRC, Office of Scientific Personnel, Postdoctoral Census Questionnaire.

[33] Medical Education in the United States: 1956-66, *Journal of the American Medical Association*, Vol. 198, No. 8, November 21, 1966.

more likely to be a candidate for a second doctors degree. Others choose not to undertake such formal training and instead undergo a more or less informal series of experiences both in the classroom and in the laboratory. Neither mode is entirely satisfactory and a number of medical schools are considering radical changes in the entire medical curriculum, partly motivated by the desire to accelerate the training of future medical faculty.

The problem of creating faculty members for the medical schools is an acute one and one that is felt by the current faculty and administration in a way that similar shortages in the arts and sciences are not felt. At the end of the 1965-66 academic year there were 672 faculty vacancies in clinical departments in existing medical schools[34] and since that time several new schools have been created or planned. In the spring of 1968 one out of six budgeted faculty positions in pediatrics across the country was unfilled, according to Dr. Ralph J. Wedgewood[35] of the University of Washington. Although there are 155 unfilled budgeted positions, only 80 pediatric faculty are trained each year.

The traditional lockstep character of medical education militates against satisfying the need for faculty. After a student has piled up debts and has acquired a family during four years of medical school, one year of internship and two years of residency, two years of a clinical fellowship and two years in the military, the prospect of two more years as a research postdoctoral (and thus an academic career) must compete with the financial advantages of private practice.

Existing programs of postdoctoral study in the clinical fields comprise both individual fellowships and varying degrees of formal traineeship activities involving groups of postdoctorals. Because the postdoctorals enter their research appointments at various stages of their medical careers (ranging from directly out of medical school, through interruption of their residency experiences, to following a year or two as assistant professors in a medical school), their backgrounds are extremely diverse. Consequently their training must be tailor-made. Some will require additional course work; others will require more clinical experience; all will require research training.

In spite of their awareness of the need, however, most medical schools have not integrated their postdoctoral activities with their other responsibilities. Faculty involvement in training postdoctorals is almost inevitably on an overload basis; there is often no lessening of their other responsibilities if faculty desire to participate in the training program. This is particularly critical when special courses are needed that are not in the regular curriculum. An example was cited by Howard Hiatt of the Harvard Medical School. He points out that

---

[34] *Journal of the American Medical Association, loc. cit.*
[35] Private communication.

most research problems in clinical medicine eventually lead to problems in biochemistry. Because of the long time span of medical training it is possible for a post-MD to have studied biochemistry as a freshman medical student before James Watson and Francis Crick unraveled DNA. There is a need for refresher courses. Under present circumstances, a biochemist must develop and teach a new course not for his own students, but for postdoctorals from a different department and almost always without special recognition.

The situation is aggravated by the fact that the medical postdoctoral is usually less useful as a research associate than the post-PhD is to his mentor. Only after several years is he able, ordinarily, to contribute actively to the research productivity of the faculty member. Whereas the major rationale given by faculty in the natural sciences for having postdoctorals in their groups is to enhance the quality and quantity of research, medical faculty seldom mention this reason unless pressed. Then they describe the assistance more in terms of that received from a graduate student than that from a colleague.

Most post-MD's, even when intending to do research eventually in a clinical field, will take their postdoctoral appointments in one of the basic medical sciences. In this setting they are clearly not as qualified as the post-PhD who probably obtained his doctorate in a basic medical science field.[36] In view of the many courses that they must take to arrive at proficiency, the additional requirements for the PhD do not seem as onerous. This, perhaps, explains why 45 percent of the U.S. post-MD's in these circumstances seek a second doctorate. Whether the long additional expenditure of time that this path requires is necessary for the eventual clinical researcher is a matter of discussion and concern among the clinical faculty.

*Post-DDS*  In dentistry the pattern of research training differs from both that of the basic medical sciences (PhD) and that of the postdoctoral in medicine. H. W. Magoun[37] has gathered statistics on these patterns, which are summarized in Figure 7. The typical individual interested in dental research completes the work for his DDS or DDM degree and then pursues a graduate program leading to a master's degree. Although some schools have PhD programs, these play a minor role. Of the 1,337 persons engaged in graduate and postdoctoral study relating to dentistry in 1966–67, 82 percent were in master's programs, 5 percent were pursuing the PhD, and 13 percent were engaged in postdoctoral study.

Magoun suggests that the emphasis on master's programs in dentistry may in part by related to the educational preparation of the dental faculty. In

---

[36] However, the post-MD is generally more familiar with human biology.
[37] H. W. Magoun, *Graduate Education for Career Teaching and Research in Dentistry*, paper presented at Workshop on Graduate Education in Sciences Related to Dentistry, Chicago, 1968. *Journal of Dental Education,* in press, 1969.

## THE DEMOGRAPHY OF POSTDOCTORAL EDUCATION

FIGURE 7
Percentage of Enrollees, by Level, in Dentistry, Medicine, and Basic Medical Sciences, 1966-67.

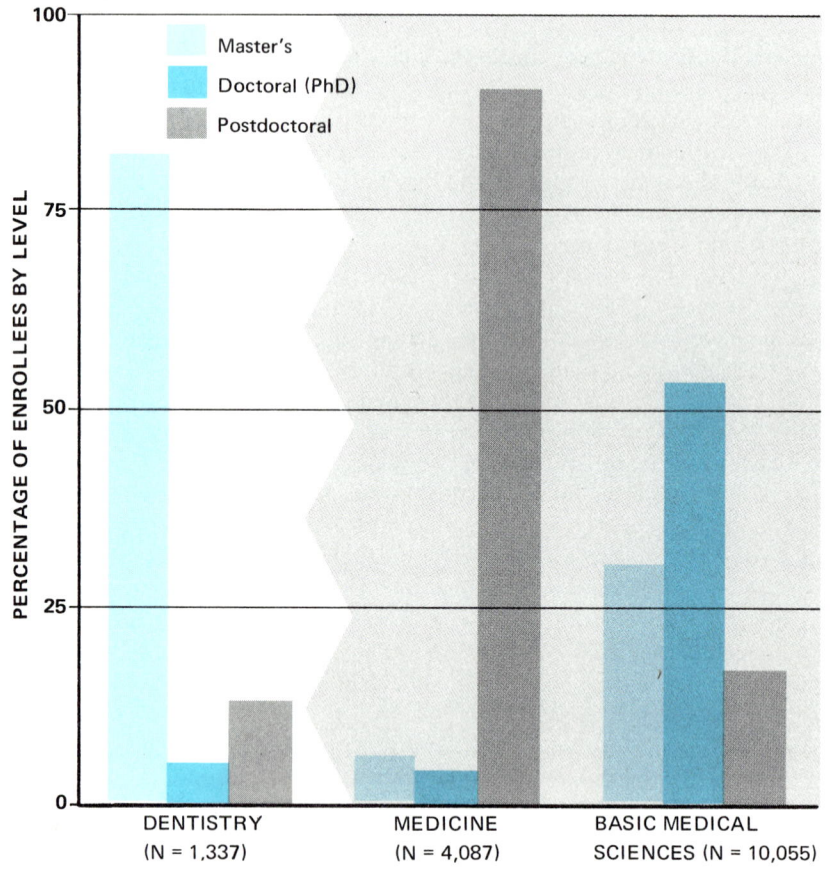

Source: H. W. Magoun, *"Graduate Education for Career Teaching and Research in Dentistry,"* paper presented at Workshop on Graduate Education in Sciences Related to Dentistry, Chicago, 1968.

1965-66 only 10 percent held the PhD with or without the professional doctorate, 21 percent held a master's degree in addition to the professional doctorate, while 69 percent held the professional doctorate only. He further points out that only half of the dental students in the United States possess the baccalaureate degree on admission to dental school. The present emphasis in dentistry on post-professional master's degree programs may rest in part on the limited preparation of many dental graduates for more advanced graduate work.

Although the National Institute of Dental Research has recently supported the establishment of a number of dental research institutes in universities over the country, the situation today is that the post-DDS is a minor participant in postdoctoral study. The statistics that follow will include him with the post-MD without altering significantly the meaning of the results.

*Post-professional-Doctorates Combined (Post-MD's)*[38]  The post-professional-doctorate does not differ significantly from his PhD counterpart in his choice of postdoctoral host institution. The university attracts three quarters of the post-MD's and the government and private hospitals account for most of the remainder. Figure 8 shows the distribution of post-MD's by host institution, by field, and by degree level. Virtually all (95 percent) of the post-MD's are in the medical sciences and in the biological sciences, although the foreign MD is more likely to be in the biological sciences than his American colleague. The recent American post-MD (within seven years of his doctorate) is almost four times as numerous as the senior post-MD, and only a few of the Americans hold both the MD and the PhD. This picture is in contrast to that for the foreign component, where one fifth of the postdoctorals hold both degrees and the older postdoctoral is almost as frequent as the younger. Again, this latter pattern is similar to that for the post-PhD population.

Table 30 gives the field distribution of the post-MD's in more detail. Among the medical sciences internal medicine and surgery are the major fields, while in the basic medical sciences biochemistry and physiology are the most attractive. Pathology, which has historically been a bridge field, is also popular.

Since the postdoctoral programs for the post-professional doctoral are the most self-consciously career motivated, the data on anticipated future employment are particularly interesting. Table 31 gives the choices of the post-MD's by level of degree. For all fields combined there is little difference between the regular and senior postdoctoral. Approximately 60 percent of both groups plan academic careers. Those who hold both the MD and the PhD are more likely to continue in academic medicine and are similar in this regard to their post-PhD associates. The column headed "other" usually describes for the post-MD an intention to enter private practice. A third of the post-MD's do not anticipate a research career.

If a man takes his postdoctoral in one of the basic medical sciences, he is much more likely to seek an academic career. Table 31 gives the choice for both biochemistry and internal medicine. Even though an MD does postdoctoral study in biochemistry, he usually returns to medicine for his research, using biochemical techniques. Presumably the prior commitment to research implied in the selection of biochemistry as a postdoctoral field enhances the likelihood that the man will remain in a research environment.

[38] Hereafter we shall use the term *post-MD's* to refer to all post-professional-doctorates.

## THE DEMOGRAPHY OF POSTDOCTORAL EDUCATION

**FIGURE 8**
Distribution of U.S. and Foreign Post-MD's by Degree Level, Postdoctoral Field, and Host Institution.

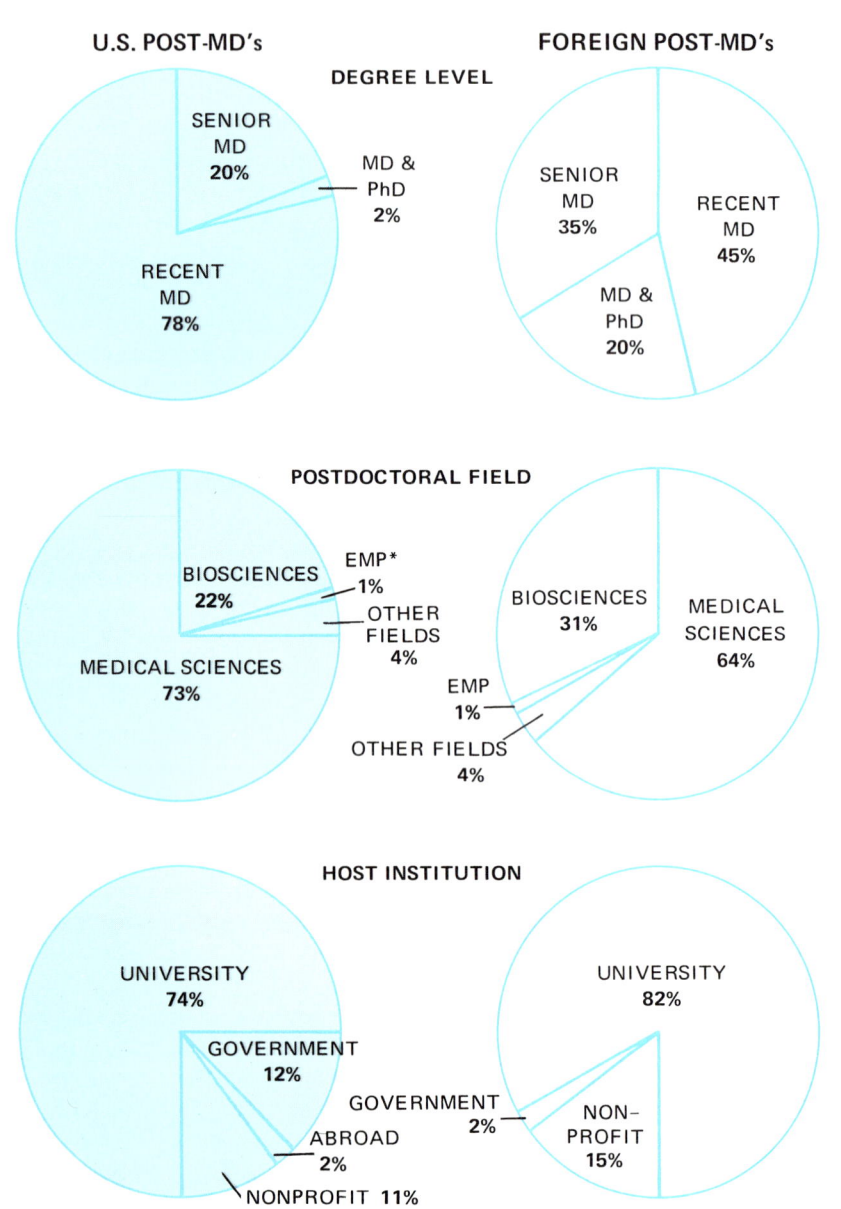

### U.S. POST-MD's

**DEGREE LEVEL**
- SENIOR MD 20%
- MD & PhD 2%
- RECENT MD 78%

**POSTDOCTORAL FIELD**
- BIOSCIENCES 22%
- EMP* 1%
- OTHER FIELDS 4%
- MEDICAL SCIENCES 73%

**HOST INSTITUTION**
- UNIVERSITY 74%
- GOVERNMENT 12%
- ABROAD 2%
- NONPROFIT 11%

### FOREIGN POST-MD's

**DEGREE LEVEL**
- SENIOR MD 35%
- RECENT MD 45%
- MD & PhD 20%

**POSTDOCTORAL FIELD**
- BIOSCIENCES 31%
- MEDICAL SCIENCES 64%
- EMP 1%
- OTHER FIELDS 4%

**HOST INSTITUTION**
- UNIVERSITY 82%
- GOVERNMENT 2%
- NON-PROFIT 15%

*Engineering, mathematics, and physical sciences.
Source: NRC, Office of Scientific Personnel, Postdoctoral Census Questionnaire.

TABLE 30  Distribution of Post-MD's among Fields by Type of Host Institution and Citizenship

### Number of Post-MD's by Type of Host Institutions and Citizenship

| Postdoctoral Field | U.S. Academic Institutions U.S. | U.S. Academic Institutions Foreign | Other Institutions U.S. | Other Institutions Foreign | Total U.S. | Total Foreign |
|---|---|---|---|---|---|---|
| Internal medicine | 455 | 271 | 163 | 64 | 618 | 335 |
| Surgery | 108 | 62 | 40 | 19 | 148 | 81 |
| Pediatrics | 70 | 62 | 29 | 19 | 99 | 81 |
| Nuclear and radiological medicine[a] | 41 | 21 | 16 | 3 | 57 | 24 |
| Social medicine[b] | 43 | 19 | 3 | 3 | 46 | 22 |
| Other medical specialties[c] | 282 | 148 | 135 | 49 | 417 | 197 |
| Other medicine[d] | 71 | 52 | 11 | 13 | 82 | 65 |
| Pathology | 120 | 38 | 17 | 11 | 137 | 49 |
| Anatomy | 23 | 23 | 1 | 1 | 24 | 24 |
| Biochemistry | 77 | 123 | 74 | 11 | 151 | 134 |
| Microbiology | 38 | 31 | 8 | 7 | 46 | 38 |
| Pharmacology | 23 | 44 | 8 | 5 | 31 | 49 |
| Physiology | 74 | 76 | 23 | 17 | 97 | 93 |
| Biology | 64 | 68 | 25 | 10 | 89 | 78 |
| Dentistry | 67 | 31 | 5 | 1 | 72 | 32 |
| Veterinary medicine | 50 | 23 | 1 | 0 | 51 | 23 |
| Other fields | 73 | 42 | 34 | 10 | 107 | 52 |
| Total | 1,679 | 1,134 | 593 | 243 | 2,272 | 1,377 |

[a] Nuclear medicine, radiobiology, clinical radioisotopes, radiology, radiological physics.
[b] Physical and medical rehabilitation, aerospace medicine, occupational medicine, public health, general preventive medicine.
[c] E.g., psychiatry, obstetrics, ophthalmology, hematology.
[d] Pharmacy, administrative medicine, unspecified medicine.

Source:  NRC, Office of Scientific Personnel, Postdoctoral Census Questionnaire.

TABLE 31  Anticipated Employment of Post-MD's by Citizenship and Level of Degree

|  |  | Percentage of Post-MD's by Anticipated Employer |  |  |  |  | Total Number (100%) |
|---|---|---|---|---|---|---|---|
| Postdoctoral Field | Degree Level | University | College | Government | Industry | Other |  |
| Biochemistry | Recent MD | 83 | 1 | 5 | 1 | 10 | 115 |
|  | Senior MD | 78 | 0 | 9 | 0 | 13 | 23 |
|  | MD and PhD | 77 | 0 | 8 | 0 | 15 | 13 |
| Internal medicine | Recent MD | 55 | 1 | 7 | 0 | 35 | 537 |
|  | Senior MD | 60 | 3 | 9 | 1 | 27 | 75 |
| *Total All Fields—U.S.* | Recent MD | 60 | 1 | 6 | 1 | 33 | 1,768 |
|  | Senior MD | 56 | 2 | 7 | 1 | 33 | 450 |
|  | MD and PhD | 74 | 2 | 6 | 2 | 17 | 54 |
| *Total All Fields—Foreign* | Recent MD | 72 | 2 | 2 | 1 | 24 | 615 |
|  | Senior MD | 72 | 3 | 4 | 0 | 21 | 482 |
|  | MD and PhD | 86 | 3 | 1 | 1 | 10 | 280 |

Source: NRC, Office of Scientific Personnel, Postdoctoral Census Questionnaire.

The foreign post-MD is much more likely to seek an academic career. In part this is a reflection of his preference, compared to the American MD, for the basic medical sciences. But even in the clinical fields almost three fourths of the foreign postdoctorals indicate a university as their career location.

## The Postdoctoral in Nonacademic Institutions

Percentage of Postdoctorals at Nonacademic and Academic Host Institutions

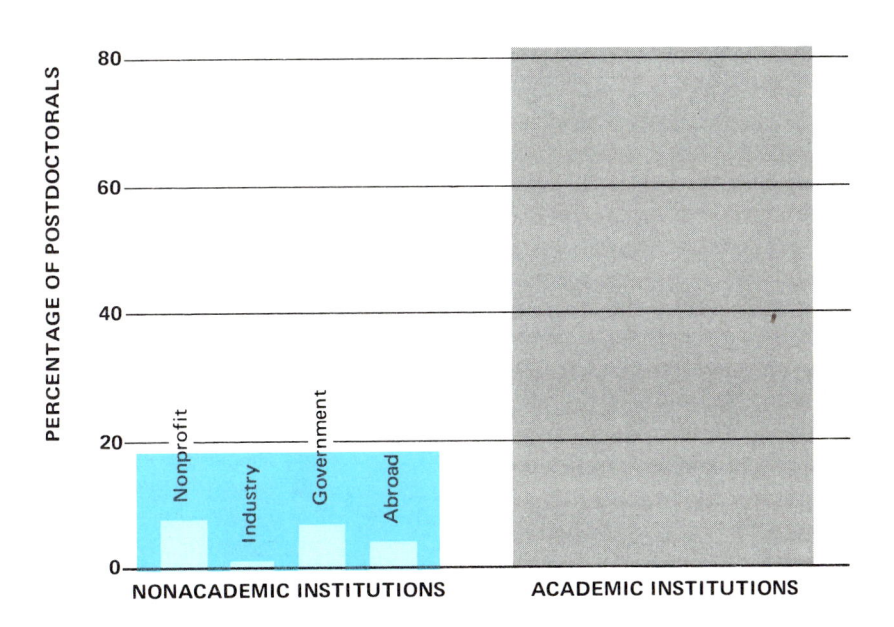

Although allusions have been made to that portion (19 percent) of the postdoctoral population not in U. S. academic institutions and occasional comparisons between the two segments have been made, the nonacademic postdoctoral activity deserves special consideration. Outside the universities, postdoctorals can be found in nonprofit institutions, in industrial laboratories, in federal government installations, and abroad. With the exception of industry, none of the above categories is homogeneous; each includes a variety of environments. Nonprofit institutions encompass hospitals, research institutes, pri-

THE DEMOGRAPHY OF POSTDOCTORAL EDUCATION

FIGURE 9
Nonacademic Host Institutions: Percentage of Postdoctorals by Field of Postdoctoral, Sex and Citizenship, and Level of Appointment.

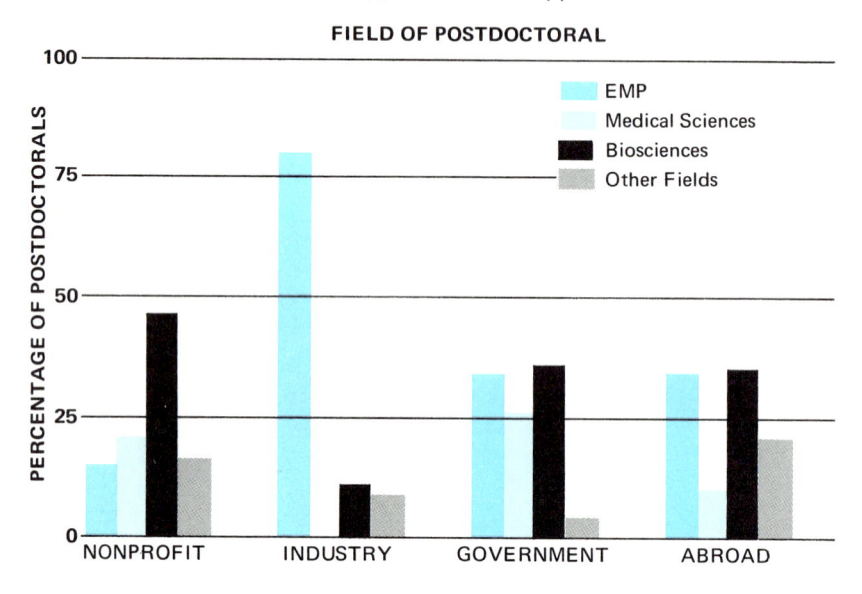

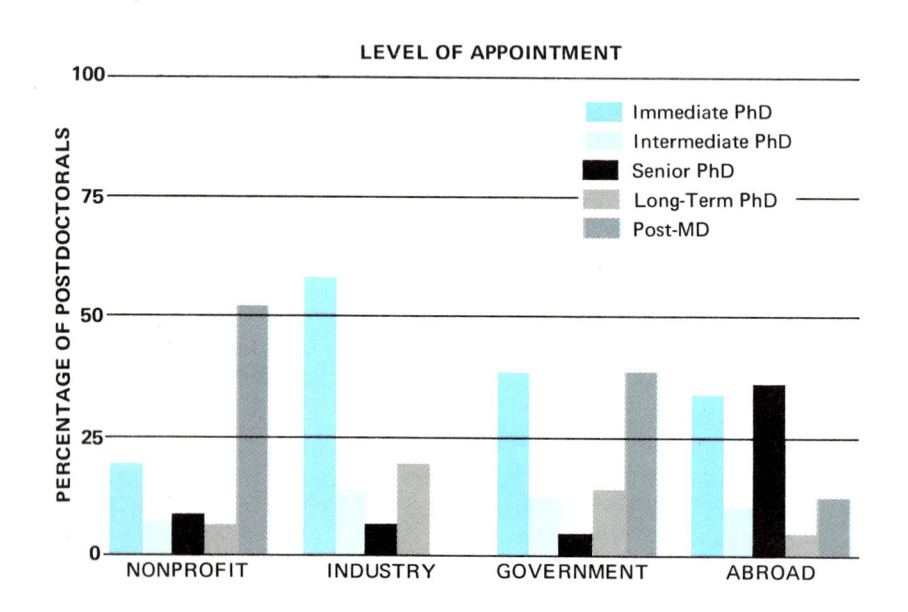

## SEX AND CITIZENSHIP

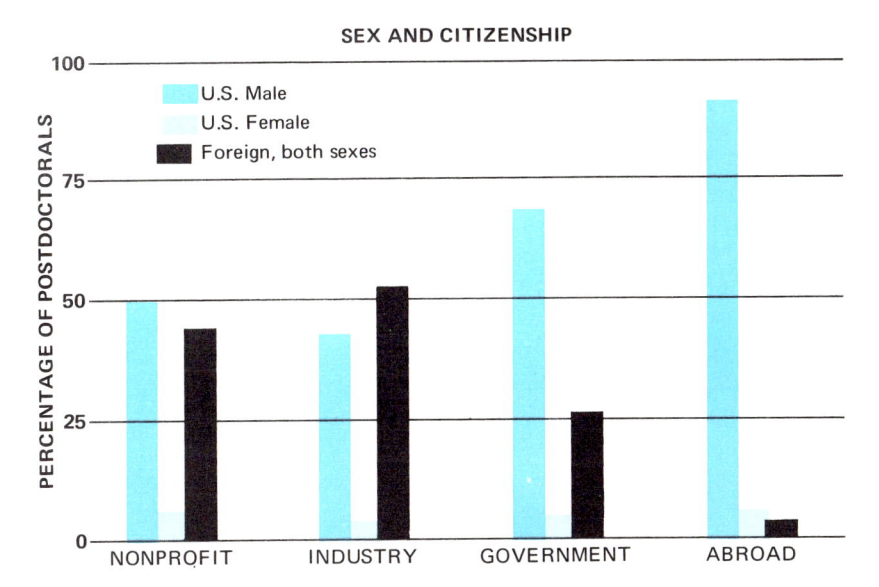

[Bar chart showing percentage of postdoctorals by U.S. Male, U.S. Female, and Foreign (both sexes) across Nonprofit, Industry, Government, and Abroad categories.]

Source: NRC, Office of Scientific Personnel, Postdoctoral Census Questionnaire.

vate laboratories, libraries, museums, and state or local government offices. The federal government installations range from the quasi-academic laboratories, such as the Lawrence Radiation Laboratory at the University of California and the Ames Laboratory at Iowa State University, through the National Bureau of Standards and the Los Alamos Scientific Laboratory, to the mission-oriented Fort Detrick Biological Laboratories of the Army and Houston Manned Spacecraft Center of NASA. Of major importance is the Bethesda campus of the National Institutes of Health. Postdoctoral activity abroad includes both appointments at foreign academic institutions and archeological field trips in uncharted territories. Other host institutions out of the country are libraries and museums.

With such a variety of institutions, little can be said that applies to all of them. Figure 9 shows the differing patterns of fields, of levels of appointment, of citizenship, and of sex among the types of nonacademic host institutions. The lack of uniformity is the most obvious feature of these charts. There are, nevertheless, some important trends and each category of host institution demonstrates interesting characteristics.

The behavior of U. S. male postdoctorals can be taken as a standard against which both the U. S. females and the foreigners can be measured. Each of the latter groups must contend with special restrictions and attitudes that modify their postdoctoral opportunities. For the U. S. female, marital ties and lingering prejudice limit her freedom of movement. The foreign postdoctoral contends not only with language problems and scarcity of support in some fields, but also is differentially attracted to the United States as one moves from field to field. Especially for more senior scholars in the humanities and in the social sciences, only those concerned mainly with American studies would find the United States a particularly fertile research environment. Similar situations, though sometimes more subtle, face the natural scientists. Although in some fields American science is preeminent, this is certainly not the case in all. The European Organization for Nuclear Research (CERN) or the Niels Bohr Institute in Copenhagen are certainly as attractive for physicists of whatever country as their American counterparts.

Academic institutions can also be used as a standard against which other host institutions may be compared. This is not to imply that the universities have the "proper" distribution of fields, sex, citizenship, or level of postdoctoral activity, but rather that, as the largest category, they represent the choice that the bulk of the postdoctorals have made. The other categories of host institutions are important for the participants but are seldom statistically significant in the total postdoctoral picture.

Nonprofit Institutions

As indicated above, this category comprises several different kinds of institutions. In terms of numbers of postdoctorals, rather than numbers of institutions, the composition of the nonprofit group is 35 percent at hospitals, 14 percent at research foundations (usually medical), 40 percent at research institutes and laboratories, and the remaining 11 percent at libraries, museums, and assorted agencies and nonprofit corporations. There are 817 postdoctorals in this group, of whom 50 percent are U. S. males, 7 percent are U. S. females, and 43 percent are foreign. By field, the proportions follow the general trends. The number of foreigners decreases as one moves from the EMP fields through biological and medical sciences to the other fields, and women are more likely to be found in the biological sciences and the other fields than in the EMP fields or the medical sciences. These patterns hold for all categories of host institutions.

The medical sciences are more predominant in nonprofit institutions than in the universities, as are the humanities and social sciences. Of course, these fields are not represented at the same institution. The heterogeneity is caused by the variety of types of institutions subsumed under the category "nonprofit." Nevertheless, some quasi-academic institutions do have several fields represented. Prominent among these are The Institute for Advanced Study on the East coast and Center for Advanced Study in the Behavioral Sciences on the West. Both are purely postdoctoral institutions offering no formal course work. Although informal seminars are regularly held, scholars work independently except for the serendipitous collaboration that each institution attempts to foster through careful selection of its scholars.

The invitational nature of the nonprofit institutions accounts for the relatively small proportion of immediate postdoctorals and the larger numbers of intermediate and senior postdoctorals. Generally, the nonmedical institutions are concerned with research rather than training. Consequently, their limited resources are reserved for established or at least budding scholars who can be expected to be productive over the short period of the appointment.

The immediate postdoctorals who are at some nonprofit institutions are there for the same reasons as those at universities, both from their own point of view and from the point of view of the institution. The president of a medical research institute states, "Nonuniversity research institutions need the services of postdoctoral scientists to the same degree that university research programs do."

Over four-fifths of the post-PhD's at nonprofit institutions are again either returning to or seeking academic employment following their postdoctoral appointments, and even 43 percent of the post-MD's are headed for the university. The nonprofit institution (whether a research institute or a hospital) is, therefore, an alternative place to do research but it is not really different from the university as a place of postdoctoral study.[39] It often has its own advantages for postdoctoral study, including special equipment or library collections and fewer distractions than a university.

Industrial Laboratories

We have been able to locate a total of 47 postdoctorals at three industrial laboratories. The three firms are Bell Telephone Laboratories, Avco-Everett Research Laboratory, and The Mitre Corporation. We know that other industrial laboratories have postdoctorals, but the number is small. Of 42 spokesmen for industry who responded to our inquiries, 17 indicated that they had formal or informal postdoctoral programs. It is characteristic, however, that even the largest corporations offer only a handful of such positions. Except for the Bell

[39] The director of a nonprofit laboratory engaged in research in the life sciences says: "I think that this laboratory behaves more like the appendage of a university than an orthodox nonprofit institution.... All our research personnel have had university postdoctoral experience." (It is not clear from the evidence that the "orthodox" nonprofit institution exists.)

Laboratories (where there are 36 postdoctorals out of the 47 who filled out our questionnaire), no firm mentioned any larger number than two or three. Most of the appointments are offered on an informal basis. One company, North American Aviation, announces the postdoctoral appointments available at its Science Center in the same fashion as a university.

A major reason why these firms have postdoctorals is the competition with universities for doctoral talent. The argument is made by the vice-president of a research corporation in the following way: "To the extent that the young PhD is strongly attracted to the university environment for postdoctoral studies, other organizations in need of PhD's must either find ways to bid competitively for their services or provide themselves by other means with equivalent learning and capability." Another vice-president says flatly: "With the advent of more industry-like research going on in universities, it becomes necessary for industry to become more university-like to attract research scientists."

Most industrial firms admit that offering postdoctoral appointments is a useful recruiting device. Only a few speak of the need to educate young PhD's in their area of research or point to the stimulus that postdoctorals can give their firm's research programs. One respondent states as a matter of course that "one purpose" of the firm's postdoctoral program is "to attract interested and promising individuals to the laboratories, with the expectation that if we feel they are outstanding, they may become interested in our work and choose to remain with us." A company spokesman who mentions another purpose first quickly lists recruiting second:

> The prime motivation for establishing the postdoctoral program was the desire to increase in our laboratory the number of young, high-class research men above the number we could afford as permanent employees for the purpose of increasing the infusion of new ideas, experiences and techniques into our research organization. In addition, we expect to hire a few of these people just as we hire postdoctorals from other establishments. Then the appointment is also a trial period for the laboratory and the man, which can be terminated by either party without prejudice.

That such a motivation is reasonable is supported by the data in Table 11 (p. 62). Thirty-five percent of the immediate postdoctorals in industry will remain in industry. This is a larger percentage by far than that from any other source.

Nevertheless, only a minor fraction of the nation's industrial firms offer postdoctoral programs. It is instructive to consider why the vast majority do not. For many firms the idea of offering short-term appointments raises serious difficulties. The research director of a major steel company argues:

> The very nature of industrial research including the possibility of involvement with proprietary matters, the dependence of fringe benefits on length of service, and other considerations militate against temporary opportunities being offered in industrial research. It is my feeling that such an arrangement would tend to encourage "floaters," employees

who move at frequent intervals from one organization to another motivated solely by the possibility of a higher salary as a result of each move.

The president of a consulting firm writes:

I find it difficult from my own experience to make a case for offering postdoctoral educational opportunities within very many industrial organizations which I have seen. The reasons for this are first, from management's point of view, I doubt that a cost effectiveness justification could be made for it; and second, from the student's point of view I doubt that he would find the climate and other motivational factors adequate. This is not to say that PhD's coming into industry do not have learning opportunities, but rather that the opportunities are too "real world" and, by definition, are therefore distracting and diverting. It seems to me that most PhD's interested in postdoctoral education are interested in acquiring greater depth rather than greater breadth, and the last thing in the world they want is distraction and diversion.

An oil company that has received many inquiries from young PhD's seeking postdoctoral experience has nevertheless felt compelled to turn them down:

For reasons that appear obvious to us we are interested in hiring "permanent" employees. An equally strong point is the great proprietary interest we seek to develop from our applied research, which represents about 90 percent of the total.

A similar statement comes from the vice-president for research of a pharmaceutical company:

We have not attempted to offer postdoctoral opportunities in the sense that the candidate would work for us for only one or a very limited number of years to enlarge his doctoral experience, and then move on. Almost without exception we select our people with the intention that they will become "permanent" members of our research organization. ... our laboratories operate on the open-door approach, with relatively free discussion of our objectives, and our successes and our failures. This community spirit flourishes best with employees who have made more than a temporary commitment to our organization.

We shall return in Chapter 7 to the relationship between postdoctoral education and the industrial world. For the present we will content ourselves with commentary on the census data.

Figure 9 shows that over half of the postdoctorals in industrial laboratories are foreign. Although the numbers are small, these postdoctorals from abroad are almost entirely from developed countries, a pattern that is significantly different than at other types of host institutions. It is also evident that most of the foreign postdoctorals are not fresh PhD's; the contrast with the American postdoctoral, who tends to be younger, is most acute in industry.

The industrial postdoctoral is also likely to be in the physical sciences and engineering. The small fraction of life scientists probably reflects the proprietary nature of the health products industry (mainly pharmaceuticals), which is particularly adverse to the "temporary employee."

## Federal Government Laboratories

One way of characterizing the postdoctoral population in the federal laboratories is to indicate the agency that supports the laboratory. If we do so, we find that 47 percent of the postdoctorals are supported by the National Institutes of Health and virtually all of them are at the main campus of NIH in Bethesda, Maryland. Thirty-two percent of the federal postdoctorals are at one or another of the Atomic Energy Commission's laboratories such as Brookhaven, Los Alamos, Oak Ridge, Argonne, or the Lawrence Radiation Laboratory at the University of California. Eight percent are at installations of the National Aeronautics and Space Administration such as the Goddard Space Flight Center, the Houston Manned Spacecraft Center, or the Jet Propulsion Laboratory at the California Institute of Technology. Five percent are at the several laboratories of the Department of Defense or of the three services. Among these laboratories are the U. S. Naval Research Laboratory, the Fort Detrick Biological Laboratory, and various laboratories of the Air Force Systems Command. The Department of Commerce supports almost 4 percent of the federal postdoctorals at its National Bureau of Standards, while the remaining 4 percent are distributed among installations of the Department of Agriculture, the National Science Foundation, and the Food and Drug Administration.

While many of the postdoctorals at NIH are similar to university project associates working on intramural research under the direction of the resident scientists, the majority are Public Health Service officers who are fulfilling selective service obligations. They are, so to speak, involuntary postdoctorals and might not properly be included in our census.

The situation at the national laboratories of the AEC is strongly university oriented. Since the Manhattan Project, the government's activity in nuclear science has been dominated by academics, and the structure of the national laboratories reflects this heritage. With the exception of the Oak Ridge National Laboratory, each of the major installations is governed by either a single university or a corporation of a group of universities. The multibillion-volt accelerators are operated predominantly for university-based physicists and the flow of people back and forth is continuous. Perhaps for this reason the AEC laboratories are highly desirable locations for postdoctoral study and do not have the problem of other government and industrial laboratories in that appointments there impede a return to the academic world. The uniqueness of the facilities, the academic atmosphere of the activities, and the abundance of basic research in fields ranging from nuclear engineering to genetics more nearly duplicates the university than most nonacademic laboratories.[40]

---

[40] It has been suggested that the identification with universities be made closer by allowing the laboratories to grant graduate degrees. See Alvin Weinberg's "The Federal Laboratories and Science Education" (*Science,* Vol. 136, April 6, 1962, p. 29).

## THE POSTDOCTORAL IN NONACADEMIC INSTITUTIONS

Postdoctoral appointments at the other federal centers are awarded for the most part by the Research Associateship Programs of the National Research Council. Since 1955, a number of federal laboratories have been hosts to postdoctorals selected by the NRC. The NRC, as well as the individual laboratories, advertises the availability of appointments at universities and elsewhere. Applications from candidates are received by the Council and its selection panels prepare rank-ordered lists of candidates approved for awards.[41]

There are actually two separate programs under this rubric. In one, the NRC makes the awards and pays the stipends out of funds supplied by a contract from the participating laboratories. In the other, appointments are made under Civil Service regulation to as many candidates as the laboratory has funds for, without departing from the rank order as determined by the NRC panels. In the latter program each laboratory has had to receive prior approval from the Civil Service Commission to participate; however, since 1967 the Commission has permitted any laboratory to make one-year postdoctoral appointments through the NRC, if the NRC approves the laboratory's research program and environment. The Commission has also authorized extensions of appointments for a second year if the laboratory determines that the extension would benefit both the individual and the laboratory.

The better-known laboratories, especially those engaged in basic research in fields of current interest, e.g., the National Bureau of Standards, have attracted increasing numbers of applicants of high caliber. Candidates are less attracted to laboratories where the emphasis is on applied research or development. Such laboratories appear to have several disadvantages: they publish less in the scientific journals, they are usually less well known, and candidates who might be attracted to them can get better-paid positions of the same sort in industry.

The federal laboratories and the National Research Council recognize a double purpose in the associateship programs: to enlist the scientific resources of the laboratories in the development of talented individuals and to contribute to the research programs of the laboratories. Care is taken to keep these purposes in balance. If, over the years, for example, more than a third of the associates in a laboratory's postdoctoral program choose to continue with the laboratory as permanent employees, this is viewed as cause for concern. It is felt that a program is failing in its educational purpose if too many of its appointees close their career options in this way.

Some ambivalence exists in the attitudes of the participating laboratories. There is a certain amount of reluctance on their part to releasing 100 percent of the exceptional talent they train. Table 11 (p. 62) indicates that almost a

---

[41] In spite of possessing all the characteristics of fellows in the selection process, these "research associates" are subject to full taxation. As in the university the distinction between fellows and research associates is more a function of legal language than operationally different treatment.

quarter of the federal postdoctorals choose to remain in government employ following their appointment. However, graduates of the program who return to the university (and 55 percent do) often motivate their students to become employees and associates in the participating laboratory.

Except in the physical sciences, the foreign postdoctoral plays a much less important role in federal laboratories than at other types of host institutions. Only 26 percent of the federal postdoctorals are foreign. In part this is a reflection of the dominance of the life sciences and the draft alternative that positions in the Public Health Service represent. Obviously only Americans are concerned with the latter and Public Health Service officers are a large fraction (approximately half) of the federal postdoctorals.

Postdoctorals Abroad

Compared to the postdoctoral at an American university, the postdoctoral abroad is much more likely to be a mature scholar on leave for a year or less to make use of the unique resources overseas or to discover what is happening in foreign laboratories. In fact, as we have seen, the senior postdoctoral is as likely to be abroad as at home. The younger man is not as ready to leave the country, since his visibility for subsequent employment is less at a foreign establishment than at a domestic one. These behavior patterns are easily discernible in the NSF postdoctoral programs, since the awardee may select his own fellowship institution. The fact that only 44 of the 120 regular postdoctorals in 1968 chose to take their appointments abroad, while 42 of the 55 senior postdoctorals did so, illustrates the behavior. Some (10 percent) of the immediate postdoctorals abroad have already been appointed to the faculty of a university, but have delayed the actual beginning of the faculty appointment to accept the fellowship. Not having to worry about their post-appointment employment, they are free to leave the country. For comparison, only 2 percent of the immediates at U. S. universities are on leave from another position.

Few object to the idea that the senior scholar should travel abroad, not only to represent United States science and learning abroad, but also to see his subject approached from another point of view and to become as familiar with foreign centers as the foreign scholars are with ours. Only the severest chauvinism assumes that the best in all fields is here and that nothing can be learned from others. The problem is whether the same values prevail for the immediate postdoctoral. Those in favor of postdoctoral opportunities abroad for the new PhD point out that for some fellows the foreign laboratory may be the best place to go because techniques and ideas there are more advanced than in the United States. Others, recognizing the indifference of science and scholarship generally to national boundaries, say that travel *per se* is not a justification but that the determining factor is where the postdoctoral can receive the best research experience. If that laboratory is not in this country, so be it.

Those opposed to the postdoctoral appointment abroad make their objection on relative grounds. Granted that in some areas superior experience can be found in foreign centers, the question is whether the additional cost is justified. If the man can receive almost as good an experience in this country, why not extend the funds by restricting the travel? Underlying these arguments is the suspicion that the move overseas will involve such a change of environment that the research will not be efficiently pursued. There are problems involved in changing institutions in this country; for the American who goes, say, to Europe there are the additional difficulties of language and custom that must be mastered.

Over 97 percent of the immediate postdoctorals abroad are supported on fellowships. The implication of this fact is that, on the whole, they are of higher quality than postdoctorals generally. They have been highly screened and are selected for their probable achievement of research leadership. On the basis of baccalaureate-to-PhD time lapse they are better than all other groups of postdoctorals. The average time lapse in the physical sciences for the immediate postdoctoral abroad is 5.0 years and for the basic medical sciences it is 5.9 years. Each is significantly below the time lapses given in Table 19 (p. 78) for the postdoctorals at U. S. institutions.

A significant point is that we are not talking about very many people. Only 7 percent of the immediate U. S. male postdoctorals are overseas—a total of 145 people by our count. What might be inappropriate for the entire group of immediate postdoctorals could be valid for a highly select subgroup of them. The subtle influences that produce the creative researcher are not understood. It would seem prudent not to foreclose the foreign experience for a few in the name of economy, as the marginal cost probably does not begin to match the value of the work that one future Nobel prizewinner among them might accomplish.

CHAPTER **5**

# Implications for the Postdoctoral

A great amount of time, effort, and financial resources has been expended on postdoctoral study, and the question "How productive has this expenditure been?" remains to be answered. As we shall see, many participants testify to the critical importance of the experience to their professional growth and performance. On the other hand, some successful nonparticipants tend to deprecate the need for the experience. It is possible that both are right, and it is impossible to know what either would have accomplished had the circumstances been different.

The evolution of a scholar or scientist is a singular process. Were it only a matter of inculcating techniques and procedures, the necessary curriculum and training exercises would have evolved by now to turn out the researchers needed for each generation. Indeed, the rather standard PhD program is an attempt to formalize the process. But even here, the dissertation research is an individual matter. A Nobel Laureate in biochemistry, Sir Hans Krebs,[1] points out that the acquisition of skills is not sufficient in the making of a scientist. "What is critical is the use of skills, how to assess their potentialities and their limitations; how to improve, to rejuvenate, to supplement them." He argues that in addition to skills, excellence in science depends on a certain attitude that fosters "... a self-critical mind and the continuous effort to learn and to improve."

The creation of the environment in which both skills and attitude are trans-

---

[1] H. A. Krebs, The Making of a Scientist, *Nature,* Vol. 215, September 30, 1967, pp. 1441-1445.

mitted from teacher to novice is the basic problem in the making of a scientist. There is general consensus that whatever else is relevant, the excellence of the incipient scientist can be enhanced by the degree of excellence of his mentor. Since excellence is relatively rare and the demand by industry, government, and higher education for trained scientists and scholars is great, many who attain the PhD are limited in their scientific capability by the fact that their mentors were competent without achieving great distinction or excellence. This is not a reflection on the standards of graduate schools or an assertion that the graduate programs have failed, but rather a consequence of the scarcity of excellence. Much of postdoctoral activity can be explained in terms of the search for a more excellent mentor.

In the article previously referred to, Krebs analyzes the scientific "genealogy" of himself as a Nobel Laureate. Each scientific ancestor is quoted as attributing his success to having worked in the laboratory of his scientific "father."

> In each case, the association between teacher and pupil was close and prolonged, extending to the mature stage of the pupil, to what we would now call postgraduate and postdoctoral levels. It was not merely a matter of attending a course of lectures but of researching together over a period of years.

Jacques Monod,[2] who received the Nobel Prize in 1965, has testified to the impact on him of a Rockefeller Fellowship that permitted him to work in the laboratory of Thomas Hunt Morgan at the California Institute of Technology.

> This was revelation to me—a revelation of what a group of scientists could be like when engaged in creative activity, and sharing in constant exchange of ideas, bold speculation, and strong criticism: it was a revelation of personalities of great stature such as George Beadle, Sterling Emerson, Bridges, Sturtevant, Jack Schultz, and Ephrussi, all of whom were working in Morgan's department.

Morgan was already a Nobel Laureate and Beadle was later to receive the Nobel Prize.

A by-product of working in the laboratory of an outstanding teacher and researcher is, as suggested by Monod, the association with extraordinary contemporaries. Krebs had a similar experience and points out that ". . . great teachers tend to attract good people. Students at all levels learn as much from their fellow students as from their seniors and this was certainly true in my case." The same phenomenon has occurred in physics where the students who were at Chicago with Enrico Fermi currently play central roles in elementary particle physics. These include Owen Chamberlain, C. N. Yang, T. D. Lee (all Nobel Laureates), Geoffrey Chew, Jack Steinberger, and Marvin Goldberger, all of whom were fellow students at the same time at Chicago.

Whether these men and others like them would have achieved what they

---

[2] Jacques Monod, *Science,* Vol. 101, 1966, p. 475.

did without their particular predoctoral and postdoctoral experiences is impossible to know. Krebs argues that scientists are not so much born as made by those who teach them research. One wonders, however, whether less innately gifted students would have fared so well. The flaw in such a speculation is that our present measures of aptitudes do not identify within the very high ranges those who are likely to be creative. Creativity is still not understood and it is only after a creative act is performed that we identify the creative person.

When we move away from the relatively small group of excellent teachers and gifted students, the situation is less clear. We generally ask for testimonials only from the successful; the much larger "merely competent" group is also much quieter. The number of postdoctorals far exceeds the number of those who will win national and international prizes and only a handful of mentors have received or will receive such honors. Is postdoctoral activity important for the less-than-exceptional student? Can a less-than-outstanding scientist serve as an adequate mentor of postdoctorals?

## Comments of Former Postdoctorals

By examining the comments of some former postdoctorals we can develop an insight into the situation from the point of view of the participants. Most reaffirm the reasons given in Chapter 5 by current postdoctorals for taking the appointment. The respondents considered their postdoctoral years valuable for permitting a transition period from student to professor, for meeting and working with eminent scholars, for starting independent research, for making field changes or acquiring breadth and perspective, and for learning specialized techniques. Many describe the postdoctoral period as the most "stimulating," "crucial," "formative," or "invaluable" experience in their careers. It is often felt to have been more important than their predoctoral training.

Not all, however, had satisfactory experiences. A number mention the exploitation of the postdoctoral by the mentor. As a chemist put it, "I was a source of cheap labor—a glorified grad student." Another called for a code of ethics to be imposed upon preceptors "regarding aspects of the training, problem selection, publication rights, etc." He felt himself to be more an employee of his mentor than a junior colleague and wished that his "preceptor had felt he also had an obligation to advance the training and experience of the postdoctoral student." A psychologist's dissatisfaction with his adviser "was in his unwillingness to guide my training, except when I entirely took the initiative in demanding guidance." In his view, "the value of postdoctoral *training,* distinguished from the opportunity to carry on research, seems to be an interaction between the disposition of the adviser to teach and the willingness of the fellow to be aggressive in seeking training." The balance between freedom and constraint is a delicate one and one which must be determined in the individual case. It is unfortunate that a professor may be insufficiently sensitive to the particular needs of his postdoctorals in their professional development.

A few former postdoctorals were disappointed in their choice of institution, either because of the inadequacy of facilities and equipment or because the faculty there had no interest in discussing problems not immediately related to their own current research. The most common theme with regard to institutional choice, however, was the mistake of some of taking their postdoctoral appointment at the same institution from which they received their PhD. A biochemist who followed this course, to his later regret, gives the following reasons for a fellow's taking his appointment in a new institution:

1. He will be exposed to new techniques and ideas.
2. He will meet other established scientists.
3. Opportunities for advancement are usually greater in a different environment.
4. He can bring new techniques and ideas to the new institution.
5. Perhaps the most important, unless the worker makes a really significant advance as a student or early in his postdoctoral work (a rare occurrence), he is not often appreciated at the institution at which he took his degree.

A physiologist echoes these remarks from his own experience and deplores the tendency to "parochial research before [the postdoctoral] has fully explored his research interests and capabilities." He also points out that the change of institution would "lead more rapidly to a more independent orientation and professional maturity."

On the positive side, the former postdoctorals urge on their successors the prime importance of the senior mentor's being a scientist of exceptional ability. A biochemist who took his postdoctoral at a national laboratory declares that his appointment was "decisive in my own personal development and the development of my subsequent career. I cannot overemphasize [its] value to me—a value more related to knowing the *man* than being at a particular place." An embryologist testified that his work with a particular scholar was crucial. "Although my experience did not result in a great number of papers, it provided something more valuable and intangible—a set of standards for excellence and contact with people who have continued to stimulate my scientific interests."

A few, speaking from their own background, attribute the value of their postdoctoral appointments to overcoming weaknesses in their graduate programs. An anatomist asserts that "I am of the opinion that the majority of young PhD's receiving their degrees from the 'average' department of biological sciences lack the research training and insight to successfully carry out a significant research program without postdoctoral training." A pharmacologist adds that "with the decrease in time for obtaining the PhD degree it is imperative that more postdoctoral positions be made available in order that recent PhD's have a chance to mature and become established in a field of research." On the other hand, most former postdoctorals saw the postdoctoral appointment as not supplementing an inferior graduate program but rather as the next stage in their development. An established zoologist writes:

> I have no hesitation in asserting that my two postdoctoral years (especially the first) were absolutely crucial for me personally in fostering the development of scientific skills and abilities, critical judgment, and intellectual perspective to a satisfactory level before I undertook a fully independent academic appointment. I do not believe my predoctoral education was deficient (indeed, I regard it as superior in nearly all respects), but the time involved in research was inadequate to permit satisfactory scholarly development as far as I personally am concerned. Possibly I would have attained the same maturation *eventually* in an academic appointment commenced directly after receipt of the doctorate but it was facilitated by postdoctoral experience first, and would have been inhibited by heavy teaching responsibilities assumed immediately after the doctorate. I also regard the postdoctoral experiences . . . as having been especially important for a variety of sustained intellectual contact with different individuals in a research context. I do not believe that I could have learned to 'do' research so easily if fully on my own at that juncture in my career.

All of the comments above were made by people between 7 and 17 years after their PhD degrees who had held an immediate postdoctoral appointment. It is interesting to compare their attitudes with those of their contemporaries who have never held a postdoctoral appointment. The scientists in the latter category divide into two factions: a small group who have no regrets (and no good words for postdoctoral education in general) and a large majority who regret not having had the experience. Many of the latter feel that their post-PhD research careers have suffered as a result. The former faction was almost exclusively composed of those presently in industry or those in fields such as geology and oceanography, where the number of available academic positions is large compared to the PhD production.

The manager of the mathematics department of an industrial firm asserts, "I feel rather strongly that a postdoctoral fellowship immediately after the PhD is detrimental to the career of an industrial scientist and not of much advantage to the future academic scientist. . . . This is not true for the exceptionally able student, but the number of postdoctorals available exceeds the number of outstanding recipients." A chemist from industry states, in partial agreement:

> I see little value in postdoctoral training for industrial careers. It would seem to me that the chief value of postdoctoral appointments lies not in the education, but in the associ-

ations. In having carried through a second research program (in addition to the doctoral research), one is undoubtedly better equipped to do further research. In industry this opportunity is always present, whereas in the academic field . . . possibly the experience comes a little more slowly.

Another industrial chemist agreed that the experience was not necessary in industry, but added, "I sincerely feel postdoctoral experience is desirable for people entering the academic profession." He saw an advantage in exposure to new and different institutions for the incipient professor who will subsequently train the next generation of students. A physiologist at a pharmaceutical corporation felt that there were only two justifications for postdoctoral work: to make up for a deficient predoctoral program and to allow a change of fields. He rather suspected that postdoctoral activity has become "a status symbol beyond its real contribution," and that many enter it to be able to refer to it in their *curriculum vitae* or to avoid facing a "real" assignment. On the other hand, a physicist at a government laboratory reports, "I am sold on the postdoctoral concept. . . . A postdoctoral would have enabled me to learn the nuclear physics that I did not have time for in graduate school."

The academic people tend to support postdoctoral education even when they did not have the experience themselves. An associate professor of anatomy said, "I feel that the personal connections with outstanding people in the field which inevitably develop as a result of postdoctoral work would have been helpful in avoiding certain pitfalls in experimental design and helpful in keeping close to the center of things. If one waits for published work to know what is going on, one tends to get left behind." A professor of pharmacology was unsuccessful in winning a fellowship immediately after his PhD and now is convinced that "one or two years of sound postdoctoral training early would have been helpful. I so advise students." Again the feeling is not unanimous. A professor of chemical engineering felt that even those new PhD's who anticipate an academic career would be better off with industrial experience than with a postdoctoral appointment in a university.

Several people whose first postdoctoral experience occurred some years after their doctorate wished that they had taken such an appointment earlier. A botanist said, "Additional research experience the first year after receiving my degree would have accelerated my 'professional development'. . . . I feel I would have advanced more rapidly with regard to academic promotion and research contribution to my field." An astronomer regrets having accepted an academic position before having had postdoctoral experience. He believes that "additional research guidance and delay of the rather extensive demands of initial teaching would have started my research efforts at a stronger and more productive level." A zoologist found his delayed postdoctoral appointment to be highly successful, but found the delay itself to have had an effect on his career. "My production of papers did not really begin until during the postdoctoral period." Other respondents favored the delayed postdoctoral appointment over the immediate. A physiologist was full of praise for his delayed appointment and had serious reservations about the value of postdoctoral work as a routine postlude to graduate training. In his opinion, "graduate school is the time in which training should be completed; I would favor a lengthening of the predoctoral span, rather than a uniform reliance on postdoctoral study." A mathematician feels that "a delayed postdoctoral fellowship usually would be better, since it takes a year or two for a person to utilize and use up his 'thesis knowledge' and mature a bit."

With regard to a delayed postdoctoral appointment taken several years after the PhD or to a senior postdoctoral appointment there is almost unanimous praise. If there is any complaint, it is that there are not sufficient opportunities for support for sabbatical-year research and study leaves. The enthusiasm was shared (and the complaint made) by academic and industrial scientists in all fields. The benefits mentioned most often concerned field changes, providing new perspectives, opportunities for contacts with other senior scholars, rekindling enthusiasm for research, keeping nonresearch professors abreast of their fields (and consequently keeping courses up-to-date), and simply providing unfettered time to do research. One professor of mathematics wrote:

The Institute for Advanced Study has repaid the United States 1,000 times the money invested in it. Since clearly not everyone can go there, it seems obvious to me that similar centers of research without teaching should be started [in several locations around the country] where a faculty member could spend a year in favorable conditions, in pure, uninterrupted scholarship, away from his natural habitat.

Others made similar remarks about the Center for Advanced Study in the Behavioral Sciences. The chairman of a political science department testified that the major advantage of such centers was contact with scholars in other disciplines. "Although one can read in disciplines other than one's own, the insights gained through conversation with others tend to be more easily assimilated into one's own thinking."

We have presented this rather lengthy recitation of reactions to show the variety of opinions and experiences. Except when the respondent was making proposals in areas where he had no experience (e.g., the industrial scientist judging the relevance of postdoctoral work for the academic scientist), one must accept the analyses at face value. Postdoctoral education may simultaneously be crucial for some and unnecessary for others. It may be appropriate in some fields and not in others. It may be more important immediately after the PhD for one scientist and not until several years have passed for another. It may be abused by some postdoctorals and some mentors, but it has clearly been productive for many.

## Quantitative Aspects of the Postdoctoral Experience

The lack of a distinct picture persists when we examine the more quantitative aspects of the impact of postdoctoral education. As indicated in the introduction and as pointed out by a respondent from industry, "Possibly the selection process, including the inclination to seek and the qualities sought in the granting of a postdoctoral position, provides the major screening as to any greater probability of future productivity. If . . . postdoctoral experience seems to yield a more productive result, this may be due to the original selection process and not to the experience." We tried in our sampling procedure to select two groups of former postdoctorals and non-former postdoctorals of equal quality as measured by the reputation of their doctoral institution and their baccalaureate-to-PhD time lapse. These two measures, of course, do not preclude potential differences; for example, motivation and encouragement to seek a postdoctoral position undoubtedly are important distinctions. Another influence in making comparisons between those who have had a postdoctoral experience and those who have not is the "halo" effect, or as Robert K. Merton[3] has put it, "the Matthew effect." Merton takes his text from the Gospel according to St. Matthew: "For unto everyone that hath shall be given, and he shall have abundance: but from him that hath not shall be taken away even that which he hath." Merton goes on to apply the principle to the system of rewards in science. The application here is in the incremental awareness one has of an award winner and in the subsequent abundance of opportunities. Given two candidates of comparable quality for a position, there is probably a tendency to favor the one who has been previously recognized by a national fellowship committee or who has worked with a particularly prestigious mentor. In this circumstance it is not the postdoctoral selection process, or even necessarily the postdoctoral experience, but the mere fact of having been a postdoctoral that turns the balance.

With these reservations in mind let us examine the comparative data among three groups of natural scientists: those who took an immediate postdoctoral appointment, those who took a delayed postdoctoral (the intermediate and senior appointee), and those who have never had a postdoctoral. The sample was selected from those who received their PhD's in 1950, 1955, or 1960 (see Appendix A-4).

The first difference among the three groups is in their current employment. Table 32 gives the type of employer in 1967, and the data indicate that those who have never had a postdoctoral are less likely to be in the academic world and are significantly more likely to be in industry. The fact that the former delayed postdoctoral is more likely to be in the university than is the former

---

[3] R. K. Merton, *Science,* Vol. 159, January 5, 1968, pp. 56–63.

TABLE 32 Type of Employer in 1967 of Natural Scientists by Postdoctoral Background, PhD's of 1950, 1955, and 1960

| Type of Employer in 1967 | Percentage of Scientists by Postdoctoral Background and PhD Year |||||||||
|---|---|---|---|---|---|---|---|---|---|
| | Immediate Postdoctoral ||| Delayed Postdoctoral ||| No Postdoctoral |||
| | 1950 | 1955 | 1960 | 1950 | 1955 | 1960 | 1950 | 1955 | 1960 |
| Academic institution | 55 | 72 | 83 | 81 | 78 | 61 | 55 | 50 | 55 |
| Nonprofit research organization | 7 | 5 | 3 | 2 | 5 | 10 | 3 | 13 | 9 |
| Industry | 13 | 10 | 5 | 4 | 3 | 0 | 25 | 21 | 16 |
| U.S. government | 15 | 10 | 4 | 11 | 6 | 13 | 9 | 14 | 15 |
| Other | 10 | 4 | 5 | 2 | 8 | 16 | 8 | 2 | 6 |
| *Total Percent* | 100 | 101 | 100 | 100 | 100 | 100 | 100 | 100 | 101 |
| *Total Number* | 40 | 83 | 127 | 47 | 65 | 31 | 65 | 111 | 115 |

Source: NRC, Office of Scientific Personnel, Postdoctoral Experience Questionnaire.

immediate postdoctoral is explained by the circumstance that sabbaticals and leaves of absence are more easily obtained and more the custom in the university setting than in other employing institutions. The immediate postdoctoral may have left the university soon after his appointment. The delayed postdoctoral remained at the university long enough to have his appointment.

In what follows we shall compare only those in the sample who are U. S. males at academic institutions. There are significant differences in the treatment of women and foreigners by all employers, and the salary scales and publication practices of the academic world differ from those of other employers. We will also often refrain from comparisons within the sciences, since our sample size is not sufficient to lend credence to the apparent differences.

Table 33 gives the academic rank or position of the sample and shows no significant differences except, of course, that the older men (PhD's of 1950) have a higher rank and are more likely to have administrative positions than are the younger men.

We begin to see some differences when we look at how the respondents' time is spent (Table 34). The former immediate postdoctoral is more involved in research and less involved in teaching and administration than the other two groups. Both research and teaching give way to administration in the case of the older respondent. It may be that the early commitment to research that the immediate postdoctoral represents is reflected in these results.

Another possible distinction is the degree of involvement with graduate education. The following table shows the percentage of academic scientists in the sample who have been graduate thesis advisers and the number of students supervised at the master's and doctoral level:

|  | Postdoctoral Background |  |  |
| --- | --- | --- | --- |
|  | Immediate | Delayed | None |
| Percent who have been graduate thesis advisers | 76 | 86 | 83 |
| Average number of MS students per year who received degrees under these advisers | .25 | .43 | .49 |
| Average number of PhD students per year who received degrees under these advisers | .38 | .23 | .29 |

At the master's level the former immediate postdoctoral is much less productive than the other two groups, but at the doctoral level he is more important. Not shown in the table but explicit in the data is a significant exception which will show up again. The man who never had a postdoctoral but who received his PhD from one of the ten leading institutions has produced on the average 0.47 masters per year and 0.40 PhD's per year. The latter number is larger than those from any other type of institution or with any other type of postdoctoral background.

When we look at the research indices (Table 35), we observe that the non-

IMPLICATIONS FOR THE POSTDOCTORAL

TABLE 33 Rank or Position in 1967 of Academic Scientists (U.S. Males Only), by Year of PhD and Postdoctoral Background

| Academic Rank or Position | Percentage of Academic Scientists ||||||
|---|---|---|---|---|---|---|
| | PhD Year ||| Postdoctoral Background |||
| | 1950 | 1955 | 1960 | Immediate | Delayed | None |
| Full professor | 70 | 45 | 13 | 41 | 47 | 40 |
| Associate professor | 10 | 36 | 52 | 31 | 34 | 33 |
| Assistant professor | – | 5 | 23 | 14 | 8 | 5 |
| Instructor, lecturer | 1 | 1 | 1 | 1 | 1 | 2 |
| Administrator | 13 | 6 | 3 | 5 | 5 | 11 |
| Research staff member | 6 | 7 | 6 | 6 | 3 | 9 |
| Postdoctoral | – | 1 | 3 | 1 | 2 | – |
| Total Percent | 100 | 101 | 101 | 99 | 100 | 100 |
| Total Number | 82 | 162 | 173 | 179 | 102 | 136 |

Source: NRC, Office of Scientific Personnel, Postdoctoral Experience Questionnaire.

postdoctoral is less likely to be doing any research than are the others. He is also less likely to have outside support for his research. However, if one subtracts those with outside support from those in research, there is no significant difference among the groups, i.e., approximately 10 percent of those doing research do not have any outside support regardless of their postdoctoral background.

The nonpostdoctoral gets his first grant slightly earlier than does the immediate. The reason may be that he can apply at an earlier date (not being on a postdoctoral appointment at the time). He is a year ahead of the delayed postdoctoral in this respect. The increase in the availability of extramural support

TABLE 34 Type of Work Activity in 1967 of Academic Scientists (U.S. Males Only) by PhD Year and Postdoctoral Background

| Type of Work Activity | Percentage of Academic Scientists ||||||
|---|---|---|---|---|---|---|
| | PhD Year ||| Postdoctoral Background |||
| | 1950 | 1955 | 1960 | Immediate | Delayed | None |
| Research | 40 | 44 | 48 | 51 | 41 | 41 |
| Teaching | 31 | 36 | 37 | 31 | 41 | 33 |
| Administration | 23 | 16 | 12 | 15 | 16 | 20 |
| Other | 6 | 4 | 3 | 3 | 2 | 6 |
| Total Percent | 100 | 100 | 100 | 100 | 100 | 100 |
| Total Number | 82 | 162 | 173 | 179 | 102 | 136 |

Source: NRC, Office of Scientific Personnel, Postdoctoral Experience Questionnaire.

TABLE 35  Research Activity of Academic Scientists (U.S. Males Only), by Year of PhD and Postdoctoral Background

| Research Indices | PhD Year 1950 | PhD Year 1955 | PhD Year 1960 | Postdoctoral Background Immediate | Postdoctoral Background Delayed | Postdoctoral Background None |
|---|---|---|---|---|---|---|
| Percent in research | 90 | 93 | 98 | 95 | 96 | 90 |
| Percent with outside support | 86 | 83 | 79 | 85 | 85 | 79 |
| Average number of years past PhD to first extramural research grants | 5.8 | 4.6 | 2.8 | 4.3 | 5.9 | 3.9 |
| Percent of those with outside support who received subsequent research grants | 94 | 88 | 85 | 89 | 91 | 87 |
| Average number of papers published per year | 2.2 | 1.8 | 2.1 | 2.1 | 1.9 | 2.2 |

Source: NRC, Office of Scientific Personnel, Postdoctoral Experience Questionnaire.

is evident in the time lag as a function of PhD class. The 1960 graduate received his first grant in half the time it took the 1950 PhD. There is no significant advantage with regard to getting a second outside grant. Approximately 90 percent of all groups who received a first grant received a second grant. Finally, there is no apparent difference in the rate of production of papers among the three groups, although the nonpostdoctoral whose degree is from one of the ten leading schools publishes an average of 2.9 papers per year—more than any other subgroup.

Such a counting of papers does not, of course, take into account the quality or importance of the paper. The Commission on Human Resources and Advanced Education of the National Research Council has used the facilities of the Science Citation Index to determine the number of times an author's work has been cited by others. Although there are many irrelevant reasons for citing a work, it is likely that on the average more important papers are cited more often than less important papers. In their latest study[4] the Commission reports the following:

The impact of research executed by postdoctoral fellowship awardees is also indicated to be greater than that by their peers who had not received a postdoctoral fellowship. In each field, the aggregate of 1957-59 male doctorates who had received a fellowship were

[4] From a draft being prepared for publication, *Human Resources and Higher Education*, Russel Sage Foundation, New York, in press.

## IMPLICATIONS FOR THE POSTDOCTORAL

found to have about twice as many recent citations to their work as those who were nonrecipients. While those who receive a postdoctoral fellowship were subsequently more likely than others to engage primarily in research and are more likely to be employed in college or university settings. Even when these factors are held "constant" the former postdoctoral fellowship holders tend to have higher citation counts than do their colleagues.

Although this result is suggestive, the Commission did not hold constant the "quality" of the two groups as we attempted to do in our sample. Citation counts for our sample show that the former immediate postdoctoral tends to be cited almost twice as often as either the former delayed postdoctoral or the non-former-postdoctoral.[5]

A final comparison among the academic scientists with different postdoctoral backgrounds is the salary that each receives. The rather surprising result is that the scientist with no postdoctoral experience receives a higher average salary than the man with previous postdoctoral experience.[6] The figures for annual income for all scientists are: $17,500 for those with no postdoctoral experience, $16,000 for those who were immediate postdoctorals, and $15,900 for those with delayed postdoctoral appointments. In part, this difference is a reflection of the somewhat heavier involvement in administration of the nonpostdoctoral, but it is probably accounted for also by the fact that the immediate postdoctoral does not begin to receive a salary as a faculty member for one or two years after the man who does not take the postdoctoral appointment. Again the nonpostdoctoral who received his PhD from one of the ten leading schools stands out. His average annual salary is $18,500, which exceeds the salary of scientists from every other academic or postdoctoral background. In general, whatever motivations a young scientist might have for seeking a postdoctoral appointment, financial advantage is not one of them.

Of those members of the PhD class of 1950 who have never had a postdoctoral appointment, 10 percent applied for such an appointment but did not receive it or did not accept the appointment when it was offered. In comparison, 21 percent of the nonpostdoctorals of the 1960 PhD class made application for an appointment. The increase in the number of postdoctoral appointments is reflected in the fact that 17 percent of the 1950 nonpostdoctorals asserted that no such appointment was available, while only 4 percent of the 1960 nonpostdoctorals were unaware of postdoctoral opportunities.

---

[5] The frequency distribution of citations in each of the groups is highly skewed. The mean number of citations does not therefore adequately describe the behavior. Nevertheless, it is clear from our data that the former immediate is cited more often than the other two groups, especially if one discounts self-citations.

[6] The figures in the humanities indicate the reverse. Here the man who has had a delayed postdoctoral appointment averages a higher salary than one who has never taken an appointment, and the former immediate postdoctoral receives a higher salary than both.

Virtually all of those who did not take a postdoctoral appointment found other opportunities more attractive at the time. In retrospect, however, approximately 40 percent of those who have not had postdoctoral experience now wish they had taken or had been offered the opportunity. Their reasons were given previously in this chapter.

The academic scientists who had had an immediate postdoctoral appointment were asked to give three reasons for choosing the institution at which they did their postdoctoral work. Regardless of where they went, the prime reason given was to work with a particular scholar (mentioned by over 60 percent of the respondents). The other reasons varied according to the type or reputation of the postdoctoral institution. Thus, those who went to one of the ten leading universities or to a nonacademic institution frequently listed the reputation of the institution as a second reason for their choice. Those who went to other academic institutions mentioned the freedom to work in the field of their choice as being the second most important consideration. The third motivating factor in their choice of institution was highly variable. Those who took their appointments at one of the ten leading schools mentioned the superior facilities, equipment, and/or libraries. Those at the 20 other major schools indicated that their choice was influenced by the recommendation of their PhD mentor. Those who went to schools of lesser reputation admitted that a favorable geographic location had influenced their decision, while those who left the academic world to take their postdoctoral appointments divided their third most important consideration between the recommendation of their PhD mentor and the freedom to work in the field of their choice. Given low priority were personal considerations or the comparative attractiveness of stipends.

The former immediate postdoctorals tended to be satisfied with their appointments. When asked to respond to various aspects of their experience on a three-point scale, ranging from *unsatisfactory* through *satisfactory* to *highly satisfactory,* their replies were distributed as shown in Figure 10. Except for the opportunity to teach, the replies in every category varied from somewhat unsatisfactory to highly satisfactory. This quantitative display correlates with the previous discussion in this chapter.

The reactions of those who had delayed appointments are shown in Figure 11. Again mention was made of the scarcity of teaching opportunities, but there was a significantly greater satisfaction with the postdoctoral experience for those who were more mature when they took the appointment. Overall, 82 percent of the delayed postdoctorals described their experience as one of enhanced productivity, as compared with 73 percent of the immediate postdoctorals.

Finally, the former immediates were asked what, if anything, they would have changed if they could have altered their first postdoctoral experience.

## IMPLICATIONS FOR THE POSTDOCTORAL

Almost two thirds would have changed nothing. Those who were less than satisfied stressed dissatisfaction mainly with the institution that they chose (23 percent) and/or the faculty mentor with whom they worked (22 percent). Almost a quarter would have stayed longer, but 6 percent would not have stayed as long. One out of five wished that they had had more guidance, while one out of fourteen would have liked more independence. Four percent would have put off the experience for a period of time, and 6 percent would have avoided it altogether.

Any attempt to summarize these comments and statistics into a few sentences would be simplistic. There is no singular impact of immediate postdoctoral education on the participants or on the nonparticipants. Even when one takes into account field differences, future employment possibilities, and the quality of academic background, there are more subtle and individual considerations such as temperament, sense of independence, and degree of impa-

### FIGURE 10

Evaluation of Immediate Postdoctoral Experience by Academic Scientists (U.S. Males Only).

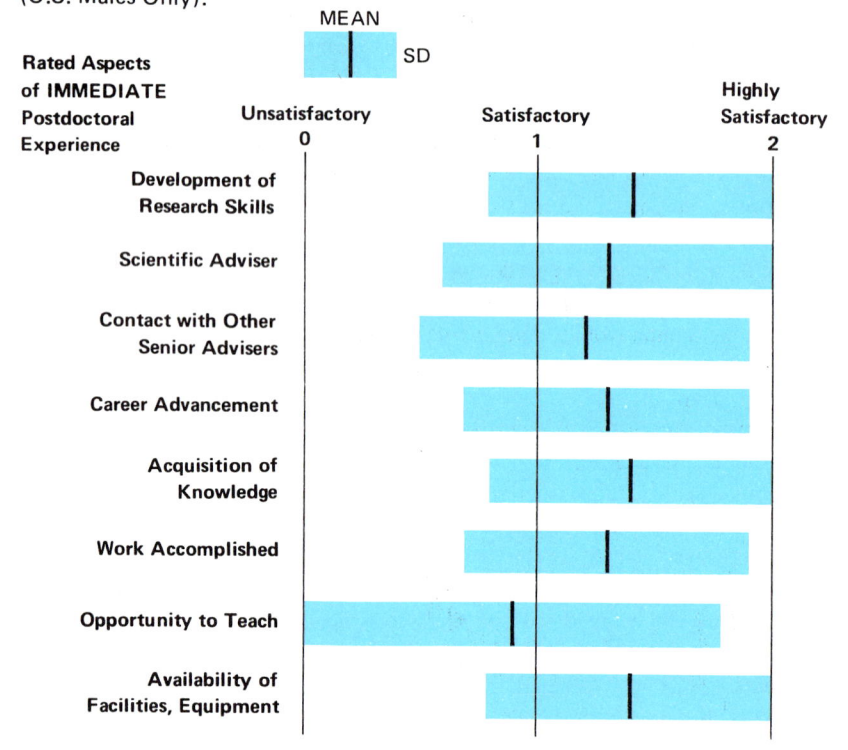

Source: NRC, Office of Scientific Personnel, Postdoctoral Experience Questionnaire.

## QUANTITATIVE ASPECTS OF THE POSTDOCTORAL EXPERIENCE

**FIGURE 11**
Evaluation of Delayed Postdoctoral Experience by Academic Scientists (U.S. Males Only).

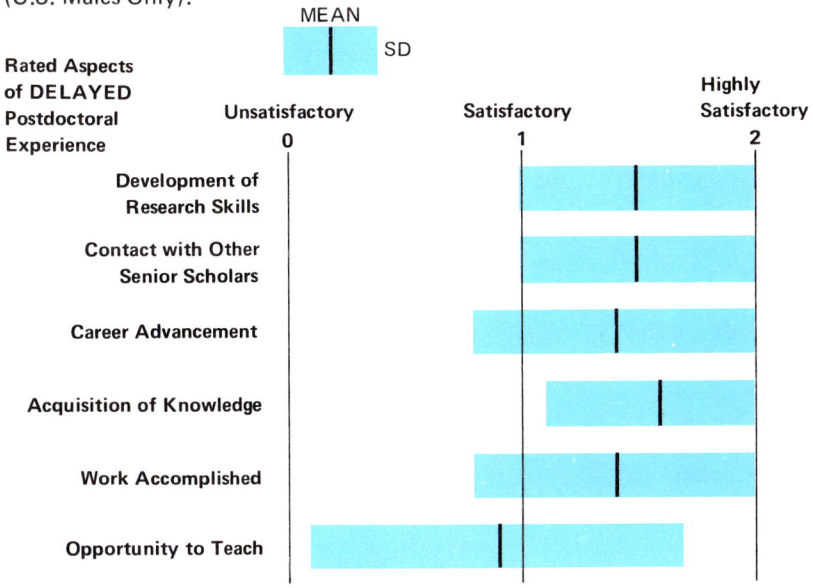

| Rated Aspects of DELAYED Postdoctoral Experience | Unsatisfactory 0 | Satisfactory 1 | Highly Satisfactory 2 |
|---|---|---|---|
| Development of Research Skills | | | |
| Contact with Other Senior Scholars | | | |
| Career Advancement | | | |
| Acquisition of Knowledge | | | |
| Work Accomplished | | | |
| Opportunity to Teach | | | |

Source: NRC, Office of Scientific Personnel, Postdoctoral Experience Questionnaire.

tience with the apprentice role. It is not necessary that the experience be a *sine qua non* in the creation of a scientist. It is sufficient that for a great many the lack of a postdoctoral opportunity would have been or is a detriment to the development of their scientific talents. Both the exceptional investigator and the more pedestrian one often benefit from the additional year or two of research under the guidance of a superior scientist and in the company of a group of similarly motivated apprentices.

Not all mentor–postdoctoral relationships are productive ones. To approve and even to encourage postdoctoral appointments for those who can benefit from them is not to condone every practice that is current. To say that 63 percent of the postdoctorals would have changed nothing in their experience is also to say that 37 percent found something amiss. Part of the reason for this absence of unanimity is the informality of postdoctoral education as it is practiced in the United States. There is no agreed-upon rationale for postdoctoral education by persons either in the individual disciplines or at the host institutions, and there are consequently no accepted criteria by which the nature of the individual experience can be judged. With this introduction we now turn to the impact of postdoctoral education on the universities.

**ACADEMIC INSTITUTIONS ARE**

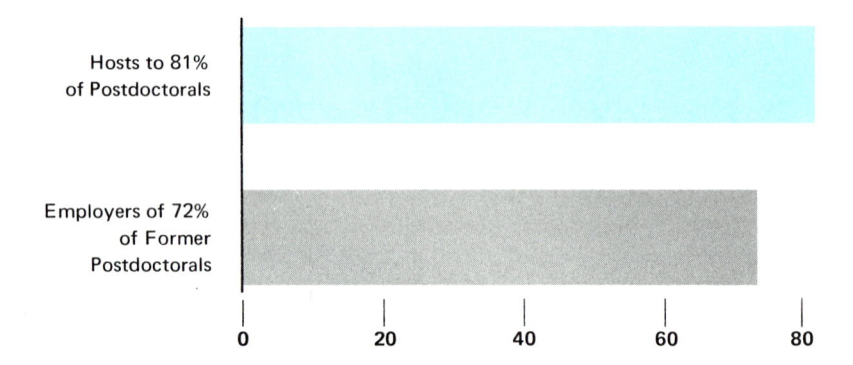

Hosts to 81% of Postdoctorals

Employers of 72% of Former Postdoctorals

0　　20　　40　　60　　80

CHAPTER **6**

# Implications for Academic Institutions

The university is central and dominant in the whole postdoctoral picture. Not only does it produce all of those who become postdoctorals and serve as host to most of the participants, but it is the major employer of most of the former postdoctorals. The impact of postdoctoral education on the universities is a pervasive one, affecting students, faculty, and administration.

On the other hand, universities participate unevenly in their relationship to postdoctorals. Generally speaking, the higher the reputation of the institution, the greater its involvement with the production, the hosting, and the recruitment for faculty positions of postdoctorals. As a consequence, it is difficult to typify the situation and to talk of "impact" in a singular sense. For many deans, faculty members, and students, acquaintanceship with postdoctoral study is by hearsay only, while for others it is a matter of daily experience. The same variability of existential knowledge can be found within a single institution as one moves from department to department and from dean to dean.

This unevenness of participation is illustrated for representative disciplines in Table 36. The distribution is even more skewed when one realizes that the number of institutions in each category gets larger as the reputation drops. While the top 30 schools produce 48 percent of the PhD's in physics, they produce 69 percent of the PhD's who take an immediate postdoctoral appointment. Similarly, these same schools serve as hosts for 68 percent of the physics postdoctorals at academic institutions. Not counting the medical schools,

TABLE 36 Participation in Postdoctoral Education in Three Fields, by Type of Academic Institution

| Measures of Participation in Postdoctoral Education | Ten Leading (10) | Twenty Other Major (20) | Established (38) | Developing (180) | Other More than half PhD faculty (104) | Less than half PhD faculty (900) |
|---|---|---|---|---|---|---|
| PHYSICS | | | | | | |
| Avg. no. of PhD's produced per inst. (1967) | 36.3 | 16.4 | 7.8 | 1.4 | 0.05 | 0.0 |
| Percent of PhD's taking postdoct. per inst. | 33 | 30 | 18 | 15 | 0 | — |
| Percent of inst. with depts having postdocts | 100 | 100 | 79 | 25 | 2 | 0 |
| Avg. no. of postdocts per dept. with postdocts | 27 | 15 | 9 | 3 | 2 | — |
| Percent new jr. faculty with postdoct. | 76 | 57 | 50 | 21 | 10 | 7 |
| BASIC MEDICAL SCIENCES | | | | | | |
| Avg. no. of PhD's produced per inst. (1967) | 25.3 | 15.2 | 8.2 | 1.9 | 0.2 | 0.0 |

| | | | | | | |
|---|---|---|---|---|---|---|
| Percent of PhD's taking postdoct. per inst. | 40 | 52 | 43 | 28 | 17 | — |
| Percent of inst. with depts having postdocts | 100 | 92 | 67 | 56 | 25 | 0 |
| Avg. no. of postdocts per dept. with postdocts | 13 | 14 | 5 | 3 | 1 | — |
| Percent new jr. faculty with postdoct. | 55 | 61 | 45 | 32 | 30 | — |
| SOCIAL SCIENCES | | | | | | |
| Avg. no. of PhD's produced per inst. (1967) | 77.7 | 46.3 | 16.8 | 4.5 | 0.1 | 0.0 |
| Percent of PhD's taking postdoct. per inst. | 5 | 4 | 1 | 2 | 0 | — |
| Percent of inst. with depts having postdocts | 60 | 32 | 13 | 5 | 0.5 | 0 |
| Avg. no. of postdocts per dept. with postdocts | 4 | 2 | 2 | 1 | 1 | 0 |
| Percent new jr. faculty with postdoct. | 6 | 7 | 5 | 5 | 4 | 1 |

Source: NRC, Office of Scientific Personnel, Postdoctoral Departmental Questionnaire.

the average number of postdoctorals from all fields per school in the ten leading institutions is 225, while the same figure for the 180 schools designated as developing institutions is only 4.6. Clearly the degree of institutional concern with postdoctorals can be expected to be much higher for those institutions with significant numbers of postdoctorals.

In the academic world then, there are two major features of postdoctoral activity. It is concentrated in a relatively few institutions and, within the institutions, it is mainly a departmental concern. Among those institutions that have sizable numbers of postdoctorals, the central administration performs essentially a "housekeeping" function. The demand for academic and research space by departments with many postdoctorals causes administrative personnel to become aware of the postdoctoral. Similarly, there is a suspicion, seldom backed by hard evidence, that the postdoctorals are costing the universities money, especially when they are not hired under faculty grants and contracts (see Chapter 9). Few universities have gathered any statistics, however, and only a few have made any concerted effort to maintain central surveillance over the postdoctoral activity on campus.

Typical of the leadership at most postdoctoral host institutions was a graduate dean of a university in the Northwest who mentioned several growing areas of concern to the administration. Among these were the selection process and the variation of stipends paid postdoctorals. He felt that the time was ripe for some formalization of departmental and institutional practices. His motivation was more pragmatic than philosophical; such a formalization was to be a consequence of the exhaustion of resources rather than an indication that there was an academic mission to be fulfilled.

In a poll of administrators at 140 universities, only three said that their institution actively promoted postdoctoral work and only about 10 percent suggested that there was considerable control by the central administration over postdoctoral appointments. The dean at a distinguished eastern university exercising considerable control, relatively speaking, over its postdoctoral appointments wrote as follows:

The extent of the review of postdoctoral fellows within individual departments varies. The principal responsibility lies with the individual faculty member who sponsors the postdoctoral fellow. . . . The department chairman is required to approve any recommendations for a postdoctoral fellow and in some departments he takes his responsibility quite seriously. In other departments, I'm sure, the process is routine. Finally the Dean of the Graduate School has to approve each appointment and each initial appointment must be accompanied by two letters of evaluation, including a letter from the supervisor of the dissertation, unless the fellow has won a national competitive postdoctoral fellowship. In this case we generally accept the fact of selection by a national committee as warrant of his credentials. The Dean has the right to refuse to appoint; but he seldom exercises this right. He has, however, raised questions of the quality of the proposed appointees.

## IMPLICATIONS FOR ACADEMIC INSTITUTIONS

The dean of another prominent eastern institution had this to say:

All postdoctorals and research associates have appointments that are approved by the Academic Council, the same body which approves all other faculty appointments. A *curriculum vitae* is submitted along with each recommendation and occasionally there is some discussion. Rarely, however, is a recommendation disapproved. Yet the existence of the mechanism is in itself a good control, probably the only one which would work.

At a west coast institution of the first rank the appointment procedure is described as follows: "Each postdoctoral fellow must have a faculty appointment that is carefully reviewed even if no salary is involved. We have three levels of appointment: research fellow, senior research fellow, and research associate. These have faculty rank as listed in our catalogue just below assistant professor, associate professor, and professor, respectively." One division of this institution has adopted rather stringent nomination procedures for postdoctorals. The faculty member who is to serve as mentor submits to the chairman a full dossier on the proposed candidate. The chairman reviews the dossier and, if he finds no critical problem, sends a memorandum to the department announcing that a person has been nominated and inviting the faculty to examine the dossier in his office. If no objection is raised, the appointment is processed through the central administration. If there is an objection, either by the chairman or by another faculty member, the question is generally talked out and resolved internally without making an issue of it. The justification given by the chairman for this rather elaborate screening is that they want to accept only those candidates they will be able to recommend highly on completion of their postdoctoral work.

But the situation at other prominent institutions is more typical. A dean at a major university in the Midwest wrote: "We have almost no controls. . . . Without question we and other universities should have controls that fit our policies. . . . The variation in qualifications of postdoctorals in a university like this one is far greater than the variation in credentials of either undergraduate or graduate students." Not only is there little central control over the quality of postdoctorals, but there is also little oversight with regard to numbers and treatment of postdoctorals. The spokesman for a major west coast university wrote: "It is a simple fact that we have no adequate control over the number or the use of postdoctoral fellows. What is needed is a recognition that they are now a fundamental part of the university community and that our procedures have to be developed to include them just as they once had to be strengthened to permit more adequate control of graduate students."

Not all administrators feel this way. Many are satisfied that the present laissez-faire approach is best. This point of view was expressed by a spokesman for a midwestern university: "The professors in a department are the only persons qualified to judge the qualifications of the postdoctoral candidate. They should be the ones to select the candidates in view of the personal relationships involved. Present departmental controls are adequate. Institution-wide controls should be avoided." The spokesman for another major midwestern university said: "The appointment of postdoctorals is initiated at the departmental level. I would not recommend changes. The academic standards of a given department are reviewed at the graduate and undergraduate level and there is a high correlation between the standards applied at these levels and at the postdoctoral level." A respondent at a distinguished eastern university concluded: "Our control is the good sense of the individual faculty member. Since the postdoctoral fellow . . . is usually recommended through the intimate and friendly relations between two faculty members, the selection process is probably as good as it can be."

There is the same general lack of anxiety over other questions that might be raised about the place of the postdoctoral in the academic community. Although a few administrators are aware of potential dangers, even fewer recommend taking any steps to mitigate them. Whether the issue is the contribution of postdoctorals to research or teaching, the competition with graduate students for space and faculty time, the adequacy of graduate programs, or the cost of postdoctoral activity to the university, most administrators believe either that what has evolved is adequate or that any steps to control or regulate the activity would do more harm than good. Such attitudes find strong support from the faculty, who currently have a relatively free hand and who doubt that institutional participation in the postdoctoral process can add anything positive. They have no desire to have the institutional invisibility of the postdoctoral removed at the expense of faculty initiative and independence. The chemistry chairman of a southern unviersity spoke for many of his faculty colleagues across the country when he stated that "the university as such does not have postdoctorals nor a policy toward postdoctorals. Individual faculty mentors have both."

If a postdoctoral were analogous to a faculty member's private library, such a statement might go unchallenged; but the postdoctoral does not exist on an academic shelf. He has a number of points of contact with students, with other faculty, and with the administration that is responsible for providing the space he occupies. In a department where the resources, both human and material, are underutilized, the addition of postdoctorals may not infringe on the activities of others. This situation (which describes many institutions) permits the indifference of the administration and the independence of the faculty. In an institution that is already crowded or at one that is being created *de novo*, there is a need to develop a rationale for postdoctoral study and a set of policies to implement it.

In a number of states, the acquisition of additional facilities from state budget committees or from legislatures requires justification in terms of enrollment. In California, for example, the planning for new buildings follows a formula that allots so many square feet for each faculty member, for each undergraduate, and for each graduate student. No space is permitted under the formula for postdoctorals. This does not mean that, after the space has been awarded, the internal division of that space cannot be made with postdoctorals in mind, but simply that the state does not recognize postdoctorals as having a legitimate claim on state resources with regard to space. The administration cannot educate the state until an institutional rationale is developed in which postdoctoral education takes its place within the complex milieu that is a modern university.

In developing that rationale the goals of the individual university will have to be taken into account. Moreover, the institution will have to consider the function and the impact of postdoctoral activity. In Chapter 4 we examined the diversity of the postdoctoral population and the motivations of the postdoctorals themselves. In Chapter 5 we described the benefits to the individual as well as some of his problems. We now examine the nature of postdoctoral activity within the university and its impact on students, on faculty, and on research.

## Effect on the Department

Since the postdoctoral makes his presence felt through the department, the degree of his impact depends on his relative number and quality compared to the other components in the department. The level of educational effort in representative fields as a function of the reputation of the school is shown in Figure 12. Since there are a number of schools not involved in research, we shall restrict ourselves in the description of the makeup of departments to those that have graduate programs, whether or not they have postdoctorals.

By almost any measure there is a strong correlation between reputation and department size. Whether one counts the full-time graduate students, full-time faculty, or postdoctorals, the average numbers of each tend to decrease as one goes down in reputation. There are, of course, excellent small departments and mediocre large ones, but these are likely to be the exception. What is more relevant to our investigation of postdoctorals is that pertinent ratios also change uniformly with reputation.

The chairman of the chemistry department of a prestigious eastern university testified to the importance of having postdoctorals in a graduate department. He suggested that fewer than one postdoctoral to every ten graduate students renders the impact of postdoctorals on the department negligible. However, he felt that the ratio in his own department of one postdoctoral

**FIGURE 12**
Percentage of Departments by Highest Level of Educational Activity, by Type of Academic Institution.

**151**

EFFECT ON THE DEPARTMENT

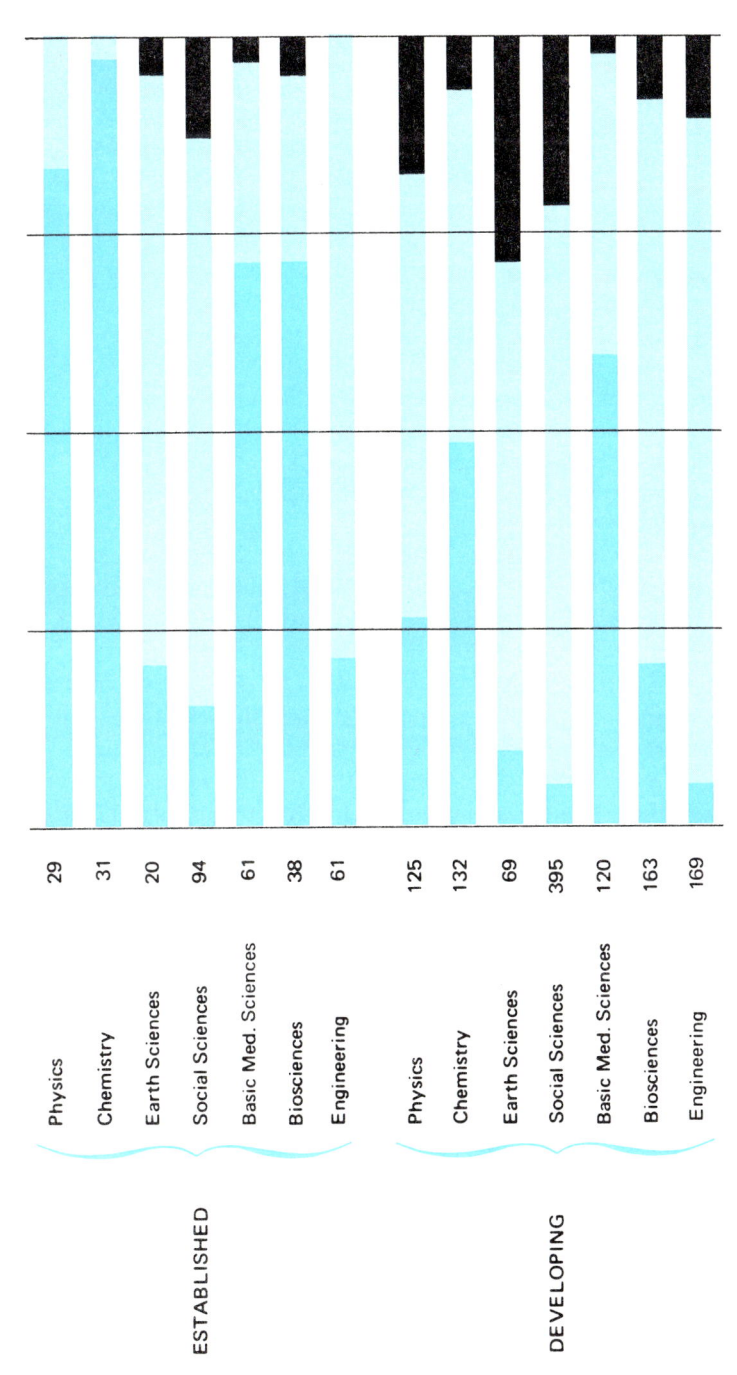

| | |
|---|---|
| Physics | 29 |
| Chemistry | 31 |
| Earth Sciences | 20 |
| Social Sciences | 94 |
| Basic Med. Sciences | 61 |
| Biosciences | 38 |
| Engineering | 61 |

ESTABLISHED

| | |
|---|---|
| Physics | 125 |
| Chemistry | 132 |
| Earth Sciences | 69 |
| Social Sciences | 395 |
| Basic Med. Sciences | 120 |
| Biosciences | 163 |
| Engineering | 169 |

DEVELOPING

Source: NRC, Office of Scientific Personnel, Postdoctoral Departmental Questionnaire.

## IMPLICATIONS FOR ACADEMIC INSTITUTIONS

for every two graduate students seemed to be somewhat larger than necessary. We shall return later to the reasons why graduate departments, qua departments, desire postdoctorals, but the chairman's suggested density is a useful one for the present. If we examine Table 37, which displays the data on departmental size and composition, we see that all of those departments of chemistry and the basic medical sciences that have postdoctorals have fewer than ten graduate students per postdoctoral, with the density of postdoctorals increasing with increasing reputation. At the other end of the scale are engineering, the social sciences, and geology (except at the ten leading institutions), where the impact of postdoctorals is small. Physics and biology occupy an intermediate position.

With few exceptions, departments without postdoctorals tend to have fewer graduate students and faculty than departments with postdoctorals. Moreover, they tend to have fewer graduate students per faculty member. This statistic bears out the contention of many respondents that the presence of postdoctorals permits the training of more graduate students. The conjectured competition between graduate students and postdoctorals for faculty time and departmental space does not seem to occur; or, if it does, it occurs within institutions already exceeding most other institutions in graduate student/faculty ratios.

The relation of postdoctorals to the production of master's degrees and doctorates is somewhat less neat (see Table 38). Although there is a definite correlation between the number of graduates per faculty member at both levels (especially at the PhD level) and the reputation of the school, there is not the clean distinction between institutions with postdoctorals and those without. Perhaps one can discern in the data a tendency of schools without postdoctorals to concentrate more on master's level work, while those with postdoctorals seem to be more involved with doctoral programs.[1]

One of the most interesting correlations between graduate study and postdoctoral study is demonstrated in Table 39. Probably because of the subfields represented in departments with postdoctorals in contrast to those research areas in departments without postdoctorals, the immediate next activities of new PhD's are strikingly different, depending on the presence or absence of postdoctorals. In particular, departments with postdoctorals are much more likely to send their graduates on to postdoctoral appointments than the other departments and less likely to send them to industry or directly into an academic post. We shall discuss the implications of this effect further when we examine the impact of postdoctoral education on the nonacademic employers

---

[1] Engineering is unique among the fields shown in attributing professional status to the baccalaureate degree. The master's degree is therefore a postprofessional degree. At some institutions the engineering program is a 5-year program ending with the master's degree.

of doctoral recipients. For the moment it is clear that graduate study in the presence of postdoctorals results in significantly more graduates who take postdoctoral appointments. As indicated earlier, it also results in more graduates.

One of the more mechanical aspects of the impact of postdoctoral study on the academic institution is the space required for the postdoctoral and the time that a faculty member spends working with him. The answer in square feet or hours per week is not as useful as the comparison of these variables for postdoctorals with those for graduate students. There is also a large dependence on the nature of the research even within the same department. A theoretical physicist requires much less space than an experimental one. An experimental solid state man may need a smaller laboratory than an experimentalist working on an accelerator. Recognizing the importance of these differences and yet not being able to make the fine distinctions required, we present in Figure 13 the responses from the faculty with regard to the comparison between postdoctorals and graduate students on time and space requirements respectively. There is surprisingly little difference among the departmental averages. To summarize the findings, a postdoctoral takes up about half as much time of the faculty as a graduate student and requires about a third more space.

It is not surprising that those institutions heavily involved in postdoctoral work are also those with faculty who themselves have had postdoctoral experience. Table 40 displays this effect. Only the earth sciences, where postdoctoral work is considered less essential, breaks the pattern of significant differences between schools with postdoctorals and those without.

This pattern of faculty backgrounds is not likely to change if the present hiring practices at institutions continue. In Table 41 we show for several fields the distribution by previous positions of newly hired junior faculty in departments having graduate programs. Except for engineering, earth sciences, and social sciences, institutions that have postdoctorals hire more of their new faculty from postdoctoral positions than from any other background. No such preference is seen for departments without postdoctorals. In fact, they tend to get their faculty straight from the PhD. Over 90 percent of the new faculty in departments with postdoctorals have the PhD degree when they join the department. Departments without postdoctorals are less successful in attracting doctorate holders.

Contrary to popular conception, however, departments on the whole do not hire their own postdoctorals for faculty positions. When the time comes to hire new faculty one's own postdoctorals are considered, of course, but along with other candidates outside the department, both postdoctoral and nonpostdoctoral. Only among certain of the ten leading institutions are more postdoctorals hired from within than from without. This occurs more often in physics and engineering and almost never in chemistry departments.

TABLE 37 Faculty and Students in Selected Graduate Departments with and without Postdoctorals, by Type of Academic Institution

<table>
<tr><th rowspan="3">Faculty and Students</th><th rowspan="3">Graduate Department</th><th colspan="8">Number of Persons by Type of Academic Institution</th></tr>
<tr><th colspan="2">Ten Leading</th><th colspan="2">Twenty Other Major</th><th colspan="2">Established</th><th colspan="2">Developing</th></tr>
<tr><th>with Postdoctorals</th><th>without Postdoctorals</th><th>with Postdoctorals</th><th>without Postdoctorals</th><th>with Postdoctorals</th><th>without Postdoctorals</th><th>with Postdoctorals</th><th>without Postdoctorals</th></tr>
<tr><td rowspan="7">Full-time faculty</td><td>Physics</td><td>44.7</td><td>—</td><td>38.5</td><td>—</td><td>23.5</td><td>14.4</td><td>19.4</td><td>10.4</td></tr>
<tr><td>Chemistry</td><td>31.2</td><td>—</td><td>28.2</td><td>—</td><td>20.9</td><td>13.0</td><td>17.0</td><td>10.5</td></tr>
<tr><td>Earth sci.</td><td>19.5</td><td>—</td><td>13.4</td><td>11.4</td><td>9.5</td><td>8.2</td><td>10.3</td><td>7.8</td></tr>
<tr><td>Social sci.</td><td>27.0</td><td>25.1</td><td>26.5</td><td>21.3</td><td>16.1</td><td>15.0</td><td>16.7</td><td>11.3</td></tr>
<tr><td>Basic med. sci.</td><td>13.4</td><td>—</td><td>15.9</td><td>—</td><td>10.9</td><td>5.8</td><td>7.3</td><td>6.7</td></tr>
<tr><td>Biosciences</td><td>19.9</td><td>15.0</td><td>21.8</td><td>11.1</td><td>19.7</td><td>13.1</td><td>14.9</td><td>11.5</td></tr>
<tr><td>Engineering</td><td>39.5</td><td>42.3</td><td>24.4</td><td>19.1</td><td>25.8</td><td>11.8</td><td>11.4</td><td>10.8</td></tr>
<tr><td rowspan="7">Full-time graduate students per full-time faculty</td><td>Physics</td><td>4.7</td><td>—</td><td>3.6</td><td>—</td><td>3.7</td><td>3.0</td><td>2.6</td><td>1.7</td></tr>
<tr><td>Chemistry</td><td>5.5</td><td>—</td><td>5.4</td><td>—</td><td>4.4</td><td>3.5</td><td>3.0</td><td>1.6</td></tr>
<tr><td>Earth sci.</td><td>3.1</td><td>—</td><td>3.3</td><td>3.2</td><td>3.2</td><td>3.4</td><td>3.3</td><td>1.9</td></tr>
<tr><td>Social sci.</td><td>4.2</td><td>4.7</td><td>4.1</td><td>3.5</td><td>3.6</td><td>3.3</td><td>3.8</td><td>2.3</td></tr>
<tr><td>Basic med. sci.</td><td>3.4</td><td>—</td><td>1.7</td><td>—</td><td>2.4</td><td>2.4</td><td>2.1</td><td>1.8</td></tr>
<tr><td>Biosciences</td><td>3.5</td><td>2.1</td><td>3.0</td><td>3.0</td><td>2.7</td><td>4.1</td><td>2.7</td><td>2.1</td></tr>
<tr><td>Engineering</td><td>4.9</td><td>3.2</td><td>4.7</td><td>3.3</td><td>3.6</td><td>2.4</td><td>3.5</td><td>1.8</td></tr>
</table>

|  |  |  |  |  |  |
|---|---|---|---|---|---|
| Postdoctorals per full-time faculty | Physics | 0.6 | — | 0.4 | — | 0.4 | — | 0.2 | — |
|  | Chemistry | 1.5 | — | 0.9 | — | 0.7 | — | 0.3 | — |
|  | Earth sci. | 0.4 | — | 0.2 | — | 0.2 | — | 0.2 | — |
|  | Social sci. | 0.2 | — | 0.1 | — | 0.1 | — | 0.1 | — |
|  | Basic med. sci. | 1.0 | — | 0.9 | — | 0.5 | — | 0.4 | — |
|  | Biosciences | 0.5 | — | 0.2 | — | 0.3 | — | 0.2 | — |
|  | Engineering | 0.2 | — | 0.1 | — | 0.1 | — | 0.1 | — |
| Full-time graduate students per postdoctoral | Physics | 7.8 | — | 9.1 | — | 9.6 | — | 16.3 | — |
|  | Chemistry | 3.7 | — | 5.7 | — | 6.8 | — | 8.7 | — |
|  | Earth sci. | 7.5 | — | 16.6 | — | 20.2 | — | 42.5 | — |
|  | Social sci. | 25.2 | — | 45.4 | — | 32.2 | — | 49.0 | — |
|  | Basic med. sci. | 3.5 | — | 1.0 | — | 5.0 | — | 4.8 | — |
|  | Biosciences | 6.8 | — | 8.3 | — | 8.9 | — | 17.5 | — |
|  | Engineering | 23.3 | — | 44.5 | — | 29.1 | — | 30.5 | — |

Source: NRC, Office of Scientific Personnel, Postdoctoral Departmental Questionnaire.

TABLE 38  Graduate Degrees Granted per Year per Faculty Member in Departments with and without Postdoctorals, by Type of Academic Institution

| Graduate Degrees per Faculty Member | Graduate Department | Ten Leading with Postdoctorals | Ten Leading without Postdoctorals | Twenty Other Major with Postdoctorals | Twenty Other Major without Postdoctorals | Established with Postdoctorals | Established without Postdoctorals | Developing with Postdoctorals | Developing without Postdoctorals |
|---|---|---|---|---|---|---|---|---|---|
| Master's degrees per faculty member | Physics | .71 | — | .48 | — | .49 | .54 | .40 | .45 |
| | Chemistry | .62 | — | .39 | — | .36 | 1.54 | .35 | .34 |
| | Earth sci. | .48 | — | .46 | .40 | .78 | .59 | .56 | .38 |
| | Social sci. | .74 | .80 | .52 | .56 | .54 | .61 | .58 | .50 |
| | Basic med. sci. | .54 | — | .11 | — | .27 | .33 | .29 | .30 |
| | Biosciences | .58 | .07 | .36 | .39 | .35 | .67 | .48 | .53 |
| | Engineering | 1.67 | 1.30 | 1.19 | 1.86 | 1.31 | .95 | 1.28 | .98 |
| PhD degrees per faculty member | Physics | .57 | — | .35 | — | .31 | .19 | .17 | .12 |
| | Chemistry | .87 | — | .67 | — | .55 | .15 | .29 | .15 |
| | Earth sci. | .47 | — | .43 | .51 | .35 | .18 | .35 | .09 |
| | Social sci. | .44 | .49 | .40 | .24 | .47 | .22 | .28 | .13 |
| | Basic med. sci. | .41 | — | .17 | — | .30 | .38 | .21 | .16 |
| | Biosciences | .39 | .18 | .35 | .40 | .21 | .36 | .18 | .12 |
| | Engineering | .49 | .29 | .39 | .35 | .29 | .15 | .22 | .10 |

Source: NRC, Office of Scientific Personnel, Postdoctoral Departmental Questionnaire.

TABLE 39  First Employment of 1967 Doctorates from Departments with and without Postdoctorals

Percentage of 1967 Doctorates by Department

| Type of First Employment | Physics with Postdoctorals | Physics without Postdoctorals | Chemistry with Postdoctorals | Chemistry without Postdoctorals | Earth Sciences with Postdoctorals | Earth Sciences without Postdoctorals | Basic Medical Sciences with Postdoctorals | Basic Medical Sciences without Postdoctorals | Biosciences with Postdoctorals | Biosciences without Postdoctorals | Engineering with Postdoctorals | Engineering without Postdoctorals | Social Sciences with Postdoctorals | Social Sciences without Postdoctorals |
|---|---|---|---|---|---|---|---|---|---|---|---|---|---|---|
| Academic appointment | 36 | 38 | 22 | 25 | 40 | 48 | 33 | 42 | 53 | 65 | 28 | 38 | 67 | 76 |
| Postdoctoral appointment | 24 | 8 | 27 | 14 | 16 | 1 | 41 | 24 | 27 | 13 | 5 | 1 | 5 | 2 |
| Industrial research | 19 | 24 | 37 | 46 | 17 | 31 | 8 | 14 | 4 | 4 | 52 | 48 | 3 | 3 |
| Government research | 15 | 18 | 8 | 5 | 15 | 12 | 12 | 12 | 8 | 13 | 8 | 7 | 12 | 9 |
| Other | 7 | 13 | 6 | 10 | 12 | 8 | 5 | 8 | 9 | 5 | 7 | 4 | 15 | 10 |
| Total | 101 | 101 | 100 | 100 | 100 | 100 | 99 | 100 | 101 | 100 | 100 | 98 | 102 | 100 |

Source: NRC, Office of Scientific Personnel, Postdoctoral Departmental Questionnaire.

TABLE 40 Percentage of Faculty with Postdoctoral Background and Percentage Who Are Postdoctoral Mentors in Departments with and without Postdoctorals

|  | Graduate Department | Percentage of Faculty by Type of Academic Institution ||||||||
|  |  | Ten Leading || Twenty Other Major || Established || Developing ||
|  |  | with Postdoctorals | without Postdoctorals | with Postdoctorals | without Postdoctorals | with Postdoctorals | without Postdoctorals | with Postdoctorals | without Postdoctorals |
| --- | --- | --- | --- | --- | --- | --- | --- | --- | --- |
| Faculty with postdoctoral background | Physics | 50 | — | 55 | — | 55 | 34 | 36 | 18 |
|  | Chemistry | 66 | — | 63 | — | 59 | 31 | 45 | 26 |
|  | Earth sciences | 34 | — | 25 | 29 | 0 | 17 | 34 | 16 |
|  | Social sciences | 44 | 32 | 29 | 24 | 23 | 14 | 21 | 10 |
|  | Basic med. sci. | 73 | — | 66 | — | 68 | 34 | 57 | 36 |
|  | Biosciences | 62 | 48 | 49 | 45 | 42 | 33 | 40 | 19 |
|  | Engineering | 20 | 8 | 18 | 9 | 21 | 5 | 8 | 5 |
| Faculty as postdoctoral mentors | Physics | 47 | — | 27 | — | 22 | — | 12 | — |
|  | Chemistry | 52 | — | 40 | — | 33 | — | 18 | — |
|  | Earth sciences | 22 | — | 17 | — | 12 | — | 15 | — |
|  | Social sciences | 12 | — | 7 | — | 8 | — | 11 | — |
|  | Basic med. sci. | 36 | — | 36 | — | 32 | — | 29 | — |
|  | Biosciences | 40 | — | 21 | — | 18 | — | 12 | — |
|  | Engineering | 11 | — | 12 | — | 10 | — | 8 | — |

Source: NRC, Office of Scientific Personnel, Postdoctoral Departmental Questionnaire.

**159**
EFFECT ON THE DEPARTMENT

## FIGURE 13
Faculty Time and Departmental Space Requirements for Postdoctorals as Compared with Requirements for Graduate Students.

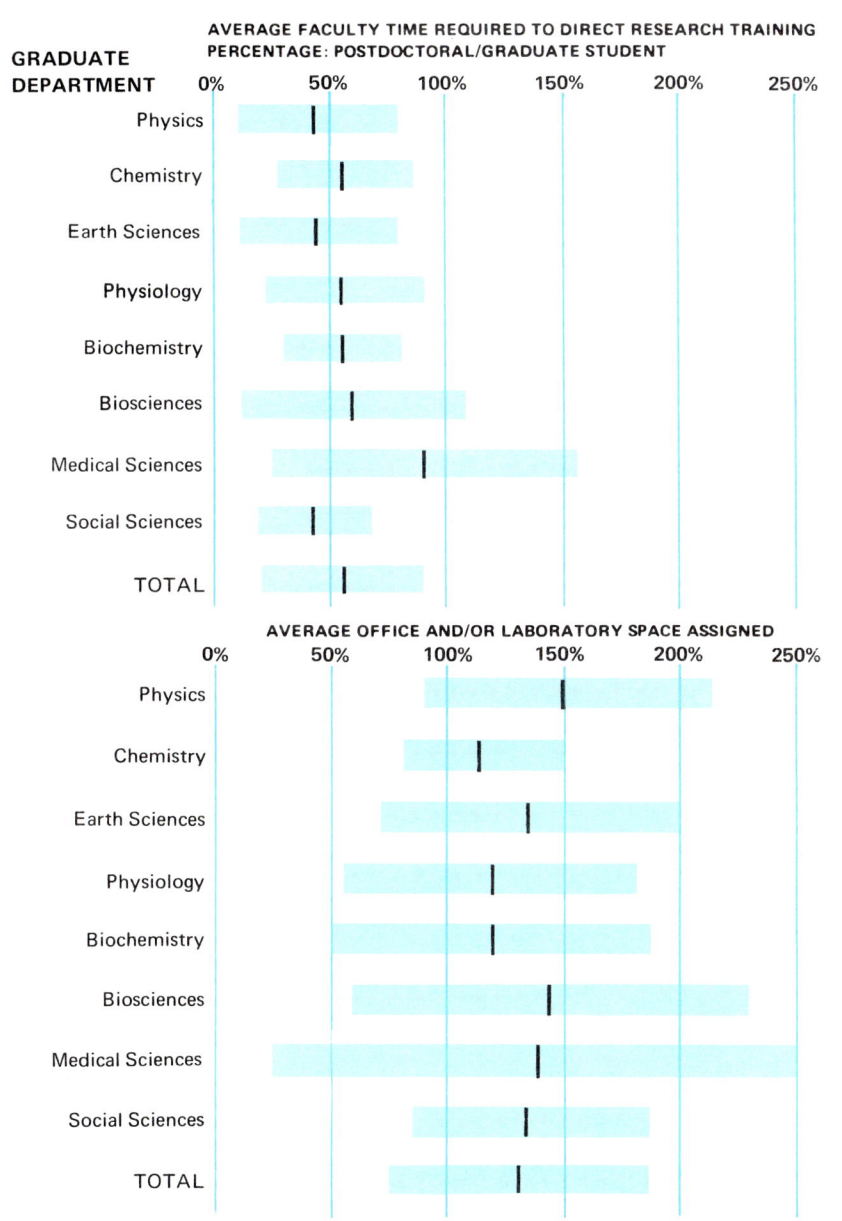

AVERAGE FACULTY TIME REQUIRED TO DIRECT RESEARCH TRAINING
PERCENTAGE: POSTDOCTORAL/GRADUATE STUDENT

GRADUATE DEPARTMENT
- Physics
- Chemistry
- Earth Sciences
- Physiology
- Biochemistry
- Biosciences
- Medical Sciences
- Social Sciences
- TOTAL

AVERAGE OFFICE AND/OR LABORATORY SPACE ASSIGNED
- Physics
- Chemistry
- Earth Sciences
- Physiology
- Biochemistry
- Biosciences
- Medical Sciences
- Social Sciences
- TOTAL

Source: NRC, Office of Scientific Personnel, Postdoctoral Faculty Questionnaire

TABLE 41 Previous Position of Newly Appointed Junior Faculty in Departments with and without Postdoctorals

| Graduate Department | Percentage of New Junior Faculty by Previous Position ||||||| New Jr. Faculty with PhD (%) |
| --- | --- | --- | --- | --- | --- | --- | --- |
| | Faculty at Other Inst. | Postdoctoral | New PhD | Still Graduate Student | Nonacademic Position | Total | |
| WITH POSTDOCTORALS | | | | | | | |
| Physics | 16 | 51 | 21 | 3 | 9 | 100 | 93 |
| Chemistry | 14 | 54 | 21 | 2 | 10 | 100 | 94 |
| Earth sciences | 12 | 22 | 41 | 5 | 20 | 100 | 91 |
| Social sciences | 17 | 9 | 46 | 23 | 4 | 99 | 70 |
| Basic med. sci. | 20 | 50 | 21 | 1 | 8 | 100 | 95 |
| Biosciences | 21 | 45 | 26 | 4 | 4 | 100 | 92 |
| Engineering | 11 | 17 | 51 | 3 | 18 | 100 | 91 |
| WITHOUT POSTDOCTORALS | | | | | | | |
| Physics | 15 | 18 | 37 | 16 | 15 | 101 | 70 |
| Chemistry | 18 | 28 | 28 | 9 | 17 | 100 | 78 |
| Earth sciences | 19 | 7 | 38 | 20 | 16 | 100 | 61 |
| Social sciences | 27 | 4 | 25 | 36 | 7 | 99 | 51 |
| Basic med. sci. | 23 | 24 | 35 | 7 | 11 | 100 | 86 |
| Biosciences | 25 | 16 | 34 | 19 | 6 | 100 | 73 |
| Engineering | 11 | 3 | 42 | 23 | 22 | 101 | 62 |

Source: NRC, Office of Scientific Personnel, Postdoctoral Departmental Questionnaire.

Finally, the difference between having and not having postdoctorals in the department is strongly reflected in the degree and intensity of the research being done in the department. Table 42 displays these differences according to three separate measures: the fraction of the faculty doing research, the fraction of the faculty receiving extramural research support, and the average number of research dollars per supported faculty member. The disparity between departments with and without postdoctorals is striking. Not displayed but again present in the data are the uniformly decreasing numbers as one goes down in reputation among the universities.

None of these results is unexpected and we might be charged with merely quantifying what everyone knew or suspected all along. More seriously, it might be suggested that we have confused the cause with the effect; it is not the presence of postdoctorals that has attracted the students, the research faculty, and the research dollars, but rather it is the faculty itself which has attracted the other three. We would agree, but go on to argue that, after a steady state situation has arisen, the department as a whole takes on the character of being involved with research and graduate education as a kind of *élan vital.* It becomes the place to be for all the components. From our data it appears that the most salient measure of the presence or absence of this *élan vital* is the presence or absence of postdoctorals. In colloquial terms, postdoctorals are "where the action is" and vice versa.

It becomes important, therefore, to understand why some departments (and, more particularly, the faculty of these departments) desire postdoctorals. It is also of interest to inquire why some departments do not have and, in some cases, do not desire postdoctorals.

## Teaching by Postdoctorals

From the department's point of view, the major reason for having postdoctorals is their contribution to teaching and research. The chairman of the department of physics at a major west coast institution expressed the attitude of most chairmen in fields where postdoctoral study is abundant by stating, "Although the postdoctoral experience is an extremely valuable one for the postdoctoral, at our university the postdoctoral contributes more than he takes away." Another chairman found the postdoctoral not only useful in carrying out research activities, but critical to the informal teaching that is valuable in a productive department. He said, "The postdoctoral is both being productive and being educated." The president of a distinguished university expressed the dominant opinion when he wrote:

TABLE 42  Degree of Faculty Involvement in Research in Departments with and without Postdoctorals

| Graduate Department | | Percentage of Faculty in Research | Percentage of Faculty with Extramural Research Support | Research Support (in $1,000's) per Faculty Member with Extramural Support |
|---|---|---|---|---|
| Physics | With postdoctorals | 91 | 76 | 53 |
|  | Without postdoctorals | 62 | 29 | 20 |
| Chemistry | With postdoctorals | 90 | 68 | 32 |
|  | Without postdoctorals | 69 | 31 | 8 |
| Earth sciences | With postdoctorals | 95 | 64 | 32 |
|  | Without postdoctorals | 81 | 47 | 21 |
| Social sciences | With postdoctorals | 88 | 52 | 26 |
|  | Without postdoctorals | 67 | 24 | 14 |
| Basic med. sci. | With postdoctorals | 94 | 86 | 35 |
|  | Without postdoctorals | 92 | 74 | 16 |
| Biosciences | With postdoctorals | 91 | 75 | 31 |
|  | Without postdoctorals | 74 | 38 | 14 |
| Engineering | With postdoctorals | 83 | 69 | 50 |
|  | Without postdoctorals | 64 | 42 | 19 |

Source: NRC, Office of Scientific Personnel, Postdoctoral Departmental Questionnaire.

## TEACHING BY POSTDOCTORALS

Postdoctoral studies have great advantages both to the individual and to the sponsoring institution. They provide a period for productive, significant research work at a most critical and creative period in a scholar's life. They not only enrich the scholarly atmosphere of the sponsoring institution and its members, but they help the institution furnish unusually gifted and well-trained supervision for graduate students. They enable the institution to evaluate exceptional individuals . . . for possible admission to the junior faculty, and they afford a stimulating association for senior scholars.

Since the definition of a postdoctoral appointment involves research, it is not surprising that one of the uses of the postdoctoral is in that area. What is less expected and less well known outside the academic world is that the postdoctoral also contributes to teaching.[2] This is particularly unexpected when many of the project associates are being paid full time for research.

Much of the teaching, however, is closely associated with the research and some of it is done unconsciously by example rather than explicitly by lecturing. A professor of chemistry commented:

> I am not sure that the teaching function of the postdoctoral within a research group has been sufficiently recognized. The postdoctorals, even the foreign ones, perform a continuous teaching function with an intimate contact that the professors cannot quite manage. The education of the graduate student is made more efficient and his knowledge gains a higher degree of sophistication because of postdoctorals in a given research group.

A colleague at another university described the process more fully by saying:

> Postdoctorals . . . set a standard and serve as an image for graduate students as well as helping them and guiding them in the laboratory. They show the graduate students what a young researcher can do and what they themselves can become.

The effectiveness of the postdoctoral as a graduate teacher is usually explained by the closeness in age and the lack of formal status that permit an identification between the two. Graduate students are "generally very happy to be able to waste a good number of silly questions on their postdoctoral colleagues rather than have to display their ignorance to their faculty research directors," as one graduate dean put it. Many faculty and chairmen have testified to the multiplying effect of postdoctorals. Many faculty members feel that the presence of postdoctorals, rather than crowding out the graduate students, permits the professor to take on more graduate students, with the postdoctoral acting as a surrogate faculty. A chemistry professor on the west coast introduced the idea of the "cascade effect," by which the professor's teaching effect is extended by the teaching of his postdoctorals and graduate students. He figured that, while a professor taught only six hours a week, the combined

---

[2] However, see Harold Orlans, *The Effects of Federal Programs on Higher Education*, The Brookings Institution, 1962, pp. 79-88, for earlier testimony to teaching by postdoctorals.

teaching by himself, his postdoctorals, and his graduate students totalled more than 30 hours a week. This group total must be compared, he insisted, with the 10 to 15 hours a week taught by professors before World War II when there were few graduate students and postdoctorals. Although this reasoning is open to question and to modification in other research groups, there is an effect here that is not usually recognized.

The dean of science at a major university suggests and then rejects three alternative ways that a university might enjoy the same teaching benefits that postdoctorals provide. These are the following: hiring more professors (rejected because of expense and the need for coordinated research projects), restoring the rank of instructor or hiring more assistant professors (rejected, since faculty members should not work for other faculty members), and hiring more technical support personnel (rejected because of the expense and commitment required to retain high quality people). In short, the postdoctoral, with his tenure of only one or two years, satisfies the needs and has none of the shortcomings of the alternatives.

In contrast to the chorus of testimony to the effectiveness of this kind of informal teaching by postdoctorals, there is much less uniformity of opinion about the desirability of a formal teaching experience for the postdoctorals. One third of the graduate deans polled indicated that as future academics, if for no other reason, postdoctorals should be involved in teaching. A characteristic reply from a dean was:

> I am concerned that postdoctoral programs keep so many of our young scholars from teaching. I am convinced that most of our present postdoctoral students could contribute to and learn from a teaching experience. I should, therefore, encourage those responsible for postdoctoral programs to permit limited teaching in the early postdoctoral years. At our institution we do use some of our postdoctoral students as teaching assistants, lecturers, etc., in both graduate and undergraduate courses. This is voluntary and remunerated with a small payment.

More deans express concern with the disassociation of postdoctorals from teaching than provide solutions for the problem. Thus, the dean at another institution wrote:

> The holder of a postdoctoral appointment during his formative years loses his awareness of the complete picture of the conventional academic man. The postdoctoral fellow misses the fact that he has personal responsibility for the running of the affairs of the community of scholars to which he belongs.

The dean at a midwestern school commented:

> For those bound toward academic positions, postdoctoral specialization unfortunately seems to intensify . . . disengagement from those institutional responsibilities and interests outside the research realm. . . . Research and scholarship are in the very nature of a

university, but the typical postdoctoral fellow is given little opportunity for or encouragement toward general involvement in other aspects of academic life.

Neither dean offered a remedy.

A few institutions have gone beyond encouragement to involve postdoctorals in teaching. Especially in medical centers, but not solely in clinical departments, teaching is seen as an integral part of the postdoctoral experience. The chairman of a department of physiology gave the following description and prescription:

> We give training in teaching to both graduate students and all postdoctorals while they are in our institution. All of those in attendance participate in all of the activities of this department and I think it should be thus everywhere. The postdoctoral who is too good to do anything except his research is not receiving proper education. . . . We do research, but we do not think of ourselves as a research institute with medical students and undergraduates as inconveniences. . . . We tend to train people to do what we do.

Some departments have appointed "research instructorships," positions that reflect a mixture of the "research postdoctoral" and the "teaching instructorship." The particular mixture and its implementation varies among departments. Of special note in this regard are the named instructorships in mathematics. A number of schools have introduced limited-term instructorships under which a man does research while teaching a reduced load. This approach is especially appropriate to mathematics, where research is a more lonely enterprise. One professor of mathematics pointed out that taking on a postdoctoral does not enhance the professor's research, but in fact lessens the amount he is able to accomplish. There is little that the postdoctoral can do to help the professor's research, and whatever time the professor spends with the postdoctoral is not spent on his own work. In expressing the benefits that the C. L. Moore Instructorships have brought to the Department of Mathematics at MIT, Professor William T. Martin said:

> They have brought a stream of exceptionally able young mathematicians here who have been a wonderful stimulus and example to the graduate students, as well as providing us with some very excellent formal teaching. The department could never have so many young men competing for tenure as assistant professors and the teaching the Moore Instructors provide is therefore a bargain at the price.

The proposition that postdoctorals should have a teaching experience during their appointment is not held unanimously, however, even among graduate deans. A number felt that the postdoctoral's chief and proper business was to devote himself to research and that it would negate the purpose of his appointment to involve him significantly in other duties. A southern dean wrote: "I believe there is no place in the postdoctoral programs for teaching. . . . The postdoctoral appointment should be primarily for research." The dean at a major university asserted: "It does not follow that postdoctorals should be awarded for the purpose of giving the student training in teaching. . . . This should be obtained by other means. . . . It would appear to spread one's postdoctoral program very thin to include teaching . . . as a part of it." The dean at another leading university put it this way:

> The central purpose of postdoctoral education is the stimulating interaction between the professor and the Fellow. As a result of this experience, both the individual and the institution can assesss, with greater validity, the nature of the Fellow's aptitude and professional interests. The central question, for both the individual and the institution, is not whether the Fellow will eventually become a suitable teacher or administrator but to what level of professional achievement he should aspire. Since this depends in a critical way on the level of his research talent, rather than his teaching or administrative ability, I do not feel there is a problem in the relative lack of attention to the latter.

The faculty tend to be more blunt about formal teaching by postdoctorals, but no less divided. One physics professor of international reputation found postdoctorals providing an interinstitutional atmosphere for the graduate students that was broadening. He felt that postdoctorals should teach and that institutions should pay them for it. "Make them light-load assistant professors, if you like." He is in a small minority among physicists, who generally agree that requiring postdoctorals to teach is one of the ways in which universities exploit them. In other fields a fair fraction of the respondents favored a light teaching load. Several biologists remarked specifically that for a man who will someday be a university professor, a year or two devoid of teaching serves only to intensify his dissatisfaction with teaching. As one remarked:

> Postdoctoral education is the backbone of the national research effort. If any change in the present system were to be made, it should be to [increase] somewhat the role of postdoctorals in teaching, since the program is also the source and strength of academic faculty.

Some of the faculty, usually those without postdoctorals, are in doubt about the benefit to be derived from interaction of postdoctorals and graduate students. One chemist expressed concern that increasing numbers of postdoctorals would reduce the amount of contact between faculty and graduate students. A number of faculty stated that they prefer working with graduate students and that the time and money spent on postdoctorals should go to predoctorals. One physicist found that where equipment was limited, the postdoctoral is often using the apparatus to the exclusion of other members of the group.

As with other aspects of postdoctoral education, the impact on the teaching responsibilities is very much a function of the experience of the observer.

TEACHING BY POSTDOCTORALS

It is too much to expect that everyone will support the concept; it is even less likely that there are no flaws. Most of the graduate students interviewed, for example, were either enthusiastic about their relationships with the postdoctorals or were at least neutral. One young chemist, who was well along with his research, however, complained that he spent all his time teaching each year's crop of postdoctorals how to use the equipment. Apparently the educational process works both ways.

In order to measure the involvement in teaching, we asked the postdoctorals to check off on a chart all the ways in which they participated in the teaching process. Table 43 gives the fraction of postdoctorals by field and citizenship who are involved in any kind of teaching and the fraction of the departments with postdoctorals that have a policy with regard to teaching by postdoctorals. Overall, 64 percent of the U. S. postdoctorals are teaching in some form or other. We can also see that the medical fields are much more concerned about teaching as a matter of policy.

TABLE 43  Involvement of Postdoctorals in Teaching, by Citizenship and Field

| Postdoctoral Field | Percentage of Postdoctorals Teaching U.S. | Foreign | Percentage of Departments Requiring Postdoctorals To Teach |
|---|---|---|---|
| Physics | 61 | 50 | 35 |
| Chemistry | 53 | 43 | 18 |
| Other physical sciences | 62 | 50 | 25 |
| Biochemistry | 57 | 41 | 54 |
| Other basic med. sci. | 72 | 55 |  |
| Biosciences | 59 | 49 | 22 |
| Internal medicine | 78 | 56 | 69 |
| Other clinical medicine | 81 | 54 |  |
| Allied medical sciences | 64 | 58 | 76 |
| Psychology | 58 | 46 | 24 |
| Social sciences | 50 | 30 |  |
| Arts and humanities | 27 | 34 | 5 |
| Education and professional | 53 | 57 | 18 |
| *Total* | 64 | 48 | 36 |

Source: NRC, Office of Scientific Personnel, Postdoctoral Census and Departmental Questionnaires.

TABLE 44  Percentage of Postdoctorals Who Teach, by Level and Types of Teaching and by Citizenship

Percentage of U.S. and Foreign Postdoctorals Who Teach, by Level and Type of Teaching

| Postdoctoral Field | Undergraduate Level Formal U.S. | Undergraduate Level Formal Foreign | Undergraduate Level Informal U.S. | Undergraduate Level Informal Foreign | Graduate Level Formal U.S. | Graduate Level Formal Foreign | Graduate Level Informal U.S. | Graduate Level Informal Foreign |
|---|---|---|---|---|---|---|---|---|
| Physics | 38 | 23 | 19 | 8 | 24 | 16 | 60 | 60 |
| Chemistry | 31 | 17 | 24 | 15 | 19 | 20 | 67 | 64 |
| Other physical sciences | 48 | 23 | 30 | 13 | 46 | 33 | 66 | 66 |
| Biochemistry | 18 | 16 | 15 | 13 | 42 | 24 | 64 | 55 |
| Other basic med. sci. | 41 | 36 | 19 | 16 | 53 | 34 | 52 | 50 |
| Biosciences | 34 | 20 | 25 | 17 | 45 | 31 | 66 | 62 |
| Internal medicine | 31 | 34 | 20 | 37 | 60 | 29 | 62 | 42 |
| Other clinical medicine | 32 | 39 | 22 | 30 | 58 | 39 | 48 | 49 |
| Allied medical sciences | 52 | 36 | 26 | 16 | 42 | 26 | 48 | 31 |
| Psychology | 41 | 46 | 28 | 18 | 28 | 27 | 49 | 64 |
| Social sciences | 37 | 16 | 21 | 5 | 23 | 16 | 54 | 58 |
| Arts and humanities | 48 | 36 | 29 | 36 | 39 | 36 | 32 | 57 |
| Education and professional | 27 | 20 | 22 | 19 | 40 | 28 | 44 | 41 |
| *Total* | 35 | 25 | 22 | 17 | 44 | 26 | 58 | 55 |

Note: The total for a field exceeds 100% because postdoctorals are doing more than one kind of teaching.

Source: NRC, Office of Scientific Personnel, Postdoctoral Census Questionnaire.

**TEACHING BY POSTDOCTORALS**

In Table 44, a breakdown of the kind of teaching that the postdoctorals do is presented (see also Figure 14). Since a postdoctoral may be involved in more than one kind of teaching, the percentages in each row sum to more than 100 percent. By formal teaching, we refer to the giving of lectures in a course, the leading of quiz or recitation sections of a course, or the giving of noncredit courses. Informal teaching includes participation in seminars, the supervision of laboratories, and the supervision of research activities. There is reason to believe that some of the postdoctorals did not recognize the informal instruction of graduate students in their group as "teaching" and as a result did not check the chart. Had they done so, the percentages would have been higher.

**FIGURE 14**

Percentage of Postdoctorals Who Teach, by Level and Type of Teaching and by Citizenship.

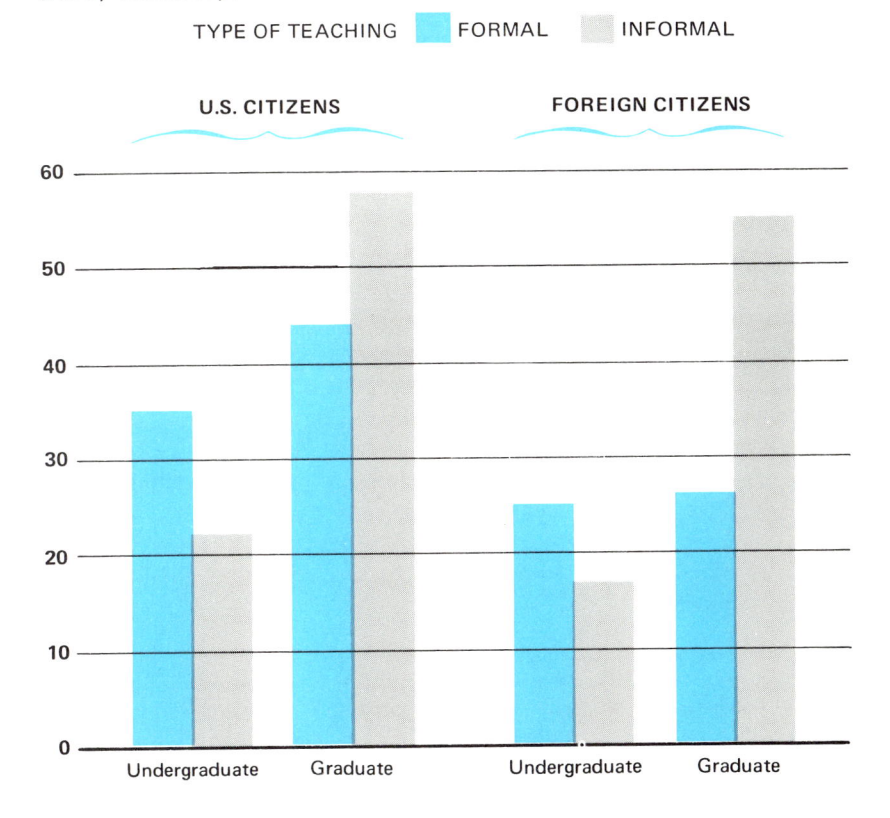

Source: NRC, Office of Scientific Personnel, Postdoctoral Census Questionnaire.

## IMPLICATIONS FOR ACADEMIC INSTITUTIONS

If the numbers in both Tables 43 and 44 are combined, we see that sizable proportions of the postdoctorals in some fields are engaged in formal undergraduate instruction. In physics, 23 percent of the U. S. postdoctorals give formal instruction to undergraduates; in the other physical sciences besides chemistry the percentage is 30. Furthermore, about 30 percent of the postdoctorals expressed a desire to have a greater opportunity to teach.

To measure how effective the teaching effort is, we asked the faculty to rank on a five-point scale the degree to which each component of his research group contributed to the effectiveness of the *faculty member's* teaching. The results are shown in Figure 15 where the bars stretch one standard deviation in each direction from the mean response.[3] It must be kept in mind that the question was phrased in relation to the professor's teaching effort, i.e., the degree to which the graduate students, postdoctorals, or research staff assisted the professor in his teaching. No evaluation is made of how well they did teaching their own formal courses. The surprising aspect of this evaluation is the light weight that professors give to the impact of postdoctorals (except in physics and chemistry) on the work with degree candidates.[4] From the verbal commentary above, one would have expected the impact to be larger. Also unexpected was the very small estimate of the influence of graduate students on each other. Most graduates tend to ascribe much of their learning to their peers.

## Contribution to Research

The other major reason departments and faculty want postdoctorals is their contribution to research. There is no doubt that the more mature postdoctoral is often able to be of greater assistance in the performance of research than the younger and as yet undeveloped graduate student. He does not have his research time cut up by courses, language study, or examinations. He often brings new points of view and new experimental techniques to the laboratory. Moreover, there is much testimony that not only do postdoctorals contribute to the quantity of research, but also to the quality. Over 73 percent of the university administrators assented to this statement. One from a midwestern university stated:

> I believe that the postdoctoral commitment has contributed significantly to the quality of research at the university. It has enhanced the level of innovation and the opportunity to gamble on novel ideas that might be less appropriate as graduate problems.

---

[3] Except where the skewness of the distribution causes the dispersion to go beyond the scale.
[4] Data on individual fields were available to the study, but do not appear in Figure 15.

**CONTRIBUTION TO RESEARCH**    171

**FIGURE 15**

Contribution of Research Group—Graduate Students, Postdoctorals, Professional Research Staff—to Natural Science Professors' Teaching Responsibilities.

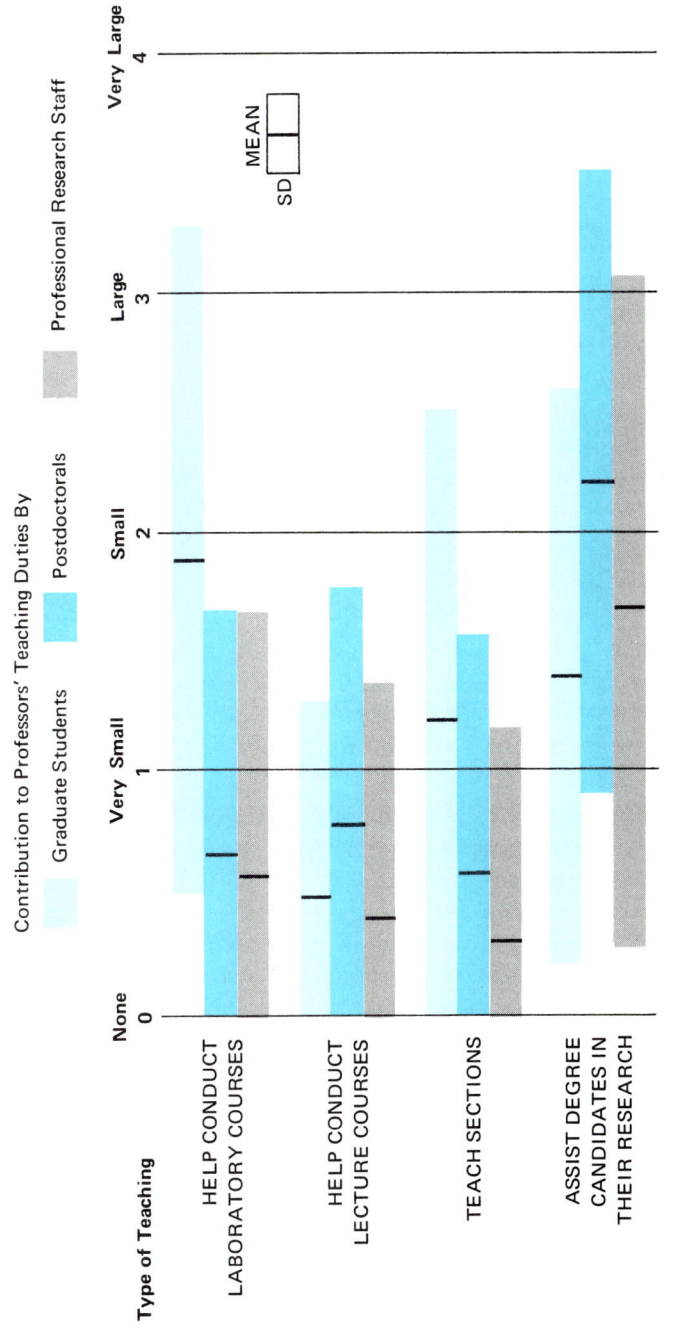

| Type of Teaching | Contribution to Professors' Teaching Duties By Graduate Students / Postdoctorals / Professional Research Staff |
|---|---|

Scale: None (0) — Very Small (1) — Small (2) — Large (3) — Very Large (4)

Categories:
- HELP CONDUCT LABORATORY COURSES
- HELP CONDUCT LECTURE COURSES
- TEACH SECTIONS
- ASSIST DEGREE CANDIDATES IN THEIR RESEARCH

Source: NRC, Office of Scientific Personnel, Postdoctoral Faculty Questionnaire.

From an eastern school we received this comment:

The presence of postdoctorals has increased the caliber and output of research at [our university]. It has also permitted more sophisticated research in many areas. The evidence which relates to this is subjective but quite persuasive. Faculty are virtually unanimous on this point. . . . Assessment of research accomplishments of various research groups makes it clear that the output of postdoctorals looms large.

The chairman of chemistry at a prestigious eastern school said that many of the faculty in his department consider the postdoctoral "indispensable." He himself felt that indispensable was too strong a word, but affirmed that they were very useful for their contribution to research. Many deans felt that postdoctorals were necessary in the department if it were to achieve the highest quality. Said one:

Since the quality of a department is often judged by the effectiveness of its research program, it is indeed hard to see how a department can achieve first rank without the intensive research work provided by postdoctorals. They lend continuity and intensiveness to the research effort of senior faculty who, because of teaching duties, committee assignments, etc., cannot spend one hundred percent of their time on their research projects.

Another dean avoided the question of indispensability, but wrote:

Research with postdoctorals can be even more adventurous than research with graduate students. The former possess more highly trained skills and broader knowledge of their subject. They do not have to produce results to quite the same specifications. These are important elements in striving for the highest quality. A good postdoctoral student should lead his faculty collaborator on an even merrier chase into new areas than a graduate student.

This element of the development of the faculty member by association with his postdoctorals is mentioned by some of the faculty as well. A chemist stated that each laboratory has its own style and approach. He found that postdoctorals contribute to the exchange of styles by bringing values from one group to another. Another chemist, in addition to attributing his increased publication rate to his postdoctorals, admitted that the direction of his research had changed with the new techniques that he had learned from his postdoctorals. A biologist confessed that, were it not for the information and the knowledge that his postdoctorals brought to him, he would have to take time off for a postdoctoral appointment himself.

Not everyone is quite so ecstatic. Some deans speak of the mixed benefits of postdoctorals and one suggested that the impact of postdoctorals on the university's research was only "on the whole favorable." Two deans had the impression that the graduate students were being squeezed out. At one institution the presence of postdoctorals "has enhanced the quality in several fields. It has enabled one professor in particular to be very productive but has had the adverse effect that he has devoted correspondingly less time to predoctoral students." At another institution, "Unquestionably it has enhanced the quality of research accomplished in most instances. However, the involvement of postdoctorals in large 'team' research efforts does not offer the same opportunity for self-development which is desirable in a training situation."[5]

Some of the faculty, probably observing the situation from the outside, are more specific. A number mention that postdoctorals are often exploited and reduced simply to another pair of hands. This situation arises, in their opinion, because the postdoctoral position is so ill-defined. The postdoctoral has no defense against being so used. Some typical responses from this less-than-enthusiastic group follow. From an organic chemist we heard:

> It is probably overdone for fiscal reasons—an occult way to increase professional personnel on external budget sources. It tends to dilute the academic community's interest in predoctoral education.

A physiologist asserted:

> The number of postdoctoral positions available is far greater than it should be. I conceive of postdoctoral education at a more advanced conceptual and intellectual level than predoctoral work, but it often turns out to be not at all better because the intellectual capacity of those guiding postdocs is limited.

A biochemist swings the biggest ax by writing:

> To some extent such programs have become a racket. Only a few of the best institutions get superior individuals. Only a limited number of professors have *real* leadership to convey to young PhD's; too much money available results in "slave labor" for inferior individuals to do "footwork" for *average* professors.

Before ascribing sentiments such as these to a few malcontents and dismissing them, it would seem more prudent to examine the present practices for possible abuses of the system. With so many expressing satisfaction with the status quo, much of what is happening must be right. It is also possible that any attempt to correct abuses will seriously damage the many favorable aspects of postdoctoral activity. Before such a statement can be made with assurance, however, there needs to be an investigation by the sponsoring and the host institutions of the style of postdoctoral education, both as sponsored and as handled locally.

Similar to the question on how much help graduate students, postdoctorals, and research staff are to a professor's teaching effort was a question to the faculty regarding the contribution to research by these same groups. The answers are summarized in Figure 16. Except for the performance of routine work, the postdoctoral is more valuable than either the graduate student or

---

[5] For a rare and persuasive defense of training in a "big science" setting, see W. K. H. Panofsky, Big Science and Graduate Education, *Science Policy and the University*, The Brookings Institution, 1968, pp. 189-201.

## IMPLICATIONS FOR ACADEMIC INSTITUTIONS

### FIGURE 16

Contribution of Research Group—Graduate Students, Postdoctorals, Professional Research Staff—to Faculty Research in the Natural Sciences.

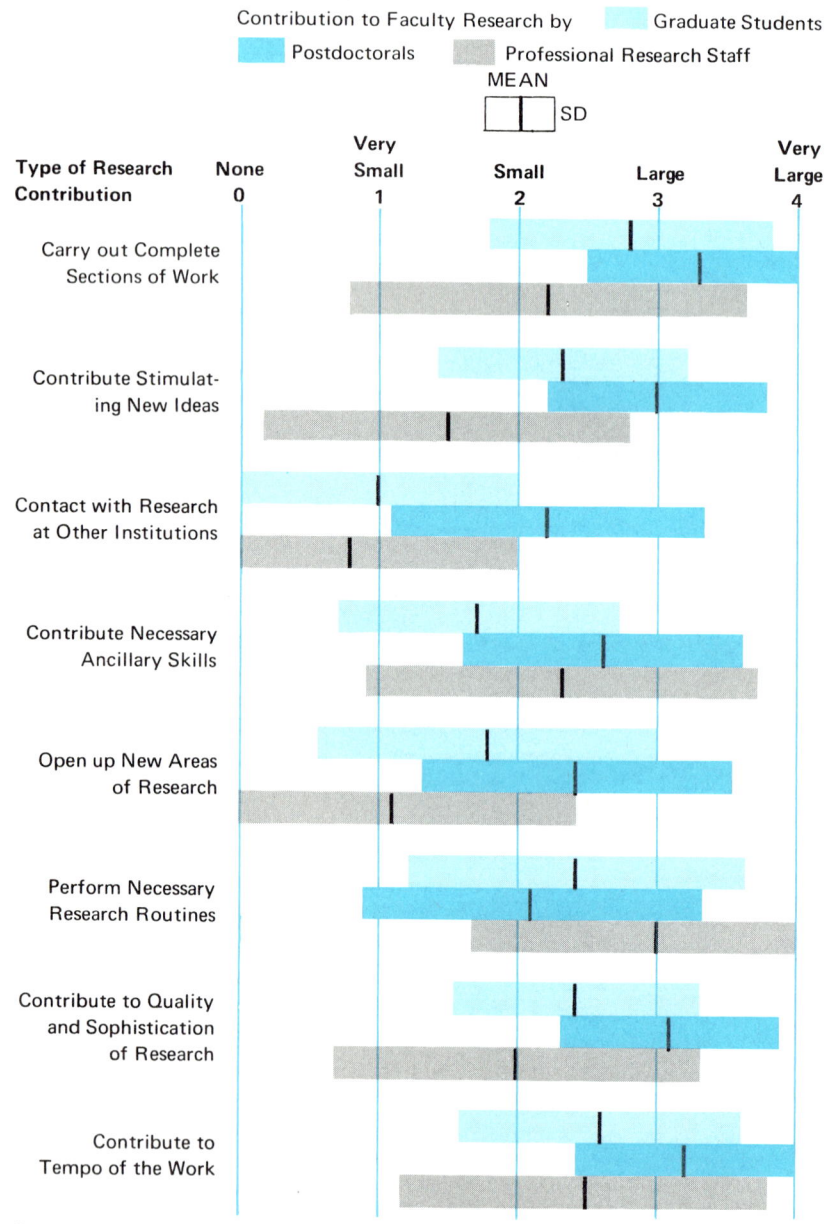

Source: NRC, Office of Scientific Personnel, Postdoctoral Faculty Questionnaire.

the professional research staff, but all three contribure heavily to the tempo of the research.

In addition to their contribution to teaching and research, postdoctorals are often welcomed at universities for other reasons. They not only bring techniques and research ideas, but they also represent an exchange of environments. Professor Derek deSolla Price of Yale has made a penetrating study[6] of the problem of the dissemination of new knowledge so vital to the growth of science, and concludes that the most efficient procedure is the rapid transit of scientists among institutions and laboratories, with short-term sojourns at one place. After making reference to this article, a graduate dean wrote: "It would appear that postdoctoral study is ideally suited to the means."

Postdoctorals also leave the university and carry with them the association with the department to which they were attached. A departmental chairman judged that 40 percent of the high reputation that his department enjoys is due to the postdoctorals that they have hosted, with 60 percent of the reputation ascribed to the PhD's produced.

In view of all the positive aspects of the impact of postdoctorals on institutions of higher education and despite the negative aspects (or perhaps in ignorance of both), most PhD-awarding departments that do not have postdoctorals at present wish they did. In Table 45 we give the response of department chairmen to the question: "If you do not now have postdoctoral stu-

TABLE 45   Evaluation by the Chairmen of Doctoral Departments without Postdoctorals of the Desirability of Having Postdoctorals

| Graduate Department | Number of Departments | Great Benefit | Some Benefit | No Significant Benefit |
|---|---|---|---|---|
| Physical sciences | 310 | 57 | 30 | 13 |
| Basic medical sciences | 61 | 72 | 25 | 3 |
| Biosciences | 129 | 55 | 33 | 12 |
| Social sciences | 376 | 44 | 35 | 21 |
| Humanities | 315 | 24 | 40 | 36 |
| Engineering | 195 | 45 | 44 | 11 |
| Education | 119 | 54 | 40 | 6 |
| Agriculture | 53 | 49 | 40 | 11 |

(Percentage of Department Chairmen Reporting Postdoctorals Would Be of)

Source: NRC, Office of Scientific Personnel, Postdoctoral Departmental Questionnaire.

[6] D. deSolla Price, The Hard Science of Science and Technology, *Proceedings of the 20th National Conference on the Administration of Research,* Denver Research Institute, 1967, pp. 45–51.

TABLE 46  Composition and Size of Research Groups with and without Postdoctorals, by Field

| Postdoctoral Field | Average Number of Persons in Research Groups ||||||||||
| | Graduate Students ||  Postdoctorals || Auxiliary Personnel[a] || Total Nonfaculty[b] || Faculty Co-Workers ||
| | with Postdoctorals | without Postdoctorals | with Postdoctorals | without Postdoctorals | with Postdoctorals | without Postdoctorals | with Postdoctorals | without Postdoctorals | with Postdoctorals | without Postdoctorals |
|---|---|---|---|---|---|---|---|---|---|---|
| Physics | 6.6 | 4.2 | 2.4 | — | 2.2 | 0.6 | 11.2 | 4.8 | 2.7 | 1.9 |
| Chemistry | 6.0 | 5.3 | 2.5 | — | 1.1 | 0.5 | 9.6 | 5.8 | 1.3 | 1.3 |
| Earth sciences | 6.6 | 6.5 | 1.8 | — | 1.6 | 1.2 | 9.9 | 7.7 | 2.1 | 2.7 |
| Biochemistry | 4.3 | 4.0 | 3.0 | — | 3.3 | 1.2 | 10.6 | 5.1 | 1.9 | 1.5 |
| Physiology | 3.9 | 4.6 | 2.6 | — | 2.7 | 0.8 | 9.1 | 5.4 | 2.5 | 1.7 |
| Biosciences | 4.7 | 5.8 | 2.2 | — | 2.9 | 1.2 | 9.8 | 7.0 | 2.4 | 1.9 |
| Medical specialities | 1.3 | 0.4 | 4.0 | — | 4.3 | 1.6 | 9.5 | 2.0 | 3.1 | 2.4 |
| Social sciences | 10.2 | 5.5 | 2.4 | — | 3.2 | 0.6 | 15.8 | 6.1 | 3.8 | 2.2 |
| *Total* | 5.6 | 5.3 | 2.5 | — | 2.2 | 0.8 | 10.3 | 6.1 | 2.1 | 1.8 |

[a]Auxiliary personnel includes professional research staff as well as technicians.
[b]Due to rounding, figures for the total nonfaculty may not equal the sum of the first three columns.

Source: NRC, Office of Scientific Personnel, Postdoctoral Faculty Questionnaire.

dents in the department, do you believe the department would benefit from the presence of such students?" Only the humanities could be described as unenthusiastic, with more saying that there would be no benefit than that the benefit would be great. When the chairmen took the opportunity to comment on their reply they generally endorsed postdoctoral education as stimulating to the research and teaching within a department. Departments of physical and biological sciences registered this sentiment most strongly, departments of engineering somewhat less, and departments of social science and education (with the exception of psychology, which registered a strong endorsement) were relatively lukewarm.

Despite this general approval of postdoctoral study, few departments reported any intention of beginning a program in the future. Departments from the ten leading institutions through the established institutions were stronger in their endorsement of postdoctoral activity and were more likely to have had experience with postdoctorals in the past. With some exceptions, most of the developing institutions' departments felt that they would have difficulty fitting postdoctorals into their organizations and challenging them academically. Departments that endorsed postdoctoral education strongly, but were not planning to initiate a program, characteristically cited reasons of organization or budget that kept them from having postdoctorals. The more lukewarm departments commonly stressed that postdoctoral study was not suitable to their departmental goals. A small percentage of these worried that postdoctorals would burden or distract their teaching staff or would not find the environment that they should have.

Implications for the Research Group

An often-repeated claim is that the presence of postdoctorals permits a faculty member to train more graduate students. In Table 46 we have collected statistics on the relative size and composition of research groups. The research group, rather than the department, is the natural unit[7] at the graduate and postdoctoral levels. It is within the group that the interaction among faculty, staff, postdoctorals, and graduate students takes place. We have separated the groups with postdoctorals from those without in order to observe the difference that postdoctorals make. Although the data could have been presented in terms of the reputation of the institution, the differences within an institution are often larger than those among institutions.

In all fields research groups with postdoctorals are larger than those without postdoctorals, by more than just the number of postdoctorals. There are

---

[7]See Warren O. Hagstrom, Competition and Teamwork in Science, Final Report to the National Science Foundation on Grant GS-657 to the University of Wisconsin.

## IMPLICATIONS FOR ACADEMIC INSTITUTIONS

more graduate students (except in physiology) as well as more auxiliary staff. There are also more faculty co-workers (except in earth sciences) in groups with postdoctorals. This last fact casts some doubt, however, on the proposition that the faculty can train more graduate students when postdoctorals are present.

We asked each group to provide us with the number of PhD's awarded to graduate students in their group in 1966 and 1967. Table 47 gives the totals for the two years and the number of PhD's per year granted per faculty member and per graduate student in the group. On the basis of these results, we would have to deny that postdoctorals make the production of PhD's more efficient. To reconcile these data with those presented in Table 38 (p. 155), it is sufficient to observe that according to Table 42 (p. 162), fewer faculty in departments without postdoctorals are involved in research. When one considers the number of PhD's produced per *research* faculty member, the ratios in Table 38 will obviously rise.

We must remember, however, that these are averages and that there are fluctuations from the average that are significant. It may well be true that the professor who is also chairman could not train as many graduate students without postdoctorals as he can with postdoctorals. There is nothing in these statistics that says anything about the quality of the doctorates granted. It may be that those graduate students who worked side-by-side with postdoctor-

TABLE 47  PhD Production by Research Groups with and without Postdoctorals, by Field

| Postdoctoral Field | PhD's Granted in 1966 and 1967 in Research Groups with Postdoctorals | without Postdoctorals | PhD's Granted per Year per Graduate Student in Research Groups with Postdoctorals | without Postdoctorals | PhD's Granted per Year per Faculty Co-Worker in Research Groups with Postdoctorals | without Postdoctorals |
|---|---|---|---|---|---|---|
| Physics | 2.8 | 2.3 | 0.22 | 0.27 | 0.52 | 0.59 |
| Chemistry | 3.0 | 2.8 | 0.25 | 0.26 | 1.14 | 1.08 |
| Earth sciences | 2.8 | 2.2 | 0.22 | 0.17 | 0.67 | 0.41 |
| Biochemistry | 1.7 | 1.9 | 0.20 | 0.24 | 0.46 | 0.63 |
| Physiology | 1.8 | 2.4 | 0.24 | 0.26 | 0.36 | 0.72 |
| Biosciences | 2.0 | 2.3 | 0.21 | 0.20 | 0.42 | 0.61 |
| Medical specialities | 0.6 | 0.4 | 0.24 | 0.47 | 0.10 | 0.08 |
| Social sciences | 4.3 | 3.0 | 0.21 | 0.27 | 0.56 | 0.67 |
| *Total* | 2.5 | 2.5 | 0.23 | 0.23 | 0.61 | 0.66 |

Source: NRC, Office of Scientific Personnel, Postdoctoral Faculty Questionnaire.

als are better prepared than those who did not. Furthermore, it may be that we are dealing with different kinds of research. There may be a correlation between the difficulty and sophistication of the research and the presence of postdoctorals. Nevertheless, the commonly held belief that the presence of postdoctorals permits more graduate education is not valid in general. It is still true, however, that it does not imply less.

As might be expected, research groups with postdoctorals are much better endowed with research funds than groups without. If there is any correlation between the quality of the research and the degree of support, then the groups with postdoctorals are doing the better research. It is more likely that we are dealing with different kinds of research. Although the customary distinction between "Big Science" and "Little Science" tends to describe the ends of a continuum rather than two distinct approaches, the postdoctorals tend to be in groups where a much higher level of effort is required. Such research is also more expensive.

In Table 48 we give the average support per research group, by field and reputation of the institution. Again, several well-known features of research support are displayed. Physics tends to be almost twice as expensive as the other fields (except the social sciences). Also, the more prestigious schools have a larger share of the money. What is new is that most of the groups with postdoctorals have more funds per research group than most of the groups without postdoctorals, regardless of the reputation of the school.

## Recruitment of Postdoctorals as Faculty

The postdoctoral appointment is a useful mechanism for having a parade of bright young men pass through the department. As we have pointed out earlier (Table 14, p. 68), a major fraction of new faculty in the science fields at the better institutions come immediately from postdoctoral positions; however, in only a few of the highly prestigious departments do the bulk of the new faculty appointments come from their own postdoctorals. The chemistry chairman at a developing institution explained why none of his new faculty had been postdoctorals in his department, although several had been postdoctorals elsewhere. At the present stage of development of his department, he was trying to broaden the areas of faculty interest. The postdoctorals in the department were in areas where he had faculty strength already.

The attractiveness of the postdoctoral as a faculty member in comparison to a man coming directly from his PhD has several components. A chemistry chairman mentioned the following: (1) The department is able to judge with

TABLE 48  Average Amount of Research Support per Research Group with and without Postdoctorals, by Field and Type of Academic Institution

| | Average Research Support (in $1,000's) per Research Group by Type of Academic Institution | | | | | | | |
|---|---|---|---|---|---|---|---|---|
| | Ten Leading | | Twenty Other Major | | Established | | Developing | |
| Postdoctoral Field | with Postdoctorals | without Postdoctorals | with Postdoctorals | without Postdoctorals | with Postdoctorals | without Postdoctorals | with Postdoctorals | without Postdoctorals |
| Physics | 307 | 98 | 171 | 42 | 137 | 47 | 107 | 37 |
| Chemistry | 163 | 34 | 64 | 29 | 53 | 24 | 54 | 21 |
| Earth sciences | 122 | 51[a] | 43 | 32 | 90[a] | 21[a] | 36[a] | 35 |
| Biochemistry | 103 | 34[a] | 87 | 38[a] | 94 | 25 | 81 | 53 |
| Physiology | 73 | 23[a] | 115 | 74[a] | 81 | 18[a] | 82 | 36[a] |
| Biosciences | 63 | 42 | 63 | 22 | 70 | 18 | 56 | 30 |
| Social sciences | 238 | 14[a] | 52[a] | 27[a] | 14[a] | 63[a] | 93[a] | 25[a] |
| Total | 170 | 50 | 96 | 31 | 83 | 28 | 70 | 32 |

[a]Less than 20 groups responding.

Source: NRC, Office of Scientific Personnel, Postdoctoral Faculty Questionnaire.

much greater chance of success how well he might perform as a faculty member, since he has had much more experience under two different mentors and (2) he is much better able to get grant support. The biology chairman at the same institution added that a new PhD is often not ready to begin independent research. He pointed out that it is difficult to determine whether a thesis reflects the candidate's abilities or those of his professor. This can cut both ways. A brilliant student working for a pedestrian professor can produce a pedestrian thesis and vice versa. The postdoctoral experience helps to resolve this dilemma.

A number of chairmen stated that the chances of a former postdoctoral's being retained on tenure are much better than those of a fresh PhD. Not only does the fresh PhD have less research experience, but he tends to have more trouble maintaining his research during the first several years. At universities complying with the American Association of University Professors' statement on tenure and academic freedom, the decision on tenure must be made at the end of the sixth year of appointment. However, since a newly appointed assistant professor is seldom appointed for more than three years, the first decision on reappointment (although not a tenure decision) must be made after only two years. This does not give the young man much time to demonstrate research potential if he has not had a postdoctoral appointment.

The attitude toward hiring former postdoctorals as faculty members depends to some degree on the field. A physics chairman indicated that his department would not even consider a new faculty member who had just finished his PhD. He felt that the transition from student to professor was too abrupt and that the postdoctoral years allow a smoother transition. Another chairman of physics from a less prestigious school agreed in principle, but found it more difficult to attract people with postdoctoral experience.

A biology chairman explained that the desirability of a postdoctoral background in faculty candidates depended upon the subfield. In more classical areas, such as population biology or ecology, he felt he could do quite well with people straight from the PhD. On the other hand, he would insist on postdoctoral experience for a biochemist.

A chemistry chairman at an established university in the South remarked that all his recent appointments to the faculty came from postdoctoral positions, but he felt that this was due to chance. He was looking for the best qualified person for each position and in each case they had been former postdoctorals. They have better *curricula vitae* in that they have more publications. Another chemistry chairman at a major eastern school explained his preference for postdoctorals as faculty candidates by pointing out that they can show two references indicating how good they are. This "stereoscopic view" of a man's promise is more reliable than the candidate's doctoral work alone.

A psychology chairman said he would prefer to have people with postdoctoral background but that there are so many employment opportunities for

## IMPLICATIONS FOR ACADEMIC INSTITUTIONS

the new PhD that few take postdoctoral appointments. An engineering chairman asserted that postdoctorals were rare in his field and that in fact he would prefer someone with industrial experience.

A number of chairmen in different fields and institutions were asked what the impact would be on recruitment of faculty if there were no postdoctorals. The usual, but not unanimous, reaction was one of horror. Chairmen used words like "disastrous" to describe what would happen to the quality of research and, ultimately, of teaching. There would seem to be four major consequences of a reduction of postdoctoral activity: (1) an extension of predoctoral work, (2) a narrowing of the research interest and capabilities of new faculty, (3) an unhealthy dependence of junior faculty on the more senior members of the department, and (4) a tendency of better departments to hire the better senior people from other institutions, with a corresponding reduction in quality of the faculty at lesser universities.

If a graduate student knew that he would have to take a teaching position immediately after his PhD, he might prefer to stay longer as a graduate student, acquiring more experience in research. Such an occurrence would seem to have two effects. The flow of students to the job market would not be any greater than it is with the existence of postdoctoral study, but the mobility that characterizes and enriches postdoctoral study would be absent. Because of the differential in stipends between the graduate student and the postdoctoral, the net effect (according to those who make this argument) would be the purchase of a lesser product with less money.

The second rationale given for seeking faculty with postdoctoral experience is that without the experience, young faculty with the pressures of teaching new courses while developing a research record tend to continue working on their thesis problems. Since the thesis topic was probably designed to be sufficiently narrow for a graduate student to accomplish, the result is an assistant professor whose research interests and techniques are not as broad as they might otherwise be. Many chairmen see little hope for creativity under these circumstances.

In some cases the search for breadth might impel a new faculty member to attach himself to a more senior colleague. This would be all the more likely if, because of his lack of research record and experience, he finds it difficult or impossible to be funded independently. Unless he is able to leave the orbit of the senior faculty member before the time for a decision on tenure, he is unlikely to be retained. Some chairmen believe that this would call too heavily on the willingness of the senior man to treat the junior man with sufficient independence.

Since the better departments can offer, in addition to salary, the amenities of distinguished colleagues and superior facilities, they are able to attract more senior people from lesser institutions than move in the opposite direction.

Should young scientists survive the pitfalls listed above and become productive researchers, they will immediately become targets for recruitment by the more prestigious schools. Under present circumstances there are more postdoctorals than the top institutions can hire and the whole range of institutions benefit. If the opposite were true, all but the top would suffer. The present postdoctorals are aware that most of them are going to be employed by institutions less prestigious than their postdoctoral host institution. As one put it, "I am going to be a much better faculty member at a developing institution after my postdoctoral than I would have been without it."

One need not accept all of the points summarized above to agree that what one chairman at a developing institution described as a "windfall" (the release of postdoctorals following a cutback in postdoctoral study) would likely be only a short-range benefit. The sudden flooding of the market would occur only once, and then the readjustment would take place. Even institutions that do not appoint many former postdoctorals as faculty recognize that light-load assistant professorships do not provide all of the benefits of a postdoctoral appointment.

Having said all this, we must recognize that there are exceptional individuals (usually from exceptional institutions) for whom the postdoctoral experience does not seem to be necessary. One professor of physics accepted his first assistant professorship immediately after his PhD in lieu of an NSF Postdoctoral Fellowship that he had been awarded. He obtained extramural support within a year and has had a productive career. Neither he nor his institution regrets his decision.

## Implications for the Disciplines

In the data already presented it is apparent that large differences exist among the various fields of study. The postdoctoral situation in chemistry is very different from that in the humanities. Engineering presents yet another picture and medicine is unique. The departments that form the educational structure for the disciplines are differentially affected by the flow of postdoctorals and by the availability of postdoctoral opportunities both for their graduates and for their faculty.

What is less obvious are the reasons for these differences. There are, of course, conditions extrinsic to the disciplines. Such conditions as the level of research funding, the availability of predoctoral fellowships, and the employment market for graduates depend only indirectly on the nature of the disciplines in the sense that these conditions could change without altering the basic nature of the discipline. It would be an error, however, to ascribe all the

IMPLICATIONS FOR ACADEMIC INSTITUTIONS

differences we have uncovered to disparate extrinsic conditions. The disciplines are also intrinsically different. Their educational goals and their research techniques set them apart. There are, of course, similarities across disciplines, but they must be discovered by observation and not extrapolated *a priori*.

An example of the failure to make disciplinary distinctions is the allegation often made that much of postdoctoral activity (especially immediately following the doctorate) reflects a weakness in graduate education. If a man were "properly" trained at the predoctoral level, would he need further training at the postdoctoral level? Has the tremendous explosion in the number of people taking graduate work led to a reduction in quality and a lowering of standards in the graduate schools?

Deans tend to be more worried about this possibility than their faculty. Up to 32 percent of the graduate deans considered that the development of postdoctoral study was an indictment of graduate education.[8] The faculty, whether or not they were working with postdoctorals, were satisfied that there were reasons for postdoctoral study even for those PhD's whose predoctoral education was excellent. When asked if the character of predoctoral training should be changed in the light of the growth of postdoctoral study, the faculty responded as follows:

|  | Predoctoral Education Should Change | Predoctoral Education Should Not Change | No Opinion |
|---|---|---|---|
| Faculty with postdoctorals | 6% | 59% | 35% |
| Faculty without postdoctorals | 5% | 46% | 49% |

Most deans and almost all professors see merit in postdoctoral education for the reasons given earlier. They would argue that, if graduate education has flaws, postdoctoral education is neither a cause nor an effect. The purpose of postdoctoral education is to accomplish something that graduate education never did and could not do without duplicating postdoctoral education itself. The disenchanted, however, are not persuaded. The graduate dean at a developing institution in the South wrote: "The growth of postdoctoral education, in my judgment, is to a large extent a reaction to the failure of graduate education to provide sufficient opportunity for specialized research." The dean at a developing university in the Midwest was more specific in his criticism:

It has been my general impression in many areas that doctoral students are frequently assigned to a segment of a problem of interest to the major adviser and, hence, serve as little more than coolie labor. As a result, they never get experience in the broad aspects

---

[8]It would be interesting to correlate the deans' responses with their predecanal field of study. To what degree are their attitudes shaped by their previous experience (or lack of experience) with postdoctorals?

of inquiry related to research. In many cases where they are given freedom to select a problem, they are expected to prepare specifications of a problem that could be self-contained. This procedure in and of itself is totally antithetical to research procedure.

Not all of the criticism comes from developing institutions. Deans at many institutions share in these misgivings "in part" or "to some extent." The dean at an eminent institution in the East wrote:

> The development of organized research means that many PhD candidates are not exposed during the predoctorate years to the threefold process of seeking out, sizing up, and carrying through a research project. Many of them simply carry out a project which is substantially defined and carefully supervised by their dissertation adviser. . . . Their PhD experience is stunted.

The dean at a respected institution in the West agreed:

> I feel, myself, that there is a very real possibility that the PhD has been downgraded in the sciences so that the dissertation has merely become an exercise in research techniques, not the original contribution to knowledge that has been the traditional standard and which is still, by and large, characteristic of the humanities and many of the social sciences.

Without denying that some students in some departments are not receiving the kind of graduate education that might be desired, there are several points that might be made in rebuttal to those quoted above. The first is that not all PhD's, in fact not even a majority of them, take postdoctoral work. To say that in 1967 26 percent of the physics PhD's went immediately into postdoctoral study implies also that 74 percent of the PhD's in physics in 1967 did *not* go into postdoctoral work. These other PhD's went to teach in colleges and universities, to do research in government and industry, and to a variety of other positions for which the employer felt that the kind of background which the PhD degree involved was the appropriate kind for the position. Each of these kinds of positions requires a different sort of person with a specific distribution of talents and motivations. If the PhD degree ever did prepare a particular kind of person for a particular kind of position, it no longer does. It would be extremely fortuitous if a single kind of predoctoral experience were appropriate for the creation of a graduate faculty member, a small college professor, an industrial researcher, and a science administrator. What is more likely is that the preparation for each of these positions will involve a postdegree internship of either a formal or informal sort. With singular exceptions, the predoctoral educational experience cannot be expected simultaneously to prepare a finished product for all of these employers, or even any one of them. One could interpret the postdoctoral experience as that internship often necessary in some fields for the preparation of a graduate faculty member. The data support such an interpretation.

The second point in response to those who feel that postdoctoral study is a reaction to the failure of graduate education has to do with the concept of "growth." Although the last decade has seen an expansion of postdoctoral activity, by 1967 the fraction of the PhD class taking postdoctoral work was just comparable to the corresponding fraction in certain fields in the 1920's (see Fig. 1, p. 18). Since it is to this period that many critics refer as a bench mark of excellence, both for graduate education and postdoctoral study, the correlation between real or apparent weaknesses in graduate education at the present time and the "growth" of postdoctoral education seems less relevant.

Finally, in those fields and subfields where the situation occurs, one must ask why faculty members urge particular thesis projects on their graduate students, thereby depriving them of the necessary experience of "seeking out, sizing up, and carrying through a research project." The answer that the professor is more interested in his own research and is looking only for contributions to it is probably limited in its applicability. To blame the phenomenon on selfishness is to foreclose the possibility that in some fields the nature of the subject and the degree of conceptual sophistication required to make "an original contribution to knowledge" are such that only after the experience of an extended and directed research project is a man ready to seek out the next project. Since not everyone is going on to a research career, it need not be appropriate for everyone to have to pursue a second research topic before attaining the degree. The present practice of granting the degree after the first project and then urging only those with research aspirations to take postdoctoral work is not only more efficient, but also does not take any longer for the participant than staying on as a predoctoral to achieve the same experience. That this is not the situation in the humanities, in the social sciences, or even in classical biology or that it once was not necessary in chemistry does not seem particularly relevant. It does not appear to be fruitful to worry whether a PhD in physics is more or less than a PhD in literature. They are not interchangeable in any practical sense.

At the risk of being somewhat repetitive, let us focus here on the disciplines and attempt to understand the differences in the degree of their involvement in postdoctoral activity in terms of their intrinsic subject matter and of their peculiar educational goals and research techniques. In what follows we shall have to make generalizations about which there are many exceptions and many shades of opinions. Our purpose is not to be definitive, but merely to indicate the variations among the disciplines.

One of the major ways in which the disciplines differ is the time at which the student first makes a commitment to the field. A student comes into contact with many fields while still in high school and enters college with at least some idea of their content and methodology. If his area of concentration is chosen from one of these fields, he is usually able to begin his study early in his college experience. After four years of undergraduate work, the student will enter graduate school with substantial background in his field.

For several fields, however, the student tends to enter the program later in his career. In psychology it will be toward the end of his undergraduate program. Biochemistry and the other basic medical sciences have almost no roots in the undergraduate program. Students who choose these fields will learn the field mainly as graduate students, with two of their four or five graduate years devoted to thesis research.

Fields also differ in the rate of development. Especially in physics, chemistry, biochemistry, and some of the biosciences, the growth of knowledge and the expansion of techniques make difficult the acquisition of the breadth of understanding necessary for fruitful research during the graduate program. While a student is working on his thesis, there is little time to keep up with developments even in contiguous areas of research. This situation in many of the sciences differs strikingly with that in the humanities and to some extent with that in the social sciences. In the humanities the pace of development of new techniques is much slower and only recently have the social sciences begun extensive application of mathematical methods that will probably exert pressures for postdoctoral study similar to those in the sciences.

In some fields the techniques and methodologies are borrowed from other fields. Thus a biochemist must learn biological concepts, chemical approaches, and lately even physical techniques. The educational experience during the graduate program is by necessity too restricted and limited to enable a student to become proficient in all of these. A similar problem exists for psychologists, especially those whose work borders on other disciplines. These may range from sociology and anthropology to mathematics, biology, chemistry, engineering, business, psychiatry, or social work. Increasingly the social sciences are experiencing the same interdisciplinary development. Only postdoctoral opportunities will enable the student to develop essential proficiency levels in these ancillary subjects.

The growth of team research has also had its impact on those fields where it is appropriate. Research problems in some areas are too complex and sophisticated to enable the lone investigator to achieve much success. Perhaps the extreme example in this regard is experimental elementary particle physics. The manpower required to operate a major multibillion volt particle accelerator is very large. Papers have been published with as many as thirty co-authors, each of whom has made an important contribution to the experiment. Clearly a student of this field cannot expect to experience the range of activities associated with the experiment without multiple opportunities to work in and around the apparatus. Again the graduate program is too short to permit him all of these opportunities before he receives the doctorate. To a lesser degree team research has developed in other parts of physics and in many of the other sciences.

In addition to the distinctions among the disciplines having to do with the time of entry to the field, with the rate of development of the field, with the interdisciplinary interactions of the field, and with the need for team research, there is one that is more subtle. Although difficult to quantify, this distinction is as important as the rest. Fields differ in the facility with which the edges of knowledge are perceived. Before a student can begin to contribute to research he must not only be able to distinguish between what is already understood and what is as yet not known, but he must also appreciate what constitutes a contribution to knowledge as opposed to an exercise in technique. In fields like theoretical physics a student may not arrive at this point until after his thesis. In fields like literature he may have grasped the essentials in his first year in graduate school. Other fields fall somewhere between these two.

As one examines each field in the light of these qualities, it is possible to understand why postdoctoral work has grown in some fields and not in others. The extrinsic conditions such as predoctoral support possibilities, of course, play a role as well. There is a high correlation (in the sciences) between the availability of predoctoral support in a field and the fraction of PhD's taking an immediate postdoctoral experience. Since there is also a relationship between the shortness of the baccalaureate-to-PhD time lapse and the availability of predoctoral support, the question is raised whether recent efforts to reduce the time lapse in the humanities will increase the demand for postdoctoral work.

Even within fields more heavily supported at the predoctoral level there are differences. Both physics and chemistry are comparable in the support possibilities available to graduate students. Yet physics PhD's take almost a year longer on the average to earn their doctorate than the chemists.[9] Apparently growing out of their earlier close association with industry, the chemistry departments consciously move their students through the doctoral program with more speed. The postdoctoral appointment is then used to supply whatever might be missing in the graduate experience for those who seek academic careers. Some physicists argue that similar approaches are possible in physics.

Some science fields do not fit the pattern. In particular, mathematics and, to a lesser degree, engineering have moderately short baccalaureate-to-PhD time lapses and yet do not participate to a great extent in postdoctoral activity. Engineering differs from most scientific disciplines in that the bachelor's de-

[9] National Academy of Sciences, *Doctorate Recipients from United States Universities,* Publ. 1489, Washington, D. C., 1967.

gree has been the professional degree. Baccalaureates who could benefit from graduate work are often drawn into industrial work by recruiters. Not until recently has graduate work become prominent. In 1940, only 108 doctorates in engineering were awarded. The number had risen to 629 in 1958 and to 2,581 in 1967. Graduates at all levels have abundant employment opportunities both in education and industry. Because the engineering doctorate is relatively new and consequently postdoctoral work is not traditional, most employers do not expect postdoctoral experience. The "chicken and egg" situation occurs where demand will not occur until there is a supply and vice versa. Finally, the graduate students in engineering tend to carry out their research with notable independence from their supervising professors.

Nevertheless, there are some in engineering who would like to see more postdoctoral work in the field. They state that many doctoral programs do not give enough maturity, self-confidence, and impetus to allow graduates to become independent investigators. In addition, a postdoctoral appointment permits the better student another research experience under a different mentor. Finally, they stress the importance of assisting foreign nationals who already possess the doctorate.

The situation in mathematics is accented by the highly independent nature of mathematics research. In this purely contemplative discipline the graduate student works very much on his own. Most great innovators in mathematics have been individualists with respect to their work. When a fruitful collaboration takes place, the work is still individual. A group exchange of ideas is followed by periods of solitary study, which are followed in turn by reports to the group or partner. The consequence of this aspect of mathematics for postdoctoral study is that the usual beneficial association of postdoctoral and mentor occurs much less frequently. Almost inevitably the professor's research is impaired by the attention he must give to the postdoctoral.

There are benefits to the young mathematician in postdoctoral study, but these are tempered by pitfalls as well. The postdoctoral appointee is able to learn about new and unsolved problems that are of interest to his new associates at the host university. He is then able to broaden his research outlook and his research program. Frequently he changes it entirely to a more promising or more fertile area in mathematics. The prestige of the appointment and the spending of time at a better institution than his own graduate school can be highly advantageous to him. On the other hand the young PhD may find his own originality and individuality considerably inhibited when he finds himself in a much more high-powered mathematical group than he was accustomed to in graduate school. Thus he may channel his further efforts more along the line of the group's interests than his own, which might have been more fruitful.

From the standpoint of the development of the individual as a potential teacher and leader, the postdoctoral program may possibly be less essential in mathematics than in some other disciplines.

The social sciences provide an example of disciplines in transition. Whereas postdoctoral activity immediately following the doctorate has been rare, there is evidence that the situation is changing.

The PhD candidate in the social sciences typically works more independently than in the sciences. This is reflected in the higher dropout rate, the longer lapsed time to complete the degree, and the fact that he frequently completes his dissertation in absentia. While the young, able PhD in the social sciences has plenty to learn, he looks upon himself (and is looked upon by his elders) as one who is competent to do independent research, upon receipt of the degree. Consequently, although he may spend a considerable part of his time in the early postdoctoral years mastering new research tools, he perceives himself as a fully-established member of the profession, and in general he is so regarded within the profession. Whether he immediately accepts a teaching appointment or joins a research term, he will be considered a junior collaborator or employee—not a trainee. There are, of course, differences among the social sciences, among subdisciplines within each of the social sciences, and among individuals within each subdiscipline. But even though postdoctoral fellowships are available, it is clear that many of the ablest young PhD's in the social sciences seek to receive a regular academic appointment early, to spend a period in government or industry, or to do a stint abroad, often with the intention of returning to a professorial rank. Many young social scientists have already been employed as full-time faculty for a year or two before they get their PhD's (Table 41, p. 160).

While the social scientist is less likely than a scientist to seek a postdoctoral appointment soon after completing his PhD, he is more likely to seek research leave at a later time. Often the social scientist will spend the first few years after completing his PhD preparing his dissertation for publication and initiating a new project. After that he will seek leave to devote time to the new project. It is apparent that while the able social scientist is always learning and needs free time for research, the needs of social scientists vary, and the immediate postdoctoral appointment is not nearly so common as in the physical and biological sciences.

There are several explanations for the differences in attractiveness of the postdoctoral appointment for social scientists as compared to scientists. Many social scientists leave their PhD institutions for teaching positions or positions in industry or government before completing their degrees, despite the efforts of graduate schools to encourage candidates to complete their dissertations in residence. This is possible because in many fields candidates are not tied to their laboratory or library until the final stage of their dissertations. Their motives for leaving are several. Often, they are financial—either the absence of financial support from the graduate school or the prospect of large financial rewards in other employment. It is also true that many social scientists seem to have a greater urge to engage immediately in teaching and that others take positions in government or industry or serve overseas, where they can observe at first hand and can participate in the world of action. For many social scientists, the world of affairs is their laboratory and participation in it is their field experience. It is not surprising, therefore, that many men wish to leave the academic world for such experience, either before or shortly after receiving their PhD's.

But there remains an important role for the postdoctoral appointment in the social sciences, both in the period immediately after the receipt of the PhD and at a later time. For example, as the social scientist makes greater use of mathematical and statistical techniques, provision should be made for training in these techniques for PhD's who did not have access to such training or did not see the need for it during their predoctoral years. Similar opportunities should be made available for those who are working in cross-cultural studies and in applied social sciences problems such as the urban communities, the underprivileged, and education.

Finally, there is the role of the research centers for more mature and even senior social scientists. The Institute for Advanced Study at Princeton, the Center for the Behavioral Sciences at Palo Alto, and the Center for Advanced Studies at Wesleyan University in Connecticut are not designed for the recent PhD or for the provision of formal training. Nor are they designed for group research. Rather, their purpose is to provide scholars of various ages with an opportunity for research, reflection, and intellectual exchange with colleagues in the same or related fields. For one fellow it will be an occasion to complete research that is already underway. For another it will be an occasion for reflection or for the starting of a new direction in his research or career. For still others it will be an occasion to study new techniques and approaches often stimulated by others at the center. Many believe that it would be desirable to provide more such opportunities than now exist.

We conclude this section by turning to the humanities. There is nothing in the humanities comparable to the extensive and well-established programs for postdoctoral work in the natural sciences. Scholars in the humanities have special opportunities for postdoctoral work through support from a variety of sources, including academic leave. The chief purpose of these forms of support and encouragement is to enable scholars in the humanities to have the free time to pursue their research and the opportunity to use library and other resources to supplement local collections. In contrast to his colleagues in the sciences, the humanistic scholar will rarely elect to spend a period of subsidized leave with a distinguished humanist under whose tutelage he will expect to grow and to develop. He will rather determine his arrangement on the basis of the resources available in a particular locality for his particular research interests.

The differences in postdoctoral activity between the humanities and science arise not simply from the recognized limitation of financial support in the humanities but from differences in the nature of the disciplines. The period of significant creative activity seems to occur at different stages in the two disciplines. Many of the most original achievements in science have been produced during the early years of a scientist's career, whereas the most impressive accomplishments in humanistic scholarship come later in a scholar's career. A young scientist is eager to continue with his research immediately after he has completed the doctorate. This impulse is encouraged at the present time by the state of scientific activity, the rapid accumulation of knowledge, the increased specialization, and the recondite nature of the art. The magnitude and complexity of some of the equipment required for many experimental problems combine to increase the desirability of continued early full-time commitment to research along with further training. Such compulsions are largely absent in humanistic scholarship. The young humanistic PhD may feel the urge to publish or to develop some useful discovery or interesting idea arising from his graduate studies but he is at the same time aware that his most important contributions will require maturing and that they lie in the future. In addition, his commitment to teaching is greater and has more bearing on his mature work as a scholar than in the case of the scientist. It is common experience that teaching even undergraduate students provides the catalyst for the humanistic scholar's studies. And, finally, the PhD degree program provides the young humanist with a reasonably good introduction to the methods and resources that he must use in his scholarly research.

Team research in the humanities, as in mathematics and in the social sciences, is not a characteristic pattern. Of course, group or team projects are not unknown. They arise chiefly in textual studies and editing, in the making of dictionaries, and in certain forms of linguistic studies. Similar enterprises could possibly be organized for special problems in, for instance, history or the history of art. There would certainly be a place in such projects for postdoctorals who could learn techniques not a part of their graduate training and at the same time advance the work of the project. It has in fact been argued that the humanities have been backward in failing to see all the advantages of group research. It might be applied to many kinds of studies now thought of as possible only by individual mature scholars. Traditional usage may dictate such a process, rather than any limitation inherent in the nature of the study. This view does not at present command general acceptance among scholars. One reason for the success of the postdoctoral appointment in science is that both the postdoctoral and his mentor profit from the arrangement. It is not yet clear how, in all but very special cases, the relations between the young scholar in the humanities and the mentor can promote equally the interests of both.

Any complete review of postdoctoral activity has to take into account the special relationship between the new PhD and the scholarly needs of the entire profession. In the humanities it must take into account the strong commitment to teaching of the humanistic scholar, his special need for breadth, and his distinctive pattern of professional growth, which often results in his finest work being accomplished during his middle and late years. For some the critical situation comes after several years of teaching and successful research when the need for greater breadth becomes apparent. Since much humanistic scholarship is by its nature interdisciplinary, the need to acquire competence in a new discipline or field of knowledge may become pressing. Both teaching and scholarship would profit from giving such men the opportunity for freedom and materials that they desire. Even the mature scholar, during what might be his most productive years, faces problems in finding support for his studies. He is not in the same position as his scientific colleagues with their sponsored research activity, summer stipends, and postdoctoral assistants.

The distinctive pattern of postdoctoral study in the sciences has grown up in response to the character of the entire scientific activity and its needs. An effective postdoctoral program in the humanities must similarly be responsive to the distinctive character of the work of humanistic scholars and the consequent diversity of their needs. Such an approach would provide the best basis for supplementing the relatively meager and uncoordinated sources of financial support available to scholars in the humanities at various stages in their careers following the doctorate.

## Summary

The impact of postdoctoral education on the universities has been great in the relatively few that are deeply involved and it has been minimal in others. Three points of contact with postdoctoral education are closely correlated. These are the production of PhD's who take postdoctoral appointments, the hosting of postdoctorals, and the recruiting of former postdoctorals as faculty. It is not accidental that the same universities that are accorded the highest reputations are also committed to the values of postdoctoral study.

The development of postdoctoral study at all levels must take into account the intrinsic nature of the field and must be responsive to the particular needs of the field. The present pattern of involvement in postdoctoral activity among the fields is partially understood in these terms. In some fields the lack of financial support has inhibited the full development of postdoctoral opportunities appropriate to those fields.

CHAPTER

# 7
# Implications for Nonacademic Institutions

The impact of postdoctoral education on the nonacademic employers of doctorates is more indirect than frontal. The fundamental issue is that despite the rapid increase in PhD production, there do not seem to be enough high-quality doctorate recipients to satisfy the demands of all employers. Every new alternative opened to the fresh PhD reduces the number of recipients available to the employers, and postdoctoral education, concentrated mainly in the universities, is another attractive alternative.

Sheer numbers, however, do not completely describe the problem. If there were a sufficient number of scientists to satisfy the demands of all consumers, nonacademic employers would still have to deal with the attitudes of the doctorate recipients. With few exceptions, nonacademic employers are involved in research in an applied science setting. Whether product-oriented as in industry or mission-oriented as in federal laboratories and federally supported portions of nonprofit or industrial laboratories, the kind of research (or the approach to it) is different from that in the universities. Although the distinction is usually made between applied and basic science, the director of a nonprofit laboratory was probably close to the core of the problem when he said: "I believe the strongest bias of most new PhD's is not for basic and against applied research, but for research problems of their own choosing and against research problems they are directed to study."

How this bias is to be overcome or how mission- or product-oriented research can use this bias to maximum benefit is of critical importance to the country. The recent report of the Committee on Science and Public Policy of the National Academy of Sciences to the Daddario Subcommittee[1] is only one of several efforts to deal with it. The postdoctoral, however, is at most a symptom of the problem, and the problem would remain even if the symptom were removed.

Although it was not the purpose of this study to investigate the distribution of PhD's among the various employers of PhD's, there are three reasons why further comment might be in order. The first is simply that we have gathered information that bears on the question and should be made available. The second is that the qualifications of the postdoctoral make his disinterest in the nonacademic world all the more significant. A third reason is that many have suggested that an increased use of the postdoctoral mechanism by nonacademic employers may be one way of resolving the problem of distribution.

## Employment of New Doctorate Recipients

There is certainly no a priori proper distribution of graduates among the several potential employers. It is impossible to say what percentage of PhD's in each field "should" go into industry or "should" go into academic institutions. It is possible, however, to examine the concomitants of different employment practices. In Table 39 (p. 156) we saw that departments with postdoctorals present graduate a smaller fraction of PhD's who choose industry for a career (at least immediately) than departments without postdoctorals. Only engineering, biology, and the social sciences have different patterns. Postdoctoral activity is minimal in engineering and in the social sciences and has little impact on the departments. In biology there is very little industrial demand. In the physical sciences, however, the effect is pronounced.

We can see a similar effect in Figure 17, where the fraction of PhD's graduating from the 30 leading universities in specific fields who enter particular employment categories is compared with the fraction of all PhD's from the same institutions and fields regardless of their subsequent employment. The other category includes, in addition to those who return to a foreign country,[2]

---

[1] National Academy of Sciences, Committee on Science and Public Policy, *Applied Science and Technological Progress*, U. S. Government Printing Office, Washington, D. C., 1967.
[2] The consistent surplus of the "other" category in Figures 17 and 18 from the 30 leading universities arises mainly from the significantly greater percentage of their graduates who go to a foreign country. In part these are foreign students going home and in part American PhD's going abroad for employment. We have no explanation for this difference in behavior of the graduates from the 30 leading universities and of those from the other universities.

IMPLICATIONS FOR NONACADEMIC INSTITUTIONS

**FIGURE 17**
Percentage of 1965-66 PhD's in Selected Fields from the 30 Leading Universities Entering Various Employment Categories.

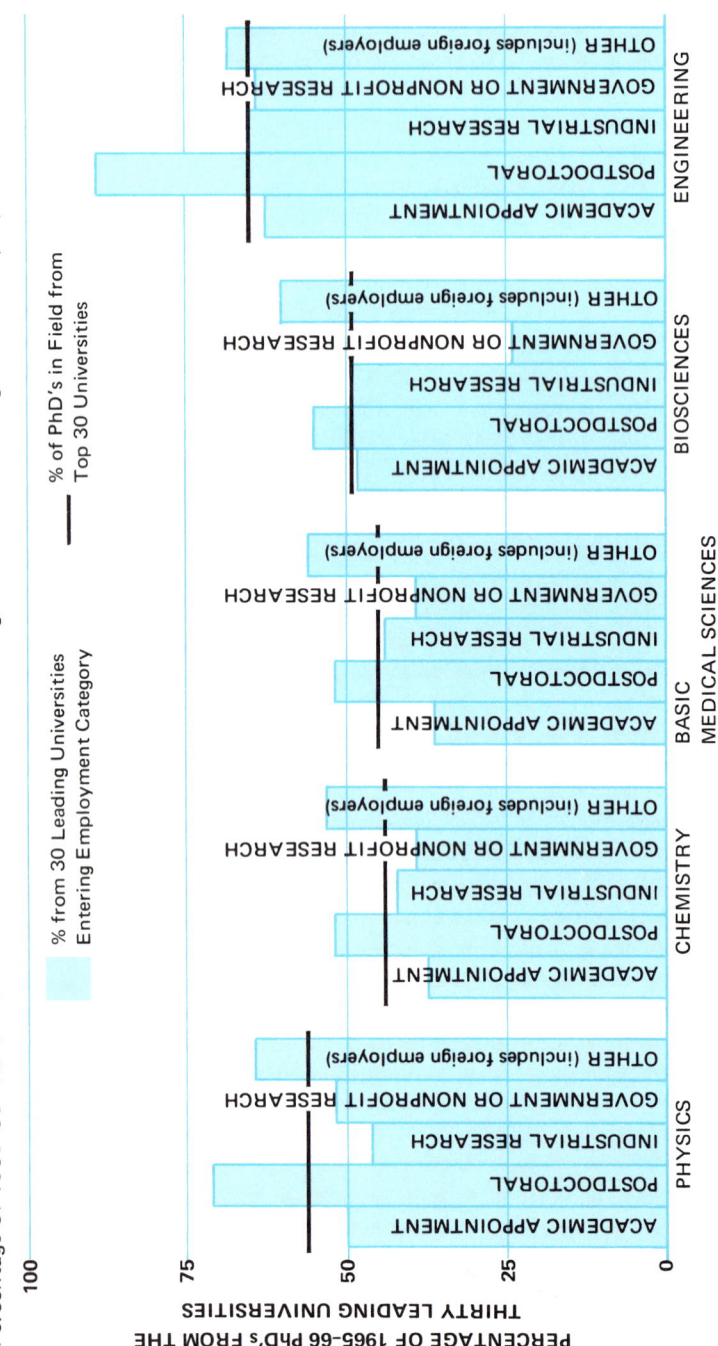

Source: NRC, Office of Scientific Personnel, Postdoctoral Departmental Questionnaire.

those who are drafted. Only in engineering do the 30 leading universities send graduates to all non-postdoctoral employers in proportion to their overall production. In physics these institutions produce 56 percent of the PhD's, but are responsible for 71 percent of the postdoctorals, only 46 percent of those who go into industry, and 50 percent of those who go into government research. The complementary view of this same phenomenon is that all the universities below the top 30 produce 44 percent of the PhD's, but are responsible for only 29 percent of the postdoctorals. They produce 54 percent of those who go into industry and 50 percent again of those who go into government research. If there is a correlation between the quality of the students and the reputation of the graduate school, industry and government are not getting their share of the top students immediately after the PhD.

As we have pointed out, however, the vast majority of postdoctorals leave that status and subsequently take up regular employment. If we assume that the postdoctorals from the PhD Class of 1965–66 behave in the same way as those who responded to the study (Table 12, p. 63), it is possible to distribute the postdoctorals of the 1965–66 PhD class among the other employment categories. Figure 18 shows the situation for the 1965–66 PhD graduates of the 30 leading universities if their postdoctorals are distributed in this way. The only differences from the overall percentages that are statistically significant (at the 95 percent confidence level) are the physicists in industrial research and the biologists in government research.[3] In the steady-state situation, therefore, each of the employers of doctorates does get its share of the graduates of the better institutions, with the exceptions just mentioned. Whether industry and government get their "proper" share of all PhD's is a separate question, and how the growth of the number of postdoctoral positions has affected this question is a matter of debate.

## Research Funds and Recruitment of Postdoctorals

It has been alleged, for example, that the involvement of universities in mission-oriented research and the use by universities of postdoctorals has created a competition between universities and nonacademic research organizations, both industrial and nonprofit, for federal funds and for superior young PhD's. Two questions immediately arise. Is the allegation true and, if so, is the situation necessarily bad for the universities, for the nonacademic employers, and for society? The answer to the first question is probably yes; at the very least, a

---

[3] Except for the "other" category, in which the statistics are significant in all fields except engineering.

198
IMPLICATIONS FOR NONACADEMIC INSTITUTIONS

FIGURE 18
Percentage of 1965-66 PhD's from the 30 Leading Universities by Type of Employer, Including Postdoctorals Distributed According to Their Subsequent Employers.

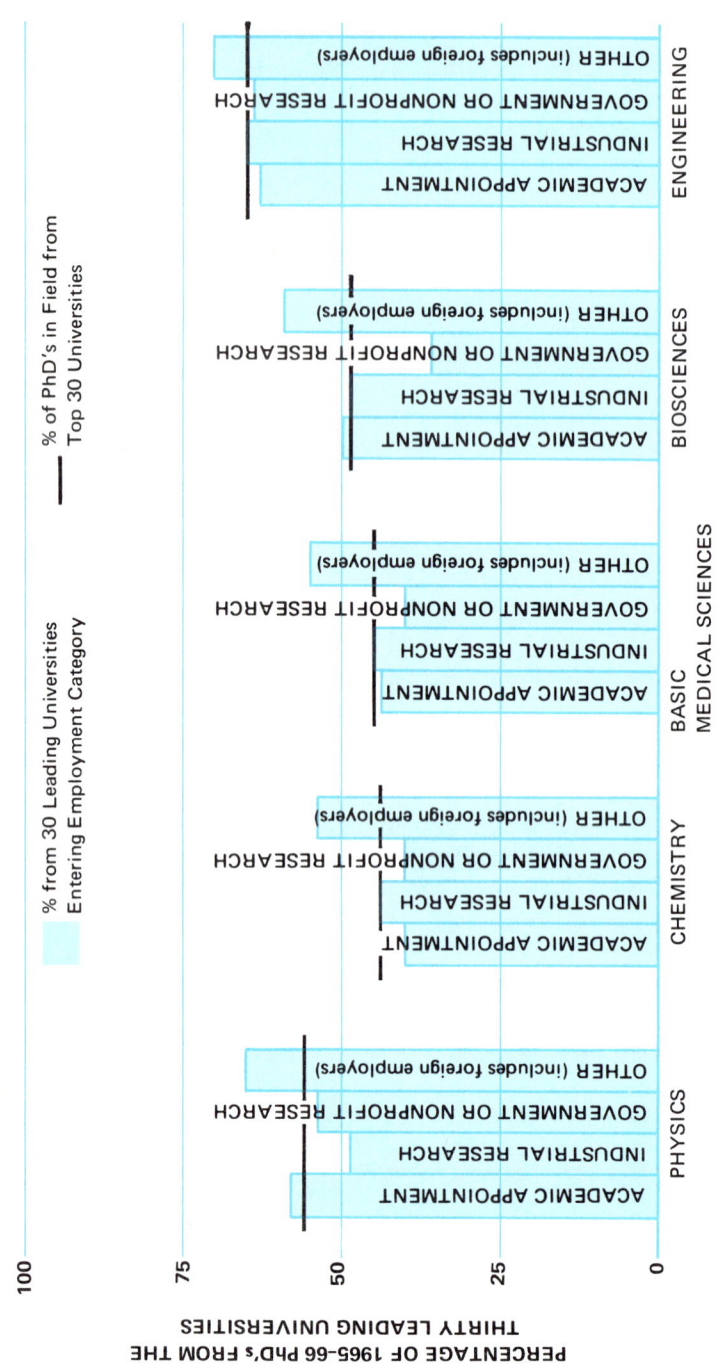

Source: NRC, Office of Scientific Personnel, Postdoctoral Census Questionnaire.

number of firms are conscious of making proposals for research contracts in competition with universities. The second question is more difficult.

A vice-president for research and development in a large and diversified company would like to reduce the competition by dividing the responsibility for various research activities more cleanly among the institutions:

> The competition for funds from mission-oriented agencies among universities and other research organizations makes it increasingly important to define some approximate roles for different kinds of places. Universities should continue to stress teaching of fundamentals, including fundamentals of research techniques [and] including the techniques of selecting research problems. Industrial laboratories should stress research fairly clearly leading to the solution of problems promptly affecting human welfare.

The vice-president for research in an oil company says:

> We believe that by engaging in specific end-product research using mission-oriented funds, universities are putting themselves in a position of directly competing with research institutes, government laboratories, and industrial research groups. They are subjecting themselves thereby to pressures to be treated in the same way as nonuniversity research institutions with respect to overhead allowances on contracts, tax treatment, etc. For the nonuniversity research institution the effects include increased competition for men with training at the doctoral level, increasing unavailability of professors for consulting, lectures, etc.

The director of research for an optical company sees postdoctoral appointments as a significant factor in the competition:

> It is not only apparent that competition has developed between universities and other research organizations for funds, it is also apparent that the funding policies have led to a competition of all the research organizations for candidates for postdoctoral appointments. This [has] created high mobility within the scientific community, although it is sometimes seriously questionable how much it has increased our scientific talent. More seriously, perhaps, this escalation of competition for postdoctoral candidates [has] caused an intensification of research programs attractive to the candidates and not necessarily leading to the training necessary, particularly in the nonuniversity or research institution. Industrial institutions therefore lack highly creative people who are motivated to accept the discipline of industrial problems.

On the other hand, some who note the competition see little harm in it or even see benefit in it. The spokesman for a consulting firm writes:

> It is true that there is competition between universities and other research organizations for funds. There has always been competition, I believe; I think there should be. Such competition is desirable if the fund-disbursing agencies have a reasonably enlightened attitude and adopt policies which have a reasonable balance and which are continuously subject to scrutiny and review. In our business . . . we are sometimes at a considerable disadvantage in respect to competition from universities and "not-for-profit" research institutions because of a peculiar attitude which has grown up to the effect that there is something unholy about the free enterprise system as applied to research and development. Other than this bit of irrationality, we find no reason to complain of the competition.

## IMPLICATIONS FOR NONACADEMIC INSTITUTIONS

The director of an aircraft company's research center comments as follows on the impact of directed research on the universities and consequently on the whole research community:

> Two different trends have arisen as a result of the competition for funds from mission-oriented agencies. In quite a few cases I feel that the universities have allowed the relative availability of funds to establish research priorities, and thereby have lost the direction of their effort, or, what is worse, have allowed research accomplishment to supplant their major mission of teaching.

But he adds:

> This has not been the case everywhere, for some have been able to use mission-oriented tasks to broaden the viewpoint and experience of people who might otherwise have become rather narrow specialists. Additionally, the pursuit of these mission-oriented problems within the university community has attracted the attention of faculty and students alike to many of the subtleties of "systems type" problems. In those cases, substantial benefits have accrued to both the universities and the students in terms of their ability to contribute to large-scale programs.

The development of postdoctoral education in the universities is put into perspective by the research vice-president of another firm:

> I see nothing wrong with postdoctoral education provided it is a bona fide attempt on the part of a postdoctoral fellow to obtain highly specialized training and experience in a field for which he feels some special long-term commitment.... I think a case for offering postdoctoral opportunities, in either a university or in nonuniversity organizations, can be made only if such organizations have on their staff recognized experts in appropriate fields. I don't think postdoctoral experience can ever be justified simply on the basis that the new PhD would like to spend a year in California, or Europe, or wherever, before he settles down to a regular job. Neither do I think that postdoctoral fellowships can ever be justified merely by the fact that a professor needs a couple of new PhD's to help him carry out a government-funded research program, although I am certain that this is not infrequently the case.... Recruitment by nonuniversity institutions (and universities, too, for that matter) is unquestionably made more difficult by any factor which increases the number of alternatives to the prospective employee, and postdoctoral fellowships are obviously one such alternative.

But he concluded: "I do not feel that this need be a problem if postdoctoral education [is] restricted to something like the criteria which I have indicated above."

The problem then is not the competition, but the failure of some universities to ensure that academic criteria are applied to the nature of the research and to the involvement of students and postdoctorals in the research. When the research is of a kind that permits the education of the junior participants, the nonacademic world is one of the ultimate beneficiaries.

That the nonacademic employers of doctorates are not opposed to mission-oriented research (or at least applied science research), in the universities is reflected in their response to another allegation. It has been charged that the university experience of the young PhD tends to motivate him away from applied research to "basic" problems. It is further suggested that the postdoctoral position only aggravates this situation. Sentiment in this regard exists not only in the nonacademic world but also appears in statements of some academicians.[4]

The vice-president for science and engineering of an electronics firm says: "The impact of postdoctoral education is to further strengthen the aloofness of the young PhD from the real world and further motivate him away from applied research." The vice-president for research of a food concern expresses the same view: "No doubt the effect is to make the postdoctoral even more academically oriented." The research vice-president of another firm agrees:

> Postdoctoral education clearly tends to accentuate this tendency. . . . However, the roots of this problem go deeper than postdoctoral education. There has arisen an unfortunate tendency for the engineering and applied sciences to slavishly imitate the cult of the pure sciences, instead of fulfilling their proper role. If this were rectified and carried through postdoctoral work, the problem of interfacing with industry would be a long way toward solution.

The chief scientist of an aircraft company makes a related point:

> The problem of motivation of the young PhD . . . is a very real one. We find that many PhD's have a completely erroneous view of the nature of applied research within industry, and that this ignorance appears to start with the student's instructor at the university. It appears on occasion that this instructor himself has developed an imaginary view of the nature of industrial research, and this deters the student from leaving the more basic research of the university. Clearly, postdoctoral education at the university will do nothing to help the situation.

The managing director of a nonprofit organization engaged in plant research has similar misgivings about the unfortunate influence of the faculty:

> Most of the professors have completely forgotten that the primary problem of research is to solve problems of benefit to society. To them, research has become an exercise in abstract exploration in an imaginative world of their own. The inevitable consequence is that their ideas are implanted in their students' thinking so strongly that they become a basic part of the students' concept of research. . . . The postdoctoral is a symptom rather than a cause of deterioration in purposefulness of modern science. It has, however, robbed development and mission-oriented research of manpower.

The senior vice-president of a nonprofit institution interested in information systems is concerned about the desire of young investigators to be undirected in their research:

[4] See The Evolution and Prospects for Applied Physical Science in the United States, by Edward Teller. *Applied Science and Technological Progress: A Report to the Committee on Science and Astronautics, U. S. House of Representatives,* by the National Academy of Sciences, 1967, p. 365.

I have in mind, particularly, the tendency to overvalue the kinds of individual freedom and isolated developments which often take place in a university. Such people may find it difficult later to integrate into a large, team-oriented activity such as major systems developments require. . . . This seems to be foreign to many of the university environments, and does not result in persons trained to become members of large, integrated efforts.

Harvey Brooks, in the lead article of the National Academy of Sciences report to the House Committee on Science and Astronautics[5] on applied science, cites a number of the problems that face a university in providing the appropriate environment for applied research and suggests a number of criteria that should be prerequisites for research of that kind in the university.

However, not all who perceive an academic aloofness from the "real world" agree that it is a serious problem, or even that it is a problem at all. The president of a consulting firm says:

I agree that the universities have a responsibility to make sure that a reasonable proportion of young PhD's should be motivated toward applied research. However, if one contrasts the attitude of young PhD's coming out of American universities with those from foreign universities and particularly British universities, we do not look so bad. Moreover, I cannot say that the trend which I see is in the wrong direction. Indeed, I have gone through periods of concern that the universities were becoming too much involved in applied research simply because mission-oriented funds were easier to come by.

Another respondent sees a balance:

Postdoctoral opportunities in universities do tend to extend the period of aloofness from human problems for some students. On the other hand, they frequently increase the degree of competence of young people who for some reason or another do turn their attention to the "real world."

Others see no problem at all:

Postdoctoral education is not harmful to industry. There is a growing need for industrial research workers who can dig into fundamental questions. There are plenty of workers who can apply what they discover.

In the words of another corporation executive:

The trend at the university level toward applied research could be dangerous for industry and for the country as a whole, if it in any way tended to limit the amount of attention given to basic research or research which might have broad relationships to many potential applications. . . . Since industry research of necessity must relate to the perpetuation of the corporation (which means a continuing, satisfactory profit/loss position), there may be difficulty in mounting research programs which do not look to the possibility of reasonably fast economic return. The postdoctoral education is no problem but, if it would imply that there would be any less activity on the part of the university in the area of economically unrewarding research, and more activity in the payoff areas of applied

---

[5]*Ibid.*

research, the trend would be unfortunate. Industry and the country should look to the universities for research of the type which profit-oriented organizations cannot afford to perform.

The president of another corporation agrees:

> Proper goals for educational institutions, I think, remain (1) training in scientific method and (2) the conduct of basic research not directed toward specific problem-solving. These goals will never be the goals of specialized research institutions, whether private and for profit or nonprofit. . . . I do not believe that the university experience of a young PhD in motivating him away from applied research and toward basic research is bad. In fact, I think it is good.

Finally, one should add the statement from the vice-president for engineering and research of an electronics company:

> I want to pay my respects to the fact that the young PhD or postdoctorate fellow from good universities has a sophisticated and up-to-date knowledge of what you consider to be the latest and the newest in your line of business. Considering that it takes an average of five years now to bring out a young PhD in the physical sciences, this speaks extremely well for the universities and the faculty.

It is not surprising in the light of these mixed views of postdoctoral education that only a minority of institutions actively recruit for new personnel among postdoctoral students. Only a third of the respondents in industry say that they actively recruit from this source, and the proportion of respondents in nonprofit research organizations and federal and federal-contract laboratories who say that they recruit postdoctorals is not much higher. Some say that they like to hire them when they can, but they do not actively seek them; others that they look for them when they need their particular expertise. But the impression remains that outside the universities postdoctorals are not at much of a premium. Some corporations that recruit among postdoctorals look for them not because they prefer them but because they would be missing good talent by overlooking them. The spokesman for a major chemical concern writes: "We actively seek but do not necessarily prefer research personnel with postdoctoral experience." The vice-chairman of the board of an electronics firm writes in the same vein:

> We do not actively seek postdoctoral experience. We look for individuals, not for categories, and we will hire any man whose experience and personal qualifications suggest that he is a good risk. If the postdoctoral category happens to relate to a particular individual with demonstrated creativity and exceptional performance, we will reach for him as a candidate for staff membership.

The following statement by the vice-president for research of a major firm in the field of graphical reproduction appears to sum up the situation for many:

> We do look for "fresh" PhD's and those with one or two years of postdoctoral experience. We have had an increasing number of individuals with postdoctoral training join the Labo-

ratories in recent years. We do not necessarily prefer such individuals; any preference is based on whether the added year or two in the university will enable a man to contribute more effectively because of the specialization which the additional training has developed.

He goes on to say:

> I have the feeling that most of the individuals taking postdoctoral work believe that today, to obtain good academic appointments, postdoctoral experience is required or, at least, is an asset in looking for a job. It is my impression resulting from our interviewing PhD candidates that those who have already developed an interest in industrial research feel that one or two years in the university will not be of much assistance to them in furthering their career. They are anxious to get on with the job where they are convinced their future lies.

The overall impression is that the implications of postdoctoral education for the nonacademic employers of doctorate recipients is slight. Whatever the failings that are perceived in the doctoral programs or in academic attitudes, they do not indict postdoctoral study, which is generally understood to be preparing PhD's for academic posts. There is, however, evidence that the coupling between the universities and the nonuniversity institutions is not as smooth as it might be. Lack of mutual understanding is apparent on both sides, and efforts should be made to educate both about needs and missions.

CHAPTER

# 8
# The Foreign Postdoctoral

From the point of view of research productivity, the question of the nationality of the investigator is irrelevant. The important question is "Can he contribute?" The answer depends on the previous training and research record of the individual, on his motivation and persistence, on his ability to work effectively with the other members of the research group, and, of course, on his native ability. It is possible in the first approximation to attribute national characteristics to the style of education, to the mode and breadth of research activities, and to the cultural attributes that describe personality and drive, but these are the components of a stereotype and are particularly inappropriate when one is looking for the creative researcher.

From the point of view of research in the American setting, which is supported mainly by tax funds and often directed toward problems arising from the American national desires, the nationality of the investigator may raise questions with political overtones. If we restrict ourselves to postdoctoral research, those questions take the following forms:

Are American scientists being displaced from postdoctoral positions by foreigners?

Is the foreign scientist being exploited by being paid a lower salary than his American counterpart for comparable work?

Is the foreign scientist merely doing our research for us, or is he being prepared for a position in his home country?

## THE FOREIGN POSTDOCTORAL

If the foreign scientist returns to his home country, have we lost in salary and research expenses more than we received in research accomplished?

If the foreign scientist wishes to stay in the United States, what is our responsibility to his home country?

It is difficult to answer these questions, due to the policy vacuum in which they are posed and in which postdoctoral study in general is supported. Except in the specific fellowship and traineeship programs (many of which exclude foreign participation), postdoctorals are essentially "hired hands" as far as the supporting agency is concerned. Although some programs of some agencies ask for names and credentials of postdoctorals supported on research grants and contracts, the majority of programs provide the necessary funds on the basis of the judgment of the agency as to what the most efficient level of effort will be for the proposed research. The professor is given a "hunting license," i.e., the funds to pay for an as yet unspecified postdoctoral. The decision on the identity of the postdoctoral is made locally by the faculty member with whatever review is provided by his departmental colleagues or the university administration. There is no federal policy or national consensus among the universities regarding the nature of the appointment except that it is to assist the research effort.

Since 81 percent of the foreign postdoctorals in the physical sciences and 68 percent of those in the biological sciences are supported from research grants, this lack of policy is particularly pertinent to the questions raised above. If the purpose of postdoctoral appointments is solely to make the research more efficient (and this is the argument made especially by the mission-oriented agencies), a professor would be derelict if he did not seek the best assistance he could find for the money. If it is possible to hire a more experienced foreign scientist for the same salary he would have to pay an inexperienced American PhD,[1] then he would be prudent to do so. The reasons that may prompt the foreign scientist to take the position, the training experience that may be present in the postdoctoral appointment, and the relevance of the research for the country from which the scientist comes are deemed not to be the responsibility of the agency program officer. The congressional mandate is to procure research to fulfill the mission of the agency.

In some cases the language of the enabling legislation explicitly excludes training as an allowable expenditure. That training takes place is, officially, serendipitous; if the appointment is structured to enhance the training at the expense of efficiency, the procedure is probably illegal.

Training does occur, however, and at the time of our census of postdoctorals almost 5,000 foreign scientists were enjoying the experience.[2] Although

---
[1] See Chapter 9.
[2] Because of the large foreign component of the postdoctoral population, many of the tables in previous chapters of this report have presented data for U. S. citizens and for-

not as a matter of national policy and not integrated with other forms of foreign assistance, the United States was in fact supporting a major fraction of this group. Unlike most foreign aid, the money was almost always spent in this country and did not contribute to the gold drain, but the long-range international implications of this activity are likely to be great. Through postdoctoral study in this country, the scientific leadership of many parts of the world has gained (or will have gained) intimate knowledge not only of our science but of our society: In addition we have gained whatever research contribution foreign postdoctorals may have made while they were here.

Perhaps each question raised at the beginning of this chapter really has no one answer. Since each participant—postdoctoral, mentor and agency officer—is permitted to define the purposes from his own point of view, one must also ask him to answer the questions from his point of view. The foreign postdoctoral is looking for training or at least experience in American laboratories. The agency program officer is purchasing research. The faculty mentor is caught in the middle, with little in the way of administrative guidelines.

## Impact on United States Universities

Approximately 55 percent of post-PhD's and 40 percent of postprofessional doctorate recipients in universities are not U. S. citizens. When asked if this proportion of foreign postdoctorals was a matter of concern, over two thirds of the university administrators expressed none. A few regretted the relative lack of American students, some worried over the brain drain and the high proportion of foreign students in certain fields, but less than 15 percent expressed concern in any general way. Even then, their alarm was tempered. The spokesman for one institution said that the foreign ratio was "somewhat high," for another it was "some cause for concern," and for another "of some concern."

Many graduate deans explain the large numbers of foreign postdoctorals in terms of the salary scale. Said one dean from a southern university:

We feel that one reason for the high incidence of foreign postdoctorals is that the usual postdoctoral stipends are attractive to foreigners, whereas they may not be very competitive with what a young PhD could earn in this country by taking a well-paying job in industry or even in higher education.

The dean at a technological institution agreed: "I suspect that, while there is a demand for postdoctoral education among United States PhD's, they are

---

eigners separately. Refer particularly to Chapter 4. Appendix B-3 presents data on foreign postdoctorals by country of origin.

## THE FOREIGN POSTDOCTORAL

also reluctant to accept stipends of $5,000 to $7,000 per year (even with tax benefits)." Still another dean suggests that:

> The large number of foreign postdoctorals on our campuses probably results from the fact that foreigners will come to work on our sponsored research projects for smaller salaries than Americans of similar qualifications would require.

It is difficult to accept this argument, however, after examining the number of American postdoctorals. In 1967 we find that 26 percent of the physics PhD's, 33 percent of the chemistry PhD's, and 58 percent of the biochemistry PhD's (Table 10, p. 60) were taking postdoctoral positions as their first post-degree activity; it is difficult to believe that Americans do not find postdoctoral appointments attractive.[3] It is more likely that the dean from a developing university was correct when he asserted:

> In the fields in which I am familiar, the large numbers of foreign postdoctorals simply reflects the fact that the capacity for directing research, measured both in terms of faculty talent and government money exceeds the supply of American candidates. I should think that this is one of the more effective uses of United States funds if it were to be regarded as a type of foreign aid. I expect it is not unlike the flow of American chemists to German universities before the first war, and that it simply reflects a response to the opportunity and the quality of what is going on in our universities.

This does not mean that there is no exploitation of the foreign postdoctoral. The dean at a midwestern university said, "It has been said that foreign postdoctoral appointees are a cheap source of labor. I am afraid that in some cases this is true." The dean at another university was more explicit:

> ... I suspect that the particular mix between foreign postdoctorals and citizens of the United States depends upon the drawing power of a particular professor. He will normally pick the most promising men applying to work with him, although he may be influenced somewhat by his desire to be known and have influence in particular foreign countries. Some of the so-called foreign postdoctorals are simply hired hands and reflect the fact that some foreigners, often with not too great ability, are willing to do kinds of work which American postdoctorals or graduate students will not do.

Table 49 shows that, among post-PhD's, the foreign postdoctorals are unevenly distributed among the universities. In the ten leading institutions the U. S. postdoctorals constitute almost half of the population, whereas in the developing institutions only 38 percent of the postdoctorals are U. S. citizens.

A related situation is demonstrated in Table 50, where the foreign postdoctorals according to the per capita GNP of their home country are distributed among the types of universities. Not only do the developing universities

---

[3] This assumes that the American postdoctorals have no less financial need or no less marketability than their classmates who do not seek postdoctoral appointments. Both assumptions are probably true.

IMPACT ON U.S. UNIVERSITIES

TABLE 49  PhD Postdoctorals at U.S. Academic Institutions, by Type of Institution and Citizenship

| Type of Academic Institution | U.S. | Foreign with U.S. PhD | Foreign with Foreign PhD | Total Percent | Number |
|---|---|---|---|---|---|
| Ten leading | 49 | 12 | 39 | 100 | 1,943 |
| Twenty other major | 46 | 10 | 43 | 100 | 1,586 |
| Established | 45 | 11 | 44 | 100 | 1,092 |
| Developing | 38 | 12 | 51 | 100 | 643 |
| Other | 64 | 11 | 25 | 100 | 362 |
| Total | 47 | 11 | 42 | 100 | 5,626 |

Source: NRC, Office of Scientific Personnel, Postdoctoral Census Questionnaire.

have a higher fraction of postdoctorals from abroad, they also tend to attract foreigners from the less-developed countries. As the dean of one of the developing universities expressed it:

I have doubts about the large number of foreign postdoctorals. One reason for this large number seems to be that they often apply to less-well-known universities to work with less-than-famous faculty members. They take positions that many American postdoctorals would not be interested in. How good this is for their training, and how much it helps the reputation of American science abroad may be questionable.

Nevertheless, the vast majority of administrators are in favor of the presence of foreign postdoctorals and feel that the expense involved in their training is more than compensated for by the benefits that are derived from having them. Not only is the research in this country enriched by the contributions that these people make while here, but they often bring to our researchers techniques and approaches to research that have been developed abroad. Beyond the cost–benefit analysis, however, is the large consensus that international education is a responsibility of the world's richest country. The dean at an eastern university asserted:

The large proportion of foreign persons among the postdoctoral population is no cause for alarm. The preponderance will phase out within a few years as the wave of the postwar population boom swells the ranks of postdoctoral fellows. The contribution that United States institutions make to the postdoctoral education of foreign nationals will be amply repaid in a continuing flow of the academic progeny which these foreign postdoctorals will produce upon their return to their native countries. Also, good talent is always a good investment and attracts its own kind.

TABLE 50  Distribution of Foreign Postdoctorals among U.S. Academic Institutions, by GNP Rating of Foreign Country of Origin

| Per Capita GNP of Foreign Countries of Origin | Percentage of Foreign Postdoctorals by Type of Academic Institution ||||| Total || Percentage of Non-USA World Population |
|---|---|---|---|---|---|---|---|---|
| | Ten Leading | Twenty Other Major | Established | Developing | Other | Percent | Number | |
| High (above $750) | 73 | 69 | 66 | 57 | 56 | 66 | 2,790 | 20 |
| Medium ($250-$749) | 6 | 7 | 5 | 5 | 13 | 7 | 317 | 12 |
| Low ($100-$249) | 10 | 11 | 11 | 11 | 22 | 13 | 541 | 37 |
| Very low (below $100) | 11 | 13 | 18 | 27 | 9 | 14 | 605 | 31 |
| Total (%) | 100 | 100 | 100 | 100 | 100 | 100 | | 100 |
| (N) | 1,158 | 1,053 | 703 | 487 | 852 | | 4,253 | |

Source: NRC, Office of Scientific Personnel, Postdoctoral Census Questionnaire.

A dean from a large midwestern university felt that the net cost of training a foreign postdoctoral is much less than that for a predoctoral. He suggested that we should limit predoctoral education of foreign nationals to those whose countries cannot provide it for them. He went on to say:

> Thus it seems to me that the best time for all concerned for a student to come to America is at the postdoctoral level. He has no degree at stake, no program, nothing to do but research, and thus is free to observe what goes on in our educational institutions at a stage at which maturity is sufficient and obligations minimal. . . . We must continue to make our contribution to the education of foreign nationals at whatever level is of most service to the world.

There was no consensus among the administrators on what might constitute a disproportionate number of foreigners. Most had no formula to suggest; a few named percentages, seemingly at random. One west coast dean, however, reported that a committee at his institution had recommended "that the proportion of foreign graduate students in a department should not be allowed to jeopardize the essentially American character of the training being given in that department." He went on to say:

> The Committee guessed that a level of about 20 percent of foreign graduate students should be the maximum. I think the same principle would apply to the postdoctoral candidates from the point of view of their really getting an effective exposure to American knowledge. In other words, if they become too high a proportion of the students in a department, they will find it increasingly hard to get what they came here for.

Leaving aside questions of policy, let us examine what the foreign postdoctoral picture looks like and why, from the point of view of the foreign postdoctoral himself and that of his faculty mentor. Science has long had an international flavor, with national boundaries or political beliefs having only minor or temporary implications for its development. The growth of American science since the turn of the century is immeasurably indebted to scientists from abroad. Not only have large numbers of our own PhD's received their postdoctoral training in Europe, but the scientists who migrated to this country during the 1930's to escape Germany included many who have added to our scientific reputation. Since 1930 the United States has received 83 of the 168 Nobel prizes awarded in physics, chemistry, and medicine. Of these, 20, or 24 percent, were won by immigrants to this country.[4]

In a fascinating account of the development of American physics in the 1920's and the subsequent rise in the numbers of refugee scientists from Germany in the 1930's, Charles Weiner[5] writes:

---

[4] Harriet Zuckerman, private communication. Included among the 83 U. S. Nobel prizes are four awarded to noncitizens who had been long-term residents of the United States.
[5] Charles Weiner, *A New Site for the Seminar: The Refugees and American Physics in the Thirties,* Perspectives in American History, Vol. 2, Harvard, 1968.

## THE FOREIGN POSTDOCTORAL

During the years immediately preceding the rise of the Third Reich, Europe was bubbling with intellectual activity in many fields of scholarship. Physics was especially ebullient. The relatively small group of scientists in this field had a profound awareness of recent radical change in the concepts of physics and expectations of more to come. European physicists and their students were constantly in motion, traveling back and forth to exchange newly born ideas. As today, travel and communication were essential aspects of the life of physicists, contrary to the folkloric image of the scientist locked up in his laboratory, uninterested in personal interactions. . . . Indeed there developed what can be described as a traveling seminar as a group of distinguished physicists attended a series of international conferences and seminars during this period, at Brussels, Leipzig, Rome, Copenhagen, Lake Como, London or elsewhere.

Young physicists traveled to learn new experimental techniques, to supplement their background by exposure to different ideas, styles, and traditions of research, and sometimes simply to meet their colleagues. Members of the group of physicists under the leadership of Enrico Fermi in Rome, for instance, were regularly dispatched to different laboratories during the heat of each summer to take advantage of larger research facilities or to learn new techniques in the relative coolness of London, Copenhagen, Hamburg, New York, or Pasadena. In the course of these migrations Emilio G. Segre visited Otto Stern in Hamburg and Pieter Zeeman in Amsterdam, Franco Rasetti visited Lise Meitner in Berlin and Robert A. Millikan in Pasadena, Edoardo Amaldi visited Peter Debye in Leipzig, and Fermi crossed the Atlantic to lecture at the University of Michigan. Reciprocally, Rome was host to other physicists from all over the world.

Since that time science has grown immensely and much of the excitement has migrated from Europe to the United States. Weiner's description of the reasons the young physicists traveled is an adequate description of the fundamental purpose of postdoctoral study in most fields and is certainly applicable to those from abroad who come here to do research.

### Countries of Origin

At the time of our census, we counted 4,845 foreign postdoctorals from 81 different countries who were in the United States at all types of host institutions (see Appendix B-3 for complete listing). Five countries (United Kingdom, India, Japan, Germany, and Canada), however, account for over half of all foreign postdoctorals and only 13 countries for three quarters of them. Thirty-seven of the countries are represented by ten or fewer postdoctorals; 24 countries by three or fewer. We are dealing, therefore, with a highly concentrated situation with relatively few countries having a significant impact. Figure 19 shows the numbers from the 13 major contributors of foreign postdoctorals.

Even though the highly developed countries of the world (per capita gross national product of $750 or more per year) account for only 20 percent of the world's population outside the United States, postdoctorals from these countries constitute 66 percent of the foreign postdoctorals (see Table 50). Among

**COUNTRIES OF ORIGIN**

### FIGURE 19
Number of Postdoctorals from the 13 Countries That Were the Source of Three-Quarters of All Foreign Postdoctorals.

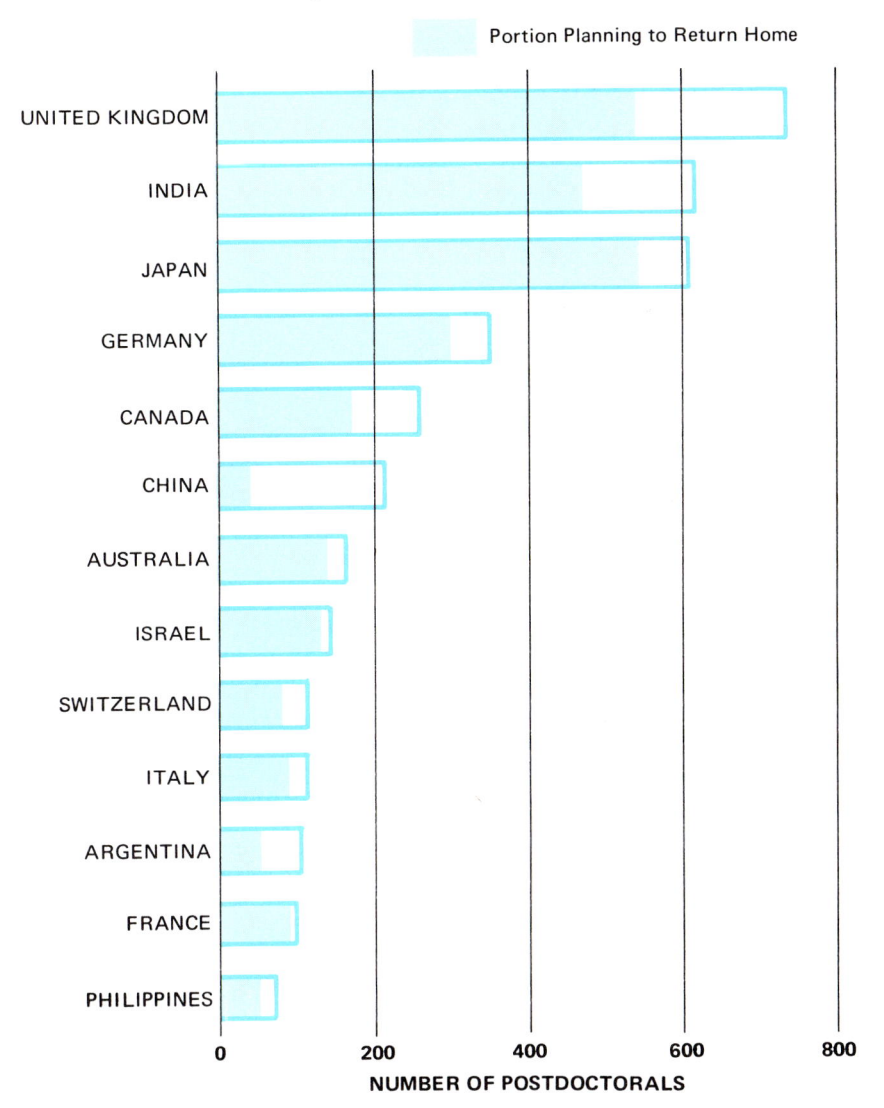

Portion Planning to Return Home

|  | |
|---|---|
| UNITED KINGDOM | ~720 |
| INDIA | ~600 |
| JAPAN | ~600 |
| GERMANY | ~360 |
| CANADA | ~260 |
| CHINA | ~210 |
| AUSTRALIA | ~170 |
| ISRAEL | ~140 |
| SWITZERLAND | ~110 |
| ITALY | ~110 |
| ARGENTINA | ~100 |
| FRANCE | ~100 |
| PHILIPPINES | ~70 |

NUMBER OF POSTDOCTORALS

Source: NRC, Office of Scientific Personnel, Postdoctoral Census Questionnaire.

TABLE 51  Percentage of Foreign Postdoctorals by Field, from Six Leading Countries

Percentage of Foreign Postdoctorals by Field from Six Leading Countries

| Postdoctoral Field | United Kingdom | India | Japan | West Germany | Canada | China | U.S. Citizens % |
|---|---|---|---|---|---|---|---|
| EMP |  |  |  |  |  |  |  |
| Physics | 56 | 51 | 35 | 57 | 33 | 54 | 27 |
| Chemistry | 15 | 13 | 7 | 20 | 14 | 20 | 11 |
|  | 32 | 30 | 19 | 25 | 10 | 23 | 10 |
| BIOSCIENCES | 30 | 35 | 36 | 28 | 21 | 30 | 30 |
| Biochemistry | 14 | 18 | 17 | 14 | 9 | 17 | 11 |
| MEDICAL SCIENCES | 10 | 9 | 23 | 7 | 40 | 9 | 30 |
| Internal medicine | 4 | 4 | 8 | 3 | 16 | 4 | 12 |
| OTHER | 5 | 5 | 6 | 8 | 6 | 7 | 13 |
| TOTAL ALL FIELDS |  |  |  |  |  |  |  |
| Percent | 100 | 100 | 100 | 100 | 100 | 100 | 100 |
| Number | 748 | 621 | 609 | 352 | 264 | 217 | 5,896 |

Source: NRC, Office of Scientific Personnel, Postdoctoral Census Questionnaire.

the 13 leading countries in the number of postdoctorals in the United States, only India, China, and the Philippines are not categorized as highly developed.

It is difficult, however, to understand the distribution of foreign postdoctorals among the fields. There is no real correlation between the categorization by GNP and the fields of research. Perhaps this is too much to expect. Postdoctoral study is sufficiently determined by individual tastes and abilities that it alone need not show such relationships. There is also the probability that local strengths in certain fields will show up as a deficit in the number of postdoctorals in those fields leaving the country to pursue their studies. In any case, Table 51 shows the distribution of postdoctorals from the six leading countries among the fields of study. Only Canada and Japan have distributions similar to that of the United States.

The large numbers of foreign postdoctorals would seem to imply that a great many faculty members find them useful to the research projects on which they work. For the most part the implication is valid. Many foreign postdoctorals are sought for the particular skills and knowledge that they possess. An often-repeated comment by chemists around the country is that European, and especially German, chemists have excellent command of laboratory techniques. A professor with research ideas found a postdoctoral from Germany especially useful in implementing them. An oceanographer with special interest in photosynthesis in a marine environment settled on a Canadian and a Dutchman for his postdoctorals, after making inquiries all over the world for people who could help him and who would be willing to work in his floating laboratory. He was particularly enthusiastic about the Dutchman, who brought an excellent knowledge of certain enzymes of interest to the professor. The physics department head at a leading midwestern university put it this way:

Postdoctorals from countries where scientific research is well developed bring to the United States novel points of view, ideas, methods and interpretations. The exchange of ideas between our department and physicists in certain countries, or even in particular laboratories, is often maintained for years by a succession of young postdoctorals or faculty on leave moving in each direction. Extensive and helpful exchanges have developed between our department and universities in England, West Germany, Italy, France, and Japan; less extensive ones with Switzerland, the Netherlands, the USSR and India.

There is evidence, however, that in other cases the foreign postdoctoral is accepted as being merely the best of a disappointing set of applicants. Although one chemist had high praise for his postdoctorals from Germany and Korea, he admitted that the Americans he was able to attract were not of a high caliber. Another chemist was able to characterize postdoctorals from specific countries with phrases like "bright but lazy," "industrious but unimaginative," "bright and hardworking, but difficult to communicate with," and "incompetent." When asked why so many of his postdoctorals were from the country he labeled as producing "incompetent" postdoctorals, he admitted that he accepted them because their applications were the best he had available.

THE FOREIGN POSTDOCTORAL

The problem appears to be one of advertising or, more accurately, the lack of advertising. A professor with a research grant that provides funds for postdoctoral assistance is often limited in his ability to make these opportunities known. If he is sufficiently renowned, he is often faced with a spontaneous flood of inquiries from interested young holders of the doctorate, both domestic and foreign. Under these circumstances he is able to be quite selective and is often able to provide names of unsuccessful but qualified prospective postdoctorals to less well-known colleagues in his department. But for many investigators the situation is quite different. A man with only limited reputation may receive no unsolicited applications from Americans. If he desires such applications, he is placed in the position of having to write or call colleagues at other institutions to ask if they have any students whom they would recommend for a postdoctoral appointment. Such a procedure is tantamount to admitting that one's professional stature is underdeveloped. On the other hand, he is quite likely to have received requests from a few foreign applicants seeking appointments in this country.

The foreign PhD is often in no position to be choosy. If his doctoral mentor is well known in international circles, the mentor will write to his equally well-known American colleague, suggesting that the student be made a postdoctoral. On the other hand, the student of a less well-known professor must write to many professors in this country, asking for an appointment. Not knowing who, other than the prestigious scientists, will have funds for postdoctorals, the foreign PhD relies on names he has seen in the literature. Although he prefers to be picked up by one of the better-known men he has written to, his desire to come to this country is such that he will accept an offer from almost anyone.

The combination of these two circumstances produces a situation in which the professor may accept a foreign postdoctoral who does not meet the standards that the professor would have liked. He is fearful that a failure on his part to fill the position with someone might result in a reduction in his grant or contract when it comes up for renewal. This "use it or lose it" syndrome, as it is called by the program officers in the federal agencies, undoubtedly plays a role in the foreign postdoctoral picture, although it is difficult to assess to what degree.[6]

It must be recalled (Table 49) that one fifth of the foreign postdoctorals received their PhD's in this country. Consequently, as far as initial postdoctoral appointments are concerned, they must be treated as Americans. If their

---

[6]The federal monitors of research grants show a mixed reaction to the foreign postdoctoral. Some are concerned with the "use it or lose it" philosophy and others are confident that the foreign postdoctorals are pulling their own weight. Most feel that the quality of the faculty they support is sufficiently high that these investigators are able to select their postdoctorals with care.

background is weak, it is a reflection on American higher education rather than that of the home country. It is of interest to know how those trained abroad compare with their American counterparts. We asked the faculty to give an overall evaluation by country of the quality of previous research training of the postdoctorals. Of course there is wide variation in individual postdoctorals, but as can be seen in Figure 20, with regard to both theoretical training and experimental training there is a definite correlation between the quality of the previous training and the degree of development of the country of origin. We have combined all fields in Figure 20 in order to enhance the statistical significance. The individual fields show the same general trend.

In every field for both theoretical and experimental training (with the sole exception of experimental training in chemistry) more faculty find the foreign postdoctoral less well trained than Americans than find him better trained. Only for theoretical training in chemistry and the medical specialties and for experimental training in physiology, in the social sciences, and in the medical specialties, however, do a majority of the faculty feel that the foreign postdoctoral is less well trained. The overall impression is that foreign postdoctorals are somewhat less desirable than Americans and that their large numbers reflect in part a shortage of Americans.

Two questions of importance with regard to the foreign postdoctoral are: Is the training he receives here relevant to the needs of his home country? and Does he go home? These two questions are related, but in neither case is the imperative clear. Should the training be relevant and should he go home? It is not the function of this study to resolve the "brain drain" issue, although we have gathered information and commentary on the subject.

## Return to Countries of Origin

To repeat an earlier statement, there is a sense in which the postdoctoral experience is aimed at individual rather than at national development. In all countries, the United States included, the postdoctoral is a member of a tiny minority; even among holders of the doctorate he is relatively rare. The experience is often important for those people who anticipate making fundamental contributions to knowledge, regardless of their citizenship. The individual who shows great promise of being able to advance our understanding of physics or biochemistry, even if he is a citizen of India or Bolivia, ought not to be denied the opportunity to make that contribution simply because his country is not yet prepared to capitalize upon it. This is not to argue that all graduates of higher education of any country should be encouraged to take postdoctoral work, but that exceptional opportunities should be made available for excep-

218

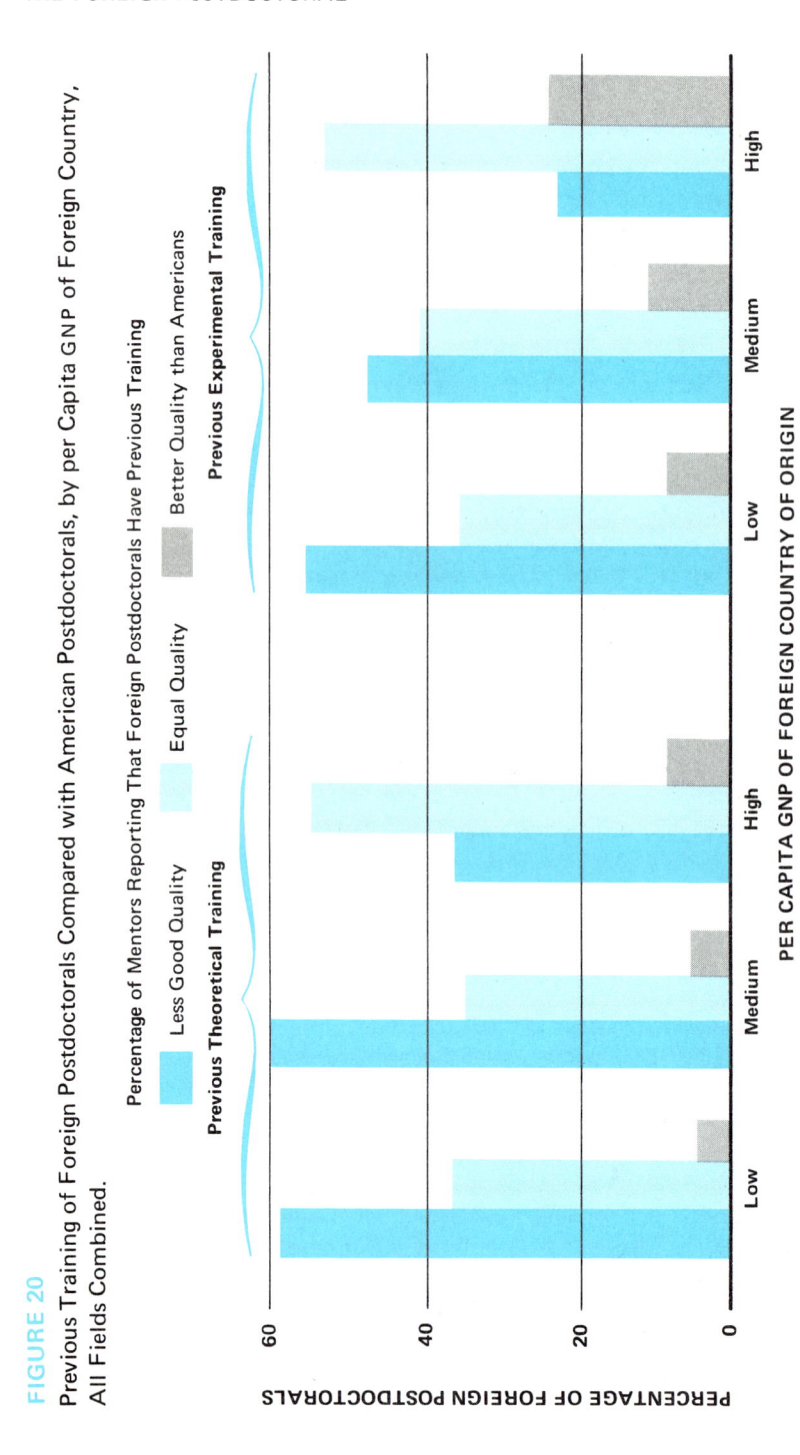

THE FOREIGN POSTDOCTORAL

**FIGURE 20** Previous Training of Foreign Postdoctorals Compared with American Postdoctorals, by per Capita GNP of Foreign Country, All Fields Combined.

Source: NRC, Office of Scientific Personnel, Postdoctoral Faculty Questionnaire

tional people. It would be unfortunate to deny a promising scientist the opportunity to develop himself to his fullest capacity, and most postdoctorals think of themselves first as scientists and then as citizens of particular countries.

At any rate, there has been little effort made to adapt the postdoctoral experience to the home country's needs. This lack of effort results, in part, from the means of support. The research that the faculty member is doing and in which the postdoctoral participates is performed in response to American national needs. Federal agencies support research that is appropriate to the stage of development of this country; if it is appropriate for another country, that circumstance is accidental. In part, the failure to make the research relevant for the home country of the foreign postdoctoral results from an ignorance of what such research might be. Even if he wished to provide relevant experience for his foreign postdoctorals, the American faculty member is unlikely to know what kind of experience would be appropriate. He is, after all, a chemist, a physicist, or a biologist, rather than an expert on the needs of a particular developing country.

Nevertheless, when polled, the faculty indicated their estimation of the relevance of the training received by foreign postdoctorals to their home countries' needs. Figure 21 presents the opinions of faculty in three fields. As might have been expected, as one moves from physics through chemistry to the biosciences the degree of relevance increases for those postdoctorals from less-developed countries. In all fields the training is more relevant for highly developed countries, i.e., countries more like the United States. As noted above, however, faculty mentors are not necessarily the best evaluators on this subject.

Accurate numbers on the extent of migration of scientific personnel are difficult to obtain. In the literature on the subject[7] various methods are used, but nearly all of them have pitfalls. It is almost impossible to distinguish the bona fide visitor who intends to go home from the disguised immigrant. Even when a man leaves the United States, it may be with the intention to return when the two-year limitation imposed by some visas has passed. This is especially likely if he goes to a third country rather than his home country. How long one should wait before deciding that a man will not immigrate is arbitrary.

We have gathered three different sorts of information pertaining to the migration question. Each postdoctoral who answered our census questionnaire was asked to indicate his probable location following his current appointment. The faculty mentor was asked to list the foreign postdoctorals who worked for him in 1961-62 and to give their current addresses, if known. They were able to locate an extraordinary 94 percent of the postdoctorals, usually with street addresses! We also asked the mentors where their current postdoctorals intended

[7] A rather complete bibliography appears in *Brain Drain and Brain Gain*, Research Policy Program, Lund, Sweden, 1967.

220
THE FOREIGN POSTDOCTORAL

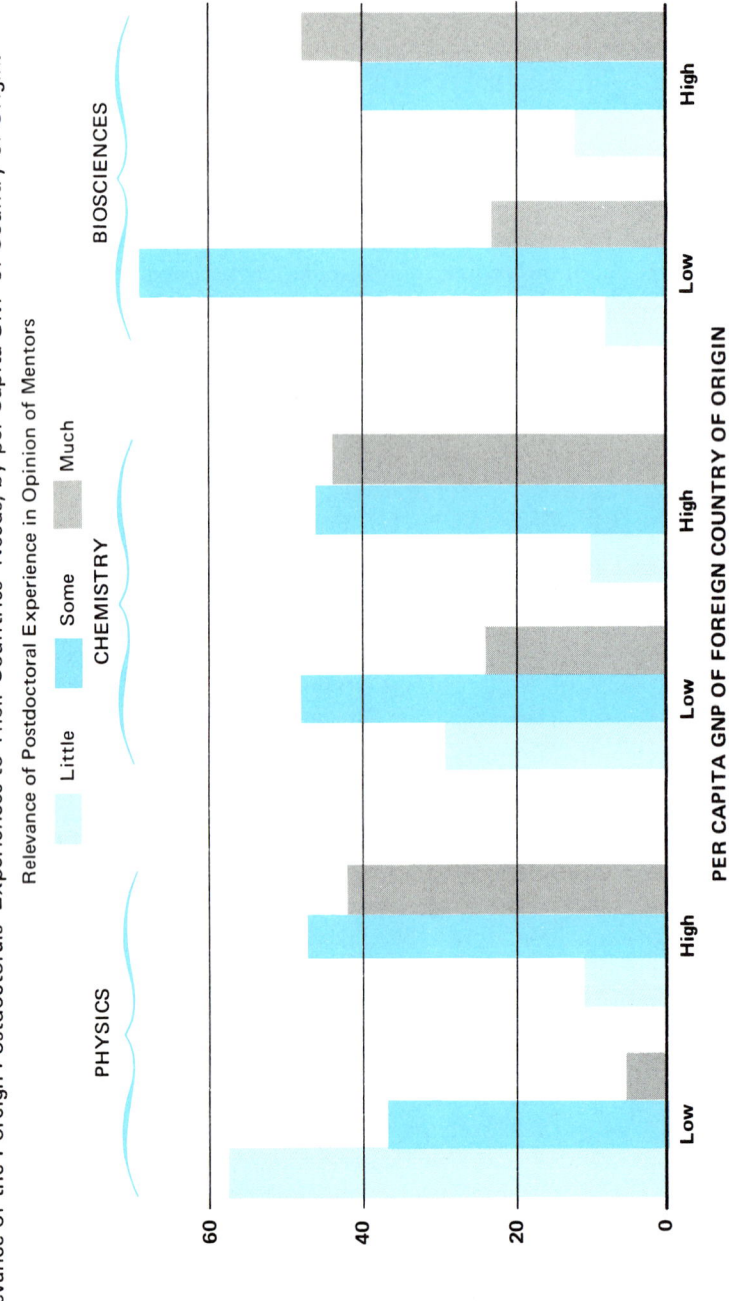

FIGURE 21
Relevance of the Foreign Postdoctorals' Experiences to Their Countries' Needs, by per Capita GNP of Country of Origin.
Relevance of Postdoctoral Experience in Opinion of Mentors

Source: NRC, Office of Scientific Personnel, Postdoctoral Faculty Questionnaire.

RETURN TO COUNTRIES OF ORIGIN

to settle. The results of these inquiries are shown in Table 52.

Rather consistently more of the 1967 foreign postdoctorals intended to return home and fewer planned to stay in the United States or go to a third country than the actual performance of the 1961-62 postdoctorals would indicate. Even if we assume that nothing had changed between 1961-62 and 1967, the two sets of data could be consistent. The postdoctoral could go home and return to the United States or another country at a later date. The relevant conditions, however, had not stayed the same; during this period there was a rapid change in the number of academic institutions abroad, both in developed and undeveloped countries. It may well be that there are more opportunities at home for people with postdoctoral backgrounds today than there were in the early 1960's.[8]

In all of the data there is a relationship between per capita GNP and the tendency to return home, with those from very low-income countries showing

TABLE 52   Future Location as Projected by 1967 Foreign Postdoctorals and Present Location of 1961-62 Foreign Postdoctorals

| Per Capita GNP of Home Country | Year of Postdoctoral Appointment | Home Country | USA | Third Country | Country Unknown | Total |
|---|---|---|---|---|---|---|
| High | 1967 | 71 | 13 | 4 | 12 | 100 |
|  | 1961-62 | 66 | 21 | 7 | 5 | 99 |
| Medium | 1967 | 65 | 21 | 4 | 11 | 101 |
|  | 1961-62 | 61 | 18 | 11 | 10 | 100 |
| Low | 1967 | 44 | 32 | 3 | 21 | 100 |
|  | 1961-62 | 35 | 53 | 4 | 8 | 100 |
| Very low | 1967 | 67 | 18 | 2 | 13 | 100 |
|  | 1961-62 | 49 | 29 | 14 | 8 | 100 |
| Total | 1967 | 66 | 17 | 4 | 13 | 100 |
|  | 1961-62 | 62 | 24 | 8 | 6 | 100 |

Source: NRC, Office of Scientific Personnel, Postdoctoral Census and Faculty Questionnaires.

[8] In the United Kingdom the number of staff members at institutions of higher education grew from 16,000 in 1961-62 to about 21,900 in 1965-66. *Annual Survey, Academic Year 1965-66,* Report of the University Grants Committee.

a surprising reversal (Table 52). The reversal would not be as severe as it appears were it not for the rather extreme figures for China (Taiwan), which is classified as "low" income and which attracts the smallest percentage of its citizens back home (only 14 percent in 1967 and 6 percent in 1961-62). Apparently, the attraction of countries other than one's own increases for the postdoctoral in rough proportion to the difference in the degree of national development. There is no significant dependence of this phenomenon on the field of research.

Because of the different ways of collecting data, it is difficult to estimate what fraction of the brain drain can be attributed to postdoctoral education as defined in this study. If, nevertheless, we combined our data with that drawn elsewhere, some interesting but possibly inconclusive consequences follow. According to testimony before a congressional committee investigating the "brain drain" from developing countries:[9]

China ... had, in 1967, 4,299 students enrolled in the sciences and engineering at U. S. educational institutions but lost through student immigration 1,137, some 26 percent of its enrollment. India had an enrollment of 5,146 but lost 1,074, or 21 percent.

Even the large percentage of Chinese postdoctorals reporting their intention of staying in this country accounts for only 116 (or 10 percent) of the 1,137 immigrants. For India, only 110 (or 10 percent) of 1,074 immigrants were postdoctorals. This means that if every foreign postdoctoral were to return home, the brain drain would still be 90 percent as large as it now is.

Our data also supports the principle well known in international educational circles, that the earlier a student from abroad begins his studies in the United States the more likely he is to remain in this country. Although two thirds of all foreign postdoctorals responding to our postdoctoral census questionnaire declared their intention to return home, only 37 percent of those who received their PhD's in this country so intend. Of those who came to the United States after receiving their doctorate, over 84 percent plan to go home. Thus not only do postdoctorals constitute a small fraction of the brain drain, but the postdoctoral experience itself does not seem to play a major role in the decision not to return home.

In terms of quality, however, the loss of a postdoctoral may be more serious. As indicated earlier in this report, the postdoctoral tends to be the more promising researcher. His failure to return home may have a larger impact than a similar move by a less able compatriot. It may be, on the other hand, that he has become overtrained in terms of his country's needs. There may be no

---

[9] *The Brain Drain of Scientists, Engineers, and Physicians from the Developing Countries into the United States,* hearing before the Research and Technical Programs Subcommittee on Government Operations of the House of Representatives, 90th Congress, January 23, 1968.

position in his home country that would permit him to exploit his specialized knowledge. His dilemma then is whether to stay where he can use what he knows or to suppress that knowledge and return home. As one young post-doctoral from England explained: "I wrote to every university in England, asking for a position in organic chemistry. None was available, so I am staying here. I don't believe there is so much a 'brain drain' as a 'brain overflow.'"

CHAPTER

# 9
# The Finances of Postdoctoral Education

The costs and benefits of postdoctoral education are shared by all of the participants: postdoctoral, host institution, and supporting agency or foundation. However, it is difficult to determine exactly how much accrues to each. Consider, first, the matter of costs. The postdoctoral, especially at the immediate and intermediate levels, receives a stipend that in most cases is substantially below what he might be earning in regular employment; the cost to him is in income foregone. The host institution pays directly in the sharing of research costs and sometimes by use of institutional funds for postdoctoral stipends. It also supports postdoctoral activity indirectly by providing additional space, faculty time, and the many ancillary services that the postdoctoral shares with other members of the university. The sponsoring agency is generally the most obvious supporter through grants to the postdoctoral or to the host institution.

As far as benefits are concerned, from the point of view of the postdoctoral himself the difference between his potential deferred income and his postdoctoral stipend is defrayed in whole or in part by his opportunity to obtain further research training under a certain mentor as well as his expectation of being able to secure a subsequent position in an institution which he respects and of being able to make significant contributions in his field. (As we saw in Chapter 5, he cannot expect a relatively higher income in his subsequent career. In this sense the income lost during his postdoctoral years is permanently lost.)

The federal government, or more generally the supporters of postdoctoral activity, also recover their costs. Many of the postdoctorals are supported on research grants and make positive contributions to scientific and scholarly knowledge. It is, in fact, this creation of knowledge that the sponsors of these postdoctorals are purchasing; under research grants postdoctoral training is a by-product. Conversely, those postdoctorals supported by fellowships or traineeships, presumably established to create or to promote new talent, are also performing research. The roles of prime purpose and by-product are reversed but the consequence is similar. To abstract the costs attributable to the postdoctoral and to identify these costs as the costs of postdoctoral education is to ignore the side benefits. The sponsors are simultaneously purchasing research and training postdoctorals.

Thus, when it comes to specifying the exact costs incurred by each of the participants the situation becomes awkward. Simply to add up the direct expenses is misleading. It is necessary to know what alternative uses of the resources would have produced. The returns on the investment must be projected and subtracted. Even if it were possible to do all this, we should also have to consider the nonquantifiable benefits of increased quality of research, of the altered environment in which graduate education takes place, of the contribution to better international relations, of the heightened sense of individual growth and achievement, etc.

Since such a comprehensive approach has not been possible, we have set a more limited objective. In what follows we shall generally ignore the question of benefits and confine our attention to an analysis of costs. However, the average figures that will be presented must not be taken out of context or extrapolated to situations not comparable to those discussed here. For example, we shall discuss the cost per postdoctoral at some selected universities. This will be the marginal cost of adding one more postdoctoral to an institution already deeply involved in research and postdoctoral education. It would be an error to presume that an institution not so involved could add postdoctorals at the same cost. The creation of the setting for postdoctoral activity, including the acquisition of equipment, the construction of research facilities, and the amassing of top level faculty, would cost quite a bit more.

## Stipends

The least ambiguous aspect of the cost of postdoctoral education concerns the stipend received by the postdoctoral. Whatever the intangible benefits of his appointment, the postdoctoral must eat and have shelter. If he had been a predoctoral fellowship holder previously, the immediate postdoctoral lived as a graduate student on an income that ranged from $2,400 to $3,600 a year. If he has no children, his wife has probably been working to augment the family income. If he has children, he is eager to see his income increased substantially. Whether it will or not depends strongly on the field, on the nature of his support, and on the employer. The nationality of the postdoctoral will have some effect, and the sex of the postdoctoral is a significant factor. If he defers his postdoctoral appointment to the intermediate or senior stage, his income will be commensurate with his seniority.

Because these variables have an effect and because the mix of support patterns, of nationality, of sex and level differs among the fields, we must not simply take field averages. On the other hand, the spread of stipends holding all the variables fixed is sufficiently great that only in a statistical sense can we speak of the dependence of the stipend on these variables. With this warning, it is of interest to note that a woman can expect about $1,400 less per year than a man and an immediate postdoctoral about $1,030 less than an intermediate postdoctoral. The difference in stipend between a fellow and a project associate is less clear from our census data since, as we have seen in Chapter 4, the postdoctoral is less sure of whether he is a fellow than he is of the size of his stipend. If we assume that his description of his type of appointment is correct, fellows on the average make $950 per year less than project associates. It is likely that the difference is really greater, but there are partial compensations that we will discuss later.

Once one eliminates the dependence on sex and level one can examine intrinsic differences in stipend among the fields. In Figure 22 we show the stipends of U. S. male immediate postdoctorals at universities and also the total annualized compensation (salary plus fringe benefits) offered to new assistant professors. Although we have not separated fellows from project associates, there remain some significant differences among the fields. Chemistry does not have proportionately more fellowships than physics, and yet there is almost a $2,000 difference in postdoctoral stipends in favor of physics. There are many more fellowships and traineeships in the biological sciences and this accounts for the relatively low stipends there. Apparently it is the pattern in chemistry to pay lower stipends even for project associateships. Similar, but smaller, differences exist in faculty salaries.

The wide differences between postdoctoral stipends and faculty salaries were not expected. Earlier commentators on the postdoctoral situation[1] suggested that the postdoctoral was paid more than the faculty. Even the departmental chairmen estimated the differences to be much smaller than shown. In physics they suggested that the postdoctoral stipend is 85 percent of the assistant professor's salary. In chemistry the ratio was given as 76 percent and in biochemistry as 74 percent. From Figure 22 the ratios of the medians are 64

---

[1] Harold Orlans, *The Effect of Federal Programs on Higher Education*, The Brookings Institution, 1962, p. 82.

STIPENDS

**FIGURE 22**
Median Annual (12-month) Stipends of Postdoctorals Compared with Salaries of Assistant Professors, by Field, 1967.

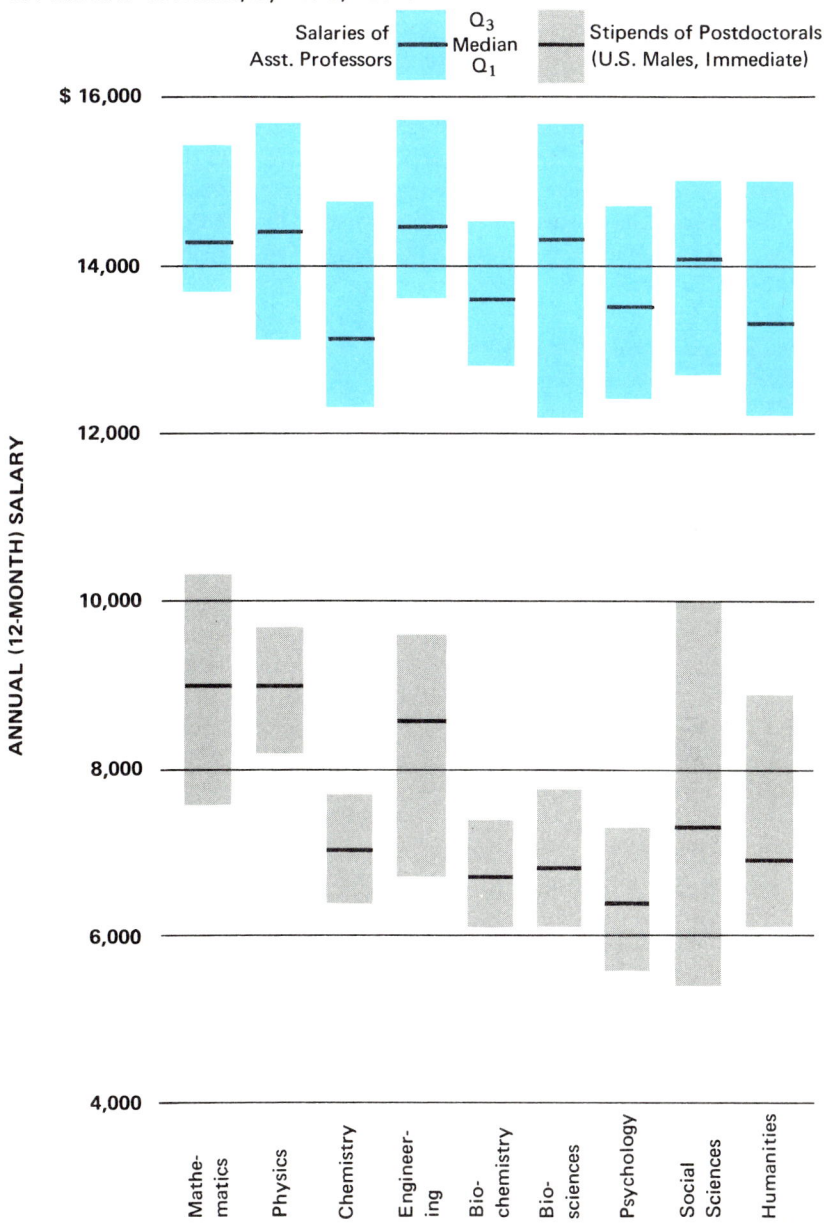

Source: NRC, Office of Scientific Personnel, Postdoctoral Census Questionnaire. American Council on Education (ACE) *Report of a Sample Survey of Salaries of New Faculty, 1967-1968*, by John Caffrey.

percent, 53 percent, and 47 percent respectively. Perhaps this difference can be explained by assuming that the chairmen were comparing academic year salaries of professors with annual stipends of postdoctorals and that they ignored the fringe benefits.

We can see the impact on the postdoctoral's stipend of the host institution, the citizenship, and the level of appointment in Figure 23. Rather consistently nonacademic host institutions offer higher stipends at each level than do the universities. The physical sciences generally pay better than the biosciences and at the universities there is some tendency for foreign postdoctorals to be paid less than Americans. In particular, foreign postdoctorals more than two years beyond the doctorate receive a stipend comparable to immediate U.S. postdoctorals. This may partially explain the large numbers of foreign postdoctorals in fields like chemistry, since for the same stipend that one pays to a relatively inexperienced American postdoctoral, one can attract a more experienced foreign scientist.

We have mentioned the difference between fellowship and project associateship stipends. At universities the largest fellowship programs at the immediate level are the National Institutes of Health Postdoctoral Research Fellowships in health and health-related fields and the National Science Foundation Postdoctoral Fellowships in the broad spectrum of sciences and social sciences. In the former program the basic annual stipend is $6,000 for an individual with no relevant experience beyond the doctorate. If he has one year of such experience the annual stipend is $6,500, and for two or more years, $7,000. In the NSF program the basic stipend is $6,500 with an increment to $7,000 if the fellowship is held beyond one year. In both programs an allowance of $500 per year is added for each dependent and a travel allowance of eight cents per mile is provided for transportation to the fellow's host institution.

These stipends must be compared with the higher salaries usually paid to project associates. The latter's salary is fixed by the market and the availability of funds in a research contract rather than by formula. The difference in income can be a source of irritation in a research group having both fellows and project associates. Comparisons with average industrial salary offers to inexperienced degree holders, even at the baccalaureate level, are more startling.[2]

|  | Industrial Salary Offers 1967-68 | | |
| --- | --- | --- | --- |
|  | Bachelor's | Master's | Doctor's |
| Chemistry | $8,748 | $10,368 | $14,160 |
| Physics | $9,012 | $10,572 | $14,724 |

It is usually argued that there are compensating features in a fellowship. The first is the tax benefits that accrue to the fellowship. An individual is

[2] *College Placement Council Salary Survey,* January 1969.

229
STIPENDS

### FIGURE 23
Annual (12-month) Stipend of Postdoctorals by Citizenship, Type of Host Institution, and Level of Postdoctoral Appointment.

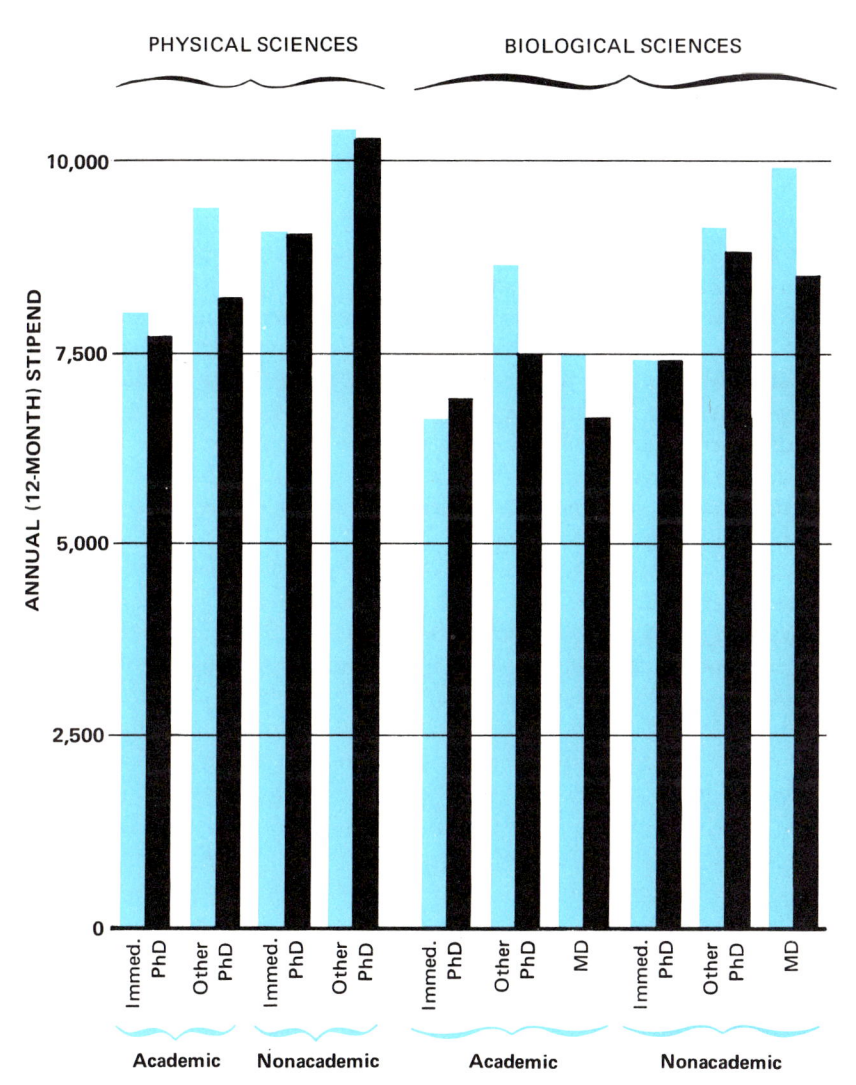

Source: NRC, Office of Scientific Personnel, Postdoctoral Census Data.

allowed to deduct $300 per month from his fellowship stipend (for a total of 36 months in his lifetime) before computing his federal income tax. This can be equivalent to as much as an additional $900 per year in taxable income.

The other compensations cited are the honor of being chosen as a fellow, the freedom of choice in selecting a fellowship institution, and the liberty to work on a research topic of one's own choosing. We have discussed the latter two elsewhere and have discovered that the freedoms are somewhat limited. The prestige derived from national recognition is a separate question and no doubt accounts for the large numbers of candidates for the fellowships. One wonders, however, how many more physicists and mathematicians would apply if the stipends were more comparable with project associate salaries.

At a time when federal support of academic science is leveling off, a decision to increase stipends implies a decision to reduce the number of fellowships. It is a matter of some debate which is greater: the pressure for higher stipends or for more fellowships. For example, the number of fellowships in the physical sciences is already very small, and most observers are unwilling to see it diminished. Commentators seem to agree that at the very least a cost-of-living escalation should be built into the programs. If there were evidence that the fellowship programs were not attracting the very best candidates—and there is no strong evidence for this yet—reassessment of the programs would be desirable because the prestige argument would be weakened considerably.

Postdoctoral appointments in nonacademic institutions such as government laboratories are much more attractive financially. The Postdoctoral Resident Research Associateships and the Postdoctoral Research Associationships operated by the National Research Council for a wide variety of government agencies have stipends (subject to income tax) ranging from $11,500 to over $12,000 at the immediate postdoctoral level. These stipends are comparable to the salaries paid new PhD's who are hired by these same laboratories. In part the differences between the university-based stipends and the government stipends is accounted for by the market. University positions are seen by most postdoctorals as being more attractive.

## University Costs

There are two kinds of costs associated with postdoctoral activity in universities. The first might be called the cost "at" the university and the other the cost "to" the university. The former could be defined as the total cost of maintaining a postdoctoral, irrespective of the source of the supporting funds. The latter would be the net unreimbursed costs incurred by the institution in providing the postdoctoral opportunity. However, as with all other attempts to define unit costs

# UNIVERSITY COSTS

at universities, these concepts present an ambiguity that arises when we try to attribute fractions of professors' time and fractions of facilities to particular groups of students. The identifiable activities of classroom teaching, of lecture preparation, of research guidance and performance, and of self-education on the part of a professor are not neatly divisible. Similar arguments can be made with regard to facilities, administration, and equipment. Either a department has an electron microscope or a cyclotron or it does not; it cannot have one half or one third of either. Faculty, graduate students, postdoctorals, and even undergraduates use the equipment, and it would be there whether or not postdoctorals were present. How much of its cost should then be attributed to the postdoctoral?

Finally, the university produces baccalaureates, master's degrees, doctorates, postdoctorals, and research. These are not independent, like the various products of a diverse industry where the unit cost per refrigerator can be separately calculated from that of a washing machine. To varying degrees students at each level contribute to the research output. Through involvement in teaching, both formally and informally, each level contributes to the production of people at each other level. It would be a major distortion to attempt to pull apart this web.

However, if we ignore the contributions of the postdoctoral to the teaching program and do not attempt to evaluate his augmentation of the research effort, it is possible to identify certain cost items associated, however fuzzily, with the postdoctoral. There is his stipend, including whatever fringe benefits (such as insurance) are involved. One can attribute certain consumable supplies and travel expenses to the postdoctoral. In principle the cost of equipment amortized over its lifetime can be partially assigned to the postdoctoral, especially if it is purchased for his use (as opposed to institutional equipment that would have been acquired in the absence of the postdoctoral). A fraction of the mentor's time can somewhat arbitrarily be assigned to the postdoctoral, although there is little evidence that additional faculty are hired on his account. It is more likely that the presence of postdoctorals causes a redistribution of faculty effort. Finally, there is a portion of the supporting services at the university that might be charged to the postdoctoral. This item includes such indirect costs as office and laboratory space, libraries, secretarial assistance, machine or glass-blowing shops, computing facilities, administration of contracts and general university management and, of course, parking facilities.[3]

If we call the total of these expenditures the cost "at" the university, it is possible to arrive at figures for individual postdoctorals and for departmental averages. Even within departments, however, the spread can be large depending

---

[3] One university official suggested that for those postdoctorals who take or audit courses to make up deficiencies, unpaid tuition represents another cost.

on the particular research projects on which the postdoctorals are working and on the type of appointment. At one university that computed these costs, the totals ranged from $9,175 to $24,573 per year in chemistry. A theoretical scientist who is not using computers is obviously not going to require the same funds as an experimentalist using expensive equipment and supplies. If we ignore these differences and consider only departmental averages, the agreement on total costs at five different universities that provided information was remarkable. Overall, the annual gross cost per postdoctoral at the universities was about $17,500 in physics; in chemistry about $15,300; and in biology about $13,000.

Except for those postdoctorals supported entirely by the university, these costs do not represent the costs "to" the university. Almost all postdoctorals bring with them some fraction of the total costs, depending on the nature of their appointments. It is probably also true that no postdoctoral entirely pays his own way in terms of the costs listed above. It is often said that a project associate does not cost the university anything, since the research grant or contract that is paying his salary also provides the funds for equipment and supplies and contains an item for indirect costs as well. Since the indirect cost rate is usually negotiated at a lower value than the actual costs and since the university must share in the cost of all grants, there is a net cost to the university of serving as host for the research. How much of this residue can or should be attributed to the postdoctoral is less clear.

Postdoctorals supported on training grants represent a larger cost to the university since the indirect cost rate is much smaller than that for research grants. On the other hand, much of their research expense, all of their stipends and fringe benefits, and incidental costs of travel to meetings are generally covered by the training grant.

The fellow is potentially the most costly since he brings little more than his stipend with him. In the NIH and NSF programs allowances of up to $1,000[4] for research expenses are also available but this seldom covers the real costs. If it were not for the research grant held by his mentor, the fellow would require more assistance from the university. In practice his research expenses are paid from research grants. As with the stipend problem, increasing the research allowance implies a reduction in the number of fellowships at the current level of federal spending. However, the case for augmentation in this area is somewhat stronger; the independence of the fellow to pursue research of his own interest is compromised to the extent that he must get support from the ongoing program of his mentor.

[4] It is puzzling in this regard that federal fellowship programs for predoctoral students carry with them a $2,500 "cost of education" allowance per fellow per year, while the federal postdoctoral programs provide much less.

Some of the issues discussed earlier with reference to the costs "at" the university complicate the estimate of costs "to" the university as well. The university is also a beneficiary of the presence of the postdoctoral. He is often involved in formal teaching; he contributes to seminars; he works with graduate students in their research; and he often frees the faculty member for other tasks. There are other costs and benefits which seem nonquantifiable. In an institution whose facilities are used to the full, the postdoctoral could in principle displace a potential graduate student. On the other hand, he no doubt contributes to the "critical size" of research groups. He stimulates research and provides an educational experience for the faculty. If we were adequately to calculate the net costs to the university, we would have to consider whether the same benefits could have been achieved in a different way and, if so, how much would have been saved.

In view of all these aspects of the cost "to" the university it is difficult to obtain meaningful numbers. The same five universities that had fair agreement on total costs could not agree at all on net costs. Their estimates ran from zero to over $8,000 for the unit cost of postdoctorals to the university. It was not possible to get agreement on costing techniques, and even within one school the estimates ranged from $540 to over $6,000.

Some schools have attempted to recover their costs by charging tuition to postdoctorals. However, the charge is usually subject to waiver by the graduate dean if the postdoctoral would have to pay tuition from his stipend. Since this generally would be the case, little money has been raised in this fashion. These schools argue, however, that they are maintaining the principle that each of the groups served by the university should at least partially pay for services received.

## Sources of Support

Although we have stated that all the components of the postdoctoral picture make some contribution to the support of the postdoctoral, it is of interest to know who is providing the basic stipend. The postdoctorals who responded to our census were asked to identify the agency that provided their salaries. Since the money is usually funneled through the host institution, we suggested that the postdoctoral discover the ultimate source by asking his research sponsor. Whether this was done in every case is rather doubtful, since 7.9 percent indicated that their stipend came from the host institution. This number seems high, although we have no direct evidence that it is incorrect.

The distribution of postdoctorals among the supporting agencies is given in Table 53. The federal government is responsible for over two thirds of the post-

## THE FINANCES OF POSTDOCTORAL EDUCATION

TABLE 53   Number and Percentage of Postdoctorals, by Reported Source of Support

| Source of Support | Postdoctorals Number | Percent |
|---|---|---|
| NSF | 906 | 8.4 |
| PHS | 4,311 | 40.1 |
| NASA | 232 | 2.2 |
| AEC | 756 | 7.0 |
| DOD | 641 | 6.0 |
| Other U.S. government agencies | 355 | 3.3 |
| Fulbright-Hays | 71 | 0.7 |
| NATO, WHO | 90 | 0.8 |
| State funds | 91 | 0.9 |
| Host institution | 850 | 7.9 |
| University other than host university | 69 | 0.7 |
| Private foundation | 610 | 5.7 |
| Other nonprofit organizations | 316 | 2.9 |
| Industry | 65 | 0.6 |
| Home country (not U.S.) | 215 | 2.0 |
| Multiple sources | 763 | 7.1 |
| Source unknown | 399 | 3.7 |
| *Total All Sources* | 10,740 | 100.0 |

Source: NRC, Office of Scientific Personnel, Postdoctoral Census Questionnaire.

doctorals and the Public Health Service (including the National Institutes of Health) alone supports 40 percent of them.

The distribution of support sources among the fields is given in Table 54. Several facts about areas of concentration become obvious. Almost all of the Public Health Service funds are concentrated in the biological and medical sciences, although a few awards are made in chemistry. The Atomic Energy Commission is predominantly concerned with physics, and both the Department of Defense and the National Aeronautics and Space Administration heavily concentrate their efforts in the physical sciences. Over two thirds of the National Science Foundation postdoctorals are in the physical sciences as well. The other government agencies, the host institutions, and all other sources (mainly the private sector) spread their support more broadly among the fields. The social sciences and the humanities[5] receive little help from the federal government and rely mainly on the private sector, including the host institutions.

[5] These data do not show the effects of the first grants of the National Endowment for the Humanities.

TABLE 54 Number of Postdoctorals, by Source of Support and Postdoctoral Field

Number of Postdoctorals by Source of Support

| Postdoctoral Field | NSF | PHS | AEC | DOD | NASA | Other Govt. | Home Country | Host Inst. | All Other | Total |
|---|---|---|---|---|---|---|---|---|---|---|
| Mathematics | 54 | 8 | 5 | 36 | 5 | 7 | 12 | 23 | 91 | 241 |
| Astronomy | 18 | 1 | 1 | 17 | 33 | 0 | 3 | 14 | 21 | 108 |
| Physics | 184 | 15 | 424 | 224 | 89 | 18 | 12 | 99 | 204 | 1,269 |
| Chemistry | 293 | 485 | 174 | 201 | 42 | 59 | 10 | 118 | 279 | 1,661 |
| Earth sciences | 53 | 2 | 4 | 16 | 27 | 3 | 9 | 15 | 60 | 189 |
| Engineering | 18 | 13 | 24 | 51 | 15 | 8 | 12 | 37 | 96 | 274 |
| Agriculture sciences | 4 | 6 | 5 | — | 2 | 10 | 2 | 4 | 22 | 55 |
| Biochemistry | 96 | 841 | 30 | 11 | 3 | 30 | 19 | 47 | 245 | 1,322 |
| Other basic med. sci. | 51 | 551 | 6 | 18 | 4 | 17 | 24 | 38 | 215 | 924 |
| Biosciences | 94 | 454 | 63 | 8 | 6 | 36 | 15 | 52 | 180 | 908 |
| Internal medicine | 5 | 725 | 3 | 12 | 1 | 26 | 29 | 72 | 186 | 1,059 |
| Clinical medicine | 1 | 701 | 10 | 15 | 1 | 95 | 20 | 132 | 298 | 1,273 |
| Allied medical sciences | 1 | 230 | 3 | 10 | — | 21 | 17 | 50 | 94 | 426 |
| Psychology | 10 | 157 | 1 | 9 | 1 | 14 | 3 | 18 | 40 | 253 |
| Social sciences | 9 | 15 | — | 3 | — | 14 | 13 | 38 | 104 | 196 |
| Arts and humanities | 3 | 5 | — | — | — | 25 | 5 | 44 | 96 | 178 |
| Education | — | 5 | — | 1 | — | 17 | — | 3 | 19 | 45 |
| All other fields | 12 | 97 | 3 | 9 | 3 | 26 | 10 | 46 | 153 | 359 |
| *Total* | 906 | 4,311 | 756 | 641 | 232 | 426 | 215 | 850 | 2,403 | 10,740 |

Source: NRC, Office of Scientific Personnel, Postdoctoral Census Questionnaire.

TABLE 55  Number of Postdoctorals, by Source of Support and Type of Host Institution

| Type of Host Institution | NSF | PHS | AEC | DOD | NASA | Other Govt. | Home Country | Host Inst. | All Other |
|---|---|---|---|---|---|---|---|---|---|
| ACADEMIC INSTITUTIONS | | | | | | | | | |
| Ten Leading | 780 | 3,474 | 641 | 589 | 165 | 254 | 189 | 612 | 1,950 |
| Twenty Other Major | 283 | 646 | 262 | 189 | 56 | 48 | 76 | 153 | 538 |
| Established | 204 | 786 | 166 | 163 | 46 | 40 | 44 | 122 | 427 |
| Developing | 177 | 422 | 141 | 131 | 39 | 34 | 13 | 57 | 250 |
| Other colleges and universities | 90 | 319 | 53 | 65 | 21 | 26 | 7 | 64 | 174 |
|  | 26 | 1,301 | 19 | 41 | 3 | 106 | 49 | 216 | 561 |
| NONACADEMIC INSTITUTIONS | | | | | | | | | |
| Nonprofit | 126 | 837 | 115 | 52 | 67 | 172 | 26 | 238 | 453 |
| Government | 32 | 328 | 9 | 20 | 7 | 40 | 12 | 138 | 231 |
| Industry | 13 | 342 | 106 | 32 | 60 | 66 | 10 | 56 | 79 |
| Abroad | — | — | — | — | — | — | — | 42 | 5 |
|  | 81 | 167 | — | — | — | 66 | 4 | 2 | 138 |
| Total | 906 | 4,311 | 756 | 641 | 232 | 426 | 215 | 850 | 2,403 |

Source: NRC, Office of Scientific Personnel, Postdoctoral Census Questionnaire.

## SOURCES OF SUPPORT

The distribution of support among the kinds of host institutions is given in Table 55. The pattern is not uniform, but in almost every case the distribution is understandable in view of the differences in mission of the several agencies and the available facilities at different institutions. The AEC, for example, has a larger fraction of postdoctorals at the ten leading institutions than does any other federal agency. This mirrors the concentration of high-energy physics research, which requires large departments in order to be efficient. Few NSF postdoctorals are at government laboratories, but NSF does not operate its own laboratories. Most of the government postdoctorals are at laboratories operated by their sponsoring agencies. Finally, only three government programs—NSF, NIH, and the Fulbright program—offer fellowships abroad.

The supporting organizations differ in the support of the various levels of postdoctoral appointment (see Table 56). If we consider only the post-PhD group, the Public Health Service, the Department of Defense, and the AEC tend to support immediate postdoctorals rather than those who take an appointment later. Quite the opposite is true for the other government category, the private sector, and the host institutions. The remaining groups fit the overall pattern, with the exception that the home-country support of the foreigners tends to favor the 2–5 years after PhD group at the expense of the immediate.

The final distribution in Table 57 gives the relationship between citizenship and source of support. The Public Health Service and the "other government" category support substantially more American than foreign postdoctorals, while DOD, NASA, and the host institutions support more foreign postdoctorals. With regard to dependence on the wealth of the country of origin, there are two anomalies. The "other government" category includes a substantially larger percentage of postdoctorals from the poorer countries than the percentage of such postdoctorals in the total population. In the case of home-country support there is an understandable relation between wealth and the ability to support postdoctoral work abroad.

It should be stressed that we have included in these tables everyone who responded to the study census and who fitted our definition of a postdoctoral. This means that we have not made distinctions here among those on fellowships, on traineeships, on project associateships, or on sabbatical leaves. As we saw in Chapter 4, there is much confusion among the postdoctorals with regard to their status. For this reason we did not trust their self-designations of the type of appointments they held. On the other hand, these distinctions are very important to the agencies and organizations responsible for providing support. Each form of support is handled by a distinct bureau or office within the several agencies, and each office has its separate mission and purpose. The Public Health Service, through the National Institutes of Health, operates both fellowship and traineeship programs. Some of its postdoctorals are supported on

TABLE 56  Number of Postdoctorals, by Source of Support and Level of Appointment

<table>
<tr><th rowspan="2">Level of Appointment</th><th colspan="8">Number of Postdoctorals by Source of Support</th></tr>
<tr><th>NSF</th><th>PHS</th><th>AEC</th><th>DOD</th><th>NASA</th><th>Other Govt.</th><th>Home Country</th><th>Host Inst.</th><th>All Other</th><th>Total</th></tr>
<tr><td>Post-PhD</td><td></td><td></td><td></td><td></td><td></td><td></td><td></td><td></td><td></td><td></td></tr>
<tr><td>Immediately after PhD</td><td>532</td><td>1,291</td><td>486</td><td>392</td><td>121</td><td>104</td><td>54</td><td>276</td><td>741</td><td>3,997</td></tr>
<tr><td>2-5 years after PhD</td><td>171</td><td>474</td><td>178</td><td>125</td><td>62</td><td>52</td><td>29</td><td>106</td><td>307</td><td>1,504</td></tr>
<tr><td>Over 5 years after PhD</td><td>149</td><td>245</td><td>47</td><td>48</td><td>36</td><td>90</td><td>19</td><td>120</td><td>441</td><td>1,195</td></tr>
<tr><td>Post-MD</td><td>6</td><td>2,036</td><td>9</td><td>46</td><td>4</td><td>167</td><td>78</td><td>268</td><td>714</td><td>3,328</td></tr>
<tr><td>Both MD and PhD</td><td>9</td><td>171</td><td>1</td><td>3</td><td>1</td><td>3</td><td>11</td><td>41</td><td>94</td><td>334</td></tr>
<tr><td>No doctorate</td><td>39</td><td>94</td><td>35</td><td>27</td><td>8</td><td>10</td><td>24</td><td>39</td><td>106</td><td>382</td></tr>
<tr><td>Total</td><td>906</td><td>4,311</td><td>756</td><td>641</td><td>232</td><td>426</td><td>215</td><td>850</td><td>2,403</td><td>10,740</td></tr>
</table>

Source: NRC, Office of Scientific Personnel, Postdoctoral Census Questionnaire.

TABLE 57  Number of Postdoctorals, by Source of Support and Citizenship

| Citizenship and GNP of Foreign Postdoctorals' Home Countries | Number of Postdoctorals by Source of Support ||||||||| |
|---|---|---|---|---|---|---|---|---|---|
| | NSF | PHS | AEC | DOD | NASA | Other Govt. | Home Country | Host Inst. | All Other | Total |
| U.S. | 450 | 2,880 | 364 | 276 | 91 | 282 | 3 | 342 | 1,167 | 5,855 |
| Foreign | 454 | 1,414 | 389 | 362 | 141 | 141 | 212 | 505 | 1,227 | 4,845 |
| High GNP | 322 | 908 | 266 | 261 | 96 | 63 | 180 | 344 | 744 | 3,184 |
| Medium GNP | 17 | 115 | 18 | 9 | 6 | 15 | 10 | 45 | 137 | 372 |
| Low GNP | 47 | 171 | 41 | 35 | 15 | 28 | 18 | 64 | 203 | 622 |
| Very low GNP | 68 | 220 | 64 | 57 | 24 | 35 | 4 | 52 | 134 | 667 |
| Unknown citizenship | 2 | 17 | 3 | 3 | — | 3 | — | 3 | 9 | 40 |
| *Total* | 906 | 4,311 | 756 | 641 | 232 | 426 | 215 | 850 | 2,403 | 10,740 |

Source: NRC, Office of Scientific Personnel, Postdoctoral Census Questionnaire.

research grants that are handled by different offices. In addition there are postdoctorals resident on the Bethesda campus. The other agencies have similar divisions of responsibility. It is probably true that no single agency has a comprehensive knowledge of the numbers and fields of the postdoctorals of various kinds that it supports. It is definitely true that there is no government-wide coordination of the numbers and fields. It is to be hoped that the annual collection of statistics by the Committee on Academic Science and Engineering of the Federal Council on Science and Technology will be a first step in this direction.

Finally, a word should be said about the nonfederal supporters of postdoctoral activity. Not counting the host institutions or the home countries, there are many foundations, health organizations, professional societies, and industrial firms that are supporting postdoctoral study. In some cases the support is direct and intentional; in others it is through research grants with less consciousness of the educational by-product. Although no single nonfederal source supports large numbers of postdoctorals, their collective support accounts for almost one quarter of all postdoctoral activity.

CHAPTER **10**
# Conclusions and Recommendations

It is often said that research and graduate education are inextricably related. For predoctoral work this statement is most applicable to the terminal or dissertation stage. However, there is no question but that the statement is true of postdoctoral education. In fact, it is fair to say that research and postdoctoral education are virtually identical. The validity of this description accounts for both the successes and the problems of postdoctoral education as it has developed in this country.

Proficiency in conducting research in most of the sciences is learned, or at least improved, in an apprenticeship to a master researcher. For a few who are exceptionally able and who take their graduate work with such a master, the graduate experience is sufficient to convert them from novice to proficiency status. For many, a longer apprenticeship is required. What form this extended experience should take depends, according to conventional wisdom, on the goal the apprentice seeks. If he desires to teach in an undergraduate college, he may want some teaching experience; further research is not as important. If he plans a career in industry, it might be wise to attach himself immediately to an industrial research laboratory where he can learn the appropriate styles of applied or project-oriented research by working with those who are committed to it. For the man who wants to become a master researcher, i.e., to train other students in research by joining the faculty of a graduate-degree-granting university, the postdoctoral appointment is the common route to follow.

The problem with the above prescriptions is that they are too neat. As we have seen, only in some of the fields is postdoctoral work a major enterprise

## CONCLUSIONS AND RECOMMENDATIONS

and a prerequisite for employment in even the better universities. Some industrial and government laboratories find that they prefer employees with postdoctoral backgrounds. In fields such as engineering, many departments seem to want faculty with "postdoctoral" experience in industry. In short, we are dealing with a complex phenomenon concerning which every statement must be qualified.

However, overemphasis on the exceptions should not be allowed to obscure the pattern. In the main, in fields like physics, chemistry, modern biology (including biochemistry), and medicine, postdoctoral education is virtually a necessity for subsequent employment in a highly research-oriented university. Furthermore, the reasons are not simply that the postdoctoral system serves as a sieve that removes the less able, but that something positive happens and that the man who completes postdoctoral study is a better researcher than he was before. He has become better prepared and more likely to succeed as a teacher of graduate students.

Whether other fields should embark on postdoctoral activities or expand them is a matter that must be decided field by field. There is danger of blind imitation, which should be avoided. The criterion should be whether only by postdoctoral study can the PhD recipient be expected to perform independent research in his chosen area of investigation. If the graduate or even the undergraduate curriculum can be arranged to make this unnecessary, then it ought to be so changed. Postdoctoral education should not be established to circumvent a needed alteration of predoctoral training.[1]

Conversely, we find no evidence that postdoctoral education has resulted from a failure of graduate education to fulfill its function. One need only read the *Proceedings of the Association of Graduate Schools,* going back to the turn of the century, to realize that many of the problems and criticisms of graduate education are seemingly insoluble and unanswerable. If the date were not printed on the page, one would find it difficult to establish the year by the tenor and content of the discussion. As Berelson seems to imply,[2] what is important is the awareness of the problems; perhaps no solutions exist. If the function of a graduate education is to produce a finished independent researcher, it has always failed in some fields. It would be more surprising if it had succeeded not only today but even earlier. There is a tendency to look at the growth of knowledge today and to explain postdoctoral education in terms of the impossibility of absorbing all that need be learned during a graduate program of standard duration. There is a concomitant tendency to look back

---

[1] There is a special place for postdoctoral work when the field is undergoing a rapid evolution. The recent surge of interest in mathematical methods in some of the social sciences, for example, has outstripped the ability of the schools to reorganize their curricula to cope with the change.

[2] Berelson, *Graduate Education in the United States,* p. 41.

## CONCLUSIONS AND RECOMMENDATIONS

to earlier times and to conceive of them as simpler and of science then as being more easily grasped. This is likely to be more nostalgic than realistic. The major advances of science have been those that consolidated knowledge by the perception of unifying principles. Before the discovery of quantum mechanics physicists had to learn the bewildering variety of atomic spectra and myriad empirical laws of limited validity. Today, atomic spectra are relegated to tables and the physicist need only know in principle how their frequencies can be deduced from the equations of quantum mechanics. To be sure other vistas have opened up, but it is far from obvious that today things are complicated whereas yesterday they were simple.

It is more likely that postdoctoral education has arisen in some fields because those fields are so rich in subtleties of technique and sophisticated ideas that the single research project required for the doctoral thesis does not provide the student with a sufficient grasp of his field to permit him to become an independent faculty member. On the other hand, not everyone who earns a PhD in those fields intends to continue in research on the frontier. To require that everyone spend another two years to acquire the mastery that is essential for further research contributions is both inefficient and redundant. The present system allows the college teacher and the nonacademic researcher to get about their business and permits the potential academic researcher to have the additional benefit of experiencing research in a new environment. If this means that the theoretical definition of the PhD degree must be changed, that might be the direction in which to move.

Our fundamental conclusion, therefore, is that postdoctoral education is a useful and basically healthy development. Although our discussion to this point has been concerned with the postdoctoral experience immediately following the PhD, the conclusion is valid for postdoctoral study at more senior levels as well. We shall return to this area in more detail later.

Having stated our favorable attitude toward postdoctoral education, we are also convinced that current practices can be improved and that changes in attitudes and policies are desirable. The merging of research and training is critical for postdoctoral education, but when the training aspect is ignored or neglected the experience may not be as useful for the postdoctoral and for his subsequent employer as it could be. The origin of the difficulties lies in the indirectness of the support of much of postdoctoral activity, both by the federal agencies and by the universities.

The problem is exposed most clearly when one tries to answer the question: "Are there too many or too few postdoctorals?" Lacking a clear statement of why there need be postdoctorals in the first place, such a question is in principle unanswerable. There are two extreme cases where the dilemma can be resolved. They are typified by considering the postdoctoral first as a "means" and second as an "end." The more realistic case where he is both means and end is more complicated.

## CONCLUSIONS AND RECOMMENDATIONS

If the postdoctoral is solely a means, i.e., he exists and is supported simply to assist a principal investigator in performing research, the number of postdoctorals will be related to the level of research activity. Once it has been decided how much research is desirable and affordable and with what urgency the research is to be done, the number of postdoctorals there "should be" can be determined. Perhaps we should not in this case refer to them as postdoctorals but as professional research-staff members who hold the doctorate. Whatever one decides about the postdoctorals, such professional researchers might be desirable. There are PhD's for whom a career as a junior associate to a principal investigator is not only attractive but possibly constitutes the best use of their talents. Support for such full-time researchers may or may not be in the country's interest, but they should not be confused with postdoctorals who are defined as seeking an appointment "of a temporary nature . . . which is intended to offer an opportunity for continued education and experience in research."

At the other extreme, if the postdoctoral is solely an end, i.e., he exists and is supported simply to prepare him for a particular kind of position (or possibly several kinds of positions), then the number of postdoctorals would sensibly be related to the number of appropriate positions expected to be available at the conclusion of his appointment. The nature of the research activities under such an appointment would be such as to provide the postdoctoral with the techniques, the vision, and the independence that are required for the successful filling of the anticipated position. Under these conditions it might not be possible to have the research program of the mentor proceed as smoothly or as efficiently as under the concept of the postdoctoral as a means. Efficiency, however, would not be the point; it would be education.

In practice neither extreme predominates, although some postdoctorals supported by faculty research grants approximate the former and some of those supported by training grants the latter. What is desired and what occurs much of the time regardless of the support mechanism is a combination of the two. The possibility of a mutually satisfactory relationship between the mentor and the postdoctoral is often realized, but grants and contracts in support of research at universities should be consciously given with the purpose of achieving simultaneously both the research objectives and the training of pre- and postdoctorals. The consciousness should extend not only to the faculty and administration of the university, but also to the granting agency. There may be some loss of efficiency implied in such a policy, but it would serve the mission of the university without hurting the mission of the agency.

In some cases congressional action would be necessary to free the agency from current restrictions on support of training or education. The only criteria that the program officers may legally apply to requests for support for research assistance at either level must relate to the "level of effort" or to the need to achieve the research goals expeditiously. The university and, more particularly,

CONCLUSIONS AND RECOMMENDATIONS

the faculty member is forced to focus its justification on these issues, not emphasizing the educational possibilities that the research might involve. Where such a practice might be appropriate for an independent or industrial research laboratory, it is a distortion of the full responsibilities of the faculty member. The fact that many program officers do in practice concern themselves with support of graduate education despite the restrictions in no way vitiates the desirability of removing the restrictions. Education on both sides of the PhD should be supported by design rather than by accident.

The training-grant approach to postdoctoral education appears to have all of the benefits and none of the drawbacks of the research-grant mechanism. Here the training is emphasized, although, since it is training in research, it implies a setting in which the faculty is fully involved in research. The trainees often play the part of research assistants and the research effort of the mentor is augmented. There is as well a more subtle, but important aspect of the training grant proposal that makes it attractive. The department or proposed training-grant faculty must justify the awarding of the grant in part because of a need for people trained in the manner proposed. Thus the faculty have an awareness of what is happening to the manpower picture in their discipline and of their responsibility to respond to it.

There is, however, a potential weakness in the training-grant approach that the research-grant mechanism does not share. Of crucial importance to the postdoctoral experience is the adequacy of the faculty member as a mentor. Unless the mentor is a master scientist capable of contributing not only skills but also a critical spirit to the relationship, the postdoctoral period may provide the apprentice with merely more research experience and not necessarily better experience. The training grant is generally awarded to an entire department or to a group of faculty. Although usually there are exceptional men in the group, few departments can boast of having only such men. In many departments there is overwhelming pressure to spread the largesse of money and trainees among the entire group, without the hard decisions that would reserve the postdoctoral support only for those investigators with something special to give. There is an aristocracy of excellence in science that is ignored only at the risk of mediocrity. The research grant tends to be awarded on the basis of such excellence. Those who construct and monitor federal programs should give thought to ways of combining the best of both approaches.

Before returning to the question of how many postdoctoral positions there should be, we must consider the third important mechanism of support, the postdoctoral fellowship. Fellowships differ from the other modes in concentrating attention on the postdoctoral himself. The great strength of the fellowships is that they identify the potential leaders in research and instruction. Since the fellow carries his own stipend with him, he is much better able to select his mentor and the mentor is usually able to accept him as an apprentice. For these exceptional people the fellowship permits, in principle, the exceptional experience.

Again, however, the real world modifies the abstract and admirable principles. Although the award is usually based not only on the scientific potential of the applicant but also on the proposed research, the grants do not in general have nearly enough support for research expenses to allow the fellow actually to carry out the anticipated research. He is forced to depend on the resources of his mentor, usually derived from research grants the mentor has won, to acquire the equipment and supplies necessary. Since the fellow is a superior individual, the mentor is usually happy to provide the funds if the purpose falls within the purview of his grant. At times, however, whether because of the restrictions on the mentor's grant or because of the mentor's own lack of interest in the research proposed by the fellow, the latter finds it to his advantage to shift his project to align it more closely with the mentor's research. The freedom of the fellow to pursue his own research is thus frustrated; nor is it clear that additional research support alone would rectify the situation. The mentor should be brought into the decision-making process, perhaps by being asked to endorse the proposed research at the time of the application for the fellowship.

Involvement of the mentor (now seen as the proposed mentor) in the application and judging process would have other advantages. Although the fellow has only himself to blame for choosing an inappropriate mentor, the review by the panels of the adequacy of the mentor as well as the quality of the applicant might avoid unfortunate experiences. Moreover, the group of possible mentors might be expanded. Present restrictions in the federal programs imposed by legislation permit fellowships to be held only at universities and at certain nonprofit and governmental institutions. If the desire is to match the fellow with the mentor, it is conceivable that the best mentor for the particular applicant is at an industrial research laboratory. Evaluation of the mentor as well as the applicant would go far to eliminate any fear that the postdoctoral might be exploited or that the program might be compromised.

We are not prepared to answer the question of how many postdoctoral positions there should be in quantitative terms, but we do have some suggestions about what should be taken into account in determining that number. The first suggestion relates to the fact that, in spite of the differences in approach, the individual postdoctoral and his mentor do not attach the significance to the special properties of the fellowship, the traineeship, and the research associateship that the sponsors of these programs often do. They are all seen as means to the same end, namely, the postdoctoral experience. We believe that this fact of life should be accepted, without suggesting that the differences among the programs are unimportant or that these different mechanisms of support should not continue. Their importance lies, however, outside of the postdoctoral–mentor relationship and nothing would seem to be gained by trying to intrude these values into that relationship. It follows that, as far as postdoctoral education is concerned, the numbers of postdoctorals is measured by considering the sum of the numbers on fellowships, on traineeships, and on project assistantships.

A second suggestion is that a distinction be made between the person hired on a research grant who is looking for a permanent position as a research associate and the bona fide postdoctoral, who is seeking a temporary educational experience. Such a distinction represents a polarization rather than a dichotomy and probably can be made only by the mentor. It depends not only on the qualifications and goals of the "postdoctoral," but also on the qualifications of the principal investigator, qua mentor, and on the nature of the research activities to be undertaken. Host institutions and faculty members must take it on themselves to evaluate each situation and to ensure that the postdoctoral is not treated simply as an employee.

The number of fellowships should be limited so that a distinctive element of the fellowship will be the recognition of exceptional quality. This means that the number of fellowships will have to be set at some modest fraction of the number of PhD's produced. The pattern in the biological sciences, where approximately one third of the postdoctorals are in each of the categories of fellowship, traineeship, and project associateship, might well be duplicated in the physical sciences. If this were done the number of fellowships in physics and chemistry would have to be increased over the number currently available and a traineeship program would have to be initiated.

In addition, the total number of postdoctoral opportunities of all kinds should have some relationship to the number of people with postdoctoral backgrounds required by universities, by specialized industries, and by government laboratories and to the number of doctorate-holders who would benefit by the experience. Such a determination would necessitate some planning of manpower requirements. We do not agree with those who argue that manpower planning is unnecessary, that the market place will determine the numbers needed, and that the society will accommodate whatever numbers of postdoctorals are available. Society will, of course, adjust to the number of postdoctorals. However, unless this number approximates the number of subsequent opportunities to utilize their special aptitudes and training, we will have one of two consequences. If there are too many postdoctorals, we will have wasted the funds required to train them; we will have raised their expectations without being able to satisfy them; and we will have created pressures in the institutions that hire them to permit them the opportunities they desire, whether there is a social need or not. If there are too few postdoctorals, the consequences are more subtle. Universities and other natural employers of postdoctorals will obviously adapt to the situation, but we can expect a drop in quality and in pro-

## CONCLUSIONS AND RECOMMENDATIONS

ductivity that will be hard to measure. Discoveries not made and excellence not realized are never missed, but we are the poorer for their absence.

An effort should also be made to ensure that a steady flow of foreign postdoctorals to the United States is maintained. We leave to those charged with foreign-policy management the task of justifying the flow in terms of our responsibility to the development of other countries less well endowed. Even if that were not an issue, the visiting and studying in our laboratories by foreign scientists could be justified by their contribution to American research alone. American science is and has been improved by the ideas and techniques these people have brought from their home countries. Our graduate students, and indeed our faculty, are better for the association. The foreign postdoctorals who return home often constitute for the mentor a network for the informal exchange of ideas and scientific news that stimulates research long after the postdoctoral experience itself.

On the other hand, some control on the numbers of foreign postdoctorals needs to be imposed, both for their benefit and for ours. The essentially American atmosphere of our graduate schools should not be lost through an excessive concentration of foreign scientists. Foreign postdoctorals of marginal quality should not be encouraged to make the investment in coming to this country when their talents might be better used at home and, in general, foreign postdoctorals should be urged to return home. However, we should not allow too great a concern for the relevance of the American postdoctoral experience to the needs of the home country to prevent an exceptional foreign scientist from participating in our programs. The next Einstein may come from Indonesia or Mali; we should welcome that possibility.

It is important that American PhD's have opportunities to work and study abroad. If the best mentor for a particular young scientist happens to be in a foreign country, then both the postdoctoral and American science will gain from his taking his appointment overseas. Familiarity with the best work being done in other countries is critical if American scholarship is not to become isolated. Moreover, the presence of American scientists in foreign laboratories will often stimulate research there. The recent reduction in the number of Fulbright fellows and the elimination for at least a year of the National Science Foundation Senior Postdoctoral Fellowship Program are severe and regrettable blows to the international character of American scholarship.

With regard to the overall support of postdoctoral activity, there is the need for more opportunities for study at the senior level. This need extends not only over all fields from the humanities to the natural sciences, but it encompasses those in industry and government as well as those in the universities. There is ample evidence that innovation and renewal take place best when individuals move into new environments and interact with new stimuli. The senior postdoctoral appointment, usually in association with a sabbatical leave with or without pay, is highly desirable both for the research and study that it permits and for the perspectives that it awakens in people who may have grown somewhat stale in their positions. This again is an area where we may not miss the benefits but we are the poorer for the lack.[3]

Finally, with regard to the numbers of postdoctorals, care must be taken that decisions made by Congress or the federal agencies to satisfy one purpose do not carry with them undesirable secondary effects. The case in point is the current budget squeeze that has resulted in a cutback in funds for research. Although the postdoctoral was not a target in this decision and the reduction of his numbers was not intended even as an accompanying side effect, there is evidence that he is one of the most vulnerable components of research budgets. In Table 58 we give the results of a survey taken in the fall of 1968 to measure the impact of federal research cutbacks on the postdoctoral population in physics and chemistry.[4] Although the reduction in numbers is not as severe as had been anticipated, it must be remembered that the demand for postdoctoral

TABLE 58 A Comparison of the Physics and Chemistry Postdoctoral Population in 1967 and 1968

| Type of Academic Institution | Physics Postdoctorals 1967 | 1968 | Percent Change | Chemistry Postdoctorals 1967 | 1968 | Percent Change |
|---|---|---|---|---|---|---|
| Ten leading | 260 | 212 | −18.5 | 379 | 356 | −6.1 |
| Twenty other major | 311 | 330 | +5.9 | 557 | 319 | −6.9 |
| Established | 233 | 221 | −5.2 | 406 | 433 | +6.7 |
| Developing | 143 | 155 | +8.3 | 358 | 415 | +16.1 |
| Total | 947 | 918 | −3.1 | 1,700 | 1,723 | +1.4 |

Source: NRC, Office of Scientific Personnel, follow-up survey for the postdoctoral study.

[3] The need for greater appreciation of the senior postdoctoral appointment is reflected in the decision of the National Science Foundation to drop their senior program temporarily in favor of the regular program during the present federal restrictions on funds. The senior program, with only 55 fellowships, represented 6 percent of all senior postdoctoral appointments, while the regular postdoctoral program with its 120 fellowships supports only 3 percent of the postdoctorals within five years of their PhD's. The relative impact of the decision on the senior postdoctorals is twice what it would have been on the more junior postdoctorals.
[4] The numbers in this Table cannot be compared with earlier data as the returns are not complete. The relative changes from 1967 to 1968 are real, however, and are probably representative. An attempt was made to obtain figures for biochemistry, but an insufficient number of responses made the data unreliable.

## CONCLUSIONS AND RECOMMENDATIONS

appointments has been increasing. If the number of positions had remained constant, the effect would be a 7 percent to 9 percent reduction in available positions. Furthermore, most of the respondents testified that in the fall of 1969 the figures will show a significant downward change. Postdoctoral positions are being excised from budgets coming up for renewal. Apparently the investigators, the agencies, and the agency review panels did not give postdoctoral education as high a priority as predoctoral education.

Most of the preceding comments and recommendations are directed at the supporters of postdoctoral education and, in particular, the federal supporters. The universities have concomitant responsibilities with regard to postdoctoral education. The primary need is for the recognition of postdoctoral activity as an activity that is as central to the university purpose as undergraduate or graduate education, on the one hand, or faculty research and public service on the other. Distinguishing again between professional researchers, who are employed more or less permanently in departments and institutes, and the education-seeking postdoctoral, the university must assure itself that it has created the proper environment for the postdoctoral–mentor relationship to take place. Because of the somewhat delicate nature of that relationship and because of the effectiveness of the informal nature of postdoctoral work, there is probably little that could be done to improve the relationship by making it more formal or by trying to structure it from the outside. Nevertheless, we have a few suggestions that should reduce abuses and possibly increase effectiveness.

Conceiving of the postdoctoral as an "end," regardless of the nature of his support, implies that the experiences provided for him will be such as to prepare him for the future. It is not self-evident that every research project or every faculty member will or can provide the proper setting. The number of qualified postdoctoral mentors is smaller than the number of all faculty qualified to direct graduate research. The university has the responsibility of identifying these people either internally or with advice from outsiders in the disciplines. In part, this is done by the review panels who recommend the grants, but not always with this particular focus.

To provide the proper setting, attention should be paid to the physical as well as intellectual environment. Because the growth of the postdoctoral population on most campuses has been relatively slow and because it was seldom planned but simply occurred, few universities have adequate space, facilities, or equipment for postdoctorals. The postdoctoral activity has had to "piggyback" on the graduate and research program, acquiring whatever space the faculty member could sequester or squeeze out of existing space. Because postdoctoral education has not received an institutional commitment, only a license to exist, the rate of acquisition of equipment or, conversely, the limiting of numbers of students and faculty members in accordance with the availability of equipment has not generally been determined with the postdoctoral in mind.

## CONCLUSIONS AND RECOMMENDATIONS

The universities are not solely to blame for these conditions. The donors and controllers of construction funds have been either indifferent or actually hostile to postdoctoral education. We know of no state legislature that permits its state university to include the anticipated number of postdoctorals along with the number of faculty and students when planning new academic buildings. Similar problems exist at private universities with their boards of trustees. These problems are not likely to be resolved until these bodies are educated by the universities concerning the importance of postdoctoral education to the university committed to research. Before that can happen, there must be a prior consensus within the university.

We hesitate to suggest imperatives for other details of the postdoctoral experience, because the making of a scientist-professor is such an individual matter. Each postdoctoral comes with his peculiar background of experiences and insights and the most effective program will be one that is tailor-made. There are, nevertheless, some aspects that should be considered. These include the opportunity to teach with supervision, the participation in administrative problem-solving, and the setting of limits on the duration of the postdoctoral appointment.

The compulsion to teach and to create knowledge in others is a strong one and one that is especially acute for the new PhD. For more than twenty years he has been taught, and he often wishes to return the favor. Some have had the experience as teaching assistants while in graduate school, but some have not. Even though the prime purpose of the postdoctoral appointment is a research apprenticeship, the ability to communicate one's new knowledge is also important. We recommend that the postdoctoral be given the opportunity to do limited teaching at some time during his appointment. It would also be helpful if his teaching could be criticized. Once he becomes a professor, he is less likely to receive peer criticism of his teaching.

One of the first tasks the postdoctoral will have when he becomes an assistant professor will be to write a proposal to some agency or foundation for support of his research. If he is successful, he will then be charged with administering the grant. He will be much better prepared for such responsibilities if he has participated in grant administration while a postdoctoral, at least to the extent of sitting in while budgets are constructed or while expenditures are being planned.

The question of how long the postdoctoral period should last is also difficult to specify uniformly for all postdoctorals. In some fields for some individuals, a year is sufficient time to make the transition from student to professor. For most fields and most postdoctorals, two years will permit the achievement of the educational objectives. Occasionally, for the rare individual, a longer period would be effective, including possibly a change of mentor and host institution. Again the question must be decided in terms of the individual. What

## CONCLUSIONS AND RECOMMENDATIONS

is important is that the postdoctoral not be kept any longer than is necessary. The decision should be made on the basis of the needs of the postdoctoral for further training, not on the needs of the faculty for further assistance.

Another question is that of the concentration of postdoctorals at relatively few institutions. If this concentration reflects the concentration of superior faculty researchers at the same institutions (and it probably does), it is not only appropriate, but any pressure to spread postdoctorals among all universities in the name of equity of geographic distribution should be strongly resisted. Egalitarian democracy cannot be the model for postdoctoral education. Only the best PhD's should be encouraged to pursue it and only the best faculty should supervise it. One of the more unfortunate ways in which a postdoctoral may be used as a means is to entice him to a weak department as a means of upgrading the department. The postdoctoral should follow excellence, not be responsible for creating it. The pattern of changes between 1967 and 1968 shown in Table 58 is not encouraging in this regard.

There are several issues regarding postdoctorals that we mention here in the hope that others will consider them either in future studies or in the routine collection of statistics.

As we have seen, postdoctoral activity makes a significant difference in the lives of the participants, in the universities that host postdoctorals, and in the flow of highly talented manpower among the universities and research institutions of the country. The collection of information on which these findings were based was a difficult process, requiring the creation of primary instruments to draw the necessary data from the sources. Very little information regarding postdoctoral work was available from compilations of statistics concerning higher education or scientific manpower. It would be a desirable consequence of this study if those responsible for collecting such information on an annual basis would include questions about postdoctorals. Some groups, such as the Graduate Traineeship Program at the National Science Foundation, the American Chemical Society, the American Medical Association, and the Committee on Academic Science and Education of the Federal Council on Science and Technology, have recently been collecting such information. Similar activity by the U. S. Office of Education would be helpful.

Similarly, recent changes in the form used by the Survey of Earned Doctorates of the National Research Council have made the data on the backgrounds of new postdoctorals much more useful. We hope that the National Register of Scientific and Technical Personnel can include explicit questions on postdoctoral experiences in its surveys of individual scientists.

We have discovered that, as far as postdoctoral education is concerned, the presentation of information in tabular form is equally as important as its collection. In the course of the study it has become evident that certain variables are particularly significant in distinguishing among universities and departments.

## CONCLUSIONS AND RECOMMENDATIONS

Major differences in hiring practices, funding, graduate enrollments, distribution of work loads, proportions of foreigners, etc., are exposed when data are distributed across these particular variables. The first is the reputation of the institution. Although valid arguments can be made against grouping by reputation, the correlation among reputation, federal obligations for research, and doctoral production is strong. The important point is that the behavior of the institutions at the graduate and research levels is much more strongly dependent on these variables than on the more classic ones of private versus public, secular versus church-related, or, within limits, large versus small.[5] To lump all universities or technical institutions together is to miss the diversity of higher education that exists within these categories and to present data that are misleading.

The second variable that has been important in presenting data is the presence or absence of postdoctorals within a department. It would be a mistake to attribute the observable differences between departments to the postdoctorals, but apparently the environment that attracts postdoctorals also produces other distinctions in the graduate and research programs. It would be interesting to determine the various correlates with postdoctoral presence.

Much more needs to be understood about the subsequent behavior of postdoctorals. Longitudinal studies, now possible with our data base, will tell us where former postdoctorals go for employment and what their achievements are. We should be able to learn how important the postdoctoral experience is in determining the course of a scientist's career. The migration of the foreign postdoctoral could be plotted and the relationship between the "brain drain" and the availability of postdoctoral appointments could be more thoroughly understood.

Beyond the longitudinal study, data should be collected periodically from postdoctorals to establish new data bases. One can expect some changes to occur in the postdoctoral picture as the means and extent of support change. More detailed information will be needed on the participants than simply a head count by discipline. It might be useful to establish a continuous record of postdoctorals similar to that made by the National Research Council's Survey of Earned Doctorates.

There is little doubt that the postdoctoral is here to stay. In fact, the current cutbacks in federal funds have awakened many to a realization of his importance in the academic world. If the academic community and the federal agencies respond to this awareness with coordinated programs of training and support, it will no longer be appropriate to refer to postdoctoral education as the "invisible university."

---

[5] A welcome contribution to this suggested manner of presentation is the National Science Board's 1969 publication, *Graduate Education: Parameters for Public Policy*.

CONCLUSIONS AND RECOMMENDATIONS

## Summary

Postdoctoral education serves a variety of purposes, differing somewhat from one discipline to another. Nevertheless, certain common themes remain as long as we restrict ourselves to the sciences, where most of the activity takes place. Only among the senior postdoctorals do the humanities play a comparable part in postdoctoral education.

Throughout this chapter a number of conclusions and recommendations have been made. We summarize them here for the convenience of the reader. (Unless otherwise specified, the word "postdoctoral" refers to the immediate postdoctoral in the sciences.)

- Postdoctoral education is a useful and basically healthy development, both immediately following the doctorate and later for more senior investigators. Its major purpose at the earlier stage is to accelerate the development of an independent investigator capable of training others in research. At the later stage it serves as a means for concentrated pursuit of research and scholarship goals and of renewal for those whose regular responsibilities do not permit them to pursue these goals.

- All those connected with postdoctoral education are urged to conceive of the postdoctoral appointee as one who is in the process of development and not primarily as the means to accomplish other ends. For the agencies and foundations, this means recognition that the educational goals of the university may be served explicitly through research support. For the university, this means that the postdoctoral is an important component of the educational scene. For the faculty member, this means that the postdoctoral should be given every opportunity and encouragement to develop his potential as an independent investigator.

- Most, but not all, postdoctorals participate in teaching and many desire more opportunities to teach. Some postdoctorals are involved in research administration. Almost all postdoctorals spend no more than two years on the appointment; some appointments are as short as one year; and a few postdoctorals find more than two years to be of benefit. Because of the individual nature of personal development, we believe that the participation of the postdoctoral in administration and teaching and the duration of the appointment should be determined in each individual case. The criterion should be whether the experience will enhance the postdoctoral's progress toward independence and excellence in research and graduate education.

- Of critical importance to the training of a postdoctoral is the ability of his mentor to provide the proper leadership and environment. In some fields the best possible mentor for a given postdoctoral may not be in a university or a national laboratory. Current restrictions should be removed to allow postdoctoral fellows to choose mentors at industrial research laboratories.

• Few universities, whether public or private, have adequate space, facilities, or equipment for postdoctorals. Both boards of trustees and funding agencies, including state legislatures and budget offices, should be apprised of the importance of postdoctoral education in the university in which research is a significant part of the educational program. The allotment of existing space and the planning for new facilities should include explicit recognition of the anticipated postdoctoral population at both the immediate and senior levels.

• Postdoctoral fellowships should carry with them sufficient support for research expenses, so that the fellow need not depend on his mentor's sources of support to carry out his proposed research.

• The number of postdoctoral opportunities available at any time should be related to the number of Ph.D.'s and professional doctorate holders who can profit from the experience. The mix between fellowships, traineeships, and project associateships in the physical sciences might mirror that in the biological sciences, where approximately one third of the postdoctorals are in each category. A distinction should be made between the postdoctoral and the employee with a doctorate who is looking for a career as a research associate.

• Support for senior and intermediate postdoctoral opportunities should be increased in all fields. In the humanities and social sciences, the senior and the intermediate postdoctoral appointments are and probably will remain the dominant modes of postdoctoral activity. In the sciences, the faculty should be encouraged to take leaves for stimulation of their research interests and renewal of their perspectives. In addition, postdoctoral activity at these levels may have the greatest subsequent impact on the quality of teaching.

• Within the bounds of maintaining the essentially American character of our institutions, the foreign postdoctoral is a most welcome visitor. In addition to the contribution to international education, the presence of foreign postdoctorals has enriched our science and has stressed the international nature of research. This exchange of persons can be stimulated by cooperating in programs that are designed to encourage the foreign postdoctorals to return to their homelands.

• Travel of American postdoctorals abroad should be encouraged and the number of opportunities increased. Not only do our people learn what is happening in other countries, but they help to further research in those countries. The recent severe limitation in Fulbright Fellowship opportunities is particularly unfortunate in this regard.

- Postdoctoral fellows tend to go to those institutions where the scientific leaders are located. Postdoctoral project associates and trainees are likewise attracted to excellence in science, since the research and training grants are generally made with a view to the scientific capability of the principal investigator or the training faculty. As institutions that do not now host postdoctorals are developed to excellence by the attraction of leadership-quality faculty, postdoctorals will follow. Postdoctorals should not be the means to the development of an institution, but the measure of its excellence.

# APPENDIXES

APPENDIX A
# The Questionnaires

## A-1 Postdoctoral Census Questionnaire

In an effort to make a census of all postdoctorals in the United States and all postdoctorals abroad who were U.S. citizens, a questionnaire was designed to elicit information on the background of the postdoctoral, the nature of his appointment, and his subsequent plans. Since the identity of these people was unknown, it was necessary that the host institutions distribute the questionnaire. A list of such institutions was compiled. These included all universities belonging to the Council of Graduate Schools in the United States (243), nonprofit institutions and government laboratories (164), independent hospitals receiving more than $25,000 in research funds from the National Institutes of Health (43), member libraries of the Association of Research Libraries (73), other institutions receiving HEW Graduate Training Grants (182), and selected industrial laboratories (28). The president or director of each of these institutions was asked to designate from his staff a coordinator with whom we might correspond. Each of these coordinators was asked to distribute the questionnaires to the postdoctorals at his institution, to collect the completed forms from them and to return the forms to the Study office. Questionnaires were also sent directly to all holders of nationally awarded fellowships (both federally and privately financed) who were not at the above institutions.

This census took place in the spring of 1967 and we received 10,740 completed forms that were sufficiently complete and not excluded by our definition of a postdoctoral appointment. The question immediately arises: How many did we miss? To estimate this we have used counts from other sources. In the application form for its Graduate Traineeship Program, the National Science Foundation asks chairmen to indicate the number of postdoctorals in their departments. Robert H. Linnell has analyzed these applications[1] and found a total of 6,352 postdoctorals in all sciences in the fall of 1966. Because the National Institutes of Health provides more funds in the health and life sciences, it is likely that many departments in these areas did not apply for training grants from NSF. Departments in the physical sciences and engineering, however, must rely almost exclusively on the NSF for locally administered funds to support graduate education. Linnell feels that almost all eligible departments in these fields in the country made a traineeship application and thus the figure in these areas for the postdoctoral population is accurate.[2] He found 3,967 postdoctorals in the EMP (engineering, mathematical, and physical) sciences.

It would have been preferable to make comparisons by individual departments to allow for differences among the return rates by discipline, but this was not possible. Our data distinguishes among fields of research; Linnell's among departments. Many postdoctorals in chemistry departments indicate that their field is molecular physics; they are included in our data as physicists. It is reasonable to assume, however, that people in EMP fields are in EMP departments. We had returns from 3,165 postdoctorals in the EMP fields at universities, which represents an 80 percent return rate.

From the clinical fields at medical schools we received 2,207 returns, whereas the American Medical Association reported[3] 4,186 postdoctorals in these areas. In this much more diffuse area of postdoctoral activity where the definition is stretched to the extreme, our rate of return is 53 percent.

If we take, as an average, a return rate of 65 percent for the basic medical sciences, assume that the fields generally associated with the arts and sciences at universities share the 80 percent return rate of the EMP fields, and assume that the return rate from postdoctorals outside of universities is the same as from those in universities, the total postdoctoral population comprised approximately 16,000 persons in the spring of 1967.

---

[1] National Science Foundation, *Graduate Manpower Resources and Education in the Sciences,* August 1967.
[2] Assuming, of course, that chairmen always report accurate figures.
[3] *Journal of the American Medical Association,* Vol. 202, No. 8, Nov. 20, 1967, p. 818.

POSTDOCTORAL CENSUS QUESTIONNAIRE

# THE STUDY OF POSTDOCTORAL EDUCATION

Sponsored by the NATIONAL RESEARCH COUNCIL
NATIONAL ACADEMY OF SCIENCES — NATIONAL ACADEMY OF ENGINEERING

If you have a postdoctoral position (see definition on the attached sheet) please fill out this questionnaire and return it to your department office (or other designated office) as soon as possible. The information provided on this form will be held in confidence by the National Research Council, and used for statistical purposes only.

1. Name ................................................................................
   (6-26)   (Last Name)        (First Name)      (Middle Name)
2. Year of Birth ............ (27-28)
3. Sex M ...... F ...... (28) (11) (12)

4. Marital status  12 ☐ Married   11 ☐ Not married (including widowed, divorced)
   (29)

5. Number of dependents. Use U.S. income tax definition, but do not include yourself ( ...... )
   (29)

6. Social Security Number (U.S.) ........................
   (30-38)

7. Of what country are you a citizen? ........................
   (39-40)

8. Please fill out the information requested below regarding your undergraduate and graduate education. Use field numbers from the attached specialties list.

| Institution and Location | Degree Received | Year | Field Number | Name |
|---|---|---|---|---|
|  |  |  |  |  |
|  |  |  |  |  |
|  |  |  |  |  |
|  |  |  |  |  |

9. Previous postdoctoral appointments (68-73, 74-9)

| Institution and Location | Period of Appointment | Department, Center, or Institute |
|---|---|---|
|  |  |  |
|  |  |  |

Please fill in the information requested below regarding your present postdoctoral appointment

10. Name and location of the institution ........................
    (6-9)

11. Department, Center, or Institute ........................
    (10-11)

12. Name of the professor or other staff member with whom you are working ........................
    (12-23)   (Last Name)          (First Name)    (Middle Initial)

13. Title of appointment ........................ If this is a part-time appointment, what
    (24-5)
    other position do you hold? ........................
    (26-7)

14. Designation of your research area, using the name and number from the accompanying specialties list:
    (28-30)
    ........................   ........................
    (name of specialty)          (number)

15. When did your postdoctoral training begin? ........ 19 .... When do you expect to complete your
    (31-33)                      (month)
    postdoctoral training? ........ 19 ....
    (34-36)      (month)

16. What agency has provided the funds for your present salary? (37-8) ........................
    (If not sure, please ask your research sponsor)

17. Which of the following general types of appointment do you hold? (39) Fellowship ..... Traineeship .....
                                                                          0                1
    Sabbatical ..... Position supported from project funds ........................
         2                              3
    Other (specify) ........................
         4

*Please turn over the page for the rest of the questions*

# APPENDIX A: THE QUESTIONNAIRES

18. Monthly salary or stipend on this postdoctoral appointment (optional) $ _____
    Additional monthly salary for teaching activities (optional) $ _____

19. Are you now on leave from another position? Yes ___ No ___ If yes, indicate the position from which you are on leave:
    _____ (position)  _____ (organization)  _____ (city)  _____ (state)

20. Are you currently receiving salary support from your home institution? Yes ___ No ___

21. What are your main reasons for taking a postdoctoral appointment?
    _____
    _____
    _____

Please answer the following with respect to the nature of your postdoctoral activities.

22. Are you a candidate for another doctoral degree? Yes ___ No ___
    Will you take or audit any regular courses during this appointment? Yes ___ No ___

23. Do you participate in the teaching of undergraduate or graduate students?

    |  | | Undergraduate | | Graduate | |
    |---|---|---|---|---|---|
    |  | | Yes | No | Yes | No |
    | Check all appropriate categories | Course lectures | | | | |
    |  | Seminars | | | | |
    |  | Laboratory supervision | | | | |
    |  | Quiz sections | | | | |
    |  | Non-credit courses | | | | |
    |  | Research supervision | | | | |

24. Do you wish this appointment provided more opportunity for teaching? Yes ___ No ___

25. Have you responsibility for the improvement of research equipment? Yes ___ No ___

26. With how many staff members do you have significant professional contact? _____

27. Do you use the library more or less than you did as a graduate student?
    Much more ___   Somewhat more ___   About the same ___   Less ___

The remaining questions ask about your career expectations after completing your present postdoctoral appointment.

28. In which of the following types of organization will you most probably be employed after your present postdoctoral work (check one)
    University ___   College ___   Federal Government ___   State or local government ___
    Business or industry ___   Non-profit organization ___   Self-employed ___
    Other (specify) _____

29. What is your most probable location? (state or country) _____

30. To what extent has your postdoctoral experience changed your career aspirations?
    _____
    _____
    _____

**THANK YOU.** Please return this completed questionnaire to your departmental office or other designated official.

## A-2 Departmental Questionnaire

In order to determine the nature of the environment in which most postdoctorals find themselves and where they are likely to be employed after their appointment, a questionnaire was designed to be answered by departmental chairmen at colleges and universities. Questionnaires were sent to the coordinators at all universities belonging to the Council of Graduate Schools (CGS) in the United States and to the presidents at a sample of all remaining colleges and universities. This sample comprised all schools at which 50 percent or more of the faculty hold the doctorate and a 10 percent random sample of all other schools. The coordinators and presidents were asked to distribute these departmental questionnaires to those departments that deal with the fields listed and to return the completed questionnaires to the Study office. The distribution of returns is as follows:

| Field | Universities in the CGS | Other Colleges and Universities — More than Half PhD Faculty | Other Colleges and Universities — Less than Half PhD Faculty | Other Institutions | Total |
|---|---|---|---|---|---|
| Humanities | 425 | 150 | 91 | — | 666 |
| Social sciences | 592 | 201 | 105 | — | 898 |
| Physical sciences | 658 | 199 | 98 | — | 955 |
| Engineering | 307 | 17 | 5 | — | 329 |
| Biological sciences | 354 | 66 | 35 | — | 455 |
| Basic medical sciences | 238 | 12 | 1 | 14 | 265 |
| Medical specialties | — | — | — | 209 | 209 |
| Education | — | — | — | 244 | 244 |
| Combined departments | — | — | — | 19 | 19 |
| *Total Departments* | 2,574 | 645 | 335 | 486 | 4,040 |

Note: Number of schools responding, 357; number of schools approached, 422.

APPENDIX A: THE QUESTIONNAIRES

# FIELDS OF STUDY COVERED BY THE DEPARTMENTAL QUESTIONNAIRE

The questionnaire should be completed at each institution by that department *chiefly responsible* for each of the following fields of study. At many institutions one department may be responsible for several of the fields listed here, e.g., a department of applied science may include all the engineering fields or a department of social studies may include the fields of economics, political science and sociology. In these cases, *even though the department is broader than the fields* listed, the response should be for the entire department. On the other hand, several fields may not be represented in any department at a given institution. In such cases, of course, the fields should be ignored. If the field is represented by two departments, e.g., in the graduate school and in the medical school, please have both respond.

If the departments are small and their circumstances similar, the form may be distributed to division, rather than department, chairmen. In extreme cases at small institutions, a single form may serve for the entire institution.

1. Agronomy
2. Animal husbandry
3. Biochemistry
4. Botany
5. Chemical engineering
6. Chemistry
7. Dentistry
8. Economics
9. Education
10. Electrical engineering
11. English
12. French
13. Genetics
14. Geology
15. History
16. Internal medicine
17. Mathematics
18. Mechanical engineering
19. Microbiology–bacteriology
20. Physics
21. Physiology
22. Political science–government
23. Preventive medicine–public health
24. Psychiatry
25. Psychology
26. Sociology
27. Surgery
28. Zoology

# DEPARTMENTAL QUESTIONNAIRE

## DEPARTMENTAL QUESTIONNAIRE: POSTDOCTORAL

1. Department ................................................ Institution ................................................

   Telephone: Area Code .......... Number .................... Extension ..........

2. *Number of faculty members in the department as of the fall term, 1966.*   Full-time   Part-time
   a. Professors            (present and on leave) ............................................
   b. Associate professors  (present and on leave) ............................................
   c. Assistant professors  (present and on leave) ............................................
   d. Lecturers ........................................................................................
   e. Instructors (other than graduate students holding this appointment) ....
   f. Visiting professors, associate professors, assistant professors, and lecturers filling regular staff positions in the department ............
   g. Other (specify) ..................................................................................
                        Total in above categories "a" through "g" ............

3. *Previous background and present functions of recent appointees to the full-time junior faculty*
   a. The last *five* members appointed to the *full-time junior* faculty (assistant professor, instructor, or equivalent) came from the following backgrounds (enter number in each appropriate category):
       Faculty appointments at other institutions .......................................
       Postdoctoral appointments at other institutions .................................
       Postdoctoral appointments at your institution ...................................
       Had just completed work for a doctor's degree (PhD, M.D., etc.) elsewhere ......
       Had just completed work for a doctor's degree at your institution ..........
       Were engaged in graduate study elsewhere, without yet completing a doctorate ....
       Were engaged in graduate study at your institution, without completing a doctorate ....
       Research in government or industry .................................................
       Private practice ..................................................................................
       Other (specify) ..................................................................................
                                                                           Total =    5
       How many of these five had completed work for a doctorate at the time of appointment? ....
       What are the normal responsibilities of a newly appointed instructor or assistant professor, measured in terms of the time he gives to each of these functions:
       Research, including training students in research ............................. %
       Instruction, including lectures, seminars, tutorials, etc. .................... %
       Administration ................................................................................ %
       Clinical service .............................................................................. %
       Other .............................................................................................. %
   d. How many full-time faculty positions in the department, of the rank of assistant professor or instructor were unfilled at the beginning of the fall term, 1966? ....

4. *Backgrounds and functions of present full-time faculty and staff*
   a. Of the professors, associate professors, and assistant professors counted in question 2 as members of your *full-time* faculty in the fall of 1966, how many . . .
       are currently on leave from the department for study or research? ......
       have at any stage in their careers had a year or more of postdoctoral study (supported either by others or by your institution)? ....
       are actively engaged in research? ....
       are engaged in research supported in whole or in part by outside grants or contracts? ....
   b. *Excluding* the faculty appointees counted in question 2, postdoctorals as defined for the Study and counted below, and technician how many *professional* research staff members were there in the department in the fall term, 1966? ....
   c. How many of these professional researchers have a PhD, M.D., or other doctor's degree? ....
   d. Please state (or estimate) the total of research funds in your department from outside grants or contracts in the fiscal year 1966-67. For the sake of uniformity, include overhead payments in the total. Do not include fellowship support or training grants. .................................................................................................... $........

5. If you do not now have postdoctoral students in the department, do you believe the department would benefit from the presence of such students? Greatly ........  To some extent ........  Not significantly ........
   Please comment:                                                                                                                *Card 1*
   ............................................................................................................
   ............................................................................................................

## APPENDIX A: THE QUESTIONNAIRES

FOR DEPARTMENTS WITH GRADUATE DEGREE PROGRAMS

6. Please enter the total number of graduate students, full and part-time, as of the fall term, 1966: A "full-time" graduate student is defined here as a graduate student who is engaged entirely in training activities in his discipline; these activities may embrace any appropriate combinations of study, teaching, and research.

|  | Full-time | Part-time |
|---|---|---|
|  | _____ | _____ |

Please state the number of *full-time* graduate students now holding:

Teaching appointments (e.g., teaching assistants, part-time instructors) ........................ _____

Research appointments (e.g., research assistants) ........................................ _____

7. How many master's and PhD degrees, or the equivalent, were awarded in the years 1964–65 and 1965–66, July 1 through June 30, to students majoring in your department?

|  | 1964–65 | 1965–66 |
|---|---|---|
| Master's degrees | _____ | _____ |
| PhD's or the equivalent | _____ | _____ |

8. How many of your PhD's in 1964–65 and 1965–66 entered each of the following occupations at their graduation?

|  | 1964–65 PhD's | 1965–66 PhD's |
|---|---|---|
| Academic appointment in a college or university | _____ | _____ |
| Postdoctoral study | _____ | _____ |
| Research in industry | _____ | _____ |
| Research in government or non-profit organizations | _____ | _____ |
| Military service | _____ | _____ |
| Foreign country, any type of employment | _____ | _____ |
| Other (specify) | _____ | _____ |
| Total | _____ | _____ |

Card 2

FOR DEPARTMENTS WITH POSTDOCTORAL STUDENTS

9a. Please enter the number of postdoctorals in the department as of the fall term, 1966.

|  | U.S. citizens | Foreigners |
|---|---|---|
| Fellowship holders | _____ | _____ |
| Trainees | _____ | _____ |
| Appointees supported on research funds | _____ | _____ |
| Visitors supported by their home institutions | _____ | _____ |
| Others (specify) | _____ | _____ |
| Total postdoctorals | _____ | _____ |

b. How many of your postdoctorals have the MD degree or equivalent? ........................ _____
How many are in residency training? ........................................ _____

10. How many of your professors, associate professors, and assistant professors counted in question 2 as members of your faculty, are the mentors or sponsors of postdoctorals? ........................ _____

11. Review of appointments
    a. Who reviews critically (other than the individual faculty member with whom he will work) the qualifications of an incoming postdoctoral student? (Check as many as apply)

    The department head ........................ _____
    A departmental committee ........................ _____
    A dean or vice-president ........................ _____
    An interdepartmental committee ........................ _____
    Other (specify) ........................ _____
    No one ........................ _____

    b. Is there any procedure for evaluating the progress and achievement of a postdoctoral student after his term of appointment? ........................ Yes _____ No _____

12. How closely does the monthly salary paid to a postdoctoral appointee by your department approach the salary paid to faculty members of the same professional experience? Please indicate by a percentage, e.g., 110%, 100%, 85%, etc. ........................ _____ %

13. How long may an individual continue in your department as a postdoctoral appointee? ........................ _____
    If there is a limit, is this institutional policy? ........................ Yes _____ No _____

14. Are there any limitations, aside from those of funds and floor space, on the number of postdoctorals your department may appoint or admit in a given year (e.g., to maintain a balance in the department, etc.)? ........................ Yes _____ No _____

15. Do you have a departmental policy of involving postdoctorals in teaching? ........................ Yes _____ No _____

Card 3

May 1967

Department Head ........................

*Please return to the college or university coordinator named on the first page.*

## A-3 Faculty Questionnaire

In order to determine the relationship of the postdoctoral to the research group a questionnaire was designed to be answered by faculty members. Two groups of faculty members were selected to be in the sample: all those in the fields listed below who were mentors of the postdoctorals responding to the census questionnaire, and the faculty advisers of all students who received the PhD in 1966 in those same fields.[4] The return rates by field are shown in the following table:

| Field | Postdoctoral Mentors Sent | Postdoctoral Mentors Returned | PhD Mentors Only Sent | PhD Mentors Only Returned |
|---|---|---|---|---|
| Physics | 654 | 430 | 488 | 127 |
| Chemistry | 785 | 625 | 614 | 217 |
| Earth sciences | 102 | 86 | 266 | 93 |
| Social sciences | 91 | 39 | 138 | 42 |
| Internal medicine | 561 | 250 | – | 7 |
| Biochemistry | 538 | 379 | 243 | 55 |
| Biosciences | 527 | 386 | 644 | 223 |
| *Total* | 3,258 | 2,195 | 2,393 | 564 |

The discrepancies and the different return rates are explainable in part by the fact that some faculty turned out to be mentors of postdoctorals who had not responded to our census. Thus those we thought were PhD mentors only were discovered to belong in the other group.

---

[4] In the social sciences a 10 percent random sample of the PhD advisers was taken to make the number comparable to the number of postdoctoral mentors.

APPENDIX A: THE QUESTIONNAIRES

# THE STUDY OF POSTDOCTORAL EDUCATION — Faculty Questionnaire

Sponsored by the NATIONAL RESEARCH COUNCIL
NATIONAL ACADEMY OF SCIENCES — NATIONAL ACADEMY OF ENGINEERING

Please correct address if changed

1. Academic Title_____

2. Principal area in which you are currently conducting research (use field number from the attached specialties list)_____
   NAME OF SPECIALITY                                    NUMBER

3. a. How many students and staff members were pursuing research with you or, if you are a member of a larger research group, in your group, as of April 1967?

   |  | U.S. Citizens | Foreign Citizens |
   |---|---|---|

   Graduate degree candidates (e.g., for S.M., Ph.D., etc.) supported on research funds of your own or of your research group. _____ _____

   Graduate degree candidates supported from other sources _____ _____

   **Postdoctorals** (including M.D.'s pursuing research under you, either by their independent planning or as part of their residency training)

   Postdoctoral fellows _____ _____

   Postdoctoral trainees (e.g., postdoctorals appointed on an N.I.H. training grant) _____ _____

   Postdoctoral appointees supported on your own or the group's research funds _____ _____

   Postdoctoral visitors supported by their home institutions or, if foreign, by their home governments _____ _____

   Other postdoctorals (specify)_____ _____ _____

   **Faculty co-workers** _____ _____

   Professional research staff including technicians with a bachelor's degree but excluding individuals separately counted above _____ _____

   Other co-workers (specify)_____ _____ _____

   b. Of your postdoctorals counted above, how many:

   Have the Ph.D. degree or equivalent? _____ _____

   Have the M.D. degree or equivalent? _____ _____

   Of these M.D.'s, how many are doing research as part of their residency training? _____ _____

4. One of our concerns is the relationship between research training and research support. Approximately what is your total research budget this fiscal year, 1966-67? For the sake of uniformity, include overhead payments in the total. $_____

5. How many students completed master's theses or doctoral dissertations under your direction in the calendar year 1966? How many are likely to finish in the calendar year 1967?

   |  | 1966 | Estimated 1967 |
   |---|---|---|
   | Master's theses completed | _____ | _____ |
   | Doctoral dissertations completed | _____ | _____ |

6. Does your department or institution limit for academic reasons

   the number of graduate degree candidates you may direct?........ Yes_____ No_____

   the number of postdoctorals you may direct?........ Yes_____ No_____

# FACULTY QUESTIONNAIRE

7. *Purpose and Character of Postdoctoral Study.*
    a. How strongly do you encourage your better graduate degree candidates, or your M.D.'s in residency training if you are in a clinical field, to take an extra year or two of postdoctoral study . . .

    if they seek an academic career     Strongly_____ Fairly strongly_____ Not strongly_____

    if they do not?     Strongly_____ Fairly strongly_____ Not strongly_____

    b. If you encourage your better graduate degree candidates or residents to take an extra year or two of postdoctoral study, please check the *three reasons* which you feel are most compelling among those listed below:

|  | Grad. degree candidates | Residents |
|---|---|---|
| To work with a particular scholar or scientist | _____ | _____ |
| To acquire additional research techniques | _____ | _____ |
| To gain further research experience | _____ | _____ |
| To carry out a piece of research on their own | _____ | _____ |
| To continue with research already started | _____ | _____ |
| To sharpen the focus of their research | _____ | _____ |
| To give them a free period of research before they become saddled with other responsibilities | _____ | _____ |
| To put them at the growing edge of current research | _____ | _____ |
| To support themselves in the academic world until a suitable faculty appointment becomes available | _____ | _____ |
| To gain some teaching experience | _____ | _____ |
| To give them a breathing spell after their formal training | _____ | _____ |
| To give them further time to mature | _____ | _____ |
| To see the work being done at other centers | _____ | _____ |
| To broaden their understanding of the field | _____ | _____ |
| **To give them** a chance to publish something | _____ | _____ |
| **Other** (specify) _____ | _____ | _____ |

   c. Should the character of predoctoral or of residency training be changed in the light of these reasons for promoting post-Ph.D. and post-residency study?    Yes_____ No_____

**PLEASE ANSWER THE FOLLOWING QUESTIONS IF YOU HAVE POSTDOCTORALS IN YOUR GROUP**
For the purpose of these questions, restrict the definition of postdoctoral to those within 5 years of the doctorate.

8. How do your postdoctorals contribute to the effectiveness of your research and teaching compared with the other students and staff working with you? Please put numbers in the spaces below to indicate the character and scale of the contribution made by each. 4 = very large; 3 = large; 2 = small; 1 = very small; 0 = no contribution.

|  | Graduate degree candidates | Post-doctorals | Continuing professional research staff (non-student non-faculty) |
|---|---|---|---|
| **A. *Research*** | | | |
| Carry out complete sections of work | _____ | _____ | _____ |
| Contribute stimulating new ideas | _____ | _____ | _____ |
| Keep us in touch with research at other institutions | _____ | _____ | _____ |
| Contribute necessary ancillary skills | _____ | _____ | _____ |
| Open up new areas of research | _____ | _____ | _____ |
| Perform necessary research routines | _____ | _____ | _____ |
| **Contribute** to the quality and sophistication of the work | _____ | _____ | _____ |
| **Contribute** to the tempo of the work | _____ | _____ | _____ |
| **B. *Teaching*** | | | |
| Help conduct laboratory courses | _____ | _____ | _____ |
| Help conduct lecture courses | _____ | _____ | _____ |
| Teach sections | _____ | _____ | _____ |
| Assist degree candidates in their research | _____ | _____ | _____ |

# APPENDIX A: THE QUESTIONNAIRES

9. *Publications by postdoctorals*

   a. How many books and papers were published in 1966 and 1967 listing your postdoctorals as author or co-author? Include publications in preparation.

   |  | Papers | Books |
   |---|---|---|
   | Postdoctorals with the Ph.D. or equivalent | _____ | _____ |
   | M.D.'s independently pursuing research training | _____ | _____ |
   | M.D.'s in residency training | _____ | _____ |

   b. What was the total number of books and papers published in 1966 and 1967 by persons under your direction? _____ _____

10. *Your foreign postdoctorals*

    a. Please list the home countries of your foreign postdoctorals, with the number of postdoctorals from each.

    | Home country | No. of individuals |
    |---|---|
    | 1. _____ | _____ |
    | 2. _____ | _____ |
    | 3. _____ | _____ |
    | 4. _____ | _____ |
    | 5. _____ | _____ |

    b. Please put checks in the appropriate spaces below to characterize your foreign postdoctorals:

    *Quality of previous research training.* Compared with your U.S. postdoctorals, they have generally had:

    | Better theoretical training | _____ | Better laboratory training | _____ |
    |---|---|---|---|
    | Equally good theoretical training | _____ | Equally good laboratory training | _____ |
    | Less good theoretical training | _____ | Less good laboratory training | _____ |

    *Relevance of their postdoctoral work to their own country's needs.* Their postdoctoral work has:

    Much relevance_____ Some relevance_____ Little relevance_____

    *Interest in returning home:*

    Most plan to return home_____ Many plan to return home_____ Few plan to return_____

11. *Your U.S. postdoctorals*

    a. How many of your present U.S. postdoctorals (excluding M.D.'s in residency training) have the qualifications you look for in an assistant professor, how many are somewhat less qualified, how many are distinctly less qualified?

    | Total number of U.S. postdoctorals (other than M.D.'s in residency training) | Number with qualifications of faculty appointees | Number who are somewhat less qualified | Number who are distinctly less qualified |
    |---|---|---|---|
    | _____ | _____ | _____ | _____ |

    b. Has the quality of awardees in the U.S. national fellowship programs (e.g. N.S.F., N.I.H.) been of a sufficiently high calibre? _____ Yes_____ No_____

12. How long should a postdoctoral (other than an M.D. in residency training or an M.D. seeking a Ph.D.) remain in your department . . .

    for his sake? _____ minimum_____ years maximum_____ years

    for the department's sake? _____ minimum_____ years maximum_____ years

13. On the unit basis that 10 = the average time required to direct the research training of a Ph.D. candidate, or of a resident if you are in a clinical field, what is your estimate of the average time required to direct the work of a postdoctoral? _____/10

14. On the unit basis that 10 = the average office and/or laboratory space you assign to a Ph.D. candidate, or to a resident if you are in a clinical field, what is your estimate of the average space occupied by a postdoctoral pursuing further training? _____/10

## FACULTY QUESTIONNAIRE

15. If you have any opinions about postdoctoral education which are not expressed above, please comment below:

16. We would like to follow up on a sample of the foreign postdoctorals holding appointments in 1961-62, to obtain their opinion of what they accomplished as postdoctorals and to trace their subsequent careers. Would you kindly list the names, and if known, the present addresses, of as many as possible of your foreign postdoctorals in 1961-62?

| Name (PLEASE PRINT) | Country of which they were a citizen | Present address, if known |
|---|---|---|
| | | |

Please return to The Study of Postdoctoral Education, National Research Council, 2101 Constitution Avenue, Washington, D.C. 20418

APPENDIX A: THE QUESTIONNAIRES

## A-4 Postdoctoral Experience Questionnaire

To determine the value of the postdoctoral experience to the individual and to compare careers of postdoctorals with those who hold the doctorate but have not been postdoctorals, a questionnaire was designed to obtain such information from a sample of PhD recipients some years after their degree. In order to avoid the possible bias that those who take postdoctoral appointments are already preselected, we attempted to make two samples of doctorate holders of apparent equal quality. For this purpose we took advantage of an existing study of the career patterns of doctorate holders[5] by Lindsey Harmon. This study has followed up the careers of some 10,000 PhD holders who received their doctorates in five-year intervals between 1935 and 1960. Of this group approximately 1,600 had had a postdoctoral appointment. By restricting our sample to those who had received their degrees in 1950, 1955, and 1960, we were left with 779 former postdoctorals. This group was matched with an equally large group of non-former postdoctorals that was similar with regard to field distribution, "quality" of PhD institution,[6] the time lapse between the baccalaureate and the doctor's degree, and age. These two groups were sent questionnaires and the return rate is given below. Some data on the nonrespondents were collected from NSF's National Register of Scientific and Technical Personnel.

|  | Former Postdoctorals | Non-former Postdoctorals |
|---|---|---|
| Questionnaires sent to: | | |
| 1950 PhD's | 199 | 199 |
| 1955 PhD's | 271 | 271 |
| 1960 PhD's | 309 | 309 |
| *Total* | 779 | 779 |
| Questionnaires returned by: | | |
| 1950 PhD's | 135 (67.8%) | 141 (70.9%) |
| 1955 PhD's | 175 (64.6%) | 186 (68.6%) |
| 1960 PhD's | 189 (60.8%) | 169 (54.7%) |
| *Total* | 498 (63.9%) | 496 (63.3%) |

It was subsequently discovered that the definition of a postdoctoral appointment in Harmon's study differed from ours. This caused some switches between the two groups. Some, who had postdoctoral experience according to their response to Harmon's study, answered our questionnaire in the negative and

---

[5] NAS–NRC, *Profiles of PhD's in the Sciences,* Publ. 1293, Washington, D. C., 1965.
[6] Allan Cartter, *An Assessment of Quality in Graduate Education,* American Council of Education, 1966.

vice versa. Furthermore, we discovered that it was important to distinguish between those who had had an immediate postdoctoral experience and those who postdoctoral appointment was delayed. When we examine the returns and separate the respondents according to their replies we get the following distribution:

|  | Respondents Who Had | | |
| --- | --- | --- | --- |
|  | Immediate Postdoctoral | Delayed Postdoctoral | No Postdoctoral |
| 1950 PhD's | 44 | 82 | 146 |
| 1955 PhD's | 94 | 87 | 173 |
| 1960 PhD's | 139 | 46 | 162 |
| *Total* | 277 | 215 | 481 |

These totals do not add to the numbers given in the previous table, since 19 respondents did not give sufficient information to allow themselves to be classified.

APPENDIX A: THE QUESTIONNAIRES

# THE STUDY OF POSTDOCTORAL EDUCATION

Sponsored by the NATIONAL RESEARCH COUNCIL
NATIONAL ACADEMY OF SCIENCES — NATIONAL ACADEMY OF ENGINEERING

POSTDOCTORAL TRAINING
AND EXPERIENCE

1. Present Title _____

2. Institution _____

   Address _____
   (CITY)                    (STATE)

3. In your present position, how is your time divided between research (including training students in research), instruction, administration, and clinical service?

   Research, including training students in research _____ %
   Instruction, including lectures, seminars, tutorials, etc. _____ %
   Administration _____ %
   Clinical service _____ %
   Other _____ %
                                    Total   100   %

4. If you are currently engaged in research, what is your field of specialization now?

   Please use field number from the attached specialities list _____
   Not currently engaged in research _____

5. If you have been successful in obtaining *outside* research support as a principal investigator or co-investigator, when did you receive your *first* grant or contract, and from what foundation or agency?

   No outside support _____
   Year 19___ Granting Agency _____
   Have you received subsequent grant(s)   Yes_____   No_____

6. How many books and papers have you published?
   Books_____   Papers_____

7. During your career, have you been a thesis adviser for any graduate students?
   Yes_____   No_____
   If "Yes," how many at master's level_____   at PhD level_____

8. What was your annual income in 1966 (or the most recent completed fiscal year) from activities related to your academic training? (optional) _____ $_____

## POSTDOCTORAL EXPERIENCE QUESTIONNAIRE

9. Have you ever sought or applied for a postdoctoral appointment (see attached definition)? Yes_____ No_____

   a. *If yes*, what reasons did you feel were the most compelling? (For your first appointment, if more than one)   Check up to 3

   | | |
   |---|---|
   | To work with a particular scholar | _____ 01 |
   | To acquire additional research techniques | _____ 02 |
   | To gain further research experience | _____ 03 |
   | To carry out a piece of research on your own | _____ 04 |
   | To develop further the research you did during your predoctoral or residency training | _____ 05 |
   | To sharpen the focus of your research | _____ 06 |
   | To give you a free period for research before you got saddled with other responsibilities | _____ 07 |
   | To put yourself at the growing edge of current research | _____ 08 |
   | To support yourself in the academic world until a suitable faculty appointment became available | _____ 09 |
   | To give you some teaching experience | _____ 10 |
   | To give yourself a breathing spell after your formal training | _____ 11 |
   | To give you further time to mature | _____ 12 |
   | To see the work being done at other centers | _____ 13 |
   | To broaden your understanding of the field | _____ 14 |
   | To give you a chance to publish something | _____ 15 |
   | Other (specify)_____ | _____ 16 |

   b. *If no*, was a postdoctoral appointment unavailable in your case? Yes_____ No_____

   Or did you feel that you would derive no benefit from it? Yes_____ No_____

   Or were other opportunities at the time more attractive? Yes_____ No_____

10. If you never had a postdoctoral appointment, do you now feel the lack of the experience it would have given you? Yes_____ No_____

    Please add any comments under question 18.

    PLEASE ANSWER THE FOLLOWING QUESTIONS IF YOU HAVE HELD AN APPOINTMENT AS A POSTDOCTORAL AS DESCRIBED IN THE ATTACHED DEFINITION. IF NOT, THANK YOU FOR THE ABOVE DATA. PLEASE RETURN THE QUESTIONNAIRE TO THE STUDY OF POSTDOCTORAL EDUCATION, NATIONAL RESEARCH COUNCIL, 2101 CONSTITUTION AVENUE, WASHINGTON, D. C. 20418

11. List below in chronological order the postdoctoral appointments (excluding clinical residencies and internships) you have held, giving the information requested.

    | Period of appointment (including renewals) | Institution | Appointment type* | R** | Field Specialization*** |
    |---|---|---|---|---|
    | (i) From_____ to_____ | _____ | ____ | ____ | ____ |
    | (ii) From_____ to_____ | _____ | ____ | ____ | ____ |
    | (iii) From_____ to_____ | _____ | ____ | ____ | ____ |

    *Insert the appropriate code from below:

    1 — Research associate: appointment under research grant funds
    2 — NIH Postdoctoral Trainee: appointment under training grant
    3 — NIH Postdoctoral Fellow: awarded in national competition
    4 — NSF Postdoctoral Fellow: awarded in national competition
    5 — NSF Senior Postdoctoral Fellow: awarded in national competition
    6 — Other government fellowship: awarded in national competition
    7 — Other non-government fellowship: awarded in national competition
    8 — Other

    **Check if part of residency training following the M. D.
    ***Use field numbers from the attached specialities list.

## APPENDIX A: THE QUESTIONNAIRES

12. Did you have a postdoctoral appointment within one year of receiving your doctorate?

    Yes_____ No_____

    If yes, please answer all questions below.    If no, please jump to question 16 and the following.

13. What led you to choose the institution you attended for your *first* postdoctoral appointment? Check three most important.

    | | |
    |---|---|
    | Recommendation of faculty adviser | _____ 0 |
    | Freedom to work in field of choice | _____ 1 |
    | Opportunity to work with eminent scholar | _____ 2 |
    | Stipend offered was most attractive | _____ 3 |
    | Superior facilities, equipment and/or library | _____ 4 |
    | Favorable geographic location | _____ 5 |
    | To complete work started there | _____ 6 |
    | The over-all reputation of the institution | _____ 7 |
    | Personal considerations | _____ 8 |
    | Other (specify)_____ | _____ 9 |

14. Looking back, how do you rate your *first* postdoctoral appointment with regard to the following aspects:

    | | highly satisfactory | satisfactory | unsatisfactory | not applicable |
    |---|---|---|---|---|
    | a. development of research skills | | | | |
    | b. your scientific adviser | | | | |
    | c. contact with other senior scholars | | | | |
    | d. your career advancement | | | | |
    | e. acquisition of knowledge | | | | |
    | f. work accomplished | | | | |
    | g. opportunity to teach | | | | |
    | h. availability of facilities and equipment | | | | |
    | i. other (specify) _____ | | | | |

15. If you could have changed your *first* postdoctoral experience, what would you have changed?   check as many as apply

    a. changed nothing _____
    b. avoided it altogether _____
    c. chosen a different institution _____
    d. chosen a different faculty sponsor _____
    e. chosen a different field _____
    f. stayed longer _____
    g. cut it shorter _____
    h. waited until you had more experience _____
    i. sought more independence _____
    j. sought more guidance _____
    k. other (specify)_____

16. Looking back, how do you rate your *delayed* or *later* postdoctoral appointment(s) with regard to:

    | | highly satisfactory | satisfactory | unsatisfactory | not applicable |
    |---|---|---|---|---|
    | a. development of research skills | | | | |
    | b. acquaintanceship with other scholars | | | | |
    | c. your career advancement | | | | |
    | d. acquisition of knowledge | | | | |
    | e. work accomplished | | | | |
    | f. opportunity to teach | | | | |
    | g. other (specify)_____ | | | | |
    | Had no such appointment_____ | | | | |

17. Were your postdoctoral appointments periods of enhanced productivity?    Yes_____ No_____

## POSTDOCTORAL EXPERIENCE QUESTIONNAIRE

18. Have you any comments on postdoctoral education not covered in the above questions?

THANK YOU FOR YOUR ASSISTANCE. PLEASE RETURN THE QUESTIONNAIRE TO THE STUDY OF POSTDOCTORAL EDUCATION, NATIONAL RESEARCH COUNCIL, 2101 CONSTITUTION AVENUE, WASHINGTON, D. C. 20418.

APPENDIX A: THE QUESTIONNAIRES

## A-5 Institutional Questionnaire

In addition to the above machine-processed questionnaires an open-ended questionnaire was designed to be answered by each institutional coordinator for the Study to determine institutional attitudes toward postdoctoral education. These were sent to the 165 schools whose postdoctorals responded to the census questionnaire. Completed returns were returned by 125 administrators.

# THE STUDY OF POSTDOCTORAL EDUCATION
Sponsored by the
**NATIONAL RESEARCH COUNCIL**
NATIONAL ACADEMY OF SCIENCES — NATIONAL ACADEMY OF ENGINEERING

INSTITUTIONAL QUESTIONNAIRE

1. Name of institution_____

2. Name and title of person completing this questionnaire_____
   _____

3. What is the rationale of your institution in promoting postdoctoral study?



4. The postdoctoral population

   a. Do you have reason to feel that you have too many or too few postdoctorals at your institution at present?



   b. Do you feel that the proportion of foreign postdoctorals in any cause of concern? Please give us any evaluation or recommendation you wish to make.



5. Selection and appointment procedures

   a. Would you like to see a change in the relative numbers of postdoctorals on national fellowships, postdoctorals on research grants, and postdoctorals on training grants? Should the funding agencies be encouraged to support one type of appointment more than another?

## APPENDIX A: THE QUESTIONNAIRES

b. Do you feel that your institution's procedures for the admission of postdoctorals on fellowships or for the appointment of postdoctorals on research or training grants are adequate to safeguard academic standards or do they need to be changed?

c. Do you feel that your institution maintains sufficient control over the duration of postdoctoral appointments, or should this control be tightened? How long should a postdoctoral be allowed to stay?

Research and teaching

a. What do you feel has been the effect of your postdoctoral commitment on the quality of research at your institution? Please cite any evidence you may have.

b. Does your institution have any policy of involving postdoctorals in teaching? Are there opportunities here which should be developed?

c. What do you feel has been the effect of your postdoctoral commitment on the quality of your undergraduate and graduate programs? Please cite any evidence you may have.

INSTITUTIONAL QUESTIONNAIRE

7. Institutional arrangements in support of postdoctoral education.

   a. Does your institution finance any postdoctoral appointments out of its own funds?

   b. To what extent do you provide to your younger faculty members opportunities for their continued education in research comparable to the opportunities for research afforded by postdoctoral appointments? To what extent can junior faculty appointments serve the same purpose as postdoctoral appointments?

   c. Have you developed any administrative structure (such as a school of advanced study) to provide for the needs of postdoctorals? Have such arrangements proved effective?

   d. What do you feel needs to be done to integrate postdoctorals into the academic community?

8. Funding

   a. What do you estimate is the net cost to your institution of accepting a postdoctoral who comes with his stipend or salary paid but with no other support?

## APPENDIX A: THE QUESTIONNAIRES

b. Does your institution place any restriction on the number of such postdoctorals, or of other postdoctorals, a department may admit? If it does not, has it considered doing so? Do you charge, or have you thought of charging, a postdoctoral fee?

c. The federal agencies provide relatively small grants ($500 to $1,000) towards the expenses of postdoctoral fellows. Can you make a case that these grants should be increased, or is it likely that the federal agencies' support in the aggregate of postdoctoral research appointees, postdoctoral trainees, and postdoctoral fellows covers the cost of their education?

9. <u>Other comments</u>:

# APPENDIX B
# Compilations of Data

## B-1 Fine Field Distribution of Postdoctorals

Each respondent to the Postdoctoral Census Questionnaire was asked to specify his postdoctoral field by using the three-digit code shown in the following Specialties List. This is the code used by the Survey of Earned Doctorates of the National Research Council. For the purpose of presentation of data, however, the three-digit codes were grouped into larger subsets and identified by generic phrases. Since these subsets do not always correspond to the groupings in the Specialties List, we present below the groupings used in this study:

| Field | Inclusive Codes |
|---|---|
| Mathematics | 000–099 |
| Astronomy | 100 |
| Physics | 110–199 |
| Chemistry | 200–299 |
| Earth Sciences | 300–399 |
| Engineering | 400–499 |
| Agricultural Sciences | 500–509 |
| Basic Medical Sciences | 520, 540, 564, 534, M42, M43, 536, 530 |
| Biosciences | All in 520–599 not listed above |
| Psychology | 600–699 |
| Social Sciences | 700–799 except 730 |
| Arts and Humanities | 800, 730, 810–830, 840, 888, 889 |
| Education | 900–999 |
| Professional and Other | 850–880, 899, unknown |
| Internal Medicine | M10–M19 |
| Other Clinical Medicine | M01–M06, L21–L50, M20–M94, except M42, M43 |
| Allied Medical Sciences | L01–L15, L60–L90, 510–519 |

APPENDIX B: COMPILATIONS OF DATA

When even coarser groupings were indicated, the following designations were used:

Engineering, Mathematical and Physical Sciences (EMP): Mathematics, Astronomy, Physics, Chemistry, Earth Sciences, Engineering
Biological Sciences: Agricultural Sciences, Basic Medical Sciences, Biosciences
Medical Sciences: Internal Medicine, Other Clinical Medicine, Allied Medical Sciences
Other Fields: Psychology, Social·Sciences, Arts and Humanities, Education, Professional and Other

Because these groupings are somewhat arbitrary we have included Table B-1, displaying information on postdoctorals by fine field. In only the following cases have we combined two or more three-digit codes:

Pathology: 534, M42, M43
Education:
    Administration: 930, 933, 935
    Educational Psychology: 630, 635, 910, 915
    Guidance and Counseling: 940, 945
    Measurement: 920, 925
    Methods: 970–996
    Philosophy: 900, 903, 905
    Special Education: 950–958
General Dentistry: 516, L60
Optometry: 515, L71
Pharmacy: 511, L80
Public Health: 512, L14
Veterinary Medicine: 513, L90
Medical Sciences, Other: 510, 514, 518, 519, L01

# FINE FIELD DISTRIBUTION OF POSTDOCTORALS

## SPECIALTIES LIST

*(For Medical Specialties, see reverse side.)*

### Mathematics

000—Algebra
010—Analysis
020—Geometry
030—Logic
040—Number Theory
050 Probability, Math Stat.
 (see also 544, 670, 725, 920)
060—Topology

080—Computing Theory & Practice
085—Applied Mathematics

098—Mathematics, General
099—Mathematics, Other

(note also 984: Math Educ.)

### Physics and Astronomy

(Note: Theoretical scientists mark "T" on questionnaire following code No.)

100—Astronomy

110—Atomic & Molec. Physics
120—Electromagnetism
130—Mechanics
132—Acoustics
134—Fluids
136—Optics
138—Thermal Physics
140—Elementary Particles
150—Nuclear Structure
160—Solid State

198—Physics, General
199—Physics, Other

### Chemistry

200—Analytical
210—Inorganic
220—Organic
230—Nuclear
240—Physical
250—Theoretical
260—Agricultural & Food
270—Pharmaceutical

298—Chemistry, General
299—Chemistry, Other

(see also Biochemistry, 540)

### Earth Sciences

300—Mineralogy, Petrology, Geochemistry
310—Stratig.; Sedimentation
320—Paleontology
330—Structural Geology
340—Solid Earth Geophysics
350—Geomorph., Glacial Geology
360—Hydrology
370—Oceanography
380—Meteorology
390—Applied Geol.: Geol. Engr.; Econ. Geol.; Petroleum Geol.

398—Earth Sciences, General
399—Earth Sciences, Other

### Fields Not Elsewhere Classified

899—Sci., General; Sci., Other; Other General Field

### Engineering

400—Aeronautical & Astronautical
410—Agricultural
420—Civil
430—Chemical
435—Ceramic
440—Electrical
445—Electronics
450—Industrial
460—Engineering Mechanics
465—Engineering Physics
470—Mechanical
475—Metallurgy & Physical Met. Engin.
480—Sanitary
485—Textile

498—Engineering, General
499—Engineering, Other

### Agricultural Sciences

500—Agronomy
502—Animal Husbandry
504—Fish & Wildlife
505—Forestry
506—Horticulture

508—Agriculture, General
509—Agriculture, Other

### Medical Sciences

510—Medicine & Surgery
511—Pharmacy
512—Public Health
513—Veterinary Medicine
514—Hospital Administration

518—Medical Sciences, General
519—Medical Sciences, Other

### Biological Sciences

520—Anatomy
522—Cytology
524—Embryology
530—Physiology, Animal
532—Physiology, Plant
534—Pathology
536—Pharmacology
540—Biochemistry
542—Biophysics
544—Biometrics, Biostatistics
 (see also 050, 670, 725, 920)
550—Botany
552—Phytopathology
560—Ecology
582—Entomology
570—Genetics
562—Hydrobiology
564—Microbiology
580—Zoology

598—Bio-Science, General
599—Bio-Science, Other

APPENDIX B: COMPILATIONS OF DATA

## SPECIALTIES LIST (CONTINUED)

### Psychology
600—Clinical
610—Counseling & Guidance
620—Developmental & Gerontological
630—Educational
641—Experimental
642—Comparative
643—Physiological
650—Industrial & Personnel
660—Personality
670—Psychometrics
  (see also 050, 544, 920)
635—School Psychology
680—Social

698—Psychology, General
699—Psychology, Other

### Social Sciences
700—Anthropology
705—Archeology
745—Area Studies (specify area)
720—Economics
725—Econometrics
  (see also 050, 544, 670, 920)
727—Statistics
730—History
740—Geography
755—International Relations
750—Political Science, Public Admin.
760—Social Work
710—Sociology

798—Social Sciences, General
799—Social Sciences, Other

### Arts & Humanities
800—Art, Fine & Applied (incl. hist. & crit.)
810-829 Lang. and Lit.
  810—Eng. & Amer.
  820—Modern Foreign, unspec.
  821—German
  822—Classical (specify)
  823—French
  824—Spanish & Portuguese
  825—Linguistics
  826—Italian
  827—Russian
  828—Other Slavic
  829—All other modern lang.

830—Music
840—Philosophy
815—Speech & Dramatic Arts

888—Arts & Humanities, General
889—Arts & Humanities, Other

### Prof. Fields Not Listed Above
850—Business Administration
855—Home Economics
860—Journalism
865—Law, Jurisprudence
870—Library & Archival Science
880—Religion & Theology

### Education
Note: For fields 900-947 and 960-967 final digit indicates level: 0—unspecified; 1—preschool; 2—elem.; 3—secondary; 4—teacher training; 5—higher educ.; 6—adult educ.; 7—other.

900—Foundations: Social, Philosoph.
908—Elem. Educ., General
909—Secondary Educ., General
910—Educational Psychology
920—Educ. Meas. & Stat.
930—Educ. Admin. & Superv.
940—Guid., Couns., Student Pers.
950-959—Special Education
  950—Field Unspecified
  952—Gifted
  954—Speech
  956—Phys. Handicapped
  958—Emot. & Ment. Handicapped
960—Audio-Visual Media

Note: For fields 970-997, and 952-959 even number is for secondary level; next odd number indicates other than secondary level.

970—Agric.
972—Art
974—Business
976—English
978—Foreign L.
980—Home Ec.
982—Ind. Arts
984—Math
986—Music
988—Phys. Ed., Health & Recreation
990—Science Educ.
992—Social Sci. Educ.
994—Vocational Educ.
996—Other Special Field
998—Educ., General
999—Educ., Other

## MEDICAL SPECIALTIES LIST

*(For use with the Postdoctoral Survey)*

| | | | |
|---|---|---|---|
| M01 | Administrative medicine | L01 | Physical medicine & rehabilitation |
| M02 | Anesthesiology | | |
| M03 | Chemotherapy | L12 | Aerospace medicine |
| M04 | Dermatology | L13 | Occupational medicine |
| M05 | General Practice | L14 | Public health |
| M06 | Geriatrics | L15 | General preventive medicine |
| M10 | Internal medicine, general | L21 | Psychiatry |
| M11 | Allergy | L22 | Neurology |
| M12 | Cardiovascular disease | L24 | Nuclear medicine |
| M13 | Endocrinology | L25 | Radiobiology |
| M14 | Gastroenterology | L26 | Clinical radioisotopes |
| M15 | Immunology | | |
| M16 | Infectious disease | L30 | Radiology |
| M17 | Metabolism | L32 | Radiological physics |
| M18 | Nephrology | | |
| M19 | Pulmonary diseases | L40 | General surgery |
| | | L41 | Cardiovascular surgery |
| M20 | Rheumatology | L42 | Colon & rectal surgery |
| | | L43 | Neurological surgery |
| M31 | Obstetrics | L44 | Orthopedic surgery |
| M32 | Gynecology | L45 | Plastic surgery |
| M35 | Oncology | L46 | Thoracic surgery |
| M36 | Ophthalmology | L47 | Urology |
| M37 | Otolaryngology | | |
| | | L50 | Tropical medicine |
| M42 | Anatomic pathology | | |
| M43 | Clinical pathology | L60 | Dentistry, general |
| M44 | Hematology | L61 | Dental public health |
| | | L62 | Endodontics |
| M90 | Pediatrics, general | L63 | Operative dentistry |
| M91 | Pediatric allergy | L64 | Oral pathology |
| M92 | Pediatric cardiology | L65 | Oral surgery |
| M93 | Pediatric hematology | L66 | Orthodontics |
| M94 | Pediatric neurology | L67 | Pedodontics |
| | | L68 | Periodontics |
| | | L69 | Prosthodontics |
| | | L71 | Optometry |
| | | L72 | Osteopathy |
| | | L73 | Podiatry (Chiropody) |
| | | L80 | Pharmacy |
| | | L90 | Veterinary medicine |

APPENDIX TABLE B-1  Postdoctorals by Field

| POSTDOCTORAL FIELD | TOTAL | ACADEMIC LEVEL ||||||| CITIZENSHIP AND SEX[a] |||| SOURCE OF SUPPORT[b] ||||| ANTICIPATED FUTURE EMPL[c] |||
|---|---|---|---|---|---|---|---|---|---|---|---|---|---|---|---|---|---|---|---|---|
| | | Immediate PhD | Intermediate PhD | Long-Term PhD | Senior PhD | Recent MD | Senior MD | PhD and MD | No Doctorate | US Male | US Female | Fgn Male | Fgn Female | Nat'l Sci Fdn | Publ Health Ser | Atom Ener Comm | Dept of Def | Other Govt | Other | Academic | Government | Industry | Other |
| MATHEMATICS | | | | | | | | | | | | | | | | | | | | | | | | |
| ALGEBRA | 19 | 12 | 2 | 3 | | | | | | 9 | 1 | 4 | | | | 2 | | 12 | 19 | | | | |
| ANALYSIS | 53 | 25 | 7 | 18 | | | | | 3 | 33 | 1 | 17 | 2 | 9 | | 12 | 3 | 27 | 46 | 1 | | 6 | |
| APPLIED MATHEMATICS | 37 | 20 | 3 | 6 | 2 | | | 1 | 2 | 14 | 1 | 19 | 2 | 5 | | 7 | 2 | 13 | 34 | | | 3 | |
| COMPUTING THEORY & PRACTICE | 32 | 19 | 4 | 3 | 1 | | 1 | | 2 | 20 | 3 | 9 | | 3 | 3 | 5 | 1 | 18 | 23 | | 5 | 4 | |
| GEOMETRY | 10 | 5 | 1 | 2 | | | | | 1 | 4 | 1 | 3 | | 3 | 1 | 1 | | 6 | 9 | | | | |
| LOGIC | 7 | 5 | | 1 | | | | | | 3 | 2 | 2 | | 3 | | | 1 | 3 | 7 | | | | |
| NUMBER THEORY | 9 | 2 | 3 | 2 | | | | | | 6 | 1 | 2 | | 3 | | | | 6 | 9 | | | | |
| PROBABILITY, MATH. STAT. | 34 | 13 | 4 | 12 | | | | | 3 | 17 | 1 | 16 | 1 | 6 | 1 | 6 | | 18 | 29 | 1 | 1 | 2 | |
| TOPOLOGY | 25 | 12 | 2 | 8 | | | | | 1 | 15 | 1 | 9 | | 13 | | 2 | | 9 | 25 | | | | |
| MATHEMATICS, GENERAL | 6 | 2 | 2 | 2 | | | | | | 4 | 1 | 1 | | 1 | 1 | | | 4 | 6 | | | | |
| MATHEMATICS, OTHER | 8 | 2 | 1 | 2 | | | | | 3 | 6 | | 2 | | 4 | | 1 | | 1 | 8 | | | | |
| TOTAL MATHEMATICS | 240 | 117 | 30 | 59 | 3 | 1 | 1 | 1 | 15 | 131 | 13 | 90 | 5 | 54 | 8 | 36 | 7 | 117 | 215 | 2 | 6 | 15 | |
| ASTRONOMY | | | | | | | | | | | | | | | | | | | | | | | |
| TOTAL ASTRONOMY | 108 | 62 | 18 | 12 | | | | | 8 | 40 | 6 | 57 | 4 | 18 | 1 | 17 | 33 | 37 | 92 | 5 | | 9 | |
| PHYSICS | | | | | | | | | | | | | | | | | | | | | | | |
| ACOUSTICS | 7 | 4 | 2 | 1 | | | | | | 4 | | 3 | | | | 4 | | 3 | 4 | | 1 | 1 | |
| ATOMIC & MOLEC. PHYSICS | 127 | 81 | 14 | 10 | | | | | 3 | 74 | | 51 | 1 | 17 | 5 | 27 | 16 | 39 | 93 | 4 | 14 | 13 | |
| ELECTROMAGNETISM | 39 | 23 | 4 | 8 | 2 | | | | 2 | 16 | 1 | 21 | 1 | 1 | 1 | 8 | 10 | 9 | 23 | 4 | 3 | 8 | |
| ELEMENTARY PARTICLES | 303 | 173 | 47 | 49 | 13 | | | | 21 | 149 | 1 | 148 | 2 | 48 | | 175 | 24 | 9 | 41 | 263 | 12 | 7 | 21 |
| FLUIDS | 43 | 23 | 6 | 6 | | | | | 2 | 19 | | 23 | 1 | 9 | | 4 | 9 | 8 | 11 | 37 | 5 | 1 | |
| MECHANICS | 2 | | 1 | 1 | | | | | | 2 | | | | | | | 1 | 1 | | 2 | | | |
| NUCLEAR STRUCTURE | 225 | 139 | 29 | 31 | 14 | | | | 12 | 110 | 4 | 109 | 2 | 39 | 1 | 106 | 31 | 3 | 38 | 181 | 15 | 11 | 10 |
| OPTICS | 12 | 6 | 2 | 3 | | | | | 1 | 5 | | 7 | | 2 | | 2 | 2 | 2 | 6 | 7 | | 1 | 3 |
| SOLID STATE | 337 | 207 | 36 | 41 | 29 | 1 | | | 22 | 153 | 1 | 173 | 9 | 41 | 5 | 81 | 13 | 98 | 241 | 17 | 42 | 28 | |
| THERMAL PHYSICS | 27 | 20 | 4 | 3 | | | | | | 15 | | 12 | | 8 | | 7 | | 8 | 6 | 20 | 2 | 2 | 2 |
| PHYSICS, GENERAL | 10 | 7 | 1 | 1 | 1 | | | | | 5 | | 5 | | | | | | 2 | 2 | 7 | 1 | | |
| PHYSICS, OTHER | 135 | 83 | 16 | 15 | | | | | 8 | 74 | 2 | 56 | 3 | 18 | 3 | 22 | 16 | 34 | 34 | 97 | 12 | 8 | 15 |
| TOTAL PHYSICS | 1267 | 766 | 152 | 178 | 98 | 1 | | | 71 | 624 | 9 | 610 | 19 | 183 | 15 | 423 | 99 | 287 | 975 | 72 | 86 | 101 | |

288

| Field | | | | | | | | | | | | | | | | | | | | | | | |
|---|---|---|---|---|---|---|---|---|---|---|---|---|---|---|---|---|---|---|---|---|---|---|---|
| **CHEMISTRY** | | | | | | | | | | | | | | | | | | | | | | | |
| AGRICULTURAL & FOOD | 15 | 10 | 1 | 2 | 2 | | | | 3 | 23 | 1 | | 7 | 1 | 14 | 15 | 10 | 6 | 5 | 5 | 3 | 16 | 38 | 7 | 2 | 4 | 6 |
| ANALYTICAL | 66 | 35 | 8 | 12 | 8 | | | | | 51 | 6 | 1 | 36 | 5 | 41 | 25 | 30 | 26 | 5 | 1 | 43 | 125 | 4 | 14 | 29 | H |
| INORGANIC | 168 | 122 | 20 | 13 | 11 | | | | 2 | 51 | 6 | 1 | 109 | 2 | 41 | 25 | 30 | 26 | 1 | 10 | 30 | 3 | 4 | 2 | 3 |
| NUCLEAR | 40 | 25 | 3 | 8 | 2 | | | | 2 | 10 | 1 | | 26 | 3 | 1 | 1 | 26 | | | | | | | | |
| ORGANIC | 664 | 421 | 77 | 97 | 45 | | | 5 | 19 | 193 | 27 | | 416 | 24 | 124 | 280 | 10 | 62 | 28 | 141 | 385 | 20 | 177 | 56 | |
| PHARMACEUTICAL | 34 | 21 | 6 | 5 | 3 | | | | | 8 | | | 24 | 2 | 1 | 23 | | 4 | 1 | 3 | 22 | 5 | 6 | 1 | |
| PHYSICAL | 478 | 304 | 64 | 66 | 31 | | | | 12 | 159 | 19 | | 279 | 18 | 74 | 96 | 83 | 79 | 34 | 101 | 336 | 24 | 70 | 34 | |
| THEORETICAL | 87 | 63 | 10 | 8 | 4 | | | | 2 | 42 | 6 | | 35 | 4 | 29 | 10 | 7 | 10 | 10 | 20 | 72 | 3 | 5 | 6 | |
| CHEMISTRY, GENERAL | 7 | 3 | 3 | 1 | | | | | | 7 | | | | | 2 | 3 | | 1 | 1 | | 4 | | 1 | 2 | |
| CHEMISTRY, OTHER | 101 | 55 | 13 | 17 | 9 | 5 | | | 2 | 44 | 6 | | 45 | 5 | 7 | 26 | 8 | 13 | 12 | 30 | 59 | 8 | 20 | 12 | |
| TOTAL CHEMISTRY | 1660 | 1059 | 204 | 229 | 115 | 6 | | 5 | 42 | 537 | 66 | | 984 | 64 | 293 | 485 | 174 | 201 | 98 | 367 | 1078 | 73 | 330 | 128 | |
| **EARTH SCIENCES** | | | | | | | | | | | | | | | | | | | | | | | | | |
| APPLIED GEOL., GEOL. ENGR. | 5 | 2 | | 1 | 1 | | | | 1 | | 1 | | 4 | | | | | | 2 | 1 | 3 | | 1 | | 1 |
| GEOMORPH., GLACIAL GEOLOGY | 5 | 2 | 1 | | 2 | | | | | 3 | | | 2 | | 1 | | | | | 3 | 5 | | | | |
| HYDROLOGY | 2 | | | | 2 | | | | | 2 | | | | | | | | | | 2 | 2 | | | | |
| METEOROLOGY | 17 | 9 | 3 | 2 | 3 | | | | | 6 | | | 11 | | 7 | | | | 4 | 4 | 12 | | | | 3 |
| MINERALOGY, GEOCHEMISTRY | 77 | 43 | 10 | 7 | 13 | | | 4 | | 33 | 1 | | 40 | 3 | 24 | 2 | 3 | 1 | 7 | 36 | 59 | 6 | 3 | 4 | |
| OCEANOGRAPHY | 15 | 9 | 3 | | 3 | | | | | 11 | | | 4 | | 6 | | | 3 | | 6 | 13 | 1 | | 1 | |
| PALEONTOLOGY | 16 | 11 | 1 | | 4 | | | | | 7 | | | 9 | | 7 | | | | 1 | 7 | 15 | | | | |
| SOLID EARTH GEOPHYSICS | 27 | 14 | 4 | 4 | 5 | | | | | 10 | | | 17 | | 3 | | | 9 | 5 | 7 | 20 | 1 | 1 | 1 | 2 |
| STRATIGRAPHY, SEDIMENTATION | 8 | 5 | 1 | 1 | 1 | | | | | 5 | | | 3 | | 3 | | | 2 | 3 | 3 | 7 | | | | 1 |
| STRUCTURAL GEOLOGY | 4 | 3 | | | 1 | | | | | 2 | | | 2 | | 1 | | | | 1 | 2 | 4 | | | | |
| EARTH SCIENCES, GENERAL | 2 | 1 | | | 1 | | | | | 1 | | | 1 | | | | | | 2 | | | 1 | | | |
| EARTH SCIENCES, OTHER | 11 | 4 | 3 | | 2 | | | 2 | 4 | | | | 6 | 1 | 1 | | 1 | | 7 | 2 | 9 | 1 | 1 | | |
| TOTAL EARTH SCIENCES | 189 | 103 | 26 | 15 | 38 | | | 7 | 84 | | 2 | | 99 | 4 | 53 | 2 | 4 | 16 | 29 | 73 | 149 | 10 | 7 | | 12 |
| **ENGINEERING** | | | | | | | | | | | | | | | | | | | | | | | | | |
| AERONAUTICAL, ASTRONAUTICAL | 13 | 12 | | 1 | 1 | | | | 8 | | | | 5 | | 1 | | | | 3 | 5 | 9 | 2 | | | 1 |
| AGRICULTURAL | 2 | | | | 2 | | | | 1 | | | | 1 | | | | | | | 2 | 2 | | | | |
| CERAMIC | 7 | 3 | 1 | 1 | 1 | | | | 2 | | | | 5 | | | | | 1 | 2 | 4 | 4 | | 2 | | 1 |
| CHEMICAL | 19 | 16 | 1 | | 1 | 1 | | | 7 | | 2 | | 12 | 1 | 1 | 3 | 1 | 2 | 2 | 12 | 12 | 2 | 2 | | 1 |
| CIVIL | 18 | 13 | | | 2 | | | 1 | 3 | | 1 | | 14 | 1 | 1 | 1 | | 2 | 2 | 13 | 13 | | 2 | 2 | 3 |
| ELECTRICAL | 28 | 19 | 3 | 3 | 2 | | | 1 | 12 | | 1 | | 15 | 3 | 3 | | | 6 | 5 | 14 | 20 | 5 | 3 | 4 | 4 |
| ELECTRONICS | 13 | 7 | 2 | 2 | 1 | | | 1 | 6 | | | | 7 | | 1 | | 1 | 3 | 3 | 7 | 6 | 1 | 2 | 1 | 2 |
| ENGINEERING MECHANICS | 27 | 22 | 2 | 1 | 2 | | | | 9 | | 1 | | 17 | 1 | 2 | | | 5 | 5 | 16 | 24 | 1 | 4 | 1 | 1 |
| ENGINEERING PHYSICS | 15 | 9 | 2 | | 2 | | | 2 | 6 | | 1 | | 9 | 1 | 1 | | 3 | 3 | 2 | 9 | 12 | | 1 | 2 | |
| INDUSTRIAL | 2 | 1 | | | | | | 1 | | | | | 2 | | | | | | | 2 | 2 | | | | |
| MECHANICAL | 25 | 15 | 5 | | 5 | | | | 13 | | 2 | | 12 | 3 | 3 | | | 5 | 5 | 16 | 16 | | 4 | 5 | |
| METALLURGY, PHYS. MET. ENGR | 81 | 54 | 10 | 10 | 4 | | | 3 | 20 | | 59 | 1 | | 4 | | 3 | 18 | 19 | 3 | 33 | 49 | 3 | 17 | 11 | |

289

## APPENDIX TABLE B-1—Continued

| POSTDOCTORAL FIELD | TOTAL | Immediate PhD | Intermediate PhD | Long-Term PhD | Senior PhD | Recent MD | Senior MD | PhD and MD | No Doctorate | US Male | US Female | Fgn Male | Fgn Female | Natl Sci Fdn | Publ Health Ser | Atom Ener Comm | Dept of Def | Other Govt | Other | Academic | Government | Industry | Other |
|---|---|---|---|---|---|---|---|---|---|---|---|---|---|---|---|---|---|---|---|---|---|---|---|
| ENGINEERING (CONTINUED) | | | | | | | | | | | | | | | | | | | | | | | |
| SANITARY | 4 | | 2 | | | | | 1 | 1 | 1 | | 3 | | | | | | | 3 | 1 | 3 | | 1 |
| ENGINEERING, GENERAL | 3 | 2 | | | 1 | | | | | | | 2 | 1 | | 1 | | | | 1 | 1 | | | |
| ENGINEERING, OTHER | 17 | 9 | 1 | | | 2 | 2 | 1 | 10 | 1 | | 7 | | 1 | 5 | | | 8 | 12 | 1 | | 1 | 4 |
| TOTAL ENGINEERING | 274 | 182 | 28 | 23 | | 2 | 2 | 12 | 98 | 1 | 170 | 4 | 18 | 13 | 24 | 2 | 51 | 20 | 143 | 185 | 7 | 39 | 36 |
| AGRICULTURE | | | | | | | | | | | | | | | | | | | | | | | |
| AGRONOMY | 24 | 16 | 2 | 1 | | | | 1 | 8 | 1 | 13 | 3 | 3 | 2 | 4 | | | 6 | 8 | 14 | 3 | 1 | 5 |
| ANIMAL HUSBANDRY | 11 | 5 | 1 | 2 | 2 | | 1 | | 7 | | 4 | 3 | | 3 | 1 | | | 1 | 6 | 9 | 2 | | |
| FORESTRY | 2 | | | 2 | | | | | 1 | | 1 | | | | | | | | 2 | 1 | 1 | | |
| HORTICULTURE | 3 | 1 | 2 | | | | | | | | 3 | | 1 | | | | | | 2 | 2 | | | 1 |
| AGRICULTURE, GENERAL | 2 | 1 | 1 | | | | | | | | 2 | | | 1 | | | | | 1 | 1 | | | 1 |
| AGRICULTURE, OTHER | 13 | 6 | 3 | 2 | 1 | | 1 | | 5 | | 8 | | 1 | | | | | 3 | 9 | 11 | 1 | | 1 |
| TOTAL AGRICULTURE | 55 | 28 | 6 | 8 | 2 | | 1 | 2 | 21 | 1 | 31 | 6 | 5 | 6 | 5 | | | 10 | 28 | 38 | 7 | 1 | 8 |
| BASIC MEDICAL SCIENCES | | | | | | | | | | | | | | | | | | | | | | | |
| ANATOMY | 63 | 6 | 3 | 1 | 26 | 16 | 6 | 3 | 32 | 5 | 21 | 5 | 39 | 30 | 1 | | 1 | 21 | 58 | | 5 | | |
| BIOCHEMISTRY | 1322 | 597 | 137 | 52 | 157 | 56 | 73 | 54 | 538 | 112 | 590 | 79 | 96 | 841 | 30 | 11 | 31 | 277 | 1045 | 62 | 53 | 137 | |
| MICROBIOLOGY | 279 | 112 | 19 | 21 | 45 | 25 | 14 | 5 | 174 | 38 | 103 | 13 | 25 | 167 | 2 | 7 | 8 | 57 | 210 | 13 | 11 | 38 | |
| PATHOLOGY | 193 | 2 | 1 | 2 | 1 | 38 | 13 | 2 | 134 | 8 | 42 | 9 | 2 | 126 | | 3 | 3 | 48 | 150 | 10 | 4 | 23 | |
| PHARMACOLOGY | 142 | 46 | 6 | 3 | 38 | 22 | 20 | 2 | 67 | 6 | 58 | 11 | 4 | 92 | 1 | | 3 | 40 | 113 | 6 | 12 | 10 | |
| PHYSIOLOGY | 353 | 106 | 21 | 15 | 102 | 62 | 25 | 8 | 178 | 23 | 141 | 11 | 21 | 197 | 3 | 10 | 6 | 109 | 294 | 18 | 3 | 31 | |
| TOTAL BASIC MEDICAL SCI. | 2352 | 869 | 187 | 93 | 502 | 219 | 151 | 74 | 1073 | 192 | 955 | 128 | 148 | 1462 | 36 | 32 | 52 | 552 | 1870 | 109 | 83 | 244 | |
| BIOSCIENCES | | | | | | | | | | | | | | | | | | | | | | | |
| BIOMETRICS, BIOSTATISTICS | 15 | 4 | 5 | 1 | 1 | 3 | | 1 | 11 | 1 | 3 | | 13 | | 1 | | 1 | 11 | 1 | 2 | | | |
| BIOPHYSICS | 205 | 92 | 29 | 12 | 20 | 11 | | 6 | 109 | 16 | 69 | 14 | 122 | 19 | 3 | 6 | 36 | 169 | 10 | 3 | 20 | | |
| BOTANY | 23 | 14 | 2 | 4 | 3 | | | | 8 | 1 | 13 | | 7 | 5 | 1 | 2 | 8 | 20 | 2 | | 1 | | |
| CYTOLOGY | 93 | 41 | 7 | 10 | 8 | 16 | 5 | 1 | 43 | 15 | 23 | 12 | 5 | 56 | 5 | | | 25 | 75 | 6 | 2 | 8 | |
| ECOLOGY | 31 | 15 | 6 | 4 | 4 | 1 | 1 | 1 | 21 | 3 | 7 | | 9 | 7 | 3 | 1 | | 11 | 26 | 1 | | 4 | |
| EMBRYOLOGY | 60 | 29 | 3 | 5 | 7 | 5 | 2 | 2 | 29 | 7 | 16 | 7 | 10 | 32 | 1 | | 1 | 15 | 51 | | | 5 | |
| ENTOMOLOGY | 26 | 8 | 5 | 9 | | | | | 5 | 2 | 16 | 3 | | 9 | | | 1 | 12 | 18 | 5 | | 2 | |

| | | | | | | | | | | | | | | | | | | | | | | |
|---|---|---|---|---|---|---|---|---|---|---|---|---|---|---|---|---|---|---|---|---|---|---|
| BIOSCIENCES (CONTINUED) | | | | | | | | | | | | | | | | | | | | | | |
| GENETICS | 180 | 68 | 15 | 27 | 10 | 27 | 22 | 1 | 10 | 78 | 23 | 59 | 18 | 12 | 109 | 7 | | 2 | 44 | 146 | 6 | 2 | 22 |
| HYDROBIOLOGY | 7 | 3 | | 3 | | | | | 1 | 5 | | 1 | 1 | 3 | 1 | | | | 2 | 6 | 1 | | |
| PHYTOPATHOLOGY | 38 | 19 | 2 | 5 | 11 | | | | 1 | 7 | 1 | 27 | 3 | 3 | 7 | 1 | | 9 | 17 | 28 | 3 | 1 | 4 |
| PLANT PHYSIOLOGY | 96 | 52 | 9 | 19 | 12 | | | | 4 | 28 | 7 | 53 | 8 | 14 | 25 | 20 | | 9 | 23 | 77 | 8 | 1 | 7 |
| ZOOLOGY | 28 | 15 | 3 | 3 | 4 | | | 3 | | 17 | 2 | 7 | 1 | 6 | 11 | 1 | | 1 | 8 | 23 | | | 3 |
| BIOSCIENCES, GENERAL | 13 | 4 | 1 | 3 | | 2 | 2 | | 1 | 7 | | 6 | | | 9 | | | | 3 | 10 | 1 | | 2 |
| BIOSCIENCES, OTHER | 92 | 47 | 9 | 6 | 5 | 15 | 8 | 1 | 1 | 43 | 14 | 33 | 2 | 7 | 47 | 4 | 1 | 3 | 29 | 72 | 1 | 1 | 14 |
| TOTAL BIOSCIENCES | 907 | 411 | 96 | 128 | 81 | 90 | 54 | 19 | 28 | 411 | 92 | 333 | 67 | 94 | 453 | 63 | 8 | 34 | 234 | 732 | 45 | 13 | 92 |
| PSYCHOLOGY | | | | | | | | | | | | | | | | | | | | | | | |
| CLINICAL | 32 | 19 | 5 | 4 | 3 | 1 | | | | 26 | 5 | 1 | | | 24 | | | 3 | 5 | 19 | 1 | | 12 |
| COMPARATIVE | 8 | 4 | | 2 | 2 | | | | | 5 | 3 | | | | 6 | | 1 | | 1 | 7 | | | 1 |
| DEVELOPMENTAL & GERONTOLOG. | 27 | 11 | 2 | 3 | 9 | | 2 | | | 17 | 8 | | 2 | | 18 | | | 2 | 6 | 21 | | | 6 |
| EXPERIMENTAL | 65 | 31 | 8 | 5 | 14 | 1 | 3 | 1 | 2 | 48 | 7 | 7 | 3 | 4 | 33 | | 2 | 3 | 22 | 52 | 2 | 1 | 10 |
| PERSONALITY | 3 | 1 | | | | 1 | 1 | | | 1 | | | | | 1 | | | 1 | 1 | 2 | | | 1 |
| PHYSIOLOGICAL | 59 | 42 | 4 | 3 | 1 | 4 | 3 | 1 | 1 | 47 | 6 | 4 | 2 | 2 | 46 | 1 | 3 | 2 | 5 | 53 | 2 | | 3 |
| PSYCHOMETRICS | 5 | | 1 | | 3 | | | | 1 | 4 | | | 1 | | 2 | | | | 3 | 5 | | | |
| SOCIAL | 19 | 6 | 4 | 1 | 6 | 1 | | | 1 | 11 | 5 | 2 | 1 | 4 | 12 | | | | 3 | 18 | | | 1 |
| PSYCHOLOGY, GENERAL | 4 | 2 | 1 | | | | 1 | | | 3 | | | | | 1 | | 1 | 1 | 2 | | | | 4 |
| PSYCHOLOGY, OTHER | 24 | 18 | 1 | 2 | 2 | 1 | 1 | | | 16 | 4 | 2 | 2 | | 10 | | 3 | 1 | 8 | 23 | | | 1 |
| TOTAL PSYCHOLOGY | 246 | 134 | 26 | 20 | 40 | 9 | 10 | 2 | 5 | 178 | 40 | 16 | 11 | 10 | 153 | 1 | 9 | 13 | 56 | 200 | 5 | 1 | 39 |
| SOCIAL SCIENCES | | | | | | | | | | | | | | | | | | | | | | | |
| ANTHROPOLOGY | 18 | 9 | 1 | 3 | 4 | 1 | | | | 10 | 3 | 4 | | 2 | 4 | | | | 11 | 18 | | | |
| ARCHEOLOGY | 6 | 2 | | 1 | 2 | | | | 1 | 3 | | 2 | 1 | | | | | | 5 | 4 | | | 2 |
| AREA STUDIES | 11 | 5 | 1 | 2 | 3 | | | | | 6 | 1 | 4 | | | | | | | 10 | 10 | | | |
| ECONOMETRICS | 6 | 1 | 2 | | 3 | | | | | 5 | | 1 | | | | | | 1 | 5 | 6 | | | |
| ECONOMICS | 48 | 7 | 13 | 3 | 20 | | | 1 | 5 | 18 | 1 | 27 | 2 | 3 | | | | | 44 | 41 | 1 | | 4 |
| GEOGRAPHY | 3 | | 1 | | 2 | | | | | 3 | | | | | | | | | 3 | 3 | | | |
| INTERNATIONAL RELATIONS | 15 | 4 | | 4 | 6 | 1 | | | 1 | 12 | | 3 | | | 1 | | 1 | | 12 | 17 | 1 | | 2 |
| POLITICAL SCI., PUBLIC ADM. | 40 | 9 | 11 | 6 | 11 | | | | 3 | 26 | 3 | 9 | 2 | 2 | 2 | | 1 | | 32 | 36 | | 1 | 3 |
| SOCIAL WORK | 1 | 1 | 1 | | | | | | | 1 | | | | | | | | | | 1 | | | |
| SOCIOLOGY | 37 | 11 | 6 | 6 | 10 | 1 | 1 | | 2 | 23 | 3 | 9 | 1 | 1 | 8 | | | 2 | 21 | 32 | | | 3 |
| STATISTICS | 3 | 2 | 1 | | | | | | | 2 | | 1 | 1 | | | | 1 | | 1 | 3 | | | |
| SOCIAL SCIENCES, GENERAL | 1 | | | | | | | | 1 | 1 | 1 | | | | 1 | | | | | 1 | | | |
| SOCIAL SCIENCES, OTHER | 7 | 3 | | 1 | 2 | | | | 1 | 3 | | 2 | 1 | | | | | 1 | 6 | 3 | | | 3 |
| TOTAL SOCIAL SCIENCES | 196 | 53 | 37 | 26 | 63 | 2 | 1 | 1 | 14 | 113 | 12 | 62 | 7 | 9 | 15 | | 3 | 4 | 151 | 170 | 2 | 1 | 17 |
| ARTS AND HUMANITIES | | | | | | | | | | | | | | | | | | | | | | | |
| ART, FINE & APPLIED | 13 | 2 | 2 | 1 | 5 | | | | 5 | 10 | 2 | 2 | 2 | | | | | | 13 | 13 | | | |
| DRAMATIC ARTS & SPEECH | 9 | 1 | 3 | 2 | 2 | 1 | | | | 7 | | 1 | 1 | | 4 | | | | 5 | 9 | | | |

## APPENDIX TABLE B-1—Continued

| POSTDOCTORAL FIELD | TOTAL | Immediate PhD | Intermediate PhD | Long-Term PhD | Senior PhD | Recent MD | Senior MD | PhD and MD | No Doctorate | US Male | US Female | Fgn Male | Fgn Female | Nat'l Sci Fdn | Publ Health Ser | Atom Ener Comm | Dept of Def | Other Gov't | Other | Academic | Government | Industry | Other |
|---|---|---|---|---|---|---|---|---|---|---|---|---|---|---|---|---|---|---|---|---|---|---|---|
| **ARTS AND HUMANITIES (CONTINUED)** | | | | | | | | | | | | | | | | | | | | | | | |
| HISTORY | 83 | 10 | 4 | 50 | | | | | 3 | 63 | 13 | 4 | 3 | | | | 2 | 76 | 77 | 1 | | | 3 |
| LANG. & LIT. - CLASSICAL | 9 | 2 | | 6 | | | | | 1 | 4 | 2 | 2 | 1 | | | | | 9 | 9 | | | | |
| LANG. & LIT. - ENG. & AMER. | 45 | 9 | 4 | 22 | | | | | 9 | 25 | 15 | 4 | 1 | | | | 3 | 41 | 44 | | | | |
| LANG. & LIT. - FRENCH | 4 | | 1 | 2 | | | | | 1 | 4 | | | | | | | | 4 | 4 | | | | |
| LANG. & LIT. - GERMAN | 3 | 1 | | | | | | | 1 | 2 | | 1 | | | | | | 2 | 2 | | | | |
| LANG. & LIT. - MOD. FOREIGN | 2 | | | 1 | | | | 1 | | 2 | | | | | | | | 2 | 2 | | | | |
| LANG. & LIT. - OTH. MODERN | 3 | | | 3 | | | | | | 3 | | | | | | | 2 | 1 | 3 | | | | |
| LANG. & LIT. - RUSSIAN | 3 | 1 | 2 | | | | | | 1 | 2 | 1 | | | | | | | 3 | 3 | | | | |
| LANG. & LIT. - SPAN., PORT. | 3 | 1 | | 2 | | | | | | 2 | | 1 | | | | | | 3 | 3 | | | | |
| LINGUISTICS | 14 | 5 | | 4 | | | | | 1 | 8 | 4 | 1 | 3 | 1 | | | 1 | 7 | 13 | | | | |
| MUSIC | 9 | 3 | | 5 | | | | | 1 | 8 | 1 | | 1 | | | | | 8 | 8 | | | | |
| PHILOSOPHY | 21 | 7 | 2 | 11 | | | | | 1 | 16 | 4 | 1 | 2 | | | | 2 | 16 | 21 | | | | |
| ARTS & HUMANITIES, GENERAL | 2 | 1 | | 1 | | | | | | | 1 | 1 | | | | | | 2 | 1 | | | 1 | |
| ARTS & HUMANITIES, OTHER | 5 | 1 | 1 | 1 | | | 2 | | 2 | 3 | 1 | 1 | | | | | 1 | 4 | 3 | | | 2 | |
| TOTAL ARTS AND HUMANITIES | 228 | 28 | 16 | 113 | 1 | | | | 24 | 159 | 44 | 9 | 5 | 5 | | | 11 | 196 | 215 | 1 | | | 6 |
| **EDUCATION** | | | | | | | | | | | | | | | | | | | | | | | |
| ADMINISTRATION | 15 | 7 | 3 | 5 | | | | | | 15 | | | | | | | 5 | 9 | 14 | | | 1 | |
| EDUCATIONAL PSYCHOLOGY | 11 | 5 | 1 | 4 | | 1 | | | | 9 | 2 | | | 4 | | 1 | 4 | 2 | 9 | 1 | | 1 | |
| ELEMENTARY EDUC., GENERAL | 1 | | | 1 | | | | | | 1 | | | | | | | 1 | | 1 | | | | |
| GUIDANCE & COUNSELING | 2 | 1 | | 1 | | | | | | 2 | | | | | | | 1 | | 2 | | | | |
| MEASUREMENT | 9 | 2 | 2 | 3 | | | 2 | | | 9 | | | | 3 | | | 2 | 2 | 7 | | | 2 | |
| METHODS | 5 | 3 | | 1 | 1 | | | | | 2 | 1 | 2 | | 1 | | | 4 | 3 | 4 | | | 1 | |
| PHILOSOPHY OF EDUCATION | 3 | | | 1 | | | | | 1 | 2 | | | | | | | 1 | 1 | 3 | | | | |
| SECONDARY EDUC., GENERAL | 1 | 1 | | | | | | | | 1 | | | | | | | | 1 | 1 | | | | |
| SPECIAL EDUCATION | 4 | 1 | | 1 | 1 | 1 | | | | 2 | 1 | | 1 | 1 | | | 1 | 3 | 3 | | | 1 | |
| EDUCATION, OTHER | 1 | | 1 | | | | | | | | 1 | | | | | | | 1 | | | | | |
| TOTAL EDUCATION | 52 | 19 | 6 | 17 | 2 | 4 | | | 1 | 44 | 5 | 5 | | 9 | | 1 | 18 | 21 | 44 | 1 | | 6 | |

| PROFESSIONAL FIELDS | | | | | | | | | | | | | | |
|---|---|---|---|---|---|---|---|---|---|---|---|---|---|---|
| ARCHITECTURE | 4 | | | | | | | | | | | 4 | 1 | 3 |
| BUSINESS ADMINISTRATION | 12 | 4 | 1 | 3 | | | | | | | | 10 | 8 | 3 |
| HOME ECONOMICS | 1 | | | 1 | | | | | | | | 1 | 1 | |
| JOURNALISM | 2 | | | 1 | | | | | | | | 2 | 2 | |
| LAW, JURISPRUDENCE | 15 | 4 | | 1 | | | 4 | 1 | 1 | | 1 | 13 | 9 | 1 |
| LIBRARY & ARCHIVAL SCIENCE | 2 | | | | 1 | | 4 | | | | 1 | 1 | 2 | |
| RELIGION & THEOLOGY | 22 | 1 | 3 | 11 | | 1 | 10 | 1 | 5 | 1 | 1 | 15 | 19 | 3 |
| TOTAL PROFESSIONAL FIELDS | 58 | 9 | 4 | 18 | 1 | 1 | 20 | 18 | 1 | 18 | 2 | 3 | 46 | 42 | 3 | 10 |
| MEDICINE | | | | | | | | | | | | | | | |
| ADMINISTRATIVE MEDICINE | 3 | | | | 2 | 1 | 1 | 3 | 1 | 7 | 2 | 1 | 7 | 9 | 2 | 1 |
| ALLERGY | 25 | | | 1 | 16 | 7 | 1 | 17 | 1 | 14 | 1 | 2 | 3 | 2 | 19 | 2 | 17 |
| ANESTHESIOLOGY | 24 | | | | 18 | 4 | 1 | 12 | 2 | 16 | 1 | | 3 | 19 | | 5 |
| CARDIOVASCULAR DISEASE | 218 | 4 | 1 | 1 | 170 | 33 | 7 | 1 | 145 | 5 | 63 | 5 | 147 | 3 | 3 | 59 | 124 | 11 | 78 |
| CHEMOTHERAPY | 39 | 4 | 2 | | 27 | 3 | | 3 | 26 | 2 | 9 | 2 | 29 | | 2 | 5 | 16 | 5 | 2 | 16 |
| DERMATOLOGY | 45 | 1 | | | 34 | 6 | 3 | 1 | 31 | 2 | 9 | 3 | 35 | | 1 | 6 | 29 | 1 | 14 |
| ENDOCRINOLOGY | 192 | 16 | 4 | 3 | 107 | 41 | 15 | 5 | 92 | 13 | 74 | 13 | 139 | 1 | 3 | 41 | 151 | 12 | 26 |
| GASTROENTEROLOGY | 109 | 1 | 1 | | 83 | 21 | 1 | 2 | 66 | 1 | 41 | 2 | 73 | | 3 | 29 | 69 | 6 | 30 |
| GERIATRICS | 2 | | | | 1 | | | | 1 | | | | 1 | | | | | | 2 |
| GYNECOLOGY | 27 | 1 | | | 14 | 12 | 1 | | 11 | 1 | 13 | 2 | 7 | | | 18 | 17 | | 4 |
| HEMATOLOGY | 115 | 1 | | | 78 | 29 | 6 | 1 | 76 | 3 | 30 | 5 | 80 | 2 | 3 | 24 | 64 | 5 | 41 |
| IMMUNOLOGY | 167 | 21 | 5 | 8 | 2 | 89 | 25 | 15 | 2 | 101 | 10 | 47 | 9 | 119 | 2 | 3 | 33 | 125 | 9 | 1 | 79 |
| INFECTIOUS DISEASE | 99 | 4 | | | 82 | 9 | 1 | 3 | 76 | 9 | 12 | 2 | 75 | 1 | 5 | 17 | 65 | 8 | 1 | 74 |
| INTERNAL MEDICINE, GENERAL | 24 | | | | 24 | | | | 13 | 2 | 9 | | 9 | | 1 | 13 | 6 | 2 | 15 |
| METABOLISM | 96 | 10 | 3 | 3 | 61 | 14 | 4 | 1 | 50 | 5 | 35 | 5 | 72 | 1 | 3 | 15 | 45 | 2 | 9 |
| NEPHROLOGY | 82 | | 1 | | 60 | 15 | 6 | 1 | 46 | 2 | 33 | 2 | 52 | 2 | 5 | 20 | 45 | 3 | 26 |
| NEUROLOGY | 75 | 1 | 1 | 1 | 50 | 17 | 5 | | 44 | 2 | 25 | 4 | 46 | 1 | 2 | 24 | 61 | 2 | 12 |
| NUCLEAR MEDICINE | 9 | | | | 3 | 4 | 1 | | 3 | | 5 | | 7 | | | 1 | 8 | | 1 |
| OBSTETRICS | 22 | | | 1 | 10 | 7 | 4 | | 9 | 1 | 10 | 2 | 8 | | | 14 | 16 | 2 | 4 |
| ONCOLOGY | 39 | 4 | 1 | | 21 | 8 | 5 | 1 | 22 | 1 | 14 | 2 | 26 | | 4 | 8 | 28 | 1 | 9 |
| OPHTHALMOLOGY | 57 | 2 | | | 36 | 16 | 2 | 1 | 39 | | 17 | 1 | 34 | | 2 | 20 | 34 | 1 | 20 |
| OTOLARYNGOLOGY | 22 | | | | 12 | 6 | 4 | | 8 | 1 | 13 | | 11 | 1 | 1 | 9 | 15 | | 6 |
| PEDIATRIC ALLERGY | 9 | | | | 6 | 3 | | | 7 | | 1 | | 5 | 1 | | 1 | 3 | 1 | 5 |
| PEDIATRIC CARDIOLOGY | 54 | | | | 35 | 16 | 1 | 2 | 22 | 7 | 22 | 2 | 30 | 2 | 6 | 16 | 37 | 2 | 14 |
| PEDIATRIC HEMATOLOGY | 29 | | | | 20 | 8 | 1 | | 14 | 5 | 9 | | 17 | 1 | 1 | 8 | 20 | 2 | 7 |
| PEDIATRIC NEUROLOGY | 16 | | | | 7 | 7 | 1 | 1 | 4 | 2 | 7 | 3 | 9 | | 1 | 4 | 11 | | 5 |
| PEDIATRICS, GENERAL | 77 | | | | 47 | 24 | 5 | 1 | 27 | 13 | 31 | 6 | 32 | 1 | 12 | 30 | 57 | 2 | 18 |
| PULMONARY DISEASES | 47 | | | | 30 | 15 | 1 | 1 | 27 | 3 | 14 | 3 | 24 | | 1 | 19 | 22 | 3 | 20 |
| PSYCHIATRY | 108 | 4 | 1 | 2 | 1 | 62 | 35 | 2 | 1 | 83 | 10 | 11 | 3 | 70 | 2 | 7 | 26 | 56 | 6 | 43 |

## APPENDIX TABLE B-1—Continued

| POSTDOCTORAL FIELD | TOTAL | Immediate PhD | Intermediate PhD | Long-Term PhD | Senior PhD | Recent MD | Senior MD | PhD and MD | No Doctorate | US Male | US Female | Fgn Male | Fgn Female | Nat'l Sci Fdn | Publ Health Ser | Atom Ener Comm | Dept of Def | Other Govt | Other | Academic | Government | Industry | Other |
|---|---|---|---|---|---|---|---|---|---|---|---|---|---|---|---|---|---|---|---|---|---|---|---|
| **MEDICINE (CONTINUED)** | | | | | | | | | | | | | | | | | | | | | | | |
| RADIOBIOLOGY | 31 | 4 | 2 | | 2 | 7 | 9 | 3 | | 13 | 2 | 14 | 2 | 14 | 6 | | 1 | 10 | 22 | 4 | | | 5 |
| RADIOISOTOPES, CLINICAL | 4 | | | | | 1 | 3 | | | 3 | | 1 | | 4 | | | | | 3 | 1 | | | |
| RADIOLOGICAL PHYSICS | 5 | | 1 | | | 2 | 2 | | | 5 | | | | 2 | 1 | | | 2 | 5 | | | | |
| RADIOLOGY | 46 | | | | | 33 | 11 | 2 | | 38 | 8 | | | 23 | | | 4 | 18 | 28 | 1 | | | 16 |
| RHEUMATOLOGY | 42 | 1 | | | | 26 | 11 | 3 | 1 | 25 | 2 | 12 | 2 | 32 | 1 | | | 9 | 29 | | | | 13 |
| SURGERY, GENERAL | 104 | | | | | 78 | 20 | 4 | 2 | 68 | 2 | 33 | | 28 | 1 | 1 | 16 | 51 | 52 | 3 | | | 45 |
| SURGERY, CARDIOVASCULAR | 52 | | | | | 24 | 21 | 3 | 4 | 23 | | 28 | | 16 | | | 6 | 25 | 31 | 1 | | | 19 |
| SURGERY, COLON & RECTAL | 1 | | | | | 1 | | | | | | | | 1 | | | | | | | | | 1 |
| SURGERY, NEUROLOGICAL | 24 | | | | | 13 | 8 | 3 | | 15 | | 9 | | 14 | 1 | | 1 | 7 | 18 | 2 | | | 4 |
| SURGERY, ORTHOPEDIC | 43 | 1 | | | | 27 | 15 | | | 32 | | 11 | | 16 | | | 10 | 14 | 19 | | | | 24 |
| SURGERY, PLASTIC | 4 | | | | | 3 | 1 | | | 4 | | | | 1 | | | 1 | 2 | 1 | | | | 3 |
| SURGERY, THORACIC | 6 | | | | | 3 | 2 | | 1 | 4 | | 2 | | 3 | | | 1 | 2 | 5 | 1 | | | |
| TROPICAL MEDICINE | 7 | 1 | | | | 2 | 3 | | 1 | 2 | | 5 | | 3 | | | | 4 | 6 | 1 | | | |
| UROLOGY | 25 | 1 | | | | 17 | 6 | 1 | | 19 | | 6 | | 9 | | | 7 | 6 | 10 | | | | 14 |
| TOTAL MEDICINE | 2225 | 81 | 20 | 25 | 10 | 1442 | 498 | 111 | 38 | 1326 | 700 | 80 | 5 | 1356 | 13 | 24 | 118 | 620 | 1421 | 109 | 5 | | 645 |
| **DENTISTRY** | | | | | | | | | | | | | | | | | | | | | | | |
| ENDODONTICS | 2 | | | | | 2 | | | | 2 | | | | | | | | 2 | 1 | | | | 1 |
| GENERAL DENTISTRY | 15 | | 1 | | | 8 | 5 | 1 | | 8 | 1 | 5 | 1 | 10 | | | | 3 | 13 | | | | 2 |
| OPERATIVE DENTISTRY | 2 | | | | | 2 | | | | 2 | | | | | | | | 2 | 2 | | | | |
| ORAL PATHOLOGY | 14 | | | | | 7 | 7 | | | 7 | 7 | | | 7 | | | | 6 | 9 | 2 | | | 3 |
| ORAL SURGERY | 10 | | | | | 8 | 2 | | | 7 | 3 | | | 2 | | 2 | | 1 | 1 | 2 | | | 7 |
| ORTHODONTICS | 24 | | | | | 14 | 6 | 1 | 3 | 16 | 5 | 2 | 1 | 11 | | 1 | 1 | 9 | 14 | 2 | | | 8 |
| PEDODONTICS | 12 | | | | | 11 | 1 | | | 10 | 1 | 1 | | 2 | | | 1 | 6 | 5 | | | | 7 |
| PERIODONTICS | 18 | | | | | 14 | 4 | | | 13 | 5 | | | 14 | | 1 | 2 | 1 | 14 | 1 | | | 3 |
| PROSTHODONTICS | 6 | | | | | 2 | 3 | 1 | | 4 | 2 | | | 2 | | 1 | | 2 | 4 | | | | 2 |
| PUBLIC HEALTH, DENTAL | 5 | | | | | 5 | | | | 5 | | | | 5 | | | | | 5 | | | | |
| TOTAL DENTISTRY | 108 | | 1 | | | 73 | 28 | 3 | 3 | 72 | 30 | 4 | | 53 | | 5 | 4 | 32 | 68 | 7 | | | 33 |

## ALLIED MEDICAL SCIENCES

| Field | | | | | | | | | | | | | | | | | | | | |
|---|---|---|---|---|---|---|---|---|---|---|---|---|---|---|---|---|---|---|---|---|
| AEROSPACE MEDICINE | 3 | | | | | 2 | | | 2 | | 1 | | | 1 | 1 | | 1 | 3 | | |
| OCCUPATIONAL MEDICINE | 5 | | | | | 2 | 1 | | 2 | | 3 | | | 1 | 1 | 1 | 2 | 2 | 1 | 2 |
| UPTOMETRY | 6 | | | | | 4 | 2 | | 4 | | 2 | | | 1 | | 2 | 3 | 2 | | 4 |
| PHARMACY | 8 | 3 | 1 | 1 | 1 | | | | 2 | | 5 | | 1 | 6 | | | 2 | 3 | | 1 |
| PREVENTIVE MEDICINE | 6 | | | | | 4 | 2 | | 5 | 1 | | | | 2 | | | 4 | 1 | 3 | 4 |
| PUBLIC HEALTH | 43 | 3 | | 1 | | 20 | 11 | 8 | 26 | 3 | 11 | 3 | | 24 | | | 17 | 29 | 3 | 10 |
| VETERINARY MEDICINE | 75 | | | | | 50 | 17 | 6 | 49 | 2 | 23 | 1 | | 48 | 1 | 1 | 20 | 52 | 5 | 10 |
| MEDICAL SCIENCES, OTHER | 171 | 9 | 1 | 2 | 2 | 92 | 46 | 14 | 87 | 11 | 60 | 12 | 1 | 94 | | 2 | 53 | 111 | 9 | 48 |
| TOTAL ALLIED MEDICAL SCI. | 317 | 15 | 3 | 3 | 3 | 174 | 80 | 32 | 177 | 17 | 105 | 17 | 1 | 177 | 3 | 5 | 102 | 203 | 19 | 79 |
| TOTAL ALL FIELDS | 10482 | 3936 | 892 | 958 | 791 | 2310 | 897 | 327 | 5125 | 580 | 4309 | 428 | 895 | 4214 | 752 | 632 | 568 | 3062 | 7697 | 477 | 582 | 1480 |
| FIELD UNKNOWN | 258 | 61 | 13 | 21 | 24 | 81 | 40 | 7 | 130 | 20 | 91 | 17 | 11 | 97 | 4 | 9 | 19 | 78 | 150 | 12 | 7 | 70 |
| GRAND TOTAL | 10740 | 3997 | 905 | 979 | 815 | 2391 | 937 | 334 | 5255 | 600 | 4400 | 445 | 906 | 4311 | 756 | 641 | 587 | 3140 | 7847 | 489 | 589 | 1550 |

[a] 40 postdoctorals did not report their sex and are not included in this listing.

[b] 399 postdoctorals did not report their source of support and are not included in this listing.

[c] 265 postdoctorals did not report their anticipated future employer and are not included in this listing.

Source: NRC, Office of Scientific Personnel, Postdoctoral Census Questionnaire.

## B-2 Distribution of Postdoctorals among Universities

For the purpose of presenting data on the distribution of postdoctorals among universities, we have grouped the universities on the basis of reputation. This grouping was determined in part by using Cartter's ranking of departments[1] and in part by the productivity of the institutions with regard to doctorates, especially in the sciences. In particular, following a compilation[2] by H. W. Magoun of Cartter's data, the top ten ranking institutions in each of six major field categories were grouped together and labeled "ten leading universities." The next twenty institutions in each of the major fields were grouped and labeled "twenty other major universities." Below these categories, the further use of Cartter's rankings seemed to us to be much less valid and another means was used to categorize institutions. Using data from the Survey of Earned Doctorates[3] the remaining universities were divided into two groups depending on their production of doctorates. If an institution had produced 200 doctorates in the physical or biological sciences between 1920 and 1961, or if it had produced 400 doctorates in all fields between 1950 and 1961, or if it had been included among either the first ten or the next twenty in any field, it was included in a group entitled "established universities." All other doctoral institutions were grouped together and labeled "developing universities." After this process was completed, the lists were scanned and several institutions that had been created in the 1950's or 1960's and that had rapidly developed into established institutions were shifted into the "established" category from the "developing" one, e.g., University of California at La Jolla. Separate rankings were compiled for the physical sciences (including mathematics), engineering, the basic medical sciences, the plant and animal sciences, the social sciences, and the humanities.

Since Cartter's ratings did not include the medical and other professional fields, a number of institutions were not rated. Also unrated were some new institutions and non-members of the Council of Graduate Schools in the United States.

Table B-2 gives the number of postdoctorals at each institution reporting postdoctorals and the number in the major fields by which institutions were rated. Associated with each institution and field is the rating used in this study (1 — ten leading, 2 — twenty other major, 3 — established, 4 — developing,

---

[1] Allan M. Cartter, *An Assessment of Quality in Graduate Education*, American Council on Education, 1966.
[2] H. W. Magoun, The Cartter Report on Quality in Graduate Education, *Journal of Higher Education*, Vol. XXXVII, No. 9, December 1966.
[3] NAS–NRC, *Doctorate Production in United States Universities, 1920–1962*, Publ. 1142, Washington, D. C., 1963.

U — unrated). Also included in the table are the numbers in clinical medicine and the numbers in all other fields.

Two points should be stressed. The numbers given represent the numbers of those postdoctorals who responded to our Census questionnaire in the spring of 1967. There probably were more postdoctorals at these institutions and, in some cases, substantially more. The other point is that the ratings by reputation are somewhat arbitrary and were determined by dated information. Disagreements with how a particular institution was rated are not only possible but even valid. The information is provided here to allow institutions to interpret where their university is represented in the tables and in the text.

APPENDIX TABLE B-2 Postdoctorals at US Academic Host Institutions by Field and Citizenship[a]

| US ACADEMIC HOST INSTITUTIONS | PHYSICAL SCIENCES Rating | PHYSICAL SCIENCES US Postdocs | PHYSICAL SCIENCES Fgn Postdocs | BIO-SCIENCES Rating | BIO-SCIENCES US Postdocs | BIO-SCIENCES Fgn Postdocs | BASIC MED SCI Rating | BASIC MED SCI US Postdocs | BASIC MED SCI Fgn Postdocs | ENGINEERING Rating | ENGINEERING US Postdocs | ENGINEERING Fgn Postdocs | SOCIAL SCIENCES Rating | SOCIAL SCIENCES US Postdocs | SOCIAL SCIENCES Fgn Postdocs | ARTS & HUMANITIES US Postdocs | ARTS & HUMANITIES Fgn Postdocs | MED SCI US Postdocs | MED SCI Fgn Postdocs | OTHER US Postdocs | OTHER Fgn Postdocs | GRAND TOTAL |
|---|---|---|---|---|---|---|---|---|---|---|---|---|---|---|---|---|---|---|---|---|---|---|
| AKRON, UNIVERSITY OF | 4 | 1 | | 4 | | | | | | 4 | | | 4 | | | | | | | 1 | | 1 |
| ALABAMA, UNIVERSITY OF | 4 | | | 4 | 4 | 5 | | | | 4 | | | 4 | | | 10 | 4 | | | 10 | | 24 |
| ALBANY, SUNY AT | 4 | 5 | 1 | 4 | | | | | | 4 | | | 4 | | | | | | | 5 | | 6 |
| ANTIOCH COLLEGE OHIO | U | | U | U | | U | | | | U | | U | 4 | | U | | | | | 1 | 1 | 1 |
| ARIZONA STATE UNIVERSITY | 4 | 7 | | 4 | 2 | | | | | 4 | | | 4 | | | | | | | 1 | | 8 |
| ARIZONA, UNIVERSITY OF | 4 | 10 | 24 | 4 | 2 | 2 | | | | 4 | | | 4 | | 1 | 1 | | | | 13 | 27 | 40 |
| ARKANSAS, UNIVERSITY OF | 4 | 2 | 1 | 4 | 1 | 1 | | | | 4 | | | 4 | | | 4 | | | | 8 | 3 | 11 |
| AUBURN UNIVERSITY ALA | 4 | | | 4 | | 1 | | | | 4 | | | 4 | | | 1 | | | | 1 | | 2 |
| BABSON INST BUS ADM MASS | U | | | U | | | | | | U | | | U | | | | | | | 1 | 1 | 1 |
| BAYLOR UNIVERSITY TEX | 4 | 1 | 1 | 4 | 6 | 10 | | | | 4 | | | 4 | | | 34 | 23 | | | 43 | 37 | 80 |
| BOSTON COLLEGE | 4 | | | 4 | | | | | | 4 | | | 4 | | | | | | | 1 | | 1 |
| BOSTON UNIVERSITY | 3 | 3 | 6 | 3 | 6 | 2 | 3 | | | 3 | 1 | | 3 | | | 6 | 3 | | | 18 | 12 | 30 |
| BRANDEIS UNIVERSITY MASS | 2 | 12 | 14 | 2 | 13 | 7 | | | | 3 | | | 2 | | | | | | | 29 | 22 | 51 |
| BROOKLYN COLLEGE | U | | | U | | | | | | U | | U | U | | U | | | | | 1 | | 1 |
| BROWN UNIVERSITY R I | 2 | 14 | 14 | 3 | | 1 | 2 | 2 | 2 | 2 | 1 | 1 | 2 | | | | 2 | | | 18 | 21 | 39 |
| BRYN MAWR COLLEGE PA | 4 | 1 | | 4 | | | 4 | | | 4 | | | 4 | | | | | | | 2 | | 2 |
| BUFFALO, SUNY AT | 4 | 15 | 4 | 3 | 4 | 10 | 4 | | 1 | 2 | | | 3 | | | 11 | 4 | | | 23 | 33 | 56 |
| CALIF INST OF TECHNOLOGY | 1 | 61 | 78 | 5 | 15 | 21 | 1 | 3 | 15 | 4 | 1 | 1 | 4 | | | | 1 | | | 90 | 133 | 223 |
| CALIF STATE COLL AT L A | 4 | 2 | | 4 | | | 4 | | | 4 | | | 4 | | | | | | | 2 | | 2 |
| CALIF, U OF, BERKELEY | 1 | 56 | 51 | 1 | 20 | 15 | 1 | 27 | 28 | 1 | 7 | 19 | 1 | 12 | 11 | 7 | 10 | 6 | | 136 | 142 | 278 |
| CALIF, U OF, DAVIS | 3 | 3 | 4 | 2 | 4 | 2 | 3 | 8 | 19 | 3 | | | 3 | | | 4 | 8 | 3 | | 19 | 38 | 57 |
| CALIF, U OF, IRVINE | U | 7 | 10 | U | 1 | | U | 2 | | U | | | U | | | | | | | 10 | 10 | 20 |
| CALIF, U OF, LA JOLLA | 3 | 22 | 29 | 3 | 5 | 3 | 3 | 11 | 13 | 3 | | | 3 | 1 | | 1 | | | | 44 | 47 | 91 |
| CALIF, U OF, LOS ANGELES | 2 | 21 | 41 | 1 | 7 | 6 | 2 | 25 | 36 | 3 | 2 | | 2 | 2 | 2 | 14 | 26 | | 2 | 80 | 115 | 195 |
| CALIF, U OF, RIVERSIDE | 3 | 8 | 16 | 3 | 3 | 3 | 3 | 1 | 6 | 3 | | | 3 | | | | | 1 | 1 | 13 | 26 | 39 |
| CALIF, U OF, SAN FRAN | U | 3 | 2 | U | 2 | 1 | U | 7 | 10 | U | 2 | 2 | 3 | | | 27 | 18 | | | 45 | 32 | 77 |
| CALIF, U OF, SANTA BARB | 4 | | 4 | 2 | 4 | 1 | 4 | 1 | 1 | 4 | | | 4 | | | | | | | 5 | 12 | 17 |

|  | | | | | | | | | | | | | | | | |
|---|---|---|---|---|---|---|---|---|---|---|---|---|---|---|---|---|
| CALIF, U OF, SANTA CRUZ | U | 2 | 5 | U | | | U | 1 | | U | | | U | | 3 | 7 | 10 |
| CANISIUS COLLEGE N Y | 4 | | | 4 | | 2 | 4 | | 1 | 4 | | | 4 | 6 | 6 | 10 | 16 |
| CARNEGIE INST OF TECH PA | 3 | 4 | 5 | 3 | | | 3 | | | 2 | | | 3 | | 5 | 10 | 15 |
| CASE INST OF TECH OHIO | 3 | 10 | 11 | 3 | 2 | 1 | 3 | | | 3 | | | 3 | | 14 | 15 | 29 |
| CATH UNIV OF AMERICA D C | 3 | 3 | 4 | 3 | | | 3 | 1 | | 3 | | | 3 | | 3 | 6 | 9 |
| CHICAGO, UNIVERSITY OF | 3 | 57 | 83 | 2 | 11 | 14 | 4 | 2 | | 3 | 1 | 1 | 3 | 4 | 105 | 130 | 235 |
| CHRIST SAV SEM JOHNSTOWN | U | | | U | | | U | | | U | | | U | | | 1 | 1 |
| CINCINNATI, UNIV OF | 3 | 2 | 3 | 3 | 15 | 11 | 3 | 2 | | 3 | | | 3 | 8 | 12 | 14 | 26 |
| CLAREMONT GR & U CEN CAL | 4 | | | 4 | 2 | | 3 | | 1 | 4 | | 1 | 3 | 7 | 2 | | 2 |
| CLARK UNIVERSITY MASS | 4 | | | 2 | | 2 | 4 | | | 2 | 1 | | 2 | | 3 | 2 | 5 |
| CLARKSON COL OF TECH N Y | 4 | 3 | 2 | 4 | | | 4 | | 2 | 4 | | | 4 | | 3 | 8 | 11 |
| CLEMSON UNIVERSITY S C | 4 | | 1 | 4 | | | 4 | | | 4 | | | 4 | | | 1 | 1 |
| COLORADO STATE UNIV | 4 | | | 4 | 8 | 4 | 4 | 1 | 1 | 3 | | | 4 | 12 | 5 | 21 | 10 | 31 |
| COLORADO, UNIVERSITY OF | 3 | 17 | 6 | 3 | 5 | 2 | 3 | 2 | 1 | 3 | | | 3 | | 26 | 11 | 37 |
| COLUMBIA COLLEGE S C | U | | | U | | | U | | | U | | | U | | 1 | | 1 |
| COLUMBIA UNIVERSITY N Y | 1 | 22 | 29 | 2 | 14 | 7 | 2 | 5 | | 1 | 2 | | 1 | 7 | 3 | 58 | 47 | 105 |
| CONNECTICUT, UNIV OF | 4 | | 7 | 4 | 8 | 1 | 4 | | | 4 | | | 4 | 3 | 1 | 13 | 12 | 25 |
| CORNELL UNIVERSITY N Y | 2 | 33 | 47 | 2 | 22 | 17 | 2 | 1 | 2 | 2 | 1 | 2 | 2 | 41 | 11 | 3 | 116 | 94 | 210 |
| DARTMOUTH COLLEGE N H | 4 | 8 | 3 | 4 | 4 | 1 | 4 | | | 1 | | | 4 | 1 | 4 | 15 | 6 | 21 |
| DELAWARE, UNIVERSITY OF | 4 | | 8 | 4 | | | 4 | | | 4 | | | 4 | | | 8 | 8 |
| DENVER, UNIVERSITY OF | 4 | | 1 | 4 | 2 | | 4 | | 2 | 4 | | | 4 | | | 3 | 3 |
| DETROIT, UNIVERSITY OF | 4 | | 1 | 4 | | | 4 | | | 4 | | | 4 | | | 1 | 1 |
| DOUGLASS COLLEGE N J | U | | | U | 1 | | U | | | U | | | U | | 1 | | 1 |
| DOWNSTATE MED CENTER N Y | 4 | | | 4 | 5 | 7 | 4 | | 1 | 4 | 1 | | 4 | 12 | 5 | 20 | 14 | 34 |
| DREXEL INST OF TECH PA | 4 | | 1 | 4 | | 1 | 4 | | | 4 | | 2 | 4 | 3 | 2 | 7 | 3 | 10 |
| DUKE UNIVERSITY N C | 2 | 14 | 16 | 1 | 21 | 20 | 3 | 3 | 1 | 2 | 6 | 1 | 2 | 64 | 9 | 121 | 53 | 174 |
| DUQUESNE UNIVERSITY PA | 4 | | 1 | 4 | | | 4 | | | 4 | | | 4 | | | | 2 | 2 |
| EMORY UNIVERSITY GA | 4 | 3 | 1 | 4 | 5 | 1 | 4 | | | 4 | | 9 | 4 | 11 | 2 | 20 | 4 | 24 |
| FLORIDA STATE UNIVERSITY | 4 | 9 | 22 | 4 | 4 | 1 | 3 | 3 | | 3 | 1 | | 3 | | 1 | 16 | 26 | 42 |
| FLORIDA, UNIVERSITY OF | 3 | 26 | 21 | 3 | 4 | 3 | 3 | | 2 | 3 | 2 | | 3 | 8 | 3 | 1 | 42 | 34 | 76 |
| FORDHAM UNIVERSITY N Y | 3 | | 3 | 3 | 4 | 1 | 3 | 2 | | 3 | 1 | | 3 | | | 1 | 4 | 5 |
| GEO PEABODY C TCHRS TENN | 4 | | | 4 | | | 4 | | | 4 | | 1 | 4 | | | 1 | | 1 |
| GEO WASHINGTON UNIV D C | 4 | | | 4 | 2 | 2 | 4 | | | 4 | | | 4 | | | 2 | 3 | 5 |
| GEORGIA INST OF TECHNOL | 4 | | 5 | 4 | | | 4 | | | 4 | | | 4 | | 1 | 4 | 6 | 10 |
| GEORGIA, UNIVERSITY OF | 4 | 2 | 8 | 4 | 5 | 3 | 4 | 2 | | 4 | | | 4 | 4 | 2 | 16 | 13 | 29 |
| HAHNEMANN MED C & HOS PA | U | | | U | 1 | 1 | U | | | U | | | U | 4 | 6 | 5 | 7 | 12 |

APPENDIX TABLE B-2—Continued

| US ACADEMIC HOST INSTITUTIONS | PHYSICAL SCIENCES Rating | PHYSICAL SCIENCES US Postdocs | PHYSICAL SCIENCES Fgn Postdocs | BIO-SCIENCES Rating | BIO-SCIENCES US Postdocs | BIO-SCIENCES Fgn Postdocs | BASIC MED SCI Rating | BASIC MED SCI US Postdocs | BASIC MED SCI Fgn Postdocs | ENGINEERING Rating | ENGINEERING US Postdocs | ENGINEERING Fgn Postdocs | SOCIAL SCIENCES Rating | SOCIAL SCIENCES US Postdocs | SOCIAL SCIENCES Fgn Postdocs | ARTS & HUMANITIES Rating | ARTS & HUMANITIES US Postdocs | ARTS & HUMANITIES Fgn Postdocs | MED SCI US Postdocs | MED SCI Fgn Postdocs | OTHER US Postdocs | OTHER Fgn Postdocs | TOTAL US Postdocs | GRAND TOTAL Fgn Postdocs |
|---|---|---|---|---|---|---|---|---|---|---|---|---|---|---|---|---|---|---|---|---|---|---|---|---|
| HARVARD UNIVERSITY MASS | 1 | 58 | 71 | 1 | 21 | 20 | 1 | 75 | 57 | 1 | 3 | 5 | 1 | 30 | 14 | 1 | 16 | 2 | 120 | 101 | 13 | 7 | 344 | 280 | 624 |
| HAWAII, UNIVERSITY OF | 4 | 1 | 3 | 4 | 2 | 4 | 4 | 1 | 4 | 4 | 4 | | 4 | | | 4 | | | 1 | 2 | | 1 | 6 | 14 | 20 |
| HOUSTON, UNIVERSITY OF | 4 | 3 | 3 | 4 | 4 | 1 | 4 | | | 4 | | | 4 | | | 4 | | | | | | | 4 | 4 | 8 |
| IDAHO, UNIVERSITY OF | 4 | 1 | 1 | 4 | 1 | | 4 | | | 4 | | | 4 | | | 4 | | | | | 1 | | 1 | 1 | 2 |
| ILLINOIS INST OF TECHNOL | 3 | 3 | 2 | 3 | | | | | | 3 | | | | | | 4 | | | | | | | 3 | 2 | 5 |
| ILLINOIS, UNIVERSITY OF | 1 | 37 | 58 | 1 | 10 | 1 | 1 | 29 | 9 | 3 | | | 3 | | | 1 | 35 | 1 | 11 | 4 | 3 | | 112 | 123 | 235 |
| INDIANA UNIVERSITY | 2 | 12 | 14 | 2 | 1 | 4 | 4 | 10 | | 2 | | | 2 | 5 | 1 | 2 | 16 | | 8 | | | | 54 | 39 | 93 |
| IOWA ST U OF SCI & TECH | 3 | 30 | 31 | 2 | 2 | 5 | 2 | 7 | 4 | 3 | 2 | | 3 | 4 | 1 | 4 | 4 | | 1 | 2 | 4 | | 50 | 52 | 102 |
| IOWA, UNIVERSITY OF | 3 | 6 | 4 | 3 | | | 3 | 5 | | 3 | | | 3 | 1 | | 3 | 16 | | 8 | 1 | | | 30 | 17 | 47 |
| JEFFERSON MED C OF PHILA | 4 | | | 4 | 1 | | 4 | 1 | | 4 | | | 4 | | | 4 | 3 | | | | 7 | | | 7 | 1 | 8 |
| JOHN CARROLL UNIV OHIO | 4 | 1 | | 4 | | | 4 | | | 4 | | | 4 | | | 4 | | | | | | | | 1 | 1 |
| JOHNS HOPKINS UNIV MD | 2 | 5 | 16 | 2 | 10 | 15 | 2 | 34 | 37 | 2 | 1 | | 2 | | | 2 | 72 | 72 | | | | | 134 | 150 | 284 |
| KANSAS, UNIVERSITY OF | 3 | 7 | 12 | 2 | 7 | 3 | 3 | 8 | 10 | 3 | | | 3 | | | 4 | 8 | | 6 | 2 | | | 33 | 33 | 66 |
| KANS CTY C OSTEOP & SURG | U | | | U | | | U | 1 | | U | | | U | | | U | | | | | 1 | | 1 | | 1 |
| KANS ST U OF AG & AP SCI | U | 1 | | U | 1 | 2 | U | | 1 | U | 2 | | U | | | U | 1 | | | 1 | | | 4 | 2 | 6 |
| KENTUCKY, UNIVERSITY OF | 4 | 3 | 4 | 4 | | 2 | 4 | | 5 | 4 | 3 | | 4 | | | 4 | 5 | | 7 | 1 | 1 | | 11 | 21 | 32 |
| LAWRENCE UNIVERSITY WISC | U | 2 | | U | | | U | | | U | | | U | | | U | | | | 1 | | | 1 | 2 | 3 |
| LEHIGH UNIVERSITY PA | 4 | 1 | 5 | 4 | | | 4 | | | 4 | | 6 | 4 | | | 4 | | | | | 1 | | 1 | 11 | 12 |
| LA ST UNIV & AG & MECH C | 4 | 8 | 23 | 3 | 3 | 1 | 3 | 1 | | 3 | | | 3 | 2 | | 4 | 2 | | 2 | 1 | 1 | | 11 | 27 | 38 |
| LOUISVILLE, UNIV OF | 4 | 1 | | 4 | | | 4 | | 3 | 4 | | | 4 | | | 4 | 5 | | 5 | | | | 13 | 8 | 21 |
| LOYOLA UNIVERSITY LA | U | | | U | | | U | | | U | 4 | | U | | | U | 1 | | | | | | 1 | | 1 |
| LUTHERAN SCH OF THEO ILL | U | | | U | | | U | | | U | | | U | | | U | | | 1 | | | | 1 | | 1 |
| MAINE, UNIVERSITY OF | 4 | | 1 | 4 | | | 4 | | | 4 | | | 4 | | | 4 | | | | | | | | 1 | 1 |
| MARQUETTE UNIV WISC | 4 | 3 | | 4 | 1 | | 4 | 2 | 5 | 4 | | | 4 | | | 4 | 11 | | 1 | | | | 14 | 6 | 20 |
| MARYLAND, UNIVERSITY OF | 2 | 18 | 16 | 3 | 3 | 1 | 3 | 1 | 2 | 3 | 3 | | 3 | 1 | | 4 | 1 | | | | 1 | | 20 | 18 | 38 |
| MASS INST OF TECHNOLOGY | 1 | 57 | 62 | 3 | 20 | 15 | 1 | 21 | 25 | 1 | 26 | 18 | 3 | 9 | 4 | 3 | 1 | 7 | | 3 | 1 | | 142 | 137 | 279 |
| MASSACHUSETTS, UNIV OF | 4 | 9 | 4 | 4 | 1 | 1 | 4 | 3 | 3 | 4 | | 1 | 4 | 1 | | 4 | | | | 3 | 1 | | 15 | 11 | 26 |

|  | | | | | | | | | | | | | | | | |
|---|---|---|---|---|---|---|---|---|---|---|---|---|---|---|---|---|
| MEDICAL COLLEGE OF GA | U | | | | U | | U | U | | | | | | 4 | 3 | 7 |
| MEDICAL C OF SO CAROLINA | U | | | | U | 2 | | U | | | 1 | | | 3 | | 3 |
| MEDICAL COLL OF VIRGINIA | 4 | | | | 4 | 6 | 1 | 4 | | | | | 8 | 14 | 3 | 17 |
| MIAMI, UNIVERSITY OF | 4 | 1 | 1 | | 4 | 5 | 4 | 4 | | | | | 1 | 12 | 6 | 18 |
| MICH ST U OF AG & AP SCI | 3 | 7 | 19 | 3 | 3 | 15 | 16 | 3 | | | 1 | | 9 | 33 | 68 | 101 |
| MICHIGAN, UNIVERSITY OF | 2 | 14 | 25 | 8 | 3 | 13 | 20 | 1 | 1 | | 4 | 7 | 12 | 56 | 73 | 129 |
| MINNESOTA, UNIVERSITY OF | 2 | 19 | 28 | 6 | 2 | 34 | 26 | 4 | 5 | 11 | 3 | 4 | 16 | 143 | 89 | 232 |
| MISSISSIPPI STATE UNIV | 4 | | | 9 | 4 | | | 2 | | 1 | 1 | | | | 2 | 2 |
| MISSISSIPPI, UNIV OF | 4 | | 6 | | 4 | 2 | 5 | 4 | | | 2 | | 2 | 4 | 16 | 20 |
| MISSOURI, U OF, COLUMBIA | 3 | 1 | 1 | | 3 | | | 3 | | | 1 | 1 | 1 | 3 | 2 | 5 |
| MISSOURI, U OF, KANS CTY | U | | 1 | | U | | | U | | | | | 5 | 5 | 1 | 6 |
| MONTANA, UNIVERSITY OF | 4 | | | 1 | 4 | | | 4 | | | | | | | 1 | 1 |
| NAZARETH COLLEGE N Y | U | | | | U | | 1 | U | | | | | | 1 | | 1 |
| NEBRASKA, UNIVERSITY OF | 3 | 1 | 7 | | 3 | 5 | 4 | 3 | | 2 | | 1 | 9 | 16 | 15 | 31 |
| NEW HAMPSHIRE, UNIV OF | 4 | 1 | 3 | | 4 | 1 | | 4 | | 2 | | | | 2 | 3 | 5 |
| N J COLL OF MED & DENT | U | | | | U | 1 | | U | 1 | 3 | | | 6 | 7 | 1 | 8 |
| N MEX INST OF MIN & TECH | 4 | | 1 | | 4 | | | 4 | | | 1 | | | 1 | | 1 |
| NEW MEXICO STATE UNIV | 4 | 2 | 3 | | 4 | | | 4 | | | | 4 | | 3 | 3 | 6 |
| NEW MEXICO, UNIV OF | 4 | 1 | 3 | | 4 | | 1 | 4 | | | | | 2 | 3 | 5 | 8 |
| NEW YORK MEDICAL COLLEGE | U | | | 1 | U | | | U | | | | | | | 1 | 1 |
| NEW YORK UNIVERSITY | 3 | 23 | 27 | 1 | 2 | 8 | 14 | 2 | 5 | 2 | 1 | | 9 | 52 | 53 | 105 |
| N C STATE UNIV RALEIGH | 4 | | 1 | 4 | 4 | | 2 | 4 | 1 | 1 | 1 | | 9 | 4 | 13 | 17 |
| NORTH CAROLINA, UNIV OF | 3 | 13 | 26 | 2 | 3 | 10 | 11 | 3 | 1 | 3 | | 1 | 30 | 72 | 57 | 129 |
| NORTH DAKOTA STATE UNIV | 4 | | 3 | 8 | 4 | | | 4 | | | | | | | 3 | 3 |
| NORTHWESTERN UNIV ILL | 2 | 16 | 26 | 1 | 3 | 7 | 21 | 2 | | | 2 | | 21 | 51 | 74 | 125 |
| NOTRE DAME, UNIV OF, IND | 3 | 8 | 18 | 4 | 3 | 21 | 1 | 3 | | | | 11 | | 9 | 22 | 31 |
| OHIO STATE UNIVERSITY | 2 | 14 | 18 | 1 | 2 | 4 | 2 | 2 | 1 | 6 | 2 | 1 | 27 | 74 | 35 | 109 |
| OKLA ST U OF AG & AP SCI | 4 | | 2 | 3 | 4 | 8 | 7 | 3 | | 1 | | | 7 | 10 | 11 | 21 |
| OKLAHOMA, UNIVERSITY OF | 3 | | | | 3 | 1 | 2 | 3 | | 1 | | 1 | | 2 | 4 | 6 |
| OREGON STATE UNIV OREG | 3 | 2 | 7 | 6 | 3 | 6 | 2 | 3 | | | | 2 | | 11 | 20 | 31 |
| OREGON, UNIVERSITY OF | 3 | | 2 | 1 | 3 | 1 | 7 | 3 | | 1 | | 4 | | 10 | 3 | 13 |
| OST MED & SURG, COL,IOWA | U | | | 3 | U | | | U | | | | | | | 1 | 1 |
| PACIFIC, U OF THE, CAL | 4 | | | | 4 | | 1 | 4 | | | | | 1 | 1 | | 1 |
| PENNSYLVANIA STATE UNIV | 2 | 11 | 30 | 2 | 4 | 1 | 1 | 2 | 3 | 1 | 1 | 1 | 57 | 19 | 42 | 61 |
| PENNSYLVANIA, UNIV OF | 2 | 12 | 16 | 2 | 2 | 29 | 25 | 2 | 2 | 2 | 2 | 1 | 25 | 118 | 85 | 203 |
| PITTSBURGH, UNIV OF | 3 | 19 | 22 | 8 | 3 | 8 | 24 | 3 | 1 | 4 | 2 | 2 | 7 | 45 | 63 | 108 |

## APPENDIX TABLE B-2—Continued

| US ACADEMIC HOST INSTITUTIONS | PHYSICAL SCIENCES Rating | PHYSICAL SCIENCES Fgn Postdocs | PHYSICAL SCIENCES US Postdocs | BIO-SCIENCES Rating | BIO-SCIENCES Fgn Postdocs | BIO-SCIENCES US Postdocs | BASIC MED SCI Rating | BASIC MED SCI Fgn Postdocs | BASIC MED SCI US Postdocs | ENGI-NEERING Rating | ENGI-NEERING Fgn Postdocs | ENGI-NEERING US Postdocs | SOCIAL SCIENCES Rating | SOCIAL SCIENCES Fgn Postdocs | SOCIAL SCIENCES US Postdocs | ARTS & HUMANITIES Fgn Postdocs | ARTS & HUMANITIES US Postdocs | MED SCI Fgn Postdocs | MED SCI US Postdocs | OTHER Fgn Postdocs | OTHER US Postdocs | TOTAL Fgn Postdocs | GRAND TOTAL |
|---|---|---|---|---|---|---|---|---|---|---|---|---|---|---|---|---|---|---|---|---|---|---|---|
| POLYTECH INST OF BROOKLN | 4 | 1 | 11 | 4 | | | 2 | | 3 | 4 | | | 4 | | | | | | | 1 | 15 | 1 | 16 |
| POMONA COLLEGE CAL | U | 1 | 2 | U | | | U | | | U | | | U | | | | | | | | 2 | 1 | 3 |
| PRINCETON UNIVERSITY | 1 | 28 | 38 | 2 | 1 | 4 | 2 | | 2 | 1 | 11 | 8 | 1 | 6 | 2 | 2 | | | | 57 | 62 | 119 | |
| PUERTO RICO, UNIV OF | U | | | U | | 1 | U | | | U | | | U | | | | | | | 11 | 1 | | 12 |
| PURDUE UNIVERSITY | 2 | 14 | 21 | 2 | 7 | 11 | 1 | | | 2 | | | 4 | | | 9 | 1 | | 1 | 6 | 28 | 55 | 83 |
| QUEENS COLLEGE N Y | U | | | U | | 1 | U | | 16 | U | | | U | | | | | | | | 1 | | 1 |
| RADCLIFFE COLLEGE MASS | U | 1 | | U | | | U | | | U | | | U | 5 | | 1 | | | | 10 | 1 | | 11 |
| RENSSELAER POLY INST N Y | 4 | 2 | 7 | 4 | | | 2 | 2 | 1 | 4 | 1 | | 4 | | | | | | | 5 | 8 | | 13 |
| RHODE ISLAND, UNIV OF | 4 | | 1 | 4 | | | 4 | | | 4 | | | 4 | | | | | | | 1 | 1 | | 2 |
| RICE UNIVERSITY TEX | 2 | 14 | 18 | 3 | 1 | | 4 | | 1 | 3 | 2 | 1 | 3 | 1 | | | | | | 24 | 22 | | 46 |
| ROCHESTER, UNIVERSITY OF | 2 | 8 | 21 | 3 | 5 | 4 | 2 | 10 | 7 | 3 | 8 | 1 | 2 | 2 | | 21 | 17 | | | 53 | 51 | | 104 |
| ROCKEFELLER UNIV N Y | 4 | 2 | 2 | 2 | 3 | 2 | 2 | 12 | 7 | 4 | 4 | | 4 | | | 2 | 2 | | | 23 | 11 | | 34 |
| RUTGERS, THE STATE U,N J | 3 | 6 | 19 | 2 | 1 | 3 | 3 | 2 | 12 | 3 | | | 3 | | | | | | | 10 | 34 | | 44 |
| ST JOHNS UNIVERSITY N Y | 4 | | 1 | 4 | | | 4 | 2 | | 3 | | | 4 | | | | | | | 2 | 1 | | 3 |
| ST LOUIS UNIVERSITY | 3 | 3 | 4 | 3 | | | 3 | | 8 | 3 | | | 3 | 3 | | 1 | 3 | | | 4 | 15 | | 19 |
| SAN FRANCISCO, UNIV OF | 4 | | | 4 | | | 4 | | | 4 | | | 4 | 1 | | | 1 | | | | 1 | | 1 |
| SOUTH CAROLINA, UNIV OF | 4 | 3 | 2 | 4 | | | 4 | | | 4 | | | 4 | | | | | | | 3 | 2 | | 5 |
| SOUTHERN CALIF, UNIV OF | 3 | 8 | 21 | 3 | 3 | | 3 | 2 | | 3 | | | 3 | | | 6 | 7 | | | 20 | 31 | | 51 |
| STANFORD UNIVERSITY CAL | 1 | 48 | 52 | 1 | 17 | 5 | 1 | 3 | 18 | 1 | 13 | 3 | 3 | 1 | 1 | 37 | 16 | 4 | 2 | 150 | 109 | | 259 |
| STEVENS INST OF TECH N J | 4 | 1 | 4 | 4 | | | 4 | | | 3 | 1 | | 4 | | | | | | | 1 | 4 | | 5 |
| STONY BROOK, SUNY AT | 4 | 4 | 12 | 3 | 1 | 1 | 4 | 1 | | 4 | 1 | | 4 | | | | | | | 9 | 15 | | 24 |
| SYRACUSE UNIVERSITY | 3 | 7 | 7 | 3 | 1 | 4 | 3 | | 5 | 3 | 1 | | 3 | | | | | | | 9 | 17 | | 26 |
| TEMPLE UNIVERSITY PA | 4 | | 4 | 4 | | 8 | 4 | | 4 | 4 | | | 4 | | | 12 | 4 | 1 | | 21 | 12 | | 33 |
| TENNESSEE, UNIVERSITY OF | 3 | 1 | 2 | 3 | 3 | 1 | 3 | | 2 | 3 | | | 3 | | | | 2 | | | 2 | 6 | | 8 |
| TEXAS A & M UNIVERSITY | 4 | 2 | 5 | 4 | 7 | 5 | 4 | | | 3 | | | 4 | | | 1 | | 1 | | 11 | 10 | | 21 |
| TEXAS CHRISTIAN UNIV | 4 | 1 | | 4 | | | 4 | | | 4 | 1 | | 4 | | | | | | | 2 | | | 2 |
| TEXAS TECHNOLOGICAL COLL | 4 | 1 | 2 | 4 | | | 4 | | | 4 | | | 4 | | | | | | | 1 | 2 | | 3 |

|  | | | | | | | | | | | | | | |
|---|---|---|---|---|---|---|---|---|---|---|---|---|---|---|
| TEXAS, UNIVERSITY OF | 2 | 21 | 34 | 2 | 14 | 4 | 4 | 11 | 18 | 2 | 2 | 2 | | 2 | 1 | 1 | 65 | 19 | | 121 | 78 | 199 |
| TUFTS UNIVERSITY MASS | 4 | 3 | 2 | 4 | 2 | | 4 | 2 | | 4 | 4 | 4 | | | | 7 | 6 | | 15 | 8 | 23 |
| TULANE UNIV OF LOUISIANA | 3 | | 2 | 3 | 1 | | 3 | 3 | 1 | 3 | 3 | 3 | | | | 20 | 4 | | 24 | 7 | 31 |
| UNION COLL & UNIV N Y | U | | | U | | | U | | 4 | U | U | U | | | | 8 | 2 | | 8 | 7 | 15 |
| UTAH ST U OF AG & AP SCI | 4 | | 2 | 4 | | 2 | 4 | | 2 | 4 | 4 | 4 | | | | | | | 7 | | 7 |
| UTAH, UNIVERSITY OF | 4 | 8 | 11 | 3 | 1 | | 2 | 11 | 7 | 3 | 3 | 3 | | 3 | | 3 | 6 | | 25 | 24 | 49 |
| VANDERBILT UNIV TENN | 3 | 5 | 8 | 3 | | 1 | 3 | 9 | 11 | 3 | 3 | 1 | 1 | 3 | | 1 | 2 | | 16 | 23 | 39 |
| VERMONT, U OF, & ST AG C | 4 | 1 | 1 | 4 | | | 4 | 1 | 2 | 4 | 4 | 1 | | 1 | | 5 | 1 | | 7 | 4 | 11 |
| VIRGINIA POLYTECH INST | 4 | 1 | 3 | 4 | | | 4 | | | 4 | | | | 1 | | 1 | | 1 | 1 | 4 | 5 |
| VIRGINIA, UNIVERSITY OF | 3 | 6 | 11 | 3 | 2 | 3 | 3 | 6 | 2 | 3 | 3 | | | 3 | 3 | 11 | 1 | | 26 | 21 | 47 |
| WASHINGTON STATE UNIV | 4 | 2 | 3 | 4 | | 4 | 4 | | 3 | 4 | 1 | | | 1 | | | 5 | | 2 | 15 | 17 |
| WASHINGTON UNIVERSITY MO | 3 | | | 4 | 2 | | 2 | 15 | 16 | 4 | 2 | | | 3 | | 25 | 21 | | 42 | 37 | 79 |
| WASHINGTON, U OF, WASH | 2 | 8 | 15 | 2 | 12 | 2 | 2 | 25 | 11 | 2 | 2 | 1 | | 2 | | 45 | 31 | | 94 | 62 | 156 |
| WAYNE STATE UNIV MICH | 4 | | | 4 | | | 4 | 1 | 3 | 4 | 4 | | 1 | 4 | | 3 | 5 | | 4 | 9 | 13 |
| WESLEYAN UNIV CONN | 4 | 3 | | 4 | | 1 | 4 | 1 | | 4 | 4 | | | 4 | | | | | 4 | 1 | 5 |
| WEST VIRGINIA UNIVERSITY | 4 | | 2 | 4 | | 1 | 4 | | 1 | 4 | 4 | 1 | | 4 | 1 | 1 | | | 1 | 6 | 7 |
| WESTERN RESERVE U OHIO | 3 | 9 | 11 | 3 | 5 | 5 | 2 | 21 | 24 | 3 | 3 | 1 | | 3 | | 17 | 19 | 1 | 56 | 60 | 116 |
| WILLIAM & MARY, C OF, VA | 4 | 1 | | 4 | | | 4 | | | 4 | 4 | | | 4 | | | | | 1 | | 1 |
| WISCONSIN, UNIVERSITY OF | 2 | 35 | 55 | 1 | 15 | 24 | 1 | 46 | 65 | 1 | 1 | 7 | 1 | 1 | 3 | 16 | 8 | 1 | 128 | 157 | 285 |
| WYOMING, UNIVERSITY OF | 4 | 1 | 1 | 4 | | | 4 | 1 | | 4 | 4 | | | 4 | | | | | 1 | 1 | 2 |
| XAVIER UNIVERSITY OHIO | 4 | | | 4 | | | 4 | | | 4 | 4 | | | 4 | | 1 | | | 1 | | 1 |
| YALE UNIVERSITY CONN | 1 | 40 | 39 | 2 | 19 | 17 | 2 | 28 | 32 | 3 | 1 | 12 | 13 | 1 | 9 | 10 | 67 | 23 | 5 | 185 | 141 | 326 |
| YESHIVA UNIVERSITY N Y | 3 | 4 | 10 | 3 | 7 | 3 | 2 | 18 | 16 | 3 | 3 | 4 | | 3 | | 19 | 15 | 2 | 55 | 45 | 100 |

[a]This table includes only those postdoctorals who reported their field of study and citizenship. If these items of information were not available, the postdoctoral was excluded from the university listing.

Source: NRC, Office of Scientific Personnel, Postdoctoral Census Questionnaire.

APPENDIX B: COMPILATIONS OF DATA

## B-3 Distribution of Foreign Postdoctorals by Country

In this study data on the foreign postdoctoral were presented for the most part by gathering the home countries into four groups determined by the per capita gross national product. The rationale was that degree of educational development is more likely to be a function of national wealth than geographical location. As with any categorization, there are flaws, and countries like Kuwait will be ranked as a rich country although its educational development does not match its wealth. (There is not much distortion in this case, however, as we detected no postdoctorals from Kuwait.) The classification of countries by per capita GNP is based on World Bank figures,[4] and the nomenclature we used is:

| Classification | Per Capita Gross National Product |
|---|---|
| High income | More than $750 |
| Medium income | $250–$749 |
| Low income | $100–$249 |
| Very low income | Less than $100 |

In Table B-3 we provide data on postdoctorals, listing each country separately. The per capita GNP classification is given with the code: High – 1, Medium – 2, Low – 3, Very Low – 4.

---

[4]Escott Reid, *The Future of the World Bank,* International Bank for Reconstruction and Development, September 1965.

APPENDIX TABLE B-3  Foreign Postdoctorals by Country of Origin[a]

| FOREIGN COUNTRY OF ORIGIN | PER CAPITA GNP CLASSIFICATION | TOTAL POSTDOCTORALS | Physical Sciences | Biosciences | Basic Med Sci | Engineering | Arts & Humanities | Social Sciences | Medical Sciences | Other | Return Home | Remain in US | Other Fgn Country | Unknown | Male | Female | University | Nonprofit | Industry | US Government | Other |
|---|---|---|---|---|---|---|---|---|---|---|---|---|---|---|---|---|---|---|---|---|---|
| AFRICA | | | | | | | | | | | | | | | | | | | | | |
| LIBYA | 2 | 1 | | 1 | | | | | | | | | 1 | | 1 | | | | | | |
| SOUTH AFRICA | 2 | 28 | 9 | 6 | | | | 9 | | 11 | 9 | 4 | 4 | 26 | 24 | 2 | 2 | | 2 | | |
| SUDAN | 4 | 2 | 1 | | 1 | | | | | 2 | | | | 2 | 2 | | | | | | |
| TUNISIA | 3 | 3 | 1 | | | | | 2 | | | 1 | 1 | 1 | 3 | 2 | 1 | 1 | | | | |
| UNITED ARAB REPUBLIC | 3 | 48 | 6 | 11 | 10 | 2 | | 14 | 4 | 34 | 8 | | 6 | 42 | 44 | 2 | 2 | | 1 | | 1 |
| ZAMBIA | 2 | 1 | 1 | | | | | | | | | | | 1 | 1 | | | | | | |
| OTHER EAST AFRICA | 3 | 4 | | 1 | | | | 2 | | 2 | 1 | 1 | | 3 | 4 | | | | | | |
| OTHER WEST AFRICA | 3 | 9 | 1 | 1 | 1 | | 1 | 5 | | 6 | 1 | | 2 | 8 | 7 | 2 | 2 | | | | |
| ASIA, EASTERN | | | | | | | | | | | | | | | | | | | | | |
| BURMA | 4 | 1 | 1 | | | | | | | | | | 1 | | 1 | | | | | | |
| CEYLON | 3 | 8 | 5 | 2 | | | | 1 | | 3 | 3 | | 2 | 8 | 8 | | | | | | |
| CHINA | 3 | 217 | 102 | 46 | 15 | 4 | | 22 | 6 | 30 | 115 | 8 | 63 | 168 | 195 | 10 | 10 | | 11 | 1 | |
| HONG KONG | 2 | 6 | 3 | 1 | | | | 1 | | 1 | 4 | | 1 | 6 | 6 | | | | | | |
| JAPAN | 1 | 609 | 190 | 173 | 24 | 14 | 7 | 139 | 6 | 500 | 56 | 4 | 49 | 581 | 541 | 50 | 50 | | 17 | 1 | |
| KOREA | 3 | 73 | 27 | 17 | 5 | 2 | | 13 | 1 | 21 | 23 | 4 | 25 | 69 | 64 | 6 | 6 | | 3 | | |
| MALAYSIA | 2 | 8 | 3 | 3 | | | | 1 | | 4 | 2 | | 2 | 7 | 8 | | | | | | |
| THAILAND | 3 | 31 | 2 | 3 | | 1 | | 22 | | 30 | | | 1 | 22 | 24 | 7 | 7 | | | | |
| VIETNAM, REPUBLIC OF | 3 | 3 | 1 | | | | 1 | 1 | | 1 | | | 2 | 3 | 3 | | | | | | |
| ASIA, WESTERN | | | | | | | | | | | | | | | | | | | | | |
| AFGHANISTAN | 4 | 1 | | | | | | | | 1 | | | | 1 | 1 | | | | | | |
| CYPRUS | 2 | 1 | | | 1 | | | | | | 1 | | | 1 | 1 | | | | | | |
| INDIA | 4 | 621 | 284 | 155 | 31 | 6 | 5 | 57 | 11 | 419 | 110 | 15 | 77 | 568 | 567 | 30 | 30 | | 24 | | |
| IRAN | 3 | 31 | 4 | 3 | | 1 | | 19 | | 17 | 8 | | 6 | 27 | 26 | 5 | 5 | | | | |
| IRAQ | 3 | 18 | 3 | 5 | | | | 7 | 2 | 8 | 4 | 1 | 5 | 16 | 17 | 1 | 1 | | | | |
| ISRAEL | 1 | 147 | 63 | 27 | 5 | 6 | | 20 | 3 | 123 | 11 | 1 | 12 | 130 | 125 | 17 | 5 | 5 | 12 | | |
| JORDAN | 3 | 3 | 2 | | 1 | | | | | 1 | | | 1 | 3 | 3 | | | | | | |

## APPENDIX TABLE B-3—Continued

| FOREIGN COUNTRY OF ORIGIN | PER CAPITA GNP CLASSIFICATION | TOTAL POSTDOCTORALS | Physical Sciences | Biosciences | Basic Med Sci | Engineering | Arts & Humanities | Social Sciences | Medical Sciences | Other | Return Home | Remain in US | Other Fgn Country | Unknown | Male | Female | University | Nonprofit | Industry | US Government | Other |
|---|---|---|---|---|---|---|---|---|---|---|---|---|---|---|---|---|---|---|---|---|---|
| ASIA, WESTERN (CONTINUED) | | | | | | | | | | | | | | | | | | | | | |
| LEBANON | 2 | 22 | 2 | 4 | 3 | | 1 | 11 | | 14 | 4 | 4 | 20 | 2 | 20 | 2 | | | | | |
| PAKISTAN | 4 | 34 | 16 | 4 | | 1 | | 7 | | 19 | 7 | 7 | 33 | 1 | 30 | 2 | | | 2 | | |
| SYRIA | 3 | 5 | 1 | | | | | 4 | | 3 | 2 | | 5 | | 5 | | | | | | |
| TURKEY | 3 | 33 | 6 | 2 | 10 | 3 | 1 | 6 | 1 | 19 | 9 | 1 | 29 | 4 | 31 | 1 | | | 1 | | |
| AUSTRALASIA | | | | | | | | | | | | | | | | | | | | | |
| AUSTRALIA | 1 | 165 | 86 | 6 | 27 | 4 | 4 | 29 | 3 | 127 | 16 | 5 | 17 | 160 | 5 | 148 | 8 | 2 | 7 | | |
| INDONESIA | 4 | 3 | 1 | | 2 | | | | | 2 | 1 | | 3 | | 3 | 2 | 1 | | | | |
| NEW ZEALAND | 1 | 47 | 20 | 6 | 10 | 2 | | 9 | | 25 | 4 | 12 | 6 | 45 | 2 | 42 | 4 | | 1 | | |
| PHILIPPINES | 3 | 75 | 3 | 3 | 16 | | | 52 | | 53 | 16 | | 6 | 56 | 19 | 58 | 12 | | 3 | 2 | |
| SAMOA | 2 | 1 | 1 | | | | | | | 1 | | | | 1 | | 1 | | | | | |
| EUROPE | | | | | | | | | | | | | | | | | | | | | |
| AUSTRIA | 1 | 32 | 19 | 4 | 2 | 2 | | 2 | | 7 | 10 | 4 | 11 | 27 | 5 | 26 | 1 | | 5 | | |
| BELGIUM | 1 | 51 | 14 | 3 | 14 | 5 | | 12 | | 34 | 4 | 4 | 9 | 45 | 6 | 41 | 6 | 1 | 3 | | |
| BULGARIA | 2 | 3 | 3 | | | | | | | 2 | | | 1 | 3 | | 2 | | | 1 | | |
| CZECHOSLOVAKIA | 1 | 46 | 15 | 3 | 13 | 3 | 1 | 11 | | 44 | | | 2 | 41 | 5 | 40 | 4 | | 1 | 1 | |
| DENMARK | 1 | 22 | 8 | 3 | 3 | 1 | | 7 | | 18 | 2 | 1 | 2 | 19 | 3 | 20 | 1 | | 1 | | |
| FINLAND | 1 | 23 | 7 | 4 | 6 | | 1 | 5 | | 20 | 1 | 1 | 1 | 19 | 4 | 18 | 4 | | 1 | | |
| FRANCE | 1 | 100 | 51 | 5 | 19 | 6 | 5 | 8 | 1 | 87 | 1 | 4 | 8 | 81 | 19 | 83 | 11 | 1 | 5 | | |
| GERMANY | 1 | 352 | 193 | 28 | 67 | 8 | 9 | 26 | 2 | 256 | 33 | 11 | 52 | 330 | 22 | 302 | 24 | 3 | 22 | 1 | |
| GREECE | 2 | 41 | 10 | 4 | 13 | 1 | | 8 | | 16 | 15 | 3 | 7 | 36 | 5 | 35 | 4 | | 2 | | |
| HUNGARY | 1 | 16 | 5 | 1 | 4 | 5 | | | | 11 | 2 | 2 | 1 | 16 | | 16 | | | | | |
| ICELAND | 1 | 2 | 2 | | | | | | | | | | 2 | 2 | | 2 | | | | | |
| IRELAND, REPUBLIC OF | 1 | 32 | 15 | 2 | 4 | 1 | | 6 | | 16 | 10 | 3 | 3 | 32 | | 28 | 2 | | 2 | | |
| ITALY | 1 | 117 | 60 | 8 | 28 | 4 | 2 | 13 | 1 | 86 | 11 | 6 | 14 | 110 | 7 | 104 | 6 | 1 | 6 | | |
| NETHERLANDS | 1 | 41 | 19 | 5 | 10 | | | 7 | | 30 | 5 | 1 | 5 | 34 | 7 | 33 | 3 | | 5 | | |

|  | | | | | | | | | | | | | | | |
|---|---|---|---|---|---|---|---|---|---|---|---|---|---|---|---|
| NORWAY | 1 | 34 | 15 | 2 | 5 | 2 | 1 | | 8 | | 25 | 4 | | 5 | 30 | 4 | 30 | | 3 |
| POLAND | 1 | 57 | 25 | 5 | 8 | 4 | 2 | 2 | 8 | 2 | 50 | 3 | 1 | 3 | 49 | 8 | 51 | 3 | 3 |
| PORTUGAL | 2 | 7 | | | 5 | | | | 1 | 1 | 5 | 1 | 1 | | 7 | | 6 | 1 | |
| ROMANIA | 2 | 3 | 2 | | 1 | | | | | | 3 | | | | 3 | | 3 | | |
| SPAIN | 2 | 41 | 8 | 2 | 12 | 2 | 1 | | 12 | 1 | 25 | 6 | 2 | 8 | 36 | 5 | 35 | 3 | 3 |
| SWEDEN | 1 | 41 | 15 | 4 | 11 | 1 | 1 | 1 | 5 | 2 | 36 | 3 | | 2 | 40 | 1 | 41 | | |
| SWITZERLAND | 1 | 117 | 62 | 10 | 21 | 1 | 2 | | 20 | | 73 | 18 | 3 | 23 | 105 | 12 | 100 | 11 | 5 |
| UNION OF SOV. SOC. REP. | 1 | 5 | 3 | | | 1 | | | 1 | | 4 | 1 | | | 4 | 1 | 5 | | |
| UNITED KINGDOM | 1 | 748 | 399 | 64 | 151 | 26 | 10 | 14 | 74 | 6 | 475 | 120 | 62 | 91 | 711 | 37 | 664 | 45 | 6 | 31 |
| YUGOSLAVIA | 2 | 52 | 30 | 2 | 7 | 1 | | 3 | 8 | | 41 | 4 | 2 | 5 | 40 | 12 | 48 | 2 | 2 |
| NORTH AMERICA EXCEPT U.S.A. | | | | | | | | | | | | | | 1 | 1 | | | | 1 |
| BERMUDA | 1 | 1 | 1 | | | | | | | | | | | 1 | | | | | |
| CANADA | 1 | 264 | 82 | 13 | 47 | 6 | 7 | 1 | 100 | 3 | 143 | 68 | 5 | 48 | 244 | 20 | 232 | 24 | 2 | 5 |
| COSTA RICA | 2 | 1 | | | | | | | 1 | | 1 | | | | 1 | | 1 | | |
| CUBA | 2 | 11 | | | 3 | | | | 6 | | | 11 | | | 9 | 2 | 9 | 2 | |
| DOMINICAN REPUBLIC | 3 | 4 | | 1 | | | | | 1 | | | 4 | | | 2 | 2 | 2 | 2 | |
| EL SALVADOR | 2 | 3 | | | 2 | | | | 1 | | 2 | 1 | | | 2 | 1 | 3 | | |
| GUATEMALA | 2 | 3 | | | | | | | 3 | | 2 | | | 1 | 3 | | 3 | | |
| HAITI | 4 | 4 | | | 1 | | | | 2 | | | 4 | | | 2 | | 2 | 2 | |
| HONDURAS | 3 | 3 | | | 1 | | | | 1 | | 2 | | | | 2 | 1 | 3 | | |
| MEXICO | 2 | 32 | 1 | 6 | 15 | | | | 9 | 1 | 30 | 2 | 1 | | 26 | 6 | 28 | 4 | |
| NICARAGUA | 2 | 1 | | | | | | | 1 | | | 1 | | | 1 | | 1 | 1 | |
| PANAMA | 2 | 1 | | | 1 | | | | | | 1 | | | | 1 | | 1 | | |
| WEST INDIES | 2 | 8 | | 1 | 3 | | 1 | | 3 | | 1 | 3 | 3 | 1 | 6 | 2 | 6 | 2 | |
| SOUTH AMERICA | | | | | | | | | | | | | | | | | | | |
| ARGENTINA | 1 | 102 | 24 | 9 | 32 | 2 | | 1 | 33 | 1 | 47 | 32 | 4 | 19 | 85 | 17 | 87 | 11 | 4 |
| BOLIVIA | 3 | 2 | | | | | | | 2 | | 2 | | | | 2 | | 1 | 1 | |
| BRAZIL | 3 | 49 | 6 | 3 | 12 | | | | 25 | 1 | 41 | 4 | | 4 | 42 | 7 | 41 | 6 | 1 | 1 |
| CHILE | 2 | 34 | 1 | 4 | 10 | 1 | 1 | | 16 | | 31 | 1 | | 2 | 33 | 1 | 30 | 2 | 2 |
| COLUMBIA | 2 | 34 | | 3 | 11 | | | | 18 | | 24 | 8 | 1 | 1 | 30 | 4 | 25 | 7 | 2 |
| ECUADOR | 3 | 2 | | 1 | | | | | 1 | | 1 | 1 | | | 2 | | 2 | | |
| PARAGUAY | 3 | 1 | 1 | | | | | | | | | | 1 | | 1 | | 1 | | |
| PERU | 2 | 23 | | 1 | 8 | | | 1 | 12 | | 19 | 3 | | 1 | 20 | 3 | 16 | 6 | |
| URUGUAY | 2 | 6 | 1 | | 4 | | | | | | 4 | 1 | | 1 | 6 | | 4 | 1 | 1 | |
| VENEZUELA | 1 | 13 | 1 | 1 | 4 | 2 | | | 4 | | 8 | 3 | | 2 | 7 | 6 | 11 | | 2 |

APPENDIX TABLE B-3—Continued

| FOREIGN COUNTRY OF ORIGIN | PER CAPITA GNP CLASSIFICATION | TOTAL POSTDOCTORALS | POSTDOCTORAL FIELD[b] Physical Sciences | Biosciences | Basic Med Sci | Engineering | Arts & Humanities | Social Sciences | Medical Sciences | Other | ANTICIPATED FUT LOCATION Return Home | Remain in US | Other Fgn Country | Unknown | SEX Male | Female | POSTDOCTORAL HOST INSTITUTION University | Nonprofit | Industry | US Government | Other |
|---|---|---|---|---|---|---|---|---|---|---|---|---|---|---|---|---|---|---|---|---|---|
| FOREIGN TOTAL[a] | 4844 | 1936 | 400 | 1083 | 174 | 96 | 53 | 935 | 59 | 3200 | 819 | 182 | 643 | 4399 | 445 | 4253 | 353 | 24 | 201 | 13 | |
| UNITED STATES TOTAL | 5855 | 1512 | 503 | 1265 | 99 | 343 | 175 | 1702 | 106 | 4865 | 72 | 918 | 5255 | 600 | 4365 | 460 | 4 | 563 | 445 | | |
| COUNTRY UNKNOWN | 41 | 16 | 4 | 4 | 1 | 3 | | 13 | | | 41 | 37 | 4 | 36 | 4 | 1 | | | | | |
| GRAND TOTAL | 10740 | 3464 | 907 | 2352 | 274 | 442 | 228 | 2650 | 165 | 3200 | 5684 | 254 | 1602 | 9691 | 1049 | 8654 | 817 | 47 | 764 | 458 | |

[a] The foreign total is 4,845. One postdoctoral was a citizen of a foreign country but did not give the country and is therefore included in "Unknown."
[b] Postdoctorals whose field was unknown were excluded from this table. In total there were 258 such cases.

Source: NRC, Office of Scientific Personnel, Postdoctoral Census Questionnaire.

APPENDIX C
# Bibliography

American Medical Association, *The Graduate Education of Physicians*, The Report of the Citizens' Commission on Graduate Medical Education, 1966.

Berelson, Bernard, *Graduate Education in the United States,* McGraw-Hill, 1960.

——— Postdoctoral Work in American Universities, *Journal of Higher Education,* March 1962.

Bush, Vannevar, *Science, the Endless Frontier,* a Report to the President, Washington, D.C., U.S. Government Printing Office, 1945. (Also reprinted by the National Science Foundation, 1960.)

Cain, Arthur S., Jr., and Lois G. Bowen, The Role of Postdoctoral Fellowships in Academic Medicine, *The Journal of Medical Education,* Vol. 36, No. 10, October 1961.

Cartter, Allan M., *An Assessment of Quality in Graduate Education,* American Council on Education, 1966.

Ingraham, Mark H., *The Outer Fringe: Faculty Benefits Other Than Annuities and Insurance,* University of Wisconsin Press, 1965.

*Journal of the American Medical Association,* annual education numbers. (Contain detailed information each year on the postdoctoral population in medical schools.)

Manpower Resources for Science and Technology, *The Brain Drain,* Her Majesty's Stationery Office, London, 1967.

Miller, John Perry, Under the Tower, the Postdoctoral Fellow, *Ventures* (magazine of Yale Graduate School), Vol. 5, No. 2, Fall 1965.

The Modern Language Association of America, Recommendations Concerning the PhD in English, *PMLA,* Vol. 82, No. 4, September 1967.

National Academy of Sciences, *Doctorate Recipients from United States Universities, 1958–1966,* Publ. 1489, Washington, D.C., 1967.

National Academy of Sciences–National Research Council, *Doctorate Production in United States Universities, 1920–1962,* Publ. 1142, Washington, D.C., 1963.

APPENDIX C: BIBLIOGRAPHY

National Academy of Sciences—National Research Council, *Profiles of PhD's in the Sciences,* Publ. 1293, Washington, D.C., 1965. (Summary report on follow-up of doctorate cohorts, 1935-1960.)

National Academy of Sciences—National Research Council, *Chemistry: Opportunities and Needs,* Publ. 1292, Washington, D.C., 1965. (A report on basic research in United States chemistry by the Committee for the Survey of Chemistry.)

National Academy of Sciences—National Research Council, *Physics: Survey and Outlook,* Publ. 1295, Washington, D.C., 1966. (A report of the present state of U.S. physics and its requirements for future growth.)

National Academy of Sciences—National Research Council, *The Plant Sciences: Now and in the Coming Decade,* Publ. 1405, Washington, D.C., 1966. (A report on the status, trends, and requirements of plant sciences in the United States.)

National Research Council, Office of Scientific Personnel, *Proceedings of the Conference on Postdoctoral Fellowships and Research Associateships in the Sciences and Engineering,* Williamstown, Mass., Sept. 10-12, 1967.

National Science Foundation, *Graduate Student Support and Manpower Resources in Graduate Science Education,* Washington, D.C., 1968 (NSF68-13).

Perkins, Dexter, John L. Snell, and the Committee on Graduate Education of the American Historical Association, *The Education of Historians in the United States,* McGraw-Hill, 1962.

Research Policy Program, *Brain Drain and Brain Gain,* Lund, Sweden, 1967.